Lecture Notes
in Business Information Processing   **511**

LNBIP reports state-of-the-art results in areas related to business information systems and industrial application software development – timely, at a high level, and in both printed and electronic form.

The type of material published includes

- Proceedings (published in time for the respective event)
- Postproceedings (consisting of thoroughly revised and/or extended final papers)
- Other edited monographs (such as, for example, project reports or invited volumes)
- Tutorials (coherently integrated collections of lectures given at advanced courses, seminars, schools, etc.)
- Award-winning or exceptional theses

LNBIP is abstracted/indexed in DBLP, EI and Scopus. LNBIP volumes are also submitted for the inclusion in ISI Proceedings.

Han van der Aa · Dominik Bork ·
Rainer Schmidt · Arnon Sturm
Editors

Enterprise, Business-Process and Information Systems Modeling

25th International Conference, BPMDS 2024
and 29th International Conference, EMMSAD 2024
Limassol, Cyprus, June 3–4, 2024
Proceedings

 Springer

Editors
Han van der Aa 🔾
University of Vienna
Vienna, Austria

Dominik Bork 🔾
TU Wien
Vienna, Austria

Rainer Schmidt 🔾
Munich University of Applied Sciences
Munich, Germany

Arnon Sturm 🔾
Ben-Gurion University of the Negev
Beer-Sheva, Israel

ISSN 1865-1348   ISSN 1865-1356 (electronic)
Lecture Notes in Business Information Processing
ISBN 978-3-031-61006-6   ISBN 978-3-031-61007-3 (eBook)
https://doi.org/10.1007/978-3-031-61007-3

This Springer imprint is published by the registered company Springer Nature Switzerland AG
The registered company address is: Gewerbestrasse 11, 6330 Cham, Switzerland

If disposing of this product, please recycle the paper.

Preface

This book contains the proceedings of two long-running events held alongside the CAiSE conference relating to the areas of enterprise, business-process, and information systems modeling: the 25th International Working Conference on Business Process Modeling, Development, and Support (BPMDS 2024) and the 29th International Working Conference on Exploring Modeling Methods for Systems Analysis and Development (EMMSAD 2024).

The two working conferences had a joint keynote given by Remco Dijkman, Full Professor in Information Systems, Eindhoven University of Technology, the Netherlands.

This year both conferences were held in Limassol, Cyprus, on June 3–4, 2024. More information on the individual events and their selection processes can be found on the following pages.

BPMDS 2024

The Business Process Modeling, Development, and Support (BPMDS) working conference has been held for more than two decades, dealing with and promoting research on BPMDS, and has been a platform for a multitude of influential research papers. In keeping with its tradition, the working conference covers a broad range of theoretical and application-based research. BPMDS started in 1998 as a recurring workshop. During this period, business process analysis and design were recognized as central issues in the area of information systems (IS) engineering. The continued interest in these topics on behalf of the IS community is reflected by the success of recent BPMDS events and the recent emergence of new conferences and workshops devoted to the theme. In 2011, BPMDS became a two-day working conference attached to CAiSE. The goals, format, and history of BPMDS can be found at www.bpmds.org.

BPMDS 2024 received 25 submissions. Each submission was reviewed by three members of the Program Committee. Finally, 8 high-quality full papers and 3 short papers were selected. These accepted papers cover a wide spectrum of topics, which we organized under four headers: (1) Large Language Model Applications, (2) Process Model Extraction, Analysis, and Visualization, (3) User Preferences and Agile Processes, and (4) Process Discovery and Analysis.

We want to thank everyone who submitted papers to BPMDS 2024 for sharing their work with us. Furthermore, we want to thank the members of the Program Committee, who made a remarkable effort in reviewing submissions, the organizers of CAiSE 2024 for their help with the organization of the event, IFIP WG8.1 for its continued support, and Springer for their assistance during the production of the proceedings.

April 2024   Han van der Aa
                                                                                                                          Rainer Schmidt

EMMSAD 2024

The objective of the EMMSAD conference series is to provide a forum for researchers and practitioners interested in modeling methods for systems analysis and development (SA&D) to meet and exchange research ideas and results. The conference aims to provide a home for a rich variety of modeling paradigms, including software modeling, business process modeling, enterprise modeling, capability modeling, service modeling, ontology modeling, and domain-specific modeling. These important modeling paradigms, and specific methods following them, continue to be enriched with extensions, refinements, and even new languages, to address new challenges. Even with some attempts at standardization, new modeling paradigms and methods are constantly being introduced, especially in order to deal with emerging trends and challenges. Ongoing changes significantly impact the way systems are analyzed and designed in practice. Moreover, they challenge the empirical and analytical evaluation of the modeling methods, which contributes to the knowledge and understanding of their strengths and weaknesses. This knowledge may guide researchers towards the development of the next generation of modeling methods and help practitioners to select the modeling methods most appropriate to their needs.

EMMSAD 2024 accepted papers in the following five tracks that emphasize the variety of EMMSAD topics: (1) Foundations of modeling & method engineering – chaired by Anne Gutschmidt, Frederick Benaben, and Istvan David; (2) Enterprise, business, process, and capability modeling – chaired by Jānis Grabis, Simon Hacks, and Monika Kaczmarek-Heß; (3) Information systems and requirements modeling – chaired by Sallam Abualhaija, Roman Lukyanenko, and Marcela Ruiz; (4) Domain-specific and knowledge modeling – chaired by Robert Clarisó, Oscar Pastor, and Tiago Prince Sales; and (5) Evaluation of models & modeling approaches – chaired by Renata Guizzardi, Qin Ma, and Monique Snoeck. More details on the current and previous editions of EMMSAD can be found at http://www.emmsad.org/.

In total, EMMSAD 2024 attracted 32 submissions. The division of submissions between the tracks was as follows: six related to foundations of modeling and method engineering, nine related to enterprise, business, process, and capability modeling, eight related to information systems and requirements modeling, seven related to domain-specific and knowledge modeling, and two related to evaluation of modeling approaches. Each paper was reviewed by three members of the program committee and received a meta-review by the track chairs. Finally, 16 high-quality papers, comprising 11 full papers and five short papers, were selected.

We wish to thank all the authors who shared their work with us, as well as the members of the EMMSAD 2024 Program Committee and Track Chairs for their valuable, detailed, and timely reviews. Finally, we thank the organizers of CAiSE 2024 for their help with the organization of the event, IFIP WG 8.1 for its support, and Springer for their continued support.

April 2024   Arnon Sturm
                                                         Dominik Bork

BPMDS 2024 Organization

Program Chairs

Han van der Aa   University of Vienna, Austria
Rainer Schmidt   Munich University of Applied Sciences, Germany

Steering Committee

Ilia Bider   Stockholm University and IbisSoft, Sweden
Selmin Nurcan   Université Paris 1 Panthéon-Sorbonne, France
Rainer Schmidt   Munich University of Applied Sciences, Germany
Pnina Soffer   University of Haifa, Israel

Program Committee

Dorina Bano   Hasso Plattner Institute, Germany
Judith Barrios Albornoz   University of Los Andes, Colombia
Iris Beerepoot   Utrecht University, the Netherlands
Karsten Boehm   FH Kufstein Tirol, Austria
Carl Corea   University of Koblenz, Germany
Johannes De Smedt   KU Leuven, Belgium
Djordje Djurica   WU Vienna, Austria
Dirk Fahland   TU Eindhoven, the Netherlands
Renata Guizzardi   University of Twente, the Netherlands
Stefan Jablonski   University of Bayreuth, Germany
Amin Jalali   Stockholm University, Sweden
Kathrin Kirchner   Technical University of Denmark, Denmark
Agnes Koschmider   University of Bayreuth, Germany
Sander J.J. Leemans   RWTH Aachen, Germany
Orlenys López-Pintado   University of Tartu, Estonia
Jan Mendling   Humboldt-Universität zu Berlin, Germany
Selmin Nurcan   Université Paris 1 Panthéon-Sorbonne, France
Luise Pufahl   TU Munich, Germany
Adrian Rebmann   University of Mannheim, Germany
Jana-Rebecca Rehse   University of Mannheim, Germany
Hajo A. Reijers   Utrecht University, the Netherlands

Michael Rosemann	Queensland University of Technology, Australia
Stefan Schönig	University of Regensburg, Germany
Ronny Seiger	University of St. Gallen, Switzerland
Pnina Soffer	University of Haifa, Israel
Vinicius Stein Dani	Utrecht University, the Netherlands
Francesco Tiezzi	Università di Firenze, Italy
Amy Van Looy	Ghent University, Belgium
Irene Vanderfeesten	KU Leuven, Belgium
Francesca Zerbato	University of St. Gallen, Switzerland

EMMSAD 2024 Organization

Program Chairs

Arnon Sturm	Ben-Gurion University of the Negev, Israel
Dominik Bork	TU Wien, Austria

Track Chairs

Anne Gutschmidt	University of Rostock, Germany
Frederick Benaben	IMT Mines Albi, France
Istvan David	McMaster University, Canada
Jānis Grabis	Riga Technical University, Latvia
Monika Kaczmarek-Heß	University of Duisburg-Essen, Germany
Oscar Pastor	Universitat Politècnica de València, Spain
Renata Guizzardi	University of Twente, the Netherlands
Qin Ma	University of Luxembourg, Luxembourg
Marcela Ruiz	Zurich University of Applied Sciences, Switzerland
Tiago Prince Sales	University of Twente, the Netherlands
Monique Snoeck	KU Leuven, Belgium
Robert Clarisó	Universitat Oberta de Catalunya, Spain
Roman Lukyanenko	University of Virginia, USA
Sallam Abualhaija	University of Luxembourg, Luxembourg
Simon Hacks	Stockholm University, Sweden

Program Committee

Alberto García	Universitat Politècnica de València, Spain
Alexander Bock	University of Duisburg-Essen, Germany
Antonio De Nicola	ENEA, Italy
Arava Tsoury	Ruppin Academic Center, Israel
Ben Roelens	Open Universiteit/Ghent University, Belgium
Carson Woo	University of British Columbia, Canada
Cesar Gonzalez-Perez	Incipit CSIC, Spain
Charlotte Verbruggen	KU Leuven, Belgium

Christophe Feltus	Luxembourg Institute of Science and Technology, Luxembourg
Claudenir M. Fonseca	University of Twente, the Netherlands
Damiano Torre	St. Mary's University, USA
Drazen Brdjanin	University of Banja Luka, Bosnia and Herzegovina
Elena Kornyshova	CNAM, France
Felix Härer	University of Fribourg, Switzerland
Francisca Pérez	Universidad San Jorge, Spain
Frederik Gailly	Ghent University, Belgium
Geert Poels	Ghent University, Belgium
George Grossmann	University of South Australia, Australia
Georgios Koutsopoulos	Stockholm University, Sweden
Giancarlo Guizzardi	University of Twente, the Netherlands
Giuseppe Berio	Université de Bretagne Sud and IRISA UMR 6074, France
Hans Weigand	Tilburg University, the Netherlands
Hans-Georg Fill	University of Fribourg, Switzerland
Jaap Gordijn	Vrije Universiteit Amsterdam, the Netherlands
Janis Stirna	Stockholm University, Sweden
Jennifer Horkoff	Chalmers University of Technology, Sweden
Jenny Ruiz de La Peña	University of Holguin, Cuba
Jesús Sánchez Cuadrado	Universidad de Murcia, Spain
Jolita Ralyté	University of Geneva, Switzerland
Jose Ignacio Panach Navarrete	Universitat de València, Spain
Juan De Lara	Universidad Autónoma de Madrid, Spain
Jürgen Jung	Frankfurt University of Applied Sciences, Germany
Kristina Rosenthal	Hochschule Niederrhein University of Applied Sciences, Germany
Kurt Sandkuhl	University of Rostock, Germany
Maria Luiza Campos	PPGI - IM/NCE - Federal University of Rio de Janeiro, Brazil
Marne de Vries	University of Pretoria, South Africa
Martin Henkel	Stockholm University, Sweden
Mohamad Gharib	University of Tartu, Estonia
Pascal Ravesteyn	Utrecht University of Applied Sciences, the Netherlands
Paul Grefen	Eindhoven University of Technology, the Netherlands
Pedro Paulo Favatos Barcelos	University of Twente, the Netherlands

Peter Fettke	German Research Center for Artificial Intelligence (DFKI) and Saarland University, Germany
Raian Ali	Hamad Bin Khalifa University, Qatar
Raimundas Matulevicius	University of Tartu, Estonia
Rebecca Deneckere	Université Paris 1 Panthéon-Sorbonne, France
Said Assar	Institut Mines-Télécom Business School, France
Stefan Strecker	University of Hagen, Germany
Sybren De Kinderen	Eindhoven University of Technology, the Netherlands
Tong Li	Beijing University of Technology, China
Tony Clark	Aston University, UK
Victoria Döller	University of Vienna, Austria
Victoria Torres	Universitat Politècnica de València, Spain
Yves Wautelet	Katholieke Universiteit Leuven, Belgium

Additional Reviewers

Sven Christ	University of Hagen, Germany
Philip Winkler	University of Hagen, Germany
Rebecca Morgan	University of South Australia, Australia
Sergio Manuel Serra Da Cruz	Federal University of Rio de Janeiro, Brazil

Contents

Process Discovery and Analysis (BPMDS 2024)

Evaluation of Modeling Methods (EMMSAD 2024)

Model-driven Engineering & AI 1 (EMMSAD 2024)

Model-driven Engineering & AI 2 (EMMSAD 2024)

Modeling and Sustainability (EMMSAD 2024)

Enterprise Modeling (EMMSAD 2024)

Joint BPMDS/EMMSAD 2024 Keynote

Resource Optimization in Business Processes

Remco Dijkman$^{(\boxtimes)}$

Eindhoven University of Technology, Eindhoven, The Netherlands
`r.m.dijkman@tue.nl`

Abstract. In administrative processes, such as financial or governmental processes, humans typically do most of the work and must be allocated to tasks in an efficient manner. This allocation is made complicated by the different authorizations and the varying effectiveness of people for tasks. Moreover, administrative processes operate under substantial uncertainty, as the customer's journey through the process typically is uncertain upon their arrival. To help solve this problem, we present a framework for resource optimization in administrative processes and delineate its differences from existing resource allocation models. We proceed to show several resource allocation solutions that have been developed with the framework. We specifically address the challenges that are encountered when implementing these solutions, some of which remain unresolved. By doing so we aim to shed light on promising avenues for future research in this domain.

1 Introduction

When designing and improving business processes one important aspect is how many resources you employ to do the work and how you assign work to resources, considering that resources are probably one of your most substantial cost factors and using them wisely may have a great impact on how efficiently and effectively the work is done. For that reason, resource allocation is a widely studied topic with many applications, such as transport resource allocation [3], job shop scheduling [2], and spare parts planning [8]. The area of business process design can both learn from and contribute to the more general area of resource optimization in two important ways.

First, business processes exist - by definition - to represent, analyze, and improve tasks in their relation to each other, while resource allocation traditionally focuses on one or a small number of tasks. The reason resource allocation traditionally has a narrow scope is understandable: solving a resource allocation problem for a single task is usually already NP-hard, extending this to multiple tasks further increases computational complexity, which makes it extremely hard to optimize processes within a feasible time frame. For example, in transport resource allocation we typically consider the allocation of transportation orders to trucks separately from the allocation of trucks to drivers to

© The Author(s), under exclusive license to Springer Nature Switzerland AG 2024
H. van der Aa et al. (Eds.): BPMDS 2024/EMMSAD 2024, LNBIP 511, pp. 3–9, 2024.
https://doi.org/10.1007/978-3-031-61007-3_1

keep computational complexity manageable. Even though considering them in their relation to each other can lead to better plans. For instance, it is easy to see that if we consider these two problems separately, it is possible to assign a transport order to a truck for which there exists no qualified driver on the day the order must be transported. Job shop scheduling probably comes closest to business process optimization. However, for jobs in a job shop, the tasks that must be performed are typically known in advance, while in business processes we typically do not know in advance which tasks we will need to perform for which customer. For those reasons, we believe that business process optimization can tackle novel resource optimization problems and can be a path forward to tackling integrated resource optimization problems.

Second, the area of business process design has a strong history of data analytics and prediction. In the more general area of resource optimization the awareness is also growing that data-driven optimization is the way forward to modeling problems that accurately represents the real world. However, while mining business processes from real data is a well-established area of research, mining resource allocation problems from data is still done in a more ad-hoc manner. Consequently, the more general area of resource allocation can benefit from techniques developed in the area of business process design and specifically process mining. Conversely, in the area of process mining, prescriptive process monitoring [5] has been pitched as a way to take data-driven decisions at run-time. However, prescriptive process monitoring focuses on suggesting optimal decisions for a single customer, neglecting constraints that typically exist between cases and resources, such as constraints on which resource can be assigned to which task, which resource is better at performing which task, and constraints with respect to resource schedules, an area that traditional resource optimization excels at. For those reasons we see a strong potential in merging techniques from the area of resource optimization and business process design to solve optimization problems that accurately represent the real world and are modeled completely, including the constraints on what is allowed.

To develop this area, we propose a framework for data-driven business process optimization that can be used to model and solve business process optimization problems, considering relations between tasks as well as constraints on resources. The vision is that the problem can be modeled using a version of a well-known notation such as BPMN or Petri nets, amended with resource constraints, and then be solved without further effort. This vision is analogous to how existing mathematical programming engines work, but while mathematical programming engines solve static problems, we aim to solve dynamic problems.

Section 2 presents the proposed framework for data-driven business process optimization and Sect. 3 shows the progress that has been made with implementing the framework as well as the open issues. Section 4 presents the conclusions.

2   Framework for Business Process Resource Optimization

Figure 1 shows a framework that can be used for resource optimization in business processes. The framework is based on the more general reinforcement learning framework and accordingly shows an environment in which decisions are made and an agent that takes the decisions. The agent receives an observation about the state of the environment and takes a decision in the form of an action. The agent then receives the next observation about the environment as well as the reward that the decision led to. In a business process resource optimization context, an observation about the state of the environment is an observation about the state of the business process, i.e., the customers that are waiting, the resources that are available to perform tasks and the resources that are busy performing tasks. A decision is which resource to assign to which task and the reward is some indication of the goodness of the assignment, such as the costs of using a resource or the time that a resource will take to perform a task.

To support the vision of modeling a resource optimization problem and then solving the problem without further effort, our framework has some additional components compared to the general reinforcement learning framework.

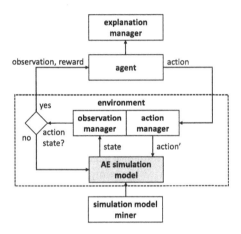

Fig. 1. A framework for business process optimization.

At the core of the framework is a simulation model. In line with the vision of easily specifying a resource allocation problem, we facilitate modeling the simulation model using a specific Petri net variant called Action-Evolution Petri Nets (AEPN) [6], which is an extension of Timed, Colored Petri Nets. Figure 2 shows an example of an assignment problem that is modeled as an AEPN. The problem is a classical resource allocation problem, where there are two types of case r_1 and r_2 and two resources, one that can perform both r_1 and r_2 cases and one that can only perform r_1 cases. The AEPN differs in two ways from classical Petri nets. First, each transition is marked as either an Action (A) or an Evolution (E) transition, where evolution transitions are regular Petri net transitions that are executed as usual, while action transitions are transitions on which a decision from the agent is requested. In the example, the transition that assigns resources to cases is an action transition. When this transition is enabled, the agent must decide which waiting case to assign to which resource. Second, a transition may have a reward function that returns a reward from the environment to the agent. In the example, the agent receives a reward of 1 each time a case completes.

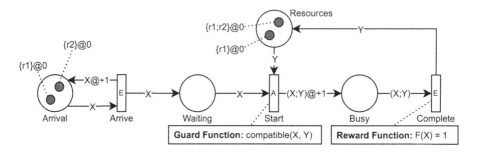

Fig. 2. Example of a resource optimization problem [6].

To realize the vision that the agent can optimize the modeled problem without additional effort, the framework has an observation manager and an action manager. The observation manager handles the translation of the state of the Petri net into an observation that can be interpreted by the agent. The action manager handles the translation of an action that is proposed by the agent into an action that can be executed in the Petri net, i.e., a binding.

There are two additional components that provide convenience functions. One is a simulation model miner. This component is capable of enhancing a process model with information that is needed to create a simulation model for resource allocation purposes, including information such as interarrival time distributions, processing time distributions, and resource schedules. The other component is the explanation manager, which provides functions that help understand resource allocation rules that the agent learns and interpret actions that the agent proposes. These functions provide assistance to process analysts and planners to help them understand what decisions they should take.

Finally, it must be noted the agent that takes the decisions in the framework is not necessarily a deep reinforcement learning agent. We have also experimented with heuristics that do resource assignment based on simple rules [3, 7] and with agents that do periodic mathematical optimization each time a decision must be made [2, 4].

3   Advances in Business Process Resource Optimization

The framework described in the previous section was made available as open source[1], but we used variations of the framework as well. Most notably, we

---

[1] https://github.com/bpogroup/aepn-project.

developed an open source library for easy modeling and simulation of Petri nets in Python[2].

In addition, we have modeled and solved various resource optimization problems to test different types of agents and build experience with how the framework can best be implemented. Table 1 presents an overview of the resource allocation problems that we have solved and the best performing algorithm that the agent used to allocate the resources.

Table 1. Winning algorithms for various problems

Problem	Best performing algorithm
Transport resource allocation [4]	Periodic Stochastic Programming
Transport resource allocation [3]	DRL (PPO)
Business process resource allocation [7]	Heuristic
Spare parts allocation [8]	DRL (DCL)
Picking order allocation [1]	DRL (PPO)
Job shop scheduling [2]	Mathematical Programming

The experience with solving resource optimization problems gives rise to three major challenges that we are working on solving.

First, as mentioned in the introduction, business processes operate under substantial uncertainty. There is uncertainty in the cases that will arrive, the properties of those cases, the tasks that must be performed on the cases, and the processing times of those tasks. We noticed that existing Deep Reinforcement Learning algorithms, and in particular the popular Proximal Policy Optimization (PPO) algorithm, encounters difficulties in learning under uncertainty. To help deal with that, we developed our own algorithm, called Deep Controlled Learning (DCL) [8], which shows a lot of promise. More research is needed to experiment with and improve on DCL in different settings.

Second, current Deep Reinforcement Learning (DRL) approaches mostly use a Multi Layer Perceptron (MLP) as a learning agent. An MLP takes vector input. However, the most logical translation of the process state to a vector easily produces an infinite number of vector features and consequently an infinite number of possible actions. For example, in Fig. 2 the logical vector interpretation of the state of the Petri net would have a feature for the number of cases of type r_1 with timestamp 0, the number of cases of type r_1 with timestamp 1, etceteras. Since this leads to an infinite number of features, it is not possible to develop a direct vector representation. While it is possible to engineer feature vectors that do not have this problem, this can be a time consuming task and the best feature vector may depend on the problem domain. Consequently, time can be saved by developing observation and action managers that can engineer

---

[2] https://github.com/bpogroup/simpn.

an observation and action space and possibly even the best neural network for a specific model.

Third, when optimizing a resource allocation problem, we typically have an objective in mind, such as minimizing the sum of completion times of cases or minimizing the total cost. However, DRL approaches take reward functions as input, rather than objective functions. Consequently, a component that can automatically engineer the reward function from an objective function would potentially save the modeler a lot of work.

4   Conclusions

We have presented a framework for resource optimization in business processes, addressing the challenges posed by the complexity and uncertainty inherent in administrative processes.

We have also identified open research problems in this domain. Specifically, we have highlighted the need for novel DRL algorithms capable of learning under substantial uncertainty, as well as the importance of developing observation and action managers to handle the complexity of process states and actions in DRL-based optimization. Additionally, we emphasize the significance of automatic engineering of reward functions from objective functions to streamline the modeling process.

By doing so we both aim to advance our understanding of resource optimization in business processes and to provide a foundation for further research in this field.

References

1. Cals, B., Zhang, Y., Dijkman, R., Dorst, C.: Solving the online batching problem using deep reinforcement learning. Comput. Ind. Eng. **156** (2021)
2. Farahani, A., van Elzakker, M.A.H., Genga, L., Troubil, P., Dijkman, R.M.: Relational graph attention-based deep reinforcement learning: an application to flexible job shop scheduling with sequence-dependent setup times. In: Proceedings of International Conference on Learning and Intelligent Optimization (LION), pp. 347–362 (2023)
3. Farahani, A., Genga, L., Dijkman, R.M.: Tackling uncertainty in online multimodal transportation planning using deep reinforcement learning. In: Proceedings of International Conference on Computational Logistics (ICCL) (2021)
4. Gumuskaya, V., van Jaarsveld, W., Dijkman, R., Grefen, P., Veenstra, A.: Integrating stochastic programs and decision trees in capacitated barge planning with uncertain container arrivals. Transp. Res. Part C **132** (2021)
5. Kubrak, K., Milani, F., Nolte, A., Dumas, M.: Prescriptive process monitoring: Quo Vadis? PeerJ Comput. Sci. **8**, e1097 (2022)
6. Lo Bianco, R., Dijkman, R.M., Nuijten, W., van Jaarsveld, W.: Action-evolution petri nets: a framework for modeling and solving dynamic task assignment problems. In: International Conference on Business Process Management (BPM), pp. 216–231 (2023)

7. Middelhuis, J., Lo Bianco, R., Scherzer, E., Bukhsh, Z.A., Adan, I.J., Dijkman, R.M.: Learning policies for resource allocation in business processes. arXiv preprint arXiv:2304.09970 (2023)
8. Temizöz, T., Imdahl, C., Dijkman, R., Lamghari-Idrissi, D., van Jaarsveld, W.: Deep controlled learning for inventory control. arXiv preprint 2011.15122 (2023)

Large Language Model Applications (BPMDS 2024)

Evaluating Large Language Models in Process Mining: Capabilities, Benchmarks, and Evaluation Strategies

Alessandro Berti[1,2]([✉]) [ID], Humam Kourani[1,2] [ID], Hannes Häfke[1] [ID], Chiao-Yun Li[1,2] [ID], and Daniel Schuster[1,2] [ID]

[1] Fraunhofer FIT, Sankt Augustin, Germany
{alessandro.berti,humam.kourani,hannes.haefke,
chiao-yun.li,daniel.schuster}@fit.fraunhofer.de
[2] Process and Data Science Chair, RWTH Aachen University, Aachen, Germany

Abstract. Using Large Language Models (LLMs) for Process Mining (PM) tasks is becoming increasingly essential, and initial approaches yield promising results. However, little attention has been given to developing strategies for evaluating and benchmarking the utility of incorporating LLMs into PM tasks. This paper reviews the current implementations of LLMs in PM and reflects on three different questions. 1) What is the minimal set of capabilities required for PM on LLMs? 2) Which benchmark strategies help choose optimal LLMs for PM? 3) How do we evaluate the output of LLMs on specific PM tasks? The answer to these questions is fundamental to the development of comprehensive process mining benchmarks on LLMs covering different tasks and implementation paradigms.

Keywords: Large Language Models (LLMs) · Output Evaluation · Benchmarking Strategies

1 Introduction

Process mining (PM) is a data science field focusing on deriving insights about business process executions from event data recorded by information systems [1]. Several types of PM exist, including *process discovery* (learning process models from event data), *conformance checking* (comparing event data with process models), and *process enhancement* (adding frequency/performance metrics to process models). Although many automated methods exist for PM, human analysts usually handle process analysis due to the need for domain knowledge. Recently, LLMs have emerged as conversational interfaces trained on extensive data [28], achieving near-human performance in various general tasks [38]. Their potential in PM lies in *embedded domain knowledge* useful for generating database queries and insights [21], *logical and temporal reasoning capabilities* [2,16], *inference abilities over structured data* [12]. Prior research has asserted

H. van der Aa et al. (Eds.): BPMDS 2024/EMMSAD 2024, LNBIP 511, pp. 13–21, 2024.
https://doi.org/10.1007/978-3-031-61007-3_2

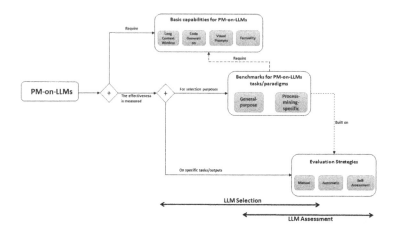

Fig. 1. Outline of the contributions of this paper.

the usage of LLMs for PM tasks [3,4]. However, a comprehensive discussion on necessary capabilities for PM, LLMs' suitability evaluation for process analytics, and assessment of LLMs' outputs in the PM context is lacking.

The three main contributions of this paper are summarized in Fig. 1. First, building upon prior work [3,4] proposing textual abstractions of process mining artifacts and an experimental evaluation of LLMs' responses, the essential capabilities that LLMs must have for PM tasks are derived in Sect. 3.1. The aforementioned capabilities allow us to narrow down the field of LLMs to those that meet these requirements. Next, evaluation benchmarks for selecting suitable LLMs are introduced in Sect. 3.2, incorporating both process-mining-specific and general criteria such as reasoning, visual understanding, factuality, and trustworthiness. Finally, we suggest automatic, human, and self-assessment methods for evaluating LLMs' outputs on specific tasks in Sect. 3.3, aiming to establish a comprehensive PM benchmark and enhance confidence in LLMs' usage, addressing potential issues like hallucination.

This paper provides an orientation to process mining researchers investigating the usage of LLMs, i.e., this paper aims to facilitate PM-on-LLMs research.

2   Background

LLMs enhance PM with superior capabilities, handling complex tasks through data understanding and natural language processing. This section covers PM tasks with LLMs (Sect. 2.1) and the adopted implementation paradigms (Sect. 2.2) along with the provision of additional domain knowledge.

2.1   Process Mining Tasks for LLMs

This subsection explores a range of PM tasks in which LLMs have already been adopted for process mining research. LLMs facilitate the automation of generating *textual descriptions* from process data, handling inputs such as event logs or formal process models [4]. They also generate *process models* from textual descriptions, with studies showing LLMs creating BPMN models and declarative constraints from text [7]. In the realm of anomaly detection, LLMs play a crucial role in identifying process data *anomalies*, including unusual activities and performance bottlenecks, offering context-aware detection that adapts to new patterns through prompt engineering. This improves versatility over traditional methods [3,4]. For *root cause analysis*, LLMs analyze event logs to suggest causes of anomalies or inefficiencies, linking delays to specific conditions or events. This goes beyond predefined logic, employing language processing for context-aware analysis [3,4] In ensuring *fairness*, LLMs identify and mitigate bias in processes, suggesting adjustments. They analyze processes like recruitment to detect disparities in rejection rates or delays by gender or nationality, aiding in fair decision-making [4,22]. LLMs can also interpret and explain *visual data*, including complex visualizations, by describing event flows in dotted charts and identifying specific patterns, such as batch processing. For process improvement, after PM tasks identify and analyze problems, LLMs can suggest actions and propose new process constraints [4,22].

2.2 Implementation Paradigms of Process Mining on LLMs

To effectively employ LLMs for PM tasks, specific implementation paradigms are required [3,4]. This section outlines key approaches for implementing LLMs in PM tasks. We distinguish three main strategies:

- *Direct provision of insights*: A prompt is generated that merges data abstractions with a query about the task. Also, interactive dialogue between the LLM and the user is possible for step-by-step analysis. The user starts with a query and refines or adjusts it based on the LLM's feedback, continuing until achieving the desired detail or accuracy, such as pinpointing process inefficiencies. For instance, to have LLMs identifying unusual behavior in an event log, we combine a textual abstraction of the log (such as the directly-follows graph or list of process variants) with a question like "Can you analyze the log to detect any unusual behavior?"
- *Code generation*: LLMs can be used to create structured queries, like SQL, for advanced PM tasks [11]. Rather than directly asking LLMs for answers, users command LLMs to craft database queries from natural language. These queries are then executed on the databases holding PM information. It is applicable to PM tasks that can be converted into database queries, such as filtering event logs or computing the average duration of process steps. Also, LLMs can be used to generate executable programs that use existing PM libraries to infer insights over the event data [9].
- *Automated hypotheses generation*: Combining the previous strategies by using textual data abstraction to prompt LLMs for autonomous hypotheses generation [3,4]. The hypotheses are accompanied by SQL queries for verification against event data. Results confirm or refute these hypotheses, with potential for LLM-suggested refinements of hypotheses.

LLMs may require additional knowledge about processes and databases to implement PM tasks, for example, in anomaly detection and crafting accurate database queries. Some strategies are used to equip LLMs with this additional domain knowledge [14], including *fine-tuning* and *prompt engineering*.

3   Evaluating LLMs in Process Mining

This section introduces criteria for selecting LLMs that are suitable for PM tasks. Moreover, we introduce criteria for evaluating their outputs. First, in Sect. 3.1, we discuss the fundamental capabilities needed for PM (long context window, acceptance of visual prompts, coding, factuality). Then, we introduce in Sect. 3.2 general-purpose and process-mining-specific benchmarks to measure the different LLMs on process-mining-related tasks. To foster the development of process-mining-specific benchmarks and to be able to evaluate a given output, we propose in Sect. 3.3 different methods to evaluate the output of an LLM.

3.1   LLMs Capabilities Needed for Process Mining

In this section, we discuss four important capabilities of LLMs for PM tasks:

- *Long Context Window*: Event logs in PM often include a vast amount of cases and events, challenging the *context window* limit of LLMs, which restricts the token count in a prompt [13]. Moreover, also the textual specification of process models requires a significant amount of information. The context window limit can be severe in many currently popular LLMs.[1] Even simple abstractions like the ones introduced in [3] (directly-follows graph, list of process variants) may exceed this limitation. The context window, which is set during model training, must be large enough for the data size. Recent efforts aim to extend this limit, though quality may decline [13,20].
- *Accepting Visual Prompts*: Visualizations in PM, such as the dotted chart and the performance spectrum [15], summarizing process behavior, empower analysts to spot interesting patterns not seen in tables. Interpreting visual prompts is key for semi-automated PM. Large Visual Models (LVMs) use architectures similar to language models trained on annotated image datasets [31]. They perform tasks like object detection and image synthesis, recognizing patterns, textures, shapes, colors, and spatial relations.[2]
- *Coding (Text-to-SQL) Capabilities*: With the context window limit preventing full event log inclusion in prompts, generating scripts and database queries is crucial for analyzing event data. As discussed in Sect. 2.2, text-to-SQL assists in filtering and analyzing event data. Key requirements for text-to-SQL in PM include understanding database schemas, performing complex joins, using database-specific operators (e.g., for calculating date differences), and

---

[1] https://community.openai.com/t/are-the-full-8k-gpt-4-tokens-available-on-chatgpt/237999.

[2] GPT-4 and Google Bard/Gemini are popular models supporting both visual and textual prompts.

translating PM concepts into queries. Overall, modern LLMs offer excellent coding capabilities [3].

– *Factuality*: LLM hallucination involves generating incorrect or fabricated information [24]. Factuality measures an LLM's ability to cross-check its outputs against real facts or data, crucial for PM tasks like anomaly detection and root cause analysis. This may involve leveraging external databases [19], knowledge bases, or internet search [32] for validation. For instance, verifying the sequence Cancel Order" followed by Deliver Order" against public data in anomaly detection. LLMs with web browsing can access up-to-date information, enhancing factuality.[3]

3.2 Relevant LLMs Benchmarks

After identifying the required capabilities for LLMs in PM, benchmarking strategies are essential to measure the quality of the textual outputs returned by the LLMs satisfying such capabilities.

Considering the wide array of available benchmarks for assessing LLMs behavior, we focus on identifying those most relevant to PM capabilities. In [5], a comprehensive collection of benchmarks is introduced. This section aims to select and utilize some of these benchmarks to evaluate various aspects of LLMs' performance in PM contexts.

– *Traditional benchmarks*: Textual prompts are crucial for LLMs evaluation in PM. Benchmarks like AGIEval assess models via standardized exams [37], and MT-Bench focuses on conversational and instructional capabilities [36]. Another benchmark evaluates LLMs on prompts of long size [6].
– *Domain knowledge benchmarks*: Domain knowledge is essential for LLMs in PM to identify anomalies using metrics and context. Benchmarks like XIEZHI assess knowledge across different fields (economics, science, engineering) [8], while ARB evaluates expertise in areas like mathematics and natural sciences [26].
– *Visual benchmarks*: Understanding PM visualizations, such as dotted charts, is essential (c.f. Section 3.1). LLMs must accurately process queries on these visualizations. MMBench tests models on image tasks [17], and MM-Vet assesses recognition, OCR, among others [35]. Yet, they may not fully meet PM visualization analysis needs, particularly in evaluating line orientations and point size/color.
– *Benchmarks for Text-to-SQL*: In PM, generating SQL from natural language is key for tasks like event log filtering. Benchmarks such as SPIDER and SPIDER-realistic test LLMs on text-to-SQL conversion [23]. The APPS benchmark evaluates broader code generation abilities [10].
– *Fairness benchmarks*: they evaluate LLM fairness in PM by analyzing group treatment and bias detection. DecodingTrust measures LLM trustworthiness, covering toxicity, bias, robustness, privacy, ethics, and fairness [30].

---

[3] https://cointelegraph.com/news/chat-gpt-ai-openai-browse-internet-no-longer-limited-info-2021.

- *Benchmarking the generation of hypotheses*: LLMs' ability to generate hypotheses from event data is vital to implement semi-autonomous PM agents. While specific benchmarks for hypothesis generation are lacking, related studies like [29, 34] evaluate LLMs using scientific papers.

Table 1. Implementation paradigms and benchmarks for LLMs in the context of different PM tasks.

Task	Paradigms			Benchmarks Classes					
	Direct Provision	Code Generation	Hypotheses Generation	Traditional	Domain Knowledge	Visual Prompts	Text-to-SQL	Fairness	Hypotheses Generation
Process Description	X			X	X				
Process Modeling	X	X	X	X	X		X		X
Anomaly Detection	X		X	X	X		X		X
Root Cause Analysis	X		X	X	X		X		X
Ensuring Fairness	X		X	X	X		X	X	X
Expl. and Interpreting	X				X	X			
Visualizations									
Process Improvement	X	X	X	X	X		X	X	X

In Table 1, we link process mining (PM) tasks to implementation paradigms and benchmarks. We discuss these tasks:

- *Process description* requires understanding technical terms relevant to the domain, crucial for accurately describing processes.
- *Process modeling* involves generating models from text, using SQL for declarative and BPMN XML for procedural models. LLMs should offer various model hypotheses.
- *Anomaly detection* and *root cause analysis* need domain knowledge to analyze process sequences or identify event attribute combinations causing issues.
- *Fairness* involves detecting biases by analyzing event attributes and values, necessitating hypothesis generation by LLMs.
- *Explaining and interpreting visualizations* requires extracting features from images and texts, offering contextual insights, like interpreting performance spectrum visualization [15].

– *Process improvement* entails suggesting text proposals or new constraints to enhance current models, leveraging code generation capabilities and understanding process limitations.

While general-purpose benchmarks are already developed and are easily accessible, they are not entirely suited for the task of PM-on-LLMs. In particular, visual capabilities (explaining and interpreting PM visualizations) and autonomous hypotheses generation require more PM-specific benchmarks. However, little research exists on PM-specific benchmarks [3,4].

3.3   How to Evaluate LLMs Outputs

This section outlines criteria for assessing the quality of outputs generated by LLMs in PM tasks, serving two primary objectives. The first objective is to assist users in identifying and addressing hallucinations and inaccuracies in LLMs' outputs. The second aim is to establish criteria for developing an extensive benchmark specifically tailored to PM applications of LLMs. The strategies follow:

– *Automatic evaluation* is particularly suited for text-to-SQL tasks. In this context, the formal accuracy and conciseness (indicated by the length of the produced query) of the SQL queries generated can be efficiently assessed. Additionally, the creation of declarative constraints, designed to enhance process execution, can also be evaluated in terms of their formal correctness.
– *Human evaluation* is essential for LLM tasks like direct querying and hypothesis generation. For direct querying tasks such as anomaly detection and root cause analysis, important criteria are *recall* (the model's ability to identify expected insights) and *precision* (the correctness of insights). These criteria also apply to hypothesis generation. Additionally, evaluating the feedback cycle's effectiveness in validating original hypotheses is crucial for these tasks.
– *Self-evaluation* in LLMs tackles hallucinations, as noted by [24]. Techniques include *chain-of-thought*, where LLMs detail their reasoning, enhancing explanations [33]. *Confidence scores* let LLMs assess their insights' reliability, discarding uncertain outputs for quality [27]. *Ensembling*, or using results from multiple LLM sessions, increases accuracy via majority voting or confidence checks [18]. *Self-reflection*, an LLM reviewing its or another's output, detects errors [25]. In anomaly detection, using confidence scores to exclude doubtful anomalies and ensembling to confirm detections across sessions improves reliability.

4   Conclusion

This paper examines LLM applications in PM, offering three main contributions: identification of necessary LLM capabilities for PM, review of benchmarks from literature, and strategies for evaluating LLM outputs in PM tasks. These strategies aim to build confidence in LLM use and establish benchmarks to assess LLM effectiveness across PM implementations.

Our discussion centers on current generative AI capabilities within PM, anticipating advancements like deriving event logs from videos. Despite future enhancements, the criteria discussed here should remain pertinent. Benchmarking for PM tasks on large language models (LLMs) will evolve, including both general and PM-specific benchmarks, yet the foundational aspects and methodologies are expected to stay consistent.

References

1. van der Aalst, W.M.P.: Process Mining - Data Science in Action, 2nd edn. Springer, Berlin (2016)
2. Bang, Y., et al.: A Multitask, Multilingual, Multimodal Evaluation of ChatGPT on Reasoning, Hallucination, and Interactivity (2023). https://doi.org/10.48550/arXiv.2302.04023
3. Berti, A., Qafari, M.S.: Leveraging Large Language Models (LLMs) for Process Mining (Technical Report) (2023). https://doi.org/10.48550/arXiv.2307.12701
4. Berti, A., Schuster, D., van der Aalst, W.M.P.: Abstractions, Scenarios, and Prompt Definitions for Process Mining with LLMs: A Case Study (2023). https://doi.org/10.48550/arXiv.2307.02194
5. Chang, Y., et al.: A Survey on Evaluation of Large Language Models (2023). https://doi.org/10.48550/arXiv.2307.03109
6. Dong, Z., et al.: BAMBOO: A Comprehensive Benchmark for Evaluating Long Text Modeling Capacities of Large Language Models (2023). https://doi.org/10.48550/arXiv.2309.13345
7. Grohs, M., et al.: Large language models can accomplish business process management Tasks. In: De Weerdt, J., Pufahl, L. (eds.) BPM 2023. Lecture Notes in Business Information Processing, vol. 492, pp. 453–465. Springer, Cham (2023). https://doi.org/10.1007/978-3-031-50974-2_34
8. Gu, Z., et al.: Xiezhi: An Ever-Updating Benchmark for Holistic Domain Knowledge Evaluation (2023). https://doi.org/10.48550/arXiv.2306.05783
9. Härer, F.: Conceptual model interpreter for large language models. In: ER 2023. CEUR Workshop Proceedings, vol. 3618. CEUR-WS.org (2023)
10. Hendrycks, D., et al.: Measuring coding challenge competence with APPS. In: NeurIPS Datasets and Benchmarks 2021 (2021)
11. Jessen, U., Sroka, M., Fahland, D.: Chit-Chat or Deep Talk: Prompt Engineering for Process Mining (2023). https://doi.org/10.48550/arXiv.2307.09909
12. Jiang, J., et al.: StructGPT: a general framework for large language model to reason over structured data. In: EMNLP 2023, pp. 9237–9251. Association for Computational Linguistics (2023)
13. Jin, H., et al.: LLM Maybe LongLM: Self-Extend LLM Context Window Without Tuning (2024). https://doi.org/10.48550/arXiv.2401.01325
14. Kampik, T., et al.: Large Process Models: Business Process Management in the Age of Generative AI (2023). https://doi.org/10.48550/arXiv.2309.00900
15. Klijn, E.L., Fahland, D.: Performance mining for batch processing using the performance spectrum. In: Di Francescomarino, C., Dijkman, R., Zdun, U. (eds.) BPM 2019. LNBIP, vol. 362, pp. 172–185. Springer, Cham (2019). https://doi.org/10.1007/978-3-030-37453-2_15
16. Liu, H., et al.: Evaluating the Logical Reasoning Ability of ChatGPT and GPT-4 (2023). https://doi.org/10.48550/arXiv.2304.03439

17. Liu, Y., et al.: MMBench: Is Your Multi-modal Model an All-around Player? (2023). https://doi.org/10.48550/arXiv.2307.06281
18. Lu, K., et al.: Routing to the Expert: Efficient Reward-guided Ensemble of Large Language Models (2023). https://doi.org/10.48550/arXiv.2311.08692
19. Pan, S., et al.: Unifying Large Language Models and Knowledge Graphs: A Roadmap (2023). https://doi.org/10.48550/arXiv.2306.08302
20. Peng, B., et al.: YaRN: Efficient Context Window Extension of Large Language Models (2023). https://doi.org/10.48550/arXiv.2309.00071
21. Petroni, F., et al.: Language models as knowledge bases? In: EMNLP-IJCNLP 2019, pp. 2463–2473. Association for Computational Linguistics (2019)
22. Qafari, M.S., van der Aalst, W.: Fairness-aware process mining. In: Panetto, H., Debruyne, C., Hepp, M., Lewis, D., Ardagna, C.A., Meersman, R. (eds.) OTM 2019. LNCS, vol. 11877, pp. 182–192. Springer, Cham (2019). https://doi.org/10.1007/978-3-030-33246-4_11
23. Rajkumar, N., Li, R., Bahdanau, D.: Evaluating the Text-to-SQL Capabilities of Large Language Models (2022). https://doi.org/10.48550/arXiv.2204.00498
24. Rawte, V., et al.: The Troubling emergence of hallucination in large language models - an extensive definition, quantification, and prescriptive remediations. In: EMNLP 2023, pp. 2541–2573. Association for Computational Linguistics (2023)
25. Ren, J., et al.: Self-Evaluation Improves Selective Generation in Large Language Models (2023)
26. Sawada, T., et al.: ARB: Advanced Reasoning Benchmark for Large Language Models (2023). https://doi.org/10.48550/arXiv.2307.13692
27. Singh, A.K., et al.: The Confidence-Competence Gap in Large Language Models: A Cognitive Study (2023). https://doi.org/10.48550/arXiv.2309.16145
28. Teubner, T., et al.: Welcome to the Era of ChatGPT et al. Bus. Inf. Syst. Eng. **65**(2), 95–101 (2023)
29. Tong, S., Mao, K., Huang, Z., Zhao, Y., Peng, K.: Automating Psychological Hypothesis Generation with AI: Large Language Models Meet Causal Graph (2023)
30. Wang, B., et al.: DecodingTrust: A Comprehensive Assessment of Trustworthiness in GPT Models (2023). https://doi.org/10.48550/arXiv.2306.11698
31. Wang, J., et al.: Review of Large Vision Models and Visual Prompt Engineering (2023). https://doi.org/10.48550/arXiv.2307.00855
32. Wang, L., et al.: A Survey on Large Language Model based Autonomous Agents (2023). https://doi.org/10.48550/arXiv.2308.11432
33. Wei, J., et al.: Chain-of-Thought Prompting Elicits Reasoning in Large Language Models. In: NeurIPS 2022 (2022)
34. Yang, Z., et al.: Large Language Models for Automated Open-domain Scientific Hypotheses Discovery (2023). https://doi.org/10.48550/arXiv.2309.02726
35. Yu, W., et al.: MM-Vet: Evaluating Large Multimodal Models for Integrated Capabilities (2023). https://doi.org/10.48550/arXiv.2308.02490
36. Zheng, L., et al.: Judging LLM-as-a-judge with MT-Bench and Chatbot Arena (2023). https://doi.org/10.48550/arXiv.2306.05685
37. Zhong, W., et al.: AGIEval: A Human-Centric Benchmark for Evaluating Foundation Models (2023). https://doi.org/10.48550/arXiv.2304.06364
38. Zhou, Y., et al.: Large Language Models are Human-Level Prompt Engineers. In: ICLR 2023. OpenReview.net (2023)

Mapping the Landscape: Exploring Large Language Model Applications in Business Process Management

Bedilia Estrada-Torres(✉)📧, Adela del-Río-Ortega📧, and Manuel Resinas📧

SCORE Lab, Universidad de Sevilla, Seville, Spain
{iestrada,adeladelrio,resinas}@us.es

Abstract. The irruption of large language models (LLMs) during the last year has prompted researchers and practitioners to explore novel scenarios for integrating LLMs, enhancing task execution efficiency across diverse domains. Among these, business process management (BPM) stands out as a fertile ground for leveraging LLM features. As organizations strive to streamline their processes throughout the BPM lifecycle, the potential benefits of incorporating LLMs become increasingly evident. In this sense, over the past year, several approaches have been proposed to incorporate LLMs in BPM-related tasks. Concurrently, research efforts have identified key research directions that can help guide the adoption of LLMs in the BPM lifecycle phases. In this article, we perform a comprehensive literature review to assess the impact and coverage of existing approaches in addressing these research directions. In addition, we deem it particularly relevant to analyze the evaluation criteria followed. By analyzing existing proposals and techniques, we aim to shed light on the most addressed BPM lifecycle phases, pinpointing the research directions they entail and the evaluation criteria utilized. Through this analysis, we provide valuable insights and recommendations to inform future research endeavors.

Keywords: LLM · Business Process Management · Lifecycle

1 Introduction

Large Language Models (LLMs) enable the development of artificial intelligence-based systems capable of analyzing and processing natural language and generating coherent texts. They facilitate, for example, the development of tasks such as translation, summarization, classification and grammatical correction of texts, extraction of relevant information, analysis of opinions, and generation of code based on natural language descriptions [3]. The recent release and ease of access to LLM versions such as *ChatGPT* [34] and *GPT-4* [35] have driven interest in LLMs across numerous users and application contexts [11,37]. From this boom, concerns arise about how LLMs can be integrated into both the development of everyday personal tasks as well as academic [26] and business activities [15].

H. van der Aa et al. (Eds.): BPMDS 2024/EMMSAD 2024, LNBIP 511, pp. 22–31, 2024.
https://doi.org/10.1007/978-3-031-61007-3_3

Regarding business process management (BPM), which concerns us in this study, some authors suggest that LLMs can help improve process management by reducing the effort and expertise required, improving data analysis, or automating tasks [22]. Vidgof et al. [38] extend this analysis and describe the possible applications of LLMs in each of the BPM lifecycle phases. They also propose six research directions to guide the adoption of LLMs in the BPM context.

Despite the novelty of LLMs proposals, and in particular, those related to BPM, in this article, we embark on a comprehensive literature review that aims to (i) identify the existing proposals, methods, and techniques, and their main characteristics (e.g., purpose, inputs, outputs), (ii) determine the most addressed BPM lifecycle phases, (iii) assess the coverage of the research directions proposed in [38], (iv) pinpoint the most used LLMs to date, and (v) recognize the evaluation criteria used in each proposal. To the best of our knowledge, this is the first of these analyses. From this information, we extract the current research trends, evaluation criteria, and areas that need more attention, providing valuable insights to inform future research endeavors.

The rest of this paper is organized as follows. Section 2 introduces preliminary concepts related to this study. The literature review process is described in Sect. 3. Our results are presented in Sect. 4. Finally, Sect. 5 concludes the paper.

2 Preliminary Concepts

The following subsections present key preliminaries to provide the necessary background for our discussion: the BPM lifecycle and LLMs.

2.1 Business Process Management Lifecycle

Several BPM lifecycle definitions can be found in BPM literature. In this article, we focus on the proposal by Dumas et al. [14] that describes six phases. It starts with the *identification* phase, which consists of distinguishing the processes relevant to the organization, as well as identifying performance measures and objectives. The *discovery* phase seeks a better understanding of the process and usually results in one or more graphic models to facilitate its comprehensibility. *Analysis* is the third phase that seeks to identify and evaluate problems and opportunities for process improvement. In the *redesign* phase, a new process version is proposed based on the previously identified problems and the alternative solutions. The fifth phase, *implementation*, involves applying the changes derived from the previous phase at the organizational and the systems level (automation). The last phase is *monitoring*, in which process data is collected and analyzed to identify whether the process is meeting expectations or adjustments are necessary. The result of monitoring can lead to a new discovery phase.

2.2 Large Language Models

LLMs are large computational models with billions of parameters that have the ability to understand and generate human language and have exceptional learning capabilities [11]. LLMs must be trained using enormous amounts of data that are used to learn complex patterns and relationships between words and phrases [3,11,38]. They rely on a (*Transformer*) architecture to extract meaning from text sequences and understand semantic relationships [3,11]. Multimodal LLMs can use, in addition to texts, other sources of information such as graphics, sounds, and photographs to produce text outputs [3].

Current LLMs have generated significant interest since the recent release of *ChatGPT* [34]. However, some of them are an evolution of language models such as Bert [13] or *GPT-1* [36], released in 2018. There are several LLMs such as *GPT-4* [35], a large-scale multimodal model; *PaLM 2* [17] that stands out for its mathematical, coding, and reasoning capabilities; *Llama 2* [20], a collection of pretrained and fine-tuned models; *Mistral* [31], an open-source model that stands out for its precise recovery of information on extensive documents; among others.

3   Review Method

We conducted a literature review on applications of LLMs related to BPM following a method inspired by the guidelines proposed in [39] and [23]. The search included proposals until December 2023 and seeks to answer the following.

- **RQ1:** What BPM lifecycle phases are addressed by the identified proposals?
- **RQ2:** What are the main input artifacts used by the identified proposals and the output artifacts generated by them?
- **RQ3:** What research directions on LLMs and BPM are being addressed by the identified proposals?
- **RQ4:** Which LLMs are most commonly used in the identified proposals?
- **RQ5:** What are the evaluation criteria used in the identified proposals?

3.1   Inclusion and Exclusion Criteria

The literature was reviewed in search of articles that relate LLM proposals to some BPM lifecycle phase, including methods, techniques, or current state analysis (e.g., positioning articles). Only articles in English were considered. We included the *arXiv*[1] articles that have not been peer reviewed due to the novelty of the topic and because the objective of our study is to know the initial trends. Articles not exclusively related to BPM but that consider BPM in some way were also included. Unavailable, repeated, and articles with different authors but with the same content were excluded, as well as bachelor and master theses.

3.2   Sources and Search Strategy

The search for articles was carried out through three bibliographic reference databases *Scopus*[2], *DBLP*[3] and *WOS*[4]. We use "large language models" and

---

[1] https://arxiv.org/.
[2] https://www.scopus.com/.
[3] https://dblp.org/.
[4] https://www.webofscience.com/wos/woscc/basic-search.

Table 1. Search in databases and articles obtained.

Databases	Query	Init.	Mod.	Rev.	Primary studies
Scopus	(TITLE(business AND process) AND ABS(large AND language AND models) AND ABS(business AND process))	1	60	3	2
DBLP	"large language models" + "business process"	3	3	2	2
WOS	(TI=(business process)) AND (AB=(large language models) AND AB=(business process))	0	62	0	0
Google Scholar	"large language models" + "business process"	-	382	25	17
Total		4	507	30	**21**

Table 2. Classification of articles according to their status and publication type.

Publication status			Categories			
Type	Num.	%	Category name	Position	Phases	Total
Unpublished	7	33%	arXiv	1	6	7
			Journal	3	1	4
Published	14	67%	Main Conference-Track	1	4	5
			Forums/Workshop/Subconferences	3	2	5
Totals	21	100%	-	8	13	**21**

"business process" as search criteria, both in the titles and abstracts. Including both phrases as mandatory in the titles and abstracts yielded very few results (Table 1, column *Init.*). The search was expanded to the *Google Scholar* database, and the queries were modified to avoid excluding articles relevant to this study (column *Query*). In total, we obtained 507 articles (column *Mod.*). The titles and abstracts were reviewed to discard those that did not meet the inclusion criteria. The complete articles were reviewed in cases where there were doubts about their inclusion, resulting in 30 articles (column *Rev.*). Finally, the complete articles were reviewed to verify the inclusion criteria, to identify the type of contribution, and the BPM lifecycle phase to which it relates, if applicable. We obtained 21 articles, called *primary studies* as in [23]. All articles obtained were from 2023, probably due to the recent rise of the LLM topic.

4   Results

The *primary studies* were classified according to the type of contribution or their relationship with the BPM lifecycle phases, their publication status, and sources.

Although all of the articles used are available online, we made a distinction between those published in journals, conferences, or other forums (*Published*, 14) and those available at *arXiv* (*Unpublished*, 7) because the latter lack prior expert review and approval. Eight *primary studies* are positioning articles on the facilities provided by LLMs in BPM, of which only one (12,5%) is *Unpublished*. The remaining 13 *primary studies* contribute to the BPM lifecycle phases, with 6 (46%) *Unpublished* articles (Table 2). Next, we describe the two main categories.

4.1   Positioning Articles

We carefully looked at the 8 positioning articles we found to analyze the potential use cases they propose for using LLMs in the BPM lifecycle phases. Regarding the *identification* phase, the use of LLMs is suggested in [38] for identifying processes from unstructured documentation. For the *discovery* phase, LLMs are suggested to generate models by mining and analyzing documentation or communication records [38], create software models in general, perform transformations between models [12], and to support the generation of process models centered on data and knowledge of workers [4]. As for the *analysis* phase, LLMs are recommended for identifying problems and bottlenecks in processes [38], *ChatGPT* for analyzing and comprehending software systems [12], and prompt engineering to enhance process explainability [9]. LLMs are proposed to *redesign* information systems and for BPM [15], to automatically extract redesign suggestions [4], although no details are provided; and to find alternatives to errors and suggestions for improvement [38]. Concerning the *implementation* phase, LLMs are proposed to support the automation and tailoring of tasks [38] and for decision making [4]. Finally, for the *monitoring* phase, LLMs are suggested to collect information on the process execution and its subsequent analysis [38]. The remaining articles do not address a particular phase: in [30], artificial intelligence is suggested to substitute modelers and code generators; in [18], a workshop is introduced but it does not provide details of its approach; while in [22], it is proposed to integrate process information with LLMs to reduce the effort and experience necessary for knowledge-based management tasks such as process data query language.

We examined the positioning papers to identify possible research directions arising from applying LLM to BPM. Out of the 8 positioning *primary studies*, only in [38] are (six) research directions proposed related to this area: *RD1-The use of LLMs in BPM practice* suggests identifying in which BPM tasks LLMs provide greater value. *RD2-Usage guidelines for researchers and practitioners* to, for example, suggest an LLM to achieve an expected value and collect best practices for creating prompts. *RD3-Creation, release, and maintenance of task variants specific to BPM* deals with the mapping of general natural language processing tasks to tasks within BPM. *RD4-Creation, release, and maintenance of data sets and benchmarks* refers, for example, whether existing natural language processing datasets and benchmarks are relevant to BPM. *RD5-LLM and BPM Artifacts* seeks to understand what artifacts are necessary for LLMs to create valuable results. Finally, *RD6-Development and release of LLMs for BPM*, seeks to study how LLMs are constructed for specific BPM tasks.

In the next section, these six research directions are used as a classification criterion to analyze the 13 articles contributing to the BPM lifecycle phases.

4.2   Articles that Contribute to the BPM Lifecycle Phases

This section addresses the research questions using information of Tables 3 and 4.

Table 3. Classification of *primary studies* related to the BPM lifecycle phases

Proposal	Purpose	Inputs	Outpus	Status	Phases	BPM	RD
Grohs et al. [19]	Generate textual BP model descrips. from textual BP descrips.	BP description Output structure	BP models textual notation and Textual BP description	UP	Discovery	√	1
Bellan et al. [6]	Extract BP info. from textual BP descrips.	BP description [Context info.]	BP elements information	P	Discovery	√	1
Zhu et al. [41]	Generate textual BP descrips. from tree notations	Conditional tree Background Restrictions	Textual BP description	UP	Discovery Analysis	√	1 & 2
Licardo et al. [27]	Generate BPM models from textual BP descrips.	BP descriptions Not detailed	Not specified	UP	Discovery	√	1
Fill et al. [16]	Generate JSON code from textual model descrips	BP descriptions Context model Example	BP model in JSON code	P	Discovery	N-E	1
Härer [21]	Generate&render models from models descrips.	Structured BP model info.	Textual and graphical models	P	Discovery	×	1
Klievtsova et al. [24]	Extract BP elements from textual BP descrips.	Textual BP descriptions taken from [29]	BP elements information	P	Discovery	√	1
Berti et al. [7]	Analysis&Process mining from event logs	Event logs	Process mining information	UP	Analysis Monitoring	√	1 & 5
Caspary et al. [10]	BP compliance	Event log Bert model PT Model traces pairs	Detected anomalies	P	Analysis	√	1
Mustroph et al. [33]	BP compliance	Event logs BP descriptions	Activity matching Compliance output	P	Analysis	√	1 & 2
Mudgal et al. [32]	Process mining from textual information	Text-tasks Extraction rules	Process mining information	P	Analysis	×	1
Lins et al. [28]	BP Follow-up	BPMN XML file	Answers to questions	UP	Analysis	√	1
Berti et al. [8]	Process mining from abstracted BP models	Event logs	Process mining info. Queries based on prompts	UP	Monitoring	√	1 & 5

To answer **RQ1**, we identify the BPM lifecycle phases addressed in each of the *primary studies (ps)*. Only for 2 of them we identified two phases, the rest address only one. For the *discovery* phase (7 *ps*), most *ps* generate a textual process model using a particular notation, by generating renderable code (e.g., JSON), using visualization software (e.g., Graphviz), or by generating textual process descriptions from semistructured process information. For the *analysis* phase, *ps* identify whether LLMs can follow the process flow based on descriptions or event logs and verify conformance of log traces from a process model. Finally, for the *monitoring* phase, *ps* focus on extracting data from processes to identify bottlenecks, throughput times, etc. No *ps* regarding the other phases were found.

Concerning **RQ2**, the *inputs* required for the *ps* vary based on their purpose, including textual or structured process model descriptions or event logs. Optional inputs are enclosed in brackets ([ ]). The *outputs* are also diverse and can include process models (textual or renderable code), process descriptions, or quantitative process information, depending on the BPM lifecycle phases addressed.

RQ3 refers to the relationship between the *ps* and the referenced research directions (Table 3, col. *RD*). We consider that the 13 *ps* address *RD1* by describing practical applications of LLMs in the BPM (lifecycle) tasks. Two *ps* address *RD2* as they present frameworks and algorithms that connect LLMs with BPM tasks and can be considered as guidelines for practitioners. *RD5* is addressed by 2 *ps*, aiming to enhance BPM tasks through prompt engi-

Table 4. Characteristics of the proposals and their evaluations.

Proposal	Impl.	LLM	Evaluation sources	Comparison		Evaluation		F-T	Resource Availability
				Internal	Ext.	Quantitative	Qualitative		
Grohs et al. [19]	Prompts by chats	GPT-4	6 PET [5] BP desc.	BP descs. Measures Measures	- [1] R. [25]	- Pre-Rec-F1S Pre-Rec-F1S	Correctness - -	-	Input Output Results
Bellan et al. [6]	Prompts by chats	GPT-3.5T	7 PET [5] BP desc.	Different contextual prompts	-	Pre-Rec-F1S	-	-	Prompts* material*
Zhu et al. [41]	Prompts by chats	GPT-3.5T	100 Cond. Trees	With & Without proposal	-	-	Subjective Evaluators opinions	-	-
Licardo et al. [27]	Prototype	GPT-3.5T GPT-4	31 BP descriptions	LLMs	-	Accuracy RGED	-	√*	-
Fill et al. [16]	Prompts by chats	GPT-4	6 models descriptions	-	-	-	-	-	Examples in paper
Härer [21]	Architecture Prototype	GPT-4 Llama 2	2 modeling scenarios	LLMs	-	-	Correctness	-	Source code
Klievtsova et al. [24]	Prompts by chats	GPT-1, GPT-2, GPT-3, GPT-3.5	21 BP descriptions	LLMs	-	KPI similarities	-	-	Results
Berti et al. [7]	pm4py	GPT-4 Bard	4 public event logs	LLMs	-	Pre-recall	-	-	pm4py library
Caspary et al. [10]	Python	Bert	BPM Acad. Init. logs [40]	-	[2]	Pre-Rec-F1S	-	√	Input Output Source
Mustroph et al. [33]	Prompts by chats	GPT-3.5 GPT-4	45 PET [5] BPIC 2020	LLMs	-	Pre-Rec	-	-	Analysis* Event logs*
Mudgal et al. [32]	Prompts by chats	GPT-3.5T*	Log messages (Log extracts)	-	-	-	Textual analysis	-	-
Lins et al. [28]	Prompts by chats	GPT-3.5 PaLM 2		LLMs	-	-	Evaluation questions (Chats)	-	Questions Answers In paper
Berti et al. [8]	pm4py	GPT-4	4 public event logs	-	-	-	Discussion	-	Event logs Questions

neering and improving task inputs. No proposed solutions related to *RD3*, *RD4*, and *RD6* were found.

To address **RQ4**, we refer to Table 4 (column *LLM*), which includes the LLMs used in the evaluation of the *ps*. Only one *ps* indicates the specific LLM version (March 2023); see [32]. Seven *ps* use a single LLM for their evaluations. Of the 21 LLM versions used in the 13 *ps*, 17 are *GPT* versions (7 are *GPT-4*, and 5 are *GPT-3.5*). *Bard*, *Llama 2*, *PaLM 2*, and *Bert* are each used only once.

To tackle **RQ5**, we rely on the remaining information in Table 4. Only 4 *ps* describe an implementation (2 as prototypes and 2 as Python libraries). Eleven *ps* indicate using datasets (process descriptions or event logs), but only 6 *ps* reference these datasets. Specific examples were prepared for testing the remaining 5 *ps*. The *Comparison* columns indicate whether the evaluation was an *Internal* comparison using measures and specified LLMs or *External*, comparing results with other articles or replicating experiments like in [19]. The evaluation of the *ps* can be *Quantitative* (7 *ps*) when it includes measures like precision or recall or *Qualitative* when based on domain experts' opinions or reviewers' assessments. Only 2 *ps* report using fine-tuning (col. *F-T*), but one does not specify the parameters used (cf. [27]). Finally, the last column of Table 4 shows the *resources available* for each evaluation. *In paper* indicates that resources are examples included in the articles, and (*) means that resources could not be accessed.

5   Discussion and Conclusions

In this article, we explore the literature to identify and analyze articles relating LLMs to the BPM lifecycle phases (positioning proposals and practical applications). Through our literature study, we explored proposals, methodologies, and techniques while identifying the primary BPM lifecycle phases addressed as well as the input and output artifacts involved. Additionally, we assessed the coverage of research directions previously outlined, pinpointed commonly used LLMs, and recognized the evaluation criteria employed across proposals.

From the initial phase of our study, we conclude that the BPM lifecycle phases currently addressed are directly related to text processing or information extraction, such as models or data, i.e., discovery, analysis, and monitoring. However, more attention needs to be devoted to those oriented to identification, implementation, and redesign. Half of the proposals analyzed have not been officially published so far. The recently released LLMs feature significantly improved capabilities compared to their predecessors, which has accelerated their adoption and accessibility. This is likely why research on integrating LLMs into BPM is still in its early stages. Although many proposals use *ChatGPT* to extract process information, they do not analyze how the quality of prompts may impact the obtained results. Regarding the LLMs used, the tendency to relate LLMs only to GPT versions is striking. To strengthen proposals outcomes, replicating experiments and comparing results among different LLMs is recommended. It is worthwhile to compare proposals with LLMs from different families, including open-source LLMs, which offer greater privacy assurances, especially in sensitive environments. Concerning evaluation, emphasizing reproducibility is crucial, and this requires accessible information sources, configurations, process stages, and outcomes for experiments. Unclear evaluation criteria (e.g. measures) can hinder reproducibility. Half of the proposals use quantitative evaluation, but evaluator-dependent qualitative assessments pose challenges in generating and comparing with new experiments. Specific LLM version codes are also crucial to reproducibility, particularly given continuous technological advancements.

Acknowledgments. This work has been partially supported by grant PID2021-126227NB-C21 funded by MCIN/AEI /10.13039/501100011033/FEDER, EU, by grant TED2021-131023B-C22 funded by MCIN/AEI/10.13039/501100011033 and by the European Union "NextGenerationEU"/PRTR.

Disclosure of Interests. The authors have no competing interests to declare that are relevant to the content of this article.

References

1. van der Aa, H., Di Ciccio, C., Leopold, H., Reijers, H.A.: Extracting declarative process models from natural language. In: Giorgini, P., Weber, B. (eds.) CAiSE 2019. LNCS, vol. 11483, pp. 365–382. Springer, Cham (2019). https://doi.org/10.1007/978-3-030-21290-2_23

2. van der Aa, H., Rebmann, A., Leopold, H.: Natural language-based detection of semantic execution anomalies in event logs. Inf. Syst. **102**(C) (2021). https://doi.org/10.1016/j.is.2021.101824
3. Amazon Web Services: What are Large Language Models (LLM)? (2024)
4. Beheshti, A., Yang, J., et al.: ProcessGPT: transforming business process management with generative artificial intelligence. In: IEEE ICWS, pp. 731–739 (2023). https://doi.org/10.1109/ICWS60048.2023.00099
5. Bellan, P., van der Aa, H., et al.: PET: an annotated dataset for process extraction from natural language text tasks. In: Cabanillas, C., Garmann-Johnsen, N.F., Koschmider, A. (eds.) BPM 2022. LNBIP, vol. 460, pp. 315–321. Springer, Cham (2022). https://doi.org/10.1007/978-3-031-25383-6_23
6. Bellan, P., et al.: Extracting business process entities and relations from text using pre-trained language models. In: Almeida, J.P.A., Karastoyanova, D., Guizzardi, G., Montali, M., Maggi, F.M., Fonseca, C.M. (eds.) EDOC 2022. LNCS, vol. 13585, pp. 182–199. Springer, Cham (2022). https://doi.org/10.1007/978-3-031-17604-3_11
7. Berti, A., et al.: Leveraging large language models for process mining (2023)
8. Berti, A., Schuster, D., van der Aalst, W.M.P.: Abstractions, Scenarios, and Prompt Definitions for Process Mining with LLMs: A Case Study. In: De Weerdt, J., Pufahl, L. (eds.) BPM 2023. LNBIP, vol. 492, pp. 427–439. Springer, Cham (2023). https://doi.org/10.1007/978-3-031-50974-2_32
9. Busch, K., et al.: Just tell me: prompt engineering in business process management. In: van der Aa, H., Bork, D., Proper, H.A., Schmidt, R. (eds.) BPMDS EMMSAD 2023 2023. LNBIP, vol. 479, pp. 3–11. Springer, Cham (2023). https://doi.org/10.1007/978-3-031-34241-7_1
10. Caspary, J., Rebmann, A., van der Aa, H.: Does this make sense? Machine learning-based detection of semantic anomalies in business processes. In: Di Francesco-marino, C., Burattin, A., Janiesch, C., Sadiq, S. (eds.) BPM 2023. LNBIP, vol. 14159, pp. 163–179. Springer, Cham (2023). https://doi.org/10.1007/978-3-031-41620-0_10
11. Chang, Y., et al.: A survey on evaluation of large language models. ACM Trans. Intell. Syst. Technol (2024). https://doi.org/10.1145/3641289
12. Combemale, B., Gray, J., Rumpe, B.: ChatGPT in software modeling. Softw. Syst. Model. **22**(3), 777–779 (2023). https://doi.org/10.1007/s10270-023-01106-4
13. Devlin, J., et al.: BERT: Pre-training of deep bidirectional transformers for language understanding (2019)
14. Dumas, M., Rosa, M.L., et al.: Fundamentals of Business Process Management, 2nd edn. Springer, Heidelberg (2018). https://doi.org/10.1007/978-3-662-56509-4
15. Feuerriegel, S., Hartmann, J., Janiesch, C., et al.: Generative AI. Bus. Inf. Syst. Eng. **66**, 111–126 (2024). https://doi.org/10.1007/s12599-023-00834-7
16. Fill, H., Fettke, P., Köpke, J.: Conceptual modeling and large language models. Enterp. Model. Inf. Syst. Archit. Int. J. Concept. Model. **18**, 1–15 (2023)
17. GoogleAI: PaLM 2 (2023). https://ai.google/discover/palm2/
18. Grisold, T., et al.: Using large language models in business processes (2023). https://bpm2023.sites.uu.nl/program/tutorials/, Tutorials of BPM
19. Grohs, M., Abb, L., Elsayed, N., Rehse, J.R.: Large language models can accomplish business process management tasks. In: De Weerdt, J., Pufahl, L. (eds.) BPM 2023. LNBIP, vol. 492, pp. 453–465. Springer, Cham (2023). https://doi.org/10.1007/978-3-031-50974-2_34
20. Touvron, H., Martin, L., Stone, K., et al.: Llama 2: Open Foundation and Fine-Tuned Chat Models. Technical report GenAI, Meta (2023)

21. Härer, F.: Conceptual model interpreter for large language models (2023)
22. Kampik, T., Warmuth, C., et al.: Large process models: business process management in the age of generative AI (2023)
23. Kitchenham, B.A.: Procedures for performing systematic reviews (2024). Keele U
24. Klievtsova, N., Benzin, J.V., Kampik, T., Mangler, J., Rinderle-Ma, S.: Conversational process modelling. In: Di Francescomarino, C., Burattin, A., Janiesch, C., Sadiq, S. (eds.) BPM 2023. LNBIP, vol. 490, pp. 319–336. Springer, Cham (2023). https://doi.org/10.1007/978-3-031-41623-1_19
25. Leopold, H., van der Aa, H., Reijers, H.A.: Identifying candidate tasks for robotic process automation in textual process descriptions. In: Gulden, J., Reinhartz-Berger, I., Schmidt, R., Guerreiro, S., Guédria, W., Bera, P. (eds.) BPMDS/EMMSAD -2018. LNBIP, vol. 318, pp. 67–81. Springer, Cham (2018). https://doi.org/10.1007/978-3-319-91704-7_5
26. Li, Q., et al.: Adapting large language models for education: foundational capabilities, potentials, and challenges. CoRR **abs/2401.08664** (2024)
27. Licardo, J.T.: A Method for Extracting BPMN Models from Textual Descriptions Using Natural Language Processing. Master's thesis, University of Pula (2023)
28. Lins, L.F., Nascimento, N., Alencar, P., Oliveira, T., Cowan, D.: Comparing generative chatbots based on process requirements (2023)
29. Mangler, J., Klievtsova, N.: - (2023). https://zenodo.org/records/7783492
30. Michael, J., Bork, D., Wimmer, M., et al.: Quo vadis modeling?. Softw. Syst. Model. **23**, 7–28 (2024). https://doi.org/10.1007/s10270-023-01128-y
31. Mistral AI: Mistral AI. Technical report, Mistral AI (2023)
32. Mudgal, P., Wouhaybi, R.: An assessment of ChatGPT on log data. In: Zhao, F., Miao, D. (eds.) AIGC 2023. CCIS, vol. 1946, pp. 148–169. Springer, Singapore (2024). https://doi.org/10.1007/978-981-99-7587-7_13
33. Mustroph, H., Barrientos, M., et al.: Verifying resource compliance requirements from natural language text over event logs. In: Di Francescomarino, C., Burattin, A., Janiesch, C., Sadiq, S. (eds.) BPM 2023. LNCS, vol. 14159, pp. 249–265. Springer, Cham (2023). https://doi.org/10.1007/978-3-031-41620-0_15
34. OpenAI: ChatGPT (2022). https://openai.com/chatgpt
35. OpenAI: GPT-4 Technical Report. Technical report, OpenAI (2023)
36. Radford, A., et al.: Improving Language Understanding by Generative Pre-Training (2018). https://openai.com/research/language-unsupervised
37. Teubner, T., Flath, C.M., Weinhardt, C., van der Aalst, W.M.P., Hinz, O.: Welcome to the Era of ChatGPT et al.: Bus. Inf. Syst. Eng. **65**(2), 95–101 (2023). https://doi.org/10.1007/s12599-023-00795-x
38. Vidgof, M., et al.: Large language models for business process management: opportunities and challenges. In: Di Francescomarino, C., Burattin, A., Janiesch, C., Sadiq, S. (eds.) BPM 2023. LNBIP, vol. 490, pp. 107–123. Springer, Cham (2023). https://doi.org/10.1007/978-3-031-41623-1_7
39. Webster, J., Watson, R.T.: Analyzing the past to prepare for the future: Writing a literature review. MIS Q. **26**(2) (2002)
40. Weske, M., Decker, G., et al.: Model collection of the business process management academic initiative (2020). https://zenodo.org/records/3758705
41. Zhu, R., Hu, Q., Li, W., Xiao, H., Wang, C., Zhou, Z.: Business process text sketch automation generation using large language model (2023)

Process Model Extraction, Analysis, and Visualization (BPMDS 2024)

Designing a User Interface to Explore Collections of Directly-Follows Graphs for Process Mining Analysis

María Salas-Urbano[1,2](✉) , Carlos Capitán-Agudo[1,2] ,
Cristina Cabanillas[1,2] , and Manuel Resinas[1,2]

[1] SCORE Lab, Universidad de Sevilla, Seville, Spain
{msurbano,ccagudo,cristinacabanillas,resinas}@us.es
[2] I3US Institute, Universidad de Sevilla, Seville, Spain

Abstract. Process mining tools use Directly-Follows Graphs (DFGs) as the main means of visualization for exploring event logs and extracting valuable insights therefrom. Extracting significant insights from DFGs is a laborious process that involves multiple data manipulation operations and comparisons between the resulting DFGs generated after each manipulation. However, current process mining tools lack the ability to uniformly manipulate and manage multiple DFGs in a consistent manner. The objective of this study is to identify the requirements for designing a user-friendly interface to handle collections of DFGs to search for interesting visualizations for process mining analysis. To achieve this, three different data sources were used: a literature review of visual query tools, the analysis of LoVizQL, a query language for process mining, and the examination of reports from Business Process Intelligence Challenges. By combining these sources, insights into interface design needs aligned with real process mining applications were obtained. As a result, we have identified 14 requirements grouped into 3 main categories. These requirements serve as the basis to build future user interfaces of visual query tools for process mining.

Keywords: directly-follows graph · process mining · query language · requirements elicitation · user interface

1 Introduction

In process mining tools, Directly-Follows Graphs (DFG) are the most common visualization means used to explore event logs and search for relevant information in them [17]. The process of discovering insights from an event log usually

This work has been funded by projects PID2022-140221NB-I00 (TAPIOCA), PID2021-126227NB-C21 (PERSEO) and TED2021-131023B-C22 (ORCHID) granted by MCIN/AEI/10.13039/501100011033/ and ERDF A way of making Europe. M. Salas-Urbano is supported by PREP2022-000372 financed by MICIN/AEI/10.13039/501100011033 and by FSE+. C. Capitán-Agudo is supported by the Spanish Ministry of Education under the FPU national plan (FPU21/03631).

H. van der Aa et al. (Eds.): BPMDS 2024/EMMSAD 2024, LNBIP 511, pp. 35–47, 2024.
https://doi.org/10.1007/978-3-031-61007-3_4

involves multiple data manipulation operations and comparisons between the resulting DFGs generated after the manipulation. For example, consider a user who wishes to explore a log of travel declarations, in which different human resources are involved, with the goal of searching for resources whose process executions are associated with process delays. First, the user filters the cases related to the process execution of one concrete resource. Then, the user filters the cases by performance and examines the resulting DFG to gain insight and detect delays in the process. This process is repeated for each resource in the dataset, and the corresponding DFG is created in each iteration. To contrast the results, the user must apply the same filters repeatedly to understand the differences between the process executions related to the resources and discover relevant insights. This makes this whole process very manual and time-consuming.

The underlying problem is that current process mining tools are not designed to explicitly consider the collection of DFGs that is created by the successive application of filters. In the previous example, the collection of DFGs would be the DFGs obtained after filtering by each resource [20]. Consequently, searching for visualizations with specific characteristics from such a collection requires several manual comparisons between visualizations. This problem is not specific to process mining, but can also be found in data analytics and is typically addressed using visual query tools [16]. In these tools, the users can generate collections of general purpose visualizations and they can query this collection to find visualizations specifying their desired patterns at high-level manner through interfaces [15,16]. For example, the users can identify line charts of products with increasing sales trends per year from a collection of line charts of all products sold by an organization. However, existing approaches are not well equipped to handle process event log data and DFGs as a visualization type.

In this work, our objective is to identify the requirements to design a user-friendly interface to explore and manipulate DFG collections intuitively. Similarly to [13], we have elicited several requirements from three different and complementary sources as can be seen in Fig. 1. Firstly, we review the literature on visual query tools that operate with collections of visualizations [14,18,21,22] and analyze the main components of their interfaces. Secondly, we analyze LoVizQL [20], the only existing process mining approach for this purpose to the best of our knowledge. LoVizQL is a Log Data Visualization Query Language that allows users to retrieve collections of DFGs that meet specific conditions. Although it does not have a user interface, the query language model enables the identification of the information items required to query a collection of DFGs. Thirdly, we analyze reports sent to the last six Business Process Intelligence Challenges (BPICs) [5–10] to extract requirements based on actual use cases. The BPICs are annual contests in which an event log of one or more processes of an organization is published together with some business questions that participants must answer through data analysis. The participants send reports informing about the analysis performed and the results. We have analyzed the use of DFGs in these reports using a mixed-methods research approach similar to that used in [2,12] to understand how DFGs are used in practice, and define requirements based on them. This variety of sources provides a better understanding of DFGs and the addition of use cases improves their alignment with its practical applications in process mining. The catalog of requirements obtained from these three sources provides the basis for the user interfaces of future visual query tools in process mining, which we use to discuss possible improvement points for current tool interfaces.

The paper is structured as follows. Section 2 outlines the literature related to this work. Section 3 describes the methodology followed to conduct the analysis. Section 4 provides details of the results. Section 5 presents the findings and limitations of this research. Section 6 summarizes the conclusions drawn and directions for future work.

2   Related Work

In process mining, different query language approaches have been developed to search for information related to specific patterns [19]. On the one hand, there are languages that take event logs as inputs and search for information such as key performance indicators or data subsets [19]. On the other hand, other languages take process models as input (e.g., BPMN models), allow to modify them, and to search for specific process models or model parts [19]. There are also mixed approaches that retrieve information from event logs and process models. However, the previous query languages are not suitable to search for specific DFGs and their properties. While the first ones search for metrics but not process models, the second ones retrieve models but lack the capacity to search for metrics. Additionally, mixed approaches do not consider DFGs. Thus, the only existing approach to search for collection of DFGs that meet certain conditions, and retrieve their properties is Log Data Visualization Query Language (LoVizQL) [20] a query language inspired by the Zenvisage Query Language [21]. However, LoVizQL lacks an interactive interface to do this search, which can be a problem for certain users. This problem is tackled in this article.

In the data visualization field, there are also query languages to search for interesting general-purpose visualizations (e.g., a scatterplot) in collections, and different approaches have been developed to facilitate this process by adding user-friendly interfaces [14,18,21,22]. This addition in query languages has resulted in visual query tools which aim to help users understand the result of a query more quickly, as well as to create the query itself [3]. In [16], three sensemaking processes followed by users are outlined which have been described as crucial for the design of a visual query tool. First, the context-creation process involves users navigating through diverse sets of visualizations and compare subsets of data to gain an understanding to search for patterns embedded within their data. Thus, this process helps users to discover the attributes that they are interested to consider in the search [15,21,22]. Once the user has discovered the attributes that she is interested, the following processes are followed (one or both): the top-down and bottom-up processes. In the first one, users have an initial intuition about the pattern that the data should follow and use it to guide the search. To support this process, visual query tools have integrated mechanisms in which users can articulate this pattern intuition to initiate queries. For example, some tools have integrated sketching boxes that allow users to draw the shape of the results of interest they want to obtain (e.g., an increasing linear trend between two attributes) [15,18,21,22]. Subsequently, they provide users with relevant results based on the described pattern. However, the findings in [11,16] indicate that sketch queries are not frequently used, because analysts often struggle to articulate their patterns of interest accurately. Consequently, some tools are integrating novel mechanisms, such as natural language search [23], where users describe their desired results in natural language and the tools generate the corresponding queries. In the bottom-up process, users use existing relevant observations in the data to define the pattern to be considered in the search. To ease this process, tools have integrated mechanisms to start the search by recommending visualizations with typical trends or data outliers [15,21].

However, the mechanisms that these visual query tools provide to support the sense-making processes in visualizations cannot be directly integrated with DFGs for several reasons. First, process mining considers filters that are not present in these tools (e.g., filters whose conditions are related to the execution order of process elements). Second, DFGs are a specific type of process mining representation that is very different from the visualization types considered in these tools. Third, the conditions to consider a pattern as interesting in process mining are different from those considered in these tools (e.g., searching for the bottlenecks of the process). Therefore, the query languages associated with these tools are not suitable for this task, as we indicated in [20].

3   Research Methodology

We aim to address the following research question:

RQ: Which requirements should be considered in the interface design of a visual query tool to facilitate discovering insights from a DFG collection and performing comparisons on them?

To answer this question we followed the research methodology illustrated in Fig. 1. Our objective is to derive the requirements for a user interface designed to manage collections of DFGs through a comprehensive requirement analysis from multiple perspectives. To address step 1 (requirements elicitation), we took inspiration from the approach followed in previous studies [13,23] and used three different data sources to analyze current tools and languages, conducted a domain analysis, and improved the understanding of the use of DFGs in practice. The diverse types of analyses performed on these data sources are outlined below. Details and materials are available in our repository[1]. Step 2 (prototyping) dealt with the design of a prototype of the user interface based on the elicited requirements, which shall be evaluated with real users, and conducting

---

[1] https://doi.org/10.5281/zenodo.10939675.

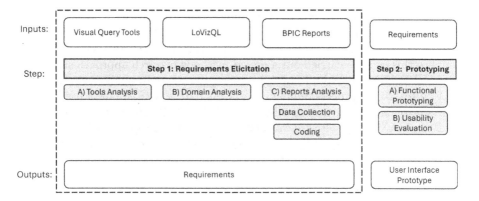

Fig. 1. Research methodology (the scope of this work is the blue dashed box) (Color figure online)

interviews with experts to validate its usability. This task is outside the scope of this paper, but we present a wireframe created with Figma[2] software of a potential user interface aimed to better illustrate the identified requirements.

Tools Analysis. We conducted an in-depth analysis of visual query tools that operate with collections of visualizations to explore the data [14,18,21,22]. Each tool was carefully examined to identify all requirements included in the interface. To this end, we extracted how each visual query tool presents the elements of its user interface (*information items*) and the purpose of each item. For example, one of the tools presented in [21] integrated a panel where the system suggested various visualizations to users based on the data context. Also, in [22] a sketch frame was included to enable users to illustrate a desired pattern.

Domain Analysis. For this analysis we relied on LoVizQL [20] as a domain model, a query language capable of handling collections of DFGs to search for those that meet specific criteria. Its queries are characterized by three main steps. In the first step, some event log subsets are created using filter operations defined by the user (e.g., filter traces in which a certain activity does not occur). Next, a DFG is created for each subset according to the metrics (e.g., average cycle time) and the attribute selected for the nodes (e.g., activities), which are defined by the user. Finally, the user can search for specific DFGs by specifying conditions related to properties or metrics of DFGs using functions (e.g., find the two DFGs with the minimum number of nodes). The DFGs that meet the conditions are displayed to the user, who can customize the resulting representation (e.g., percentage of nodes displayed). Using LoVizQL as a domain model helped us to identify the information items that are necessary in a user interface of a visual query tool for searching in collections of DFGs.

---

[2] https://www.figma.com/.

Reports Analysis. The goal of this analysis was to identify the use cases that the user interface must support. In this paper, we tackle this goal by analyzing how DFGs were used in practice and what insights could be extracted from them. To this end, we carried out a mixed-methods research approach similar to that used in [2,12], based on multiple coding iterations to analyze the usage of DFGs in real-world process mining reports. As data source, we have used the 92 reports belonging to the last six editions of BPICs: 2015, 2016, 2017, 2018, 2019, and 2020. MAXQDA[3] software was utilized for the coding, and the approach for these iterations was inspired by the Grounded Theory methodology [1]. Before the analysis, we followed a deductive approach and created two types of codes to interpret the use of DFGs: descriptive codes and identification codes. Descriptive codes were used to identify what was represented in the DFG, such as the main process flow or the two most frequent process variants. Identification codes were used to signal when the analyst drew a conclusion or insight from the DFG (e.g., identifying a bottleneck as a result of a transition between activities with high cycle time depicted in the DFG).

Afterwards, we followed an inductive approach and coded the information related to DFGs provided in the reports to figure out the codes related to each code type. Concerning the descriptive codes, we exclusively took into account the DFGs whose figures were included in the report. The DFGs mentioned in the text without illustration were disregarded in the coding process. In total, we coded 391 DFGs. Of the 92 available reports, 74 of them include DFGs with the respective figures. So, we considered six of nine reports in 2015, four of five in 2016, 23 of 23 in 2017, two of three in 2018, ten of 15 in 2019, and 29 of 37 in 2020. Furthermore, it was possible to assign multiple descriptive codes to the same figure to represent various features. Regarding the identification codes, we considered the insights that were clearly referred to a DFG, even though it was not explicitly mentioned.

The coding process was iterative and we created a total of 42 codes: 20 descriptive codes and 22 identification codes. Subsequently, we grouped some of them by similarity, creating more general codes. So, finally, six more general codes were created for the descriptive category and seven for the identification category. Examples of descriptive codes are *Show a filtered DFG* and *Zoom in the process*. These general codes include more specific codes, such as *Show a DFG filtered by an activity existence* or *Zoom in a transition between activities*, respectively. Examples of general identification codes are *Identify bottlenecks* and *Identify deviations from the happy path*. Furthermore, specific codes are included, such as *Identify activities as bottlenecks* or *Identify loops*, respectively.

Finally, we derived specific requirements for each descriptive code identified in the BPIC reports analysis, and we used the identification codes to define the mechanisms of pattern search and the parameters that can be customized in the search for patterns by the users (e.g., thresholds to identify bottlenecks).

---

[3] https://www.maxqda.com/es/.

4   Results

Table 1 shows all the requirements identified. For each row, which represents one requirement, we include: the necessary information elements in the user interface for that requirement, the source from which the requirement was extracted, the user story [4] to describe in natural language what is the user need and why, and finally a usage example obtained from the coded BPIC reports with its corresponding code to illustrate the need in real cases. Additionally, the requirements depicted in the table are grouped into three categories (represented with different colors) that have been identified from the current visual query tools based on the three sense-making processes described in Sect. 2. These categories include *Context Creation*, *Pattern Search*, and *Results Information*. Next, we detail each of these categories.

4.1   Context Creation

The *Context Creation* group comprises requirements related to the specification of a collection of DFGs. A collection of DFGs is obtained from a set of event log subsets by performing some manipulation actions on them. First, this specification requires selecting the input data to generate the collection, which can be one or multiple event logs, as highlighted in the BPIC reports (e.g., to compare similar processes). This is the *Event log* requirement in Table 1. Second, it is necessary to indicate the filter parameters: *Filter type* and *Filter condition* requirements. The former indicates the type of filter that will be applied. There are different types of filters for event logs: those based on event attributes or those based on the process control flow, between others. The latter represents the need to express which data will be selected in the filter. Third, users can perform multiple consecutive filters by adding additional filters, which is indicated with the *Number of filters* requirement.

Furthermore, the information included in the collection of DFGs also falls under the *Context Creation* group. This includes the attribute used for nodes (e.g., activity, phase, resource), and the metrics displayed in the nodes and transitions like cycle time or frequency (*Node information* and *Node and transition metric* requirements in Table 1).

4.2   Results Information

This group includes requirements for visualizing the results of queries, that is, a collection of DFGs. To differentiate each DFG shown in this collection, it is necessary to use an identifier related to the data source (*Data source identifier* and *Visualization of a collection of DFGs* requirements in Table 1). Furthermore, in order to abstract away details in the DFGs, it is necessary to include the *Activity threshold* and *Transition threshold* requirements, which set thresholds that limit the nodes and transitions that appear in the DFG based on their frequencies, as it is usually done in most process mining tools. Finally, to visualize a DFG in more detail, it is required to define a zoom percentage that indicates the level of detail to go through (*Zoom percentage* requirement).

Table 1. Elicited requirements. The Source column refers to Tools Analysis (T), Domain Analysis (D), and Reports Analysis (R). Screen numbers correspond to the wireframe in Fig. 2.

Information Item (Wireframe mapping)		Source	User need	Code and Example
Context Creation (screen 1A)	Event log	R	As a user, I want to load more than one dataset into the system so that I can analyze and explore both at the same time.	*Show some DFGs in the same figure* **R1 BPI 2020:** Declaration processes with median and mean durations based on the Domestic Declarations and International Declarations log.
	Filter type	D,R	As a user, I want to apply a filter on the event log, so that I can get a event log subset.	*Show the filtered DFG* **R21 BPI 2017:** Likewise, we applied the filter of directly followed between A_Complete and W_Validate application (Fig.15).
	Filter condition	T,D,R		
	Number of filters	T,D,R	As a user, I want to apply different filters one after another so that I can get event log subsets by combining some attributes.	*Show the filtered DFG* **R7 BPI 2015:** Table 16: Process flow per Municipality for "Kap" and filtered on 01_HOOFD_*
	Node information	D,R	As a user, I want to determine which attribute involved in the process to use as nodes in the DFGs, so that I can visualize the process associated with the values of that attribute.	*Show a DFG with atypical nodes* **R2 BPI 2015:** Fig. 6: Handover of work network in M1 (50% of resources, 25% of paths)
	Node and transition metric	D,R	As a user, I want to visualize performance time metrics in the DFGs, so that I can identify the nodes and transitions that take more time.	*Show the animation of the flow of cases* **R2 BPI 2020:** Figure 5: Disco's replay function of Permit Log permit requests
Results Information (screen 1B and 2D)	Data source identifier	R	As a user, I want to visualize more than one DFG (from the same or different data sources) in the same tab so that I can compare both processes.	*Show some DFGs in the same figure* **R3 BPIC 2015:** Figure 7. Extract of the objection lodging path from the process maps of municipality 2 (a) and 5 (b)
	Visualization of a collection of DFGs	R		
	Activity threshold	D,R	As a user, I want to determine the percentage of activities and transitions that appear in the main process flow so that I can visualize the DFGs according to their frequency.	*Show the main process flow* **R13 BPI 2019:** Figure 6: 3-way-matching after GR (100% of the activities and 40% of the paths)
	Transition threshold	D,R		
	Zoom percentage	R	As a user, I want to visualize some parts of the process in more detail, so that I can study the behavior of those parts in depth.	*Zoom the DFG* **R9 BPI 2017:** Fig. 25. Time duration of arc A_Pending O_Cancelled
Pattern Search (screen 2 and 3)	Bottom-up (3)	Pattern description	R	As a user, I want to see the resulting DFGs of some queries recommended by the system so that I can select a pattern of interest.	*All identification codes* **R29 BPI 2020:** After all this analysis, a bottleneck was identified, which occurs in the permission sub-process, specifically in the activities of "Permit FINAL APPROVED by SUPERVISOR" and "Permit FINAL APPROVED by DIRECTOR" which takes 39 and 55 days respectively (see figure 4).
	Top-down (2A)	Pattern function	T,D,R	As a user, I want to select the target of some queries recommended by the system, so that I can visualize a pattern of interest.	
		Pattern condition	T,D,R	As a user, I want to set some parameters for the pattern visualizations and specification, so that I can customize the patterns to my needs.	

Table 2. Identification codes.

General identification code (Specific identification codes)
Identify activities (Identify activities with high duration, Identify infrequent activities, Identify the most frequent activities, Identify startpoint activities, Identify endpoint activities, Identify group of activities, Identify the activities belonging to a fragment)
Identify resources (Identify resources with high workload, Identify resources by performed activities, Identify cluster of resources)
Identify fragments (Identify the most frequent fragment, Identify a frequent sequence of fragments)
Identify transitions (Identify transitions with high duration)
Identify bottlenecks (Identify resources as bottlenecks, Identify activities as bottlenecks, Identify transitions as bottlenecks, Identify activity loops as bottlenecks)
Identify deviations from the happy path (Identify activity loops, Identify outliers, Identify decision point activities)
Identify differences (Identify differences between process flow and process model, Identify differences of throughput)

4.3   Pattern Search

Requirements associated with the search of interesting visualizations are included in the *Pattern Search* group. These requirements are divided into two groups according to the search mechanism used.

The bottom-up search group is required to display visualizations that may be relevant for users based on the current data context. These recommendations include a DFG collection with the corresponding description of the pattern based on the identification codes obtained from the BPIC reports analysis (*Pattern description* requirement in Table 1). The identification codes extracted are shown in Table 2. This allows the user to express interest in some pattern and obtain the corresponding query by selecting the desired visualization. For instance, the system could show DFGs where resources are identified as bottlenecks as shown on the third screen in Fig. 2.

The top-down search group includes requirements about the specification of the patterns. The purpose is to present interesting query objectives to users based on the data context. Thus, some parameters associated with the specification of the pattern are required. It is necessary to specify the pattern function of interest based on identification codes extracted from the analysis of the BPIC reports (*Pattern function* requirement), such as: *Identify transitions with high cycle time*, *Identify activity loops*, or *Identify resources with high workload* (cf. Table 2). Additionally, it is required to customize this pattern determining some conditions (*Pattern condition* requirement). For example, the system could display visualizations that highlight transitions with high cycle times. However, determining what qualifies as a high cycle time lacks a universal criterion. There-

Fig. 2. Initial wireframe for exploring and visualizing DFGs interface. Screen numbers and characters correspond to Table 1.

fore, in addition to using default values, users are allowed to define their own criteria.

5   Discussion and Limitations

The set of requirements obtained from this research provides the basis for building user interfaces of future visual query tools in process mining. These requirements indicate which information is needed to search in collections of DFGs. Therefore, process mining tool developers who want to include visual query capabilities in their tools should consider these requirements to ensure that their interfaces successfully cover the needs of their users.

Complementary to these requirements, we have also obtained, from the analysis of BPIC reports, a set of use cases for DFGs captured through the identification codes summarized in Table 2. This collection of use cases could be used by current process mining tools to consider the process behind these identifications and provide a similar approach to bottom-up mechanisms. Thus, different pre-customized DFGs would be presented to the user after loading the event log in the tool.

Finally, the methodology employed in this study has the potential to be generalized to consider other scopes than the use of DFGs. BPIC reports contain other types of visualizations that have not been included in this analysis but could also be very useful to help the user to find relevant insights from the event data. This highlights a gap for future research that could analyze these other visualizations in a similar way. This research will improve our understanding of the use of visualizations in process mining.

As limitations, we have been inspired by grounded theory for the coding of DFGs in the Reports Analysis, which implies a subjective interpretation of the figures and the description by the users in the report. However, it is important to note that the coding process was iterative and the authors met to discuss the codes for some figures or descriptions that were not so clear. In addition, the extraction of requirements in our study only considers the use of DFGs within the BPIC reports, which could be a bias in the study. Nevertheless, we analyzed a large amount of data consisting of 391 figures extracted from 74 reports belonging to 6 challenges. This information is very extensive and diverse because each BPIC has unique contextual nuances and presents different research objectives for participants. Furthermore, the authors of the reports belong to different domains, including students, professionals, and academics, and they use different process mining tools to obtain DFGs, such as Disco, ProM or Celonis, among others. For the tools analysis, we did not consider commercial process mining tools because they are not equipped to manage multiple DFGs and compare them at the same time in a homogeneous manner. However, LoVizQL includes most of the features necessary to manipulate the data and preferences for displaying DFGs of these tools. Furthermore, we have considered the manipulation actions carried out in the BPIC reports by these tools to obtain DFGs.

6   Conclusions

In this work, we aimed to identify the requirements to design a user-friendly interface to handle collections of DFGs intuitively. To achieve this objective, we have gathered several information items from three distinct sources: current visual query tools, a query language to manage collections of DFGs, and real-world cases. This collection of sources enhances the understanding of DFGs, and the inclusion of use cases also aligns them with real applications of process mining. As a result, we have extracted 14 requirements from the collection of the elicited information items. Additionally, we have grouped these requirements into three categories: *Context Creation*, *Pattern Search*, and *Results Information*. These requirements provide the basis for future interfaces focused on handling DFGs. As future work, we plan to focus on designing a new version of the user interface, developing the visual query tool, and evaluating its usability and usefulness through interviews with process mining experts and academic users in a real-world scenario.

References

1. Alman, A., Di Ciccio, C., Maggi, F.M., Montali, M., van der Aa, H.: RuM: declarative process mining, distilled. In: Polyvyanyy, A., Wynn, M.T., Van Looy, A., Reichert, M. (eds.) BPM 2021. LNCS, vol. 12875, pp. 23–29. Springer, Cham (2021). https://doi.org/10.1007/978-3-030-85469-0_3
2. Capitán-Agudo, C., Salas-Urbano, M., Cabanillas, C., Resinas, M.: Analyzing how process mining reports answer time performance questions. In: Di Ciccio, C., Dijkman, R., del Río Ortega, A., Rinderle-Ma, S. (eds.) BPM 2022. LNCS, vol. 13420, pp. 234–250. Springer, Cham (2022). https://doi.org/10.1007/978-3-031-16103-2_17
3. Catarci, T., Costabile, M.F., Levialdi, S., Batini, C.: Visual query systems for databases: a survey. J. Vis. Lang. Comput. **8**(2), 215–260 (1997). https://doi.org/10.1006/jvlc.1997.0037
4. Cohn, M.: User Stories Applied: For Agile Software Development. Addison-Wesley Professional, Boston (2004)
5. van Dongen, B.: BPI Challenge 2015. 4TU.ResearchData (2015). https://doi.org/10.4121/uuid:31a308ef-c844-48da-948c-305d167a0ec1
6. van Dongen, B.: BPI Challenge 2016. 4TU.ResearchData (2016). https://doi.org/10.4121/uuid:360795c8-1dd6-4a5b-a443-185001076eab
7. van Dongen, B.: BPI Challenge 2017. 4TU.ResearchData (2017). https://doi.org/10.4121/uuid:5f3067df-f10b-45da-b98b-86ae4c7a310b
8. van Dongen, B.: BPI Challenge 2018. 4TU.ResearchData (2018). https://doi.org/10.4121/uuid:3301445f-95e8-4ff0-98a4-901f1f204972
9. van Dongen, B.: BPI Challenge 2019. 4TU.ResearchData (2019). https://doi.org/10.4121/uuid:d06aff4b-79f0-45e6-8ec8-e19730c248f1
10. van Dongen, B.: BPI Challenge 2020. 4TU.ResearchData (2020). https://doi.org/10.4121/uuid:52fb97d4-4588-43c9-9d04-3604d4613b51
11. Imani, S., Alaee, S., Keogh, E.: Qute: query by text search for time series data. In: Arai, K., Kapoor, S., Bhatia, R. (eds.) FTC 2020. AISC, vol. 1289, pp. 412–427. Springer, Cham (2021). https://doi.org/10.1007/978-3-030-63089-8_27
12. Klinkmüller, C., Müller, R., Weber, I.: Mining process mining practices: an exploratory characterization of information needs in process analytics. In: International Conference on Business Process Management, pp. 322–337 (2019). https://doi.org/10.1007/978-3-030-26619-6_21
13. Kubrak, K., Milani, F., Nolte, A., Dumas, M.: Design and evaluation of a user interface concept for prescriptive process monitoring. In: Indulska, M., Reinhartz-Berger, I., Cetina, C., Pastor, O. (eds.) Advanced Information Systems Engineering, CAiSE 2023. Lecture Notes in Computer Science, vol. 13901, pp. 347–363. Springer, Cham (2023). https://doi.org/10.1007/978-3-031-34560-9_21
14. Lee, D.J.L., Kim, J., Wang, R., Parameswaran, A.: Scattersearch: Visual querying of scatterplot visualizations. arXiv preprint arXiv:1907.11743 (2019)
15. Lee, D.J.L., Lee, J., Siddiqui, T., Kim, J., Karahalios, K., Parameswaran, A.: You can't always sketch what you want: understanding sensemaking in visual query systems. IEEE Trans. Vis. Comput. Graph. **26**(1), 1267–1277 (2020). https://doi.org/10.1109/TVCG.2019.2934666
16. Lee, D.J.L., Siddiqui, T., Karahalios, K., Parameswaran, A.: Three lessons from accelerating scientific insight discovery via visual querying. Patterns **1**(7), 100126 (2020). https://doi.org/10.1016/j.patter.2020.100126

17. Leemans, S.J., Poppe, E., Wynn, M.T.: Directly follows-based process mining: exploration & a case study. In: International Conference on Process Mining, pp. 25–32. IEEE (2019). https://doi.org/10.1109/ICPM.2019.00015
18. Mannino, M., Abouzied, A.: Expressive time series querying with hand-drawn scale-free sketches. In: Proceedings of the 2018 CHI Conference on Human Factors in Computing Systems, pp. 1–13 (2018). https://doi.org/10.1145/3173574.3173962
19. Polyvyanyy, A.: Process Querying Methods. Springer, Cham (2022). https://doi.org/10.1007/978-3-030-92875-9
20. Salas-Urbano, M., Capitán-Agudo, C., Cabanillas, C., Resinas, M.: LoVizQL: a query language for visualizing and analyzing business processes from event logs. In: Monti, F., Rinderle-Ma, S., Ruiz Cortés, A., Zheng, Z., Mecella, M. (eds.) ICSOC 2023. LNCS, vol. 14420, pp. 13–28. Springer, Cham (2023). https://doi.org/10.1007/978-3-031-48424-7_2
21. Siddiqui, T., et al.: Fast-forwarding to desired visualizations with zenvisage. In: 8th Biennial Conference on Innovative Data Systems Research (2017)
22. Siddiqui, T., Luh, P., Wang, Z., Karahalios, K., Parameswaran, A.: Shapesearch: a flexible and efficient system for shape-based exploration of trendlines. In: Proceedings of ACM SIGMOD International Conference on Management of Data, pp. 51–65 (2020). https://doi.org/10.1145/3318464.3389722
23. Siddiqui, T., Luh, P., Wang, Z., Karahalios, K., Parameswaran, A.G.: From sketching to natural language: expressive visual querying for accelerating insight. ACM SIGMOD Rec. **50**(1), 51–58 (2021). https://doi.org/10.1145/3471485.3471498

Precision-Guided Minimization
of Arbitrary Declarative Process Models

Eduardo Goulart Rocha[1,2](✉) [ID] and Wil M.P. van der Aalst[1,2] [ID]

[1] Celonis Labs GmbH, Munich, Germany
[2] Process and Data Science (PADS) Chair, RWTH Aachen University,
Aachen, Germany
e.goulartrocha@celonis.com, wvdaalst@pads.rwth-aachen.de

Abstract. Declarative model minimization is a computationally expensive task. State-of-the-art approximation techniques rely on hard-coded heuristic functions based on properties of constraint templates, which requires rework when new templates are added and cannot handle models expressed as arbitrary logical formulas. We present a precision-based heuristic function that requires no pre-configuration and can handle arbitrary constraints, provided they can be mapped to a finite automaton. The approach is evaluated on real-world datasets, where it outperforms state-of-the-art methods while accepting a wider range of inputs.

Keywords: Process Mining · Declarative Process Mining · Constraint Minimization · Redundant Constraints

1 Introduction

Declarative process models are a popular modeling paradigm for processes with high variability [14]. Figure 1a shows a declarative model for a procurement process. It consists of constraints to which the process must adhere. The constraints mandate that the process starts with the approval of the purchase (c_1), that the payment is booked/the goods are collected if and only if the purchase was approved (c_5, c_6), and that all activities happen exactly once (c_2, c_3, c_4).

Declarative models may contain redundancies. In Fig. 1a, constraint c_3 can be inferred from c_1, c_2, and c_5 (if a happens exactly once at the beginning and a must be followed by b, then b must happen exactly once). Redundant constraints express hidden dependencies. These are often inserted by an unwary user or by automated process discovery methods. Redundant constraints bloat the model, affecting its understandability, without adding extra information. Thus, it is important to minimize process models by removing as much redundancy as possible.

Redundancy resolution is a difficult task. State-of-the-art techniques approximate its solution by checking for redundant constraints according to a specific order [7]. The ordering criterion affects the approximation quality. State-of-the-art ordering criteria consist of a hard-coded heuristic tailored specifically for the underlying declarative language [7]. However, this approach has a few drawbacks:

© The Author(s), under exclusive license to Springer Nature Switzerland AG 2024
H. van der Aa et al. (Eds.): BPMDS 2024/EMMSAD 2024, LNBIP 511, pp. 48–56, 2024.
https://doi.org/10.1007/978-3-031-61007-3_5

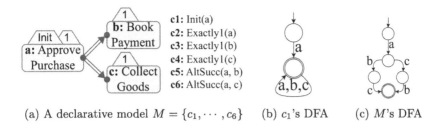

| (a) A declarative model $M = \{c_1, \cdots, c_6\}$ | (b) c_1's DFA | (c) M's DFA |

Fig. 1. A declarative procurement process (1a) and some related DFAs (1b, 1c).

1. The method can only be applied to declarative languages based on templates
2. The heuristic must be redesigned every time the language is changed
3. Designing the heuristic function requires domain expertise
4. The heuristic might lead to suboptimal pruning

We present a heuristic function based on model precision for *consistent* declarative models. The precision function measures the "excess behavior" allowed by each constraint with respect to the model. More precise constraints are closer to the model's language and thus also stricter. Stricter constraints are prioritized as they are less likely to be redundant. The proposed method requires no user input and is applicable to any set of constraints expressible as DFAs, including arbitrary $\text{LTL}_f/\text{LDL}_f$ formulas, thus going beyond the DECLARE language. A preliminary evaluation on real-world datasets shows that the approach outperforms the state-of-the-art in terms of runtime and pruning efficiency.

2   Preliminaries

Given a set of activity labels Σ, a trace $\sigma \in \Sigma^*$ is a finite sequence of activities. A *constraint* c is an object whose language $\mathcal{L}(c) \subseteq \Sigma^*$ defines its accepted traces. A *declarative process model* M is a set of constraints M with language $\mathcal{L}(M) = \bigcap_{c \in M} \mathcal{L}(c)$. A model M is *consistent* if $\mathcal{L}(M) \neq \emptyset$, i.e. constraints do not contradict each other. In this work, we consider constraints expressing *regular languages*, which can be defined using Deterministic Finite Automata:

Definition 1. (Deterministic Finite Automaton (DFA)) *Is a tuple* $(Q, \Sigma, \delta, q_0, F)$ *where* Q *is the set of states,* Σ *is a set of symbols,* $\delta : Q \times \Sigma \nrightarrow Q$ *is the transition function,* q_0 *is the initial state and* $F \subseteq Q$ *is the set of final states.*

A DFA $D = (Q, \Sigma, \delta, q_0, F)$ accepts a trace $\sigma = l_1 \cdots l_n \in \Sigma^*$ iff. there is a path $(q_0, l_1, q_1) \cdots (q_{n-1}, l_n, q_n) \in (Q \times \Sigma \times Q)^*$ s.t. $q_n \in F$ and $\delta(q_{i-1}, l_i) = q_i$ $\forall 1 \leq i \leq n$. The language of D is the set $\mathcal{L}(D) = \{\sigma \in \Sigma^* | \sigma$ is accepted by $D\}$.

Template-based declarative languages such as DECLARE [14] are backed by a set of logical formula templates, e.g. LTL_f formulas. Table 1 shows a snippet of

Table 1. A snippet of DECLARE templates [9]. See [4] for the LTL_f semantics.

Template		LTL_f
1. Position		
Init(x)	Trace must start with x	$\Box(start \rightarrow x)$
End(x)	Trace must end with x	$\Box(end \rightarrow x)$
2. Cardinality		
AtMost1(x)	x occurs at most once	$\Box(x \rightarrow \neg \bigcirc \Diamond x)$
Exactly1(x)	x occurs exactly once	$\Diamond x \wedge \Box(x \rightarrow \neg \bigcirc \Diamond x)$
3. Bidirectional Coupling		
AltSucc(x, y)	x and y occur in indirect sequence	$\Box((x \rightarrow \bigcirc(\neg x \text{ U } y)) \wedge (y \rightarrow \blacklozenge x))$
Choice(x, y)	x or y must occur, but not both	$(\Diamond x \wedge \neg \Diamond y) \vee (\neg \Diamond x \wedge \Diamond y)$

the DECLARE language. Templates can be instantiated with concrete parameters, yielding a constraint. For example, setting x = "*Approve Purchase*" for template $Init(x)$ yields constraint c_1 from Fig. 1a. We refer to [6] for a discussion on the expressiveness of LTL_f. For now, it suffices to know that LTL_f (thus also DECLARE) is strictly less expressive than DFAs.[1] And that given an LTL_f formula φ, there exists a DFA D accepting exclusively the traces satisfying φ, i.e. $\sigma \models \varphi \iff \sigma \in \mathcal{L}(D)$. Furthermore, reasoning tasks can also be mapped to DFA operations. Particularly, given a set of formulas $\Phi = \{\varphi_1, \varphi_2, \cdots, \varphi_n\}$ and its respective DFAs $\mathcal{D} = \{D_1, D_2, \cdots, D_n\}$, then $\sigma \models \Phi \iff \sigma \in \bigcap_{D_i \in \mathcal{D}} \mathcal{L}(D_i)$.

Figure 1 shows the minimal DFAs for constraint c_1 (1b) and model M (1c). Notice how $\mathcal{L}(M) \subset \mathcal{L}(c_1)$, i.e. does not fully describe M. The next section presents an approach for redundancy resolution based on model precision, which aims at preserving constraints that provide the most information.

3   Minimizing Arbitrary Declarative Models

We formalize the problem of declarative model minimization:

Definition 2. (Declarative Model Minimization Problem) *Given a declarative process model M, the model minimization problem is defined as:*

$$M_{min} = \underset{M' \subseteq M, \mathcal{L}(M') = \mathcal{L}(M)}{\arg \min} |M'| \tag{1}$$

Model minimization searches for a minimal equivalent sub-model. Its exact computation requires checking all subsets $M' \subseteq M$, which is intractable. Therefore, state-of-the-art methods approximate it by greedily checking for redundant constraints based on a specific constraint ordering criterion. In this work, we consider the minimization procedure from [7]. Algorithm 1 presents a simplified and slightly more general version of this algorithm for redundancy resolution.

---

[1] [6] introduces the Linear Dynamic Logic over Finite Traces (LDL_f), which is as expressive as DFAs. We do not discuss LDL_f formulas, but we notice that methods presented here work with arbitrary DFAs and hence are directly applicable to them.

Algorithm 1: Adaptation of the MINERful minimization algorithm [7]. The steps related to conflict resolution were removed and the checks for the subsumption hierarchy were replaced by a generic inclusion check.

---

1 **input** A declarative model $M \subseteq \mathcal{C}$ and an ordering criterion $<_h$

2 **output** A declarative model $M' \subseteq M$ s.t. $M' \Rightarrow M$

3 $\Gamma \leftarrow \emptyset$;

4 **foreach** $(c_i, c_j) \in (M \times M) \wedge c_i \neq c_j$ **do**

5 $\quad$ **if** $c_i, c_j \notin \Gamma \wedge \mathcal{L}(c_i) \Rightarrow \mathcal{L}(c_j)$ **then** $\Gamma \leftarrow \Gamma \cup \{c_j\}$;

6 $M_0 \leftarrow sort([c_i \in M | c_i \notin \Gamma], <_h)$

7 **foreach** $i \in [1, 2, \cdots, |M_0|]$ **do**

8 $\quad$ **if** $\mathcal{L}(\{c_1, c_2, \cdots, c_{i-1}\}) \subseteq \mathcal{L}(c_i)$ **then** $\Gamma \leftarrow \Gamma \cup \{c_i\}$;

9 $M_1 \leftarrow sort([c_i \in M' | c_i \notin \Gamma], <_h)$

10 **foreach** $i \in [|M_1|, \cdots, 2, 1]$ **do**

11 $\quad$ **if** $\mathcal{L}(M \setminus (\Gamma \cup \{c_i\})) \subseteq \mathcal{L}(c_i)$ **then** $\Gamma \leftarrow \Gamma \cup \{c_i\}$;

12 $M_2 \leftarrow M \setminus \Gamma$

13 **return** M_2

The procedure accepts a model M and an ordering criteria $<_h$. Initially, a preliminary pass (lines 4-6) removes trivial constraint implication pairs. Next, a first redundancy resolution pass (line 7-9) removes constraints that are implied by constraints preceding it in $<_h$. Finally, a second pass (lines 10-12) ensures that the returned set is redundancy-free by checking each constraint against all others. This is done starting from the largest (according to $<_h$) constraints.

The correctness of Algorithm 1 follows directly from the fact that only redundant constraints are removed. Its optimality depends on $<_h$. A good ordering criterion $<_h$ should sort constraints with the highest pruning potential first. In [7], a series of ordering criteria are presented based on properties of the constraint templates such as constraint type, activation linkage, and relevance metrics (see [7] for more details). This approach requires a redesign of $<_h$ every time the set of templates is extended, which is time-consuming and error-prone. Furthermore, it is only applicable to models built from a set of fixed templates. To address these deficiencies, we propose to define $<_h$ using a precision function. A precision function is a function $p : \Sigma^* \times \Sigma^* \to \mathbb{R}$, where $p(L_1, L_2)$ estimates the fraction $\frac{|L_2 \setminus L_1|}{|L_1|}$. A precision function p induces an ordering criteria $<_{M,p}$ as follows:

Definition 3. (Precision-Based Constraint Ordering) *Let M be a declarative model and $p : \Sigma^* \times \Sigma^* \to \mathbb{R}$ a precision function. The ordering $<_{M,p}$ induced by p with respect to M is defined as:*

$$c_1 <_{M,p} c_2 \iff p(\mathcal{L}(M), \mathcal{L}(c_1)) > p(\mathcal{L}(M), \mathcal{L}(c_2)) \qquad (2)$$

Intuitively, the more precise a constraint $c_i \in M$ with respect to M, the stricter it is and the more likely it is to prune subsequent constraints. Multiple precision measures have been proposed in the process mining literature (see

Table 2. Comparison of pruning efficiency using the hard-coded function from [7] that orders constraints by increasing type priority and decreasing activation linkage, and the precision-based Escaping Edges Precision (ETC).

$<$	prio.	link.	const.	$\in M_1(M_2)$	$ETC(M, c_i)$	const.	$\in M_1(M_2)$
-	1	3	Init(a)	$\checkmark(\checkmark)$	0.46	AltSucc(a, b)	$\checkmark(\checkmark)$
	2	3	Exactly1(a)	$\checkmark(\checkmark)$	0.46	AltSucc(a, c)	$\checkmark(\checkmark)$
	2	2	Exactly1(b)	$\checkmark(\checkmark)$	0.40	Exactly1(a)	$\checkmark(\checkmark)$
	2	2	Exactly1(c)	$\checkmark(\checkmark)$	0.40	Exactly1(b)	$\times(\times)$
	3	3	AltSucc(a, b)	$\times(\times)$	0.40	Exactly1(c)	$\times(\times)$
+	3	3	AltSucc(a, c)	$\times(\times)$	0.35	Init(a)	$\times(\times)$

Sect. 5 for an in-depth discussion). We propose using the Escaping Edges Precision (ETC) [11] as it accepts arbitrary DFAs as inputs, it can be efficiently computed given both DFAs and it performs well when $\mathcal{L}(M) \subseteq \mathcal{L}(c_i)$. A drawback is that the ETC precision only works when the model is consistent.

Table 2 compares both heuristics when minimizing the model M from Fig. 1. Notice that the ETC heuristic leads to better pruning. Both heuristics differ in how they order the *Init* and *AltSucc* constraints.

4   Experimental Evaluation

We evaluate the proposed approach on the example task of discovering a declarative model from a procedural specification. Given a procedural model and a set of constraint templates, we instantiate all templates with all possible parameter combinations and check if the procedural model satisfies the constraints. The result is an "equivalent" declarative version of the original model. We use manually designed process models for the Road Fines (RF), and BPI Challenge 2020 (BPI-20) processes, derived from their respective process specifications, and a model discovered from the BPI Challenge 2017 log (BPI-17).[2]

We consider the DECLARE[3] (DEC) templates [9] with the hard-coded heuristic function specified in [7] (HC), as well as the templates by Ramezani et al. [16] (RMZ). The latter includes constraint templates with varying numbers of arguments (k) and subsumes the set of DECLARE templates. For that, we design a heuristic function inspired by the one described in [7]. We consider the minimization with the ETC precision function ([11]) and with a random shuffle of the constraints as a baseline (RND).

Quantitative Evaluation We assess the pruning and runtime efficiency of each heuristic. We report the number of constraints after the preliminary pass ($|M_0|$), and after the first/second minimization passes (1st/2nd #min), along with the runtime for each run. The approach is implemented in pure Python and each experiment is assigned a memory limit of 4 GBs. Table 3 summarizes the results.

---

[2] The datasets can be found at github.com/EduardoGoulart1/BPMDS24.
[3] Extracted from github.com/cdc08x/MINERful/commit/8311258.

Table 3. Comparison of random (RND), hard-coded (HC), and precision-based (ETC) heuristic functions in terms of pruning performance (#min) and computation time in seconds. We report the numbers for two runs of the algorithm, performing only a first pass and performing both passes over the constraints.

DS	LIB	K	$|M_0|$	RND [1st—2nd]				HC [1st—2nd]				ETC [1st—2nd]			
				#min		time(s)		#min		time(s)		#min		time(s)	
RF	DEC	2	77	56	26	11.3	20.5	50	**23**	4.6	27.9	**36**	**23**	17.3	43.8
		2	151	109	72	7.9	38.0	105	**68**	7.6	42.2	**82**	69	5.6	13.7
	RMZ	3	197	94	62	4.8	48.8	98	**59**	4.0	22.4	**86**	60	3.3	7.4
		4	2623	!	!	!	!	**173**	58	17.4	283.6	!	!	!	!
BPI-20	DEC	2	37	30	**17**	0.15	1.24	36	23	0.61	12.6	**19**	18	1.34	2.16
		2	85	59	35	0.24	2.41	53	**34**	0.78	2.30	**41**	35	0.49	0.58
	RMZ	3	92	60	33	0.48	2.81	49	**31**	0.30	1.30	**36**	**31**	0.38	0.52
		4	122	76	32	2.25	3.17	74	32	0.48	2.44	**35**	**31**	0.66	1.25
BPI-17	DEC	2	79	65	!	7.8	!	67	**32**	2.6	47.5	**44**	33	8.2	41.1
		2	138	88	**62**	5.8	201	95	**62**	7.5	118.6	**81**	**62**	10.2	26.8
	RMZ	3	145	91	**57**	11.1	83	81	59	3.6	43.0	**78**	58	8.3	19.1
		4	416	121	66	83.1	735	123	**59**	4.8	90.1	**84**	60	36.6	50.9

For the single-pass minimization procedure, the ETC heuristic achieves the best pruning efficiency, being the best-performing method in all but one situation where it ran out of memory. Perhaps most surprisingly, the hard-coded heuristic frequently performs similar or worse than the random heuristic. After the second pass, the difference between the hard-coded and the ETC heuristics diminishes.

The runtime of the single pass for the ETC-based heuristic is dominated by the computation of $\bigcap_{c \in M} \mathcal{L}(c)$ (this is also the step where it runs out of memory). In comparison, the hard-coded heuristic is cheap to compute, and consequentially faster for the single pass. However, when considering the second pass, the situation flips. The time to compute $\bigcap_{c \in M} \mathcal{L}(c)$ is compensated by a subsequent speedup in pruning. Making the ETC heuristic faster than the hard-coded in all but one situation (excluding the out-of-memory). Overall, the experiments show that the ETC-based heuristic provides better pruning than the hard-coded heuristic. With a single pass, ETC prunes almost as many constraints as the hard-coded with two passes, while being much faster. Therefore, the ETC heuristic surpasses the state-of-the-art in terms of pruning efficiency and performance.

Comparing the Orders We now compare the orderings induced by the hard-coded and the ETC-based heuristics. We consider the Road Fines (RF) model and the DECLARE templates (DEC). Figure 2 compares the results of the single-pass minimization procedure produced by the hard-coded and ETC-based heuristics.

Figures 2a and 2b plot the position of each constraint and their ranks according to the hard-coded/ETC heuristics. Constraints colored red are marked as redundant. The hard-coded function contains large plateaus of multiple con-

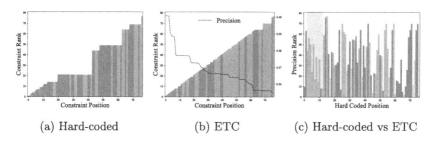

(a) Hard-coded   (b) ETC   (c) Hard-coded vs ETC

Fig. 2. HC vs ETC heuristics on the DEC-2 templates for the Road Fines dataset.

straints with the same rank, which explains why it performs similarly to the random ordering. In comparison, ETC can better distinguish the rank of each constraint. However, notice that the ETC precision varies in a relatively small range from 0.35 to 0.40. Sometimes, the difference in precision between two constraints is $< 10^{-5}$. This shows the problem with the *low-resolution* of the ETC function and motivates the development of higher-resolution metrics.

Finally, Fig. 2c compares the position assigned by the hard-coded ordering criterion with the rank assigned by the ETC function. Constraints colored green are marked as redundant by the ETC heuristic, but not by the hard-coded. Constraints colored orange are marked as redundant by the hard-coded ordering but not the ETC-based. Both orderings seem to have little agreement between them. More interestingly, in Fig. 2c there is a cluster of green constraints at the beginning encompassing almost all DECLARE cardinality constraints (gray background). The ETC heuristic assigns them high ranks and marks them as minimal. This suggests that the hard-coded function could be improved by lowering the type priority of cardinality constraints. We tried that in our experiments. To our surprise, the minimization using this modified function ran out of memory. A possible explanation is that not all cardinality constraints are trivial. Assigning a low priority to all cardinality constraints misses important constraints that help to reduce the size of intermediate models, causing out-of-memories. In contrast, the ETC-based heuristic can separate constraints of the same type if it deems that they are not equally relevant in the given context.

Overall, the experiments from this section show that the ETC-based ordering criterion produces fewer ties in the constraint ordering and that even a heuristic function designed by domain experts can be sub-optimal. A possible argument in favor of hard-coded heuristics is that they can incorporate other aspects such as understandability, ensuring that more understandable constraints are prioritized. However, even in these situations, a precision-based heuristic could be used as a secondary ordering criterion, to break ties between constraints.

5   Related Work

DECLARE [14] is the de-facto standard language for declarative process mining. Its greatest advantages are usability and simplicity. Using constraint templates facilitates tasks such as discovery [9,12] and reasoning [7]. More recently, as the limitations of DECLARE in terms of expressiveness and the link between DECLARE, LTLf/LDLf, and DFAs became clear [6], more general reasoning methods aiming at the full LTLf/LDLf specifications have been proposed [8,10].

Most precision metrics in process mining require that at least one of its inputs is finite [1,2,5,13]. The ETC precision was first proposed in [13] and later refined in [2] to handle unfitting behavior by using trace alignment. In [11], the approach is extended to handle infinite languages by comparing their respective DFAs. Furthermore, [11] suggests projecting both languages' DFAs to subsets of activities to handle language mismatches. In our setting, the projection step is not necessary since the model's language always fits the constraint's language.

In [15], a family of precision metrics is proposed based on the quotient $\frac{\|\mathcal{L}(M) \cap \mathcal{L}(c)\|}{\|\mathcal{L}(c)\|}$, where $\|.\|$ is a (monotone) language measure, e.g. the language's topological entropy. This metric did not lead to satisfactory results in our experiments since $\mathcal{L}(M) \cap \mathcal{L}(c_i) = \mathcal{L}(M) \ \forall c_i \in M$, and multiple constraints have the same topological entropy $\|c_i\|$, leading to multiple ties in their ordering criteria. In [3] a precision metric based on the comparison of the sets of k-trimmed subtraces (the Markovian abstraction) of M and c_i is proposed. This metric also performed poorly in our experiments since many constraints have very similar abstractions. Similarly, techniques based on behavioral relations [17] also perform poorly in our setup since many constraints have very similar behavioral relations.

6   Conclusion

This paper proposed a method for the minimization of arbitrary declarative process models using model precision. The approach is in itself competitive with state-of-the-art techniques even when applied to declarative models for which a hard-coded heuristic function exists. Moreover, it is the only alternative for models containing arbitrary LTLf/LDLf formulas. This paves the way for the usage of declarative models that go beyond template-based declarative languages.

In future work, we plan to develop "higher resolution" precision functions that produce fewer ties between constraints, to investigate more efficient precision functions that do not require the intersection of all constraint DFAs, and to extend it to inconsistent declarative models. Finally, we would like to evaluate the proposed approach on sets of arbitrary LTLf/LDLf formulas, which is so far not possible due to a lack of suitable LTLf/LDLf miners.

Acknowledgements. We thank the Alexander von Humboldt (AvH) Stiftung for supporting our research.

References

1. Adriansyah, A., van Dongen, B., van der Aalst, W.M.P.: Conformance checking using cost-based fitness analysis. In: 2011 IEEE 15th International Enterprise Distributed Object Computing Conference, pp. 55–64 (2011)

2. Adriansyah, A., Munoz-Gama, J., Carmona, J., Dongen, B., Aalst, W.M.P.: Measuring precision of modeled behavior. Inf. Syst. e-Bus. Manage. **13** (2014)
3. Augusto, A., Armas-Cervantes, A., Conforti, R., Dumas, M., Rosa, M.L.: Measuring fitness and precision of automatically discovered process models: a principled and scalable approach. IEEE Trans. Knowl. Data Eng. **34**(4), 1870–1888 (2022)
4. Cecconi, A., Di Ciccio, C., De Giacomo, G., Mendling, J.: Interestingness of Traces in declarative process mining: the Janus LTLp$_f$ approach. In: Weske, M., Montali, M., Weber, I., vom Brocke, J. (eds.) BPM 2018. LNCS, vol. 11080, pp. 121–138. Springer, Cham (2018). https://doi.org/10.1007/978-3-319-98648-7_8
5. Chatain, T., Carmona, J.: Anti-alignments in conformance checking – the dark side of process models. In: Kordon, F., Moldt, D. (eds.) PETRI NETS 2016. LNCS, vol. 9698, pp. 240–258. Springer, Cham (2016). https://doi.org/10.1007/978-3-319-39086-4_15
6. De Giacomo, G., Vardi, M.Y.: Linear temporal logic and linear dynamic logic on finite traces. In: Proceedings of the Twenty-Third International Joint Conference on Artificial Intelligence, pp. 854–860. IJCAI 2013, AAAI Press (2013)
7. Di Ciccio, C., Maggi, F.M., Montali, M., Mendling, J.: Resolving inconsistencies and redundancies in declarative process models. Inf. Syst. **64**, 425–446 (2017)
8. Di Ciccio, C., Maggi, F.M., Montali, M., Mendling, J.: On the relevance of a business constraint to an event log. Inf. Syst. **78**, 144–161 (2018)
9. Di Ciccio, C., Mecella, M.: On the discovery of declarative control flows for artful processes. ACM Trans. Manage. Inf. Syst. **5**(4) (2015)
10. De Giacomo, G., De Masellis, R., Grasso, M., Maggi, F.M., Montali, M.: Monitoring business metaconstraints based on LTL and LDL for finite traces. In: Sadiq, S., Soffer, P., Völzer, H. (eds.) BPM 2014. LNCS, vol. 8659, pp. 1–17. Springer, Cham (2014). https://doi.org/10.1007/978-3-319-10172-9_1
11. Leemans, S.J.J., Fahland, D., van der Aalst, W.M.P.: Scalable process discovery and conformance checking. Softw. Syst. Model. **17**, 599–631 (2016)
12. Maggi, F.M., Bose, R.P.J.C., van der Aalst, W.M.P.: Efficient discovery of understandable declarative process models from event logs. In: Ralyté, J., Franch, X., Brinkkemper, S., Wrycza, S. (eds.) CAiSE 2012. LNCS, vol. 7328, pp. 270–285. Springer, Heidelberg (2012). https://doi.org/10.1007/978-3-642-31095-9_18
13. Munoz-Gama, J., Carmona, J.: A fresh look at precision in process conformance, vol. 6336, pp. 211–226 (2010)
14. Pesic, M., Schonenberg, H., van der Aalst, W.M.P.: Declare: Full support for loosely-structured processes. In: 11th IEEE International Enterprise Distributed Object Computing Conference (EDOC 2007), pp. 287–287 (2007)
15. Polyvyanyy, A., Solti, A., Weidlich, M., Di Ciccio, C., Mendling, J.: Monotone precision and recall measures for comparing executions and specifications of dynamic systems. ACM Trans. Softw. Eng. Methodol. **29**(3) (2020)
16. Ramezani, E., Fahland, D., van Dongen, B., van der Aalst, W.M.P.: Diagnostic information in temporal compliance checking. Technical report, BPM Cent. Rep (2) (2012)
17. Weidlich, M., Polyvyanyy, A., Desai, N., Mendling, J., Weske, M.: Process compliance analysis based on behavioural profiles. Inf. Syst. **36**, 1009–1025 (2011)

Leveraging Data Augmentation for Process Information Extraction

Julian Neuberger$^{(\boxtimes)}$, Leonie Doll, Benedikt Engelmann, Lars Ackermann ,
and Stefan Jablonski

University of Bayreuth, Bayreuth, Germany
{julian.neuberger,leonie.doll,benedikt.engelmann,lars.ackermann,
stefan.jablonski}@uni-bayreuth.de

Abstract. Business Process Modeling projects often require formal process models as a central component. High costs associated with the creation of such formal process models motivated many different fields of research aimed at automated generation of process models from readily available data. These include process mining on event logs and generating business process models from natural language texts. Research in the latter field is regularly faced with the problem of limited data availability, hindering both evaluation and development of new techniques, especially learning-based ones.

To overcome this data scarcity issue, in this paper we investigate the application of data augmentation for natural language text data. Data augmentation methods are well established in machine learning for creating new, synthetic data without human assistance. We find that many of these methods are applicable to the task of business process information extraction, improving the accuracy of extraction. Our study shows, that data augmentation is an important component in enabling machine learning methods for the task of business process model generation from natural language text, where currently mostly rule-based systems are still state of the art. Simple data augmentation techniques improved the F_1 score of mention extraction by 2.9% points, and the F_1 of relation extraction by 4.5. To better understand how data augmentation alters human annotated texts, we analyze the resulting text, visualizing and discussing the properties of augmented textual data.

We make all code and experiments results publicly available (Code for our framework can be found at https://github.com/JulianNeuberger/pet-data-augmentation, detailed results for our experiments as MySQL dump can be downloaded from https://zenodo.org/doi/10.5281/zenodo.10941423.).

Keywords: Business Process Extraction · Data Augmentation · Natural Language Processing

1 Introduction

It has been shown that a major share of time planned for Business Process Management (BPM) projects is spent on the acquisition of formal business process

H. van der Aa et al. (Eds.): BPMDS 2024/EMMSAD 2024, LNBIP 511, pp. 57–70, 2024.
https://doi.org/10.1007/978-3-031-61007-3_6

models [14]. This fact motivated a whole host of work done on automated generation of business process models from varying, readily available sources, such as event logs, or natural language process descriptions. The latter area has seen increasing attention in recent years [1,2,13,14,23,24]. Most of these approaches can be formulated as a two-step process, where first the business process relevant information is extracted from text, and then a concrete model is generated from this information.

Many approaches proposed for the task of business process information extraction (BPIE) from texts are still rule-based. This means they extract the information needed for building a formal business process model by applying rules defined by human experts. These rules are usually optimized for a specific dataset, industry sector, or language. For this reason, such systems usually achieve impressive results for their intended, very limited, application domain, but are difficult to transfer to new ones. Alternative approaches like data driven approaches, often called machine learning (ML) methods, infer rules directly from data, making them a lot easier to be adapted to new datasets, domains, or languages. Ideally, adapting an ML approach involves only training on new data. However, this need for data, both for the initial development, as well as for potential adaptations, is what typically impedes application of ML methods at first. Compared to other disciplines also using machine learning, datasets in BPM are relatively small, especially for the task of generating business process models from natural language text. Data sets for this task are expensive to generate, as time-consuming manual annotation by experts is required, in which raw text data is enriched with the desired results (e.g. process entities) in order to provide the ML methods with a basis for learning. Previous work tried to solve this issue by leveraging out-of-domain data, e.g., via pretrained word embeddings [2], or less expressive models, which are easier to train [23] on small datasets. Other fields of related research, such as computer vision, natural language processing (NLP), or audio analysis, tackle the issue by synthesizing new data samples from the existing dataset. This concept is called data augmentation (DA), injecting controlled perturbations. These perturbations can be structural changes (e.g., rotations), as well as added noise.

Data augmentation has already been shown to be useful in a BPM context, such as for the task of next activity prediction, where it is proposed as a solution for the problem of rare process executions, as well as for extrapolating gradual changes in the way processes are executed [18,19]. The authors show that

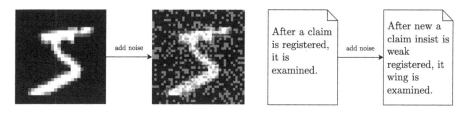

Fig. 1. Example for adding noise to an image (left) and to a sentence (right). The image keeps its semantics, while the sentence looses it.

simple data augmentation strategies like swapping, inserting, or deleting events in the record of a process execution can result in significant accuracy gains [18]. Encouraged by those results, we want to analyze how data augmentation can be applied to improve existing methods for generating process models from text. Due to the nature of natural language, introducing noise without changing the semantics of a data sample is much harder, compared to, for example, computer vision tasks. See Fig. 1 for an example, where introducing noise into an image still keeps its semantics (image of a handwritten "5") intact. Introducing noise in the form of random words into a single sentence on the other hand, can change its semantics significantly, to a point, where it is hard to understand even for humans. We will discuss this fact in more detail in Sect. 2 and give examples for data augmentation techniques, which preserve semantics.

To further structure our understanding of applying data augmentation in the context of generating business process models from natural language text, we pose three research questions.

RQ1 Can simple data augmentation techniques, including swapping, deleting, or randomly inserting words into sentences increase the performance of machine learning methods for BPIE, measured as the harmonic mean of precision and recall?

RQ2 Does the use of large language models in data augmentation, such as for so called *Back Translation* techniques, provide a significant advantage over simpler, rule-based methods?

RQ3 What characteristics of the natural language text data are changed by augmentations, and how do they affect different extraction tasks?

The rest of this paper is structured in the following way: Sect. 2 describes the background of data augmentation in a NLP environment. In Sect. 3 we give an overview of work related to our study. Section 4 defines the setup for our experiments. We then present our results in Sect. 5. Finally, in Sect. 6 we discuss limitations, describe future work, and draw a conclusion.

2 Background

Data augmentation describes a suite of techniques originally popularized in computer vision [25], where simple operations, such as cropping, rotating, or introducing noise into images greatly improved performance of machine learning algorithms used for classification of images. These operations usually preserve the semantics of input data, meaning that an image containing an object will still depict the same object after its data have been augmented, for example, they have been overlaid with noise. This property is called *invariance* [28], and is harder to hold for NLP data [12]. An example for this fact is depicted in Fig. 2. Changing random tokens (e.g., words) in a sentence may alter semantics to a point, where relevant elements or relations between those elements are no longer present after augmentation. Additionally, annotations may be lost, if transformations are applied and afterwards these changes cannot be traced. This might happen, when, for example, an entire sentence is translated into another language and then is back-translated typically leading to a rephrased version of the original text. Since it is not clear, which parts of the new sample correspond to the original one, annotations of process-relevant elements do not apply to the new sample. For this reason, research on data augmentation techniques has been conducted, which are specifically designed for information extraction tasks in the NLP domain[11,15,21]. These techniques use additional resources, such as pretrained large language models, to augment training samples, while keeping their semantics intact.

Fig. 2. Examples for four different data augmentation techniques. *Random deletion, random swap, random insertion* (all written in red), are all not preserving the semantics of a sample and its label. *Rephrasing* (green) is an example for a technique that does. (Color figure online)

Process Relevant Information Extraction from natural language is a research field immediately relevant for information systems, as business process models are often a central part for process aware information systems. Discovering and creating these process models is an expensive task [14] and a lot of work has been done on extracting them from natural language text directly [1,2,5,13,14]. These texts describe a business process in natural language as technical documentation, maintenance handbooks, or interview transcripts. Sequences of words (spans) in these texts contain information that is relevant to the business process, such as *Actors* (persons or departments involved in the process), *Activities* (tasks that are executed), or *Data Objects* (physical or digital objects involved in the process). Extracting this information is therefore a sequence tagging task, and can be framed as *Mention Detection* (MD). Mentions relate to each other, e.g., defining the order of execution for two Activities, or which Actor executes the Activity. Predicting and classifying these relations is called *Relation Extraction* (RE). Refer to Fig. 3 for an example of this process. It shows a fragment of a larger description of a process from the insurance domain, where insurance claims have to be registered in a system and subsequently examined by an employee. The spans *claim* and *it* are annotated as Data Objects (the claim in question, in green). Activities executed by a process participant are marked in orange. These four spans can now be transformed into business process model elements for a target notation language (here BPMN[1]). How these elements interact with each other can also be extracted from the text

---

[1] See specification at https://www.bpmn.org/.

fragment, e.g., the *Flow* of activity execution between the mentions *registered* and *examined*, depicted as an orange arrow.

Fig. 3. Example for a fragment of a natural language business process description and its corresponding business process model fragment in BPMN. (Color figure online)

Developing approaches towards automated extraction of process relevant information requires data to test performance, and train models, if applicable. The currently largest collection of human-annotated process descriptions is called PET [6]. It contains 45 natural language process descriptions, and is annotated with 7 types of process relevant entities (e.g., Actors, Activities, Data Objects), as well as 6 types of relations between them (e.g., Flow between Activities). In total the dataset contains less than 2,000 examples for both relations and entity mentions. For comparison, typical datasets for related tasks, like Knowledge Graph completion contain more than 200 times as many. For example, the popular *FB15k* dataset comprises more than 500,000 relation examples [8]. Datasets for extraction of named entities and their relations have similar extents, e.g., the DocRed dataset, which contains more than 1,500,000 relation examples [27]. This fact makes PET a prime candidate for data augmentation techniques, in order to make the most out of the limited amount of training examples. We show this in our experiments using PET for the tasks MD and RE in BPIE. To our knowledge our work is the first to attempt applying NLP data augmentation to the BPIE task.

3 Related Work

Data augmentation techniques applied in this paper are largely based on the ones available in the *NL-Augmenter* framework [10]. NL-Augmenter provides a list of more than 100 data augmentation techniques, which are suitable for varying tasks like text classification, sentiment analysis, and even tagging. We discuss how we adapted these transformations to the PET data format in more detail in Sect. 4. Not all transformations are relevant for this work, and we have to exclude most of them, as they are not fitting for BPIE. Details of our exclusion criteria can be found in Sect. 4.

In [17] the authors evaluate nine simple data augmentation techniques (e.g., random deletion) on a total of seven event logs, using seven different models. Our paper follows a similar line of thought for BPIE, instead of predictive process monitoring. The transformations we employ differ significantly from theirs in two core aspects. First, transformations used in this paper are more complex, owing to the more complex character of natural language. While their work focused on reordering events in a log of a process execution, our work uses transformations that are concerned with replacing, extending, or modifying sequences of text, while preserving any annotations present in the data. Second, transformations used in our work often require external resources. These resources can be explicit, i.e., databases like WordNet [22], which contains lexical information such as synonyms, antonyms, or hypernyms of words. They can also be implicit, such as large language models, which contain knowledge about natural language, obtained by unsupervised training on huge amounts of textual data [9].

The techniques we present in our paper mainly benefit work that already exists in the field of BPIE. Therefore, approaches towards BPIE based on machine learning are related to this work. These approaches can be separated into two main fields of research. *(1)* learning approaches, which use the data to train a machine learning models, e.g., a neural network [2], conditional random fields [6], or decision trees [23]. *(2)* prompting based approaches that use the data for engineering input for large language models (e.g., GPT) [16,20], or use the data for so called *in context learning*, by providing examples in the input itself [5].

Automated extraction of information relevant to business processes from natural language text descriptions can be seen as a special case of automated knowledge graph construction or completion [4]. We therefore consider techniques for automated knowledge graph construction and completion as distantly related work, which could still benefit from the augmentation techniques we analyze in this paper. Nonetheless, we focus on methods of BPIE in this paper, as potential solution for this field's small datasets.

4   Experiment Setup

The NL Augmenter framework provides a total of 119 data augmentation techniques, but not all of them are applicable to the task at hand. We therefore define four criteria for exclusion: **(EC1)** The technique does not apply to the English language. **(EC2)** The technique alters the spelling of tokens. **(EC3)** The data augmentation technique does not work for supervised data, e.g., it corrupts target annotations. **(EC4)** The technique uses task-, and/or domain-specific resources, such as dictionaries, or databases, which often do not exist for BPM data, and are hard to create given the diversity of BPM application domains. Applying these exclusion criteria results in 19 data augmentation techniques relevant for the task of business process information extraction from natural language text.

4.1   Data Augmentation Effects

The data augmentation techniques we selected synthesize samples with three core characteristics.

(1) Increased linguistic variability, i.e., augmented text uses a larger vocabulary to describe the same, or at least, a similar business process[2]. The most prominent examples for such techniques are the *Back-Translation* techniques. These use a large language model, e.g., BERT [9] to translate the process description to a different language and subsequently translate it back to the original language – here English. Since data augmentation techniques must not alter the annotations of entities, we only translated spans of text, not the entire document at once. Take for example, the running example *After a claim is registered, it is examined*. Here four spans are annotated as entities – *a claim, registered, examined*, and *it*. Additionally there are three remaining spans, that do not correspond to entities: *After a, is, is*. By back-translating these seven spans separately, we obtain variation in their wording (*surface form*), but are still able to preserve annotations. Samples synthesized in this way are especially useful for making methods for the MD task generalize better and more robust.

(2) Variations in span length. Many spans of a given entity type, e.g., Actors are very uniform in length across examples. This is a result of several factors, but most apparent actors are often identified by their job title, e.g., *the clerk*, or the department, e.g., *the secretary office*. These titles and departments are very short phrases, and longer ones are abbreviated, reducing their length to two or less tokens, e.g., *the MPOO*. Even though their expanded form may not be known, expanding some of these spans to suitable phrases, e.g., *Manager, Post Office Operations*, creates samples with longer surface forms. This in turn, may improve the robustness of the MD extractors, as well as the generalization capabilities of RE methods.

(3) Directionality of relations between mentions. The order of appearance for mentions that form a relation, is very uniform in the current version of PET. This is especially apparent, when looking at the base-line extraction rules defined by the original authors of PET: Here the order of appearance of Activities and Actors is exploited, to form the *Actor Performer* and *Actor Recipient* relations [6]. These relations define the Actor, that performs an Activity, and the Actor, on which an Activity is performed. The Actor left of an Activity is assigned the former, while the Actor right of that Activity is assigned the latter. In this example order uniformity can lead to less robust models, as they rely on this and subsequently make wrong predictions given different linguistic constructs. Synthesizing samples with a different order may encourage models to consider linguistic features (context) rather than just the order of mentions in a sentence during prediction.

4.2 Finding Optimal Configurations

Each of the data augmentation techniques we selected can potentially be adjusted by several parameters, which control how augmented samples are synthesized. A typical example for such a parameter is the number of inserted

---

[2] The augmentation technique might change information in the text, which changes the process overall, e.g., by replacing original actors with new, artificial ones.

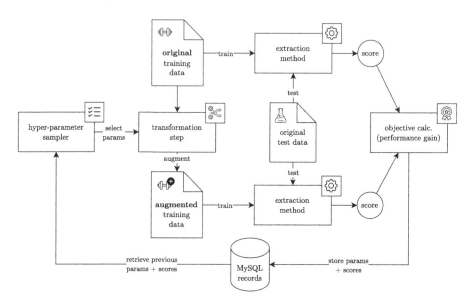

Fig. 4. Choosing optimal configurations for data augmentation techniques.

tokens. Increasing this number would result in a sample, which is more perturbed compared to a sample where fewer tokens are inserted. We consider optimally choosing such parameters for a given technique a *hyper-parameter optimization* problem. Hyper-parameter optimization is defined as finding a configuration of parameters so that a given objective (metric to optimize) is minimal or rather maximal, depending on the case. Here, we want to maximize the performance gain that the application of a data augmentation technique has. To that end we run a 5-fold cross-validation of the extraction step (MD, RE) with the original, unaugmented data. We then select a configuration for the given technique and run the same 5-fold cross-validation, but augment the training data of each fold with the data augmentation technique. We define the difference between the scores of these two models on the (unaugmented) test dataset as the *performance gain* and use it as maximization objective for our hyper-parameter optimization. Each data augmentation technique is optimized in 25 runs (*trials*) using Optuna [3] and a Tree-Structured Parzen Estimator for selecting parameter values [7]. We depict this process in Fig. 4.

The most effective data augmentation techniques can then be used to supplement the existing PET dataset, as well as any future datasets used for BPIE. In the following Sect. 5 we present the results of the experiment described here and discuss their implications.

5   Results

In this section we will discuss results for the experiments we defined in the previous section. Table 1 lists the differences of all data augmentation techniques

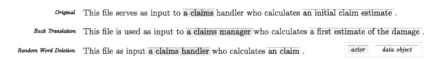

Fig. 5. Two examples for the effects of data augmentation techniques.

compared to a run on un-augmented data. All differences are measured as the micro-averaged F_1 score. Concluding from our results, we find that the RE task can benefit significantly from most of the data augmentation techniques we selected and tested. Transformations that reorder tokens, like *Shuffle Within Segments*, *Sentence Reordering*, or *English Mention Replacement* seem to be less useful, compared to other techniques. This is most likely rooted in the change in directionality of relations (effect **(3)** from Sect. 4). Since these transformations do not take any context into account, such changes may be breaking semantics of relations in a sentence.

Transformations based on large language models, especially back translation techniques, like *Multilingual Back Translation*, which translate a sentence fragment twice, are very time-intensive. Yet, improvements in relation extraction performance is not significant, when comparing them to more lightweight approaches, e.g., *Synonym Substitution*, which uses WordNet to rephrase text sequences. In our experiments using these large language model based methods is not worth the increase in computing power and time. While the MD task can still benefit from all data augmentation techniques, it does so to a lesser extent when compared to the RE task. This indicates a model, that is already more stable, and generalizes better. Transformations that alter the amount of tokens in mentions, such as *Random Word Deletion*, *Synonym Insertion*, or *Subsequence Substitution for Sequence Tagging*, result in lesser improvements, compared to paraphrasing methods, such as *AntonymsSubstitute*, *BackTranslation*, or *Synonym Substitution* (Fig. 5). Similar to the RE task, the MD task does not benefit significantly more from resource and time intensive, large language model based augmentation techniques for paraphrasing, compared to their simpler counterparts.

Based on our observations, we can answer research question RQ1, with "Yes". Simple data augmentation techniques like swapping tokens, deleting them, or inserting random tokens do have a significant benefit. The RE task benefits more from them, than the MD task does. Since nearly all augmentations have a net positive impact, we argue that the perturbations act as controlled noise, very similar to techniques used for training deep neural networks. There, models that are more robust and generalize better are created, simply by adding noise to the training data [26].

The use of large language models in data augmentation techniques brings with it a significant increase in resources needed, both in terms of computing time, hardware requirements, and power consumption. Based on our experiments, this is not worthwhile for improving the business process information

Table 1. Detailed results for all transformation steps, for both the MD and RE task. Column *Id* refers to the identifier defined in [10]. It links to the source code for this technique. Top three results are set in **bold** face. All results are the averages of a 5-fold cross validation on the entire dataset.

Technique	Id	Description	MD	RE
Unaugmented		results for un-augmented data	0.695	0.759
Adjectives Antonyms Switch	B.3	use antonyms of adjectives	+0.024	**+0.045**
AntonymsSubstitute (Double Negation)	B.5	substitute even number of words with antonyms	**+0.025**	+0.042
Auxiliary Negation Removal	B.6	remove negated auxiliaries	**+0.025**	+0.039
BackTranslation	B.8	translate to German, then back to English	**+0.025**	+0.036
Concatenate Two Random Sentences	B.24	remove punctuation between sentences	+0.023	+0.042
Contextual Meaning Perturbation	B.26	replace words with use of pretrained language model	+0.004	+0.040
English Mention Replacement for NER	B.39	replace mention with one of the same type in document	+0.015	+0.036
Filler Word Augmentation	B.40	introduce "uhm", "I think",	+0.021	**+0.043**
Multilingual Back Translation	B.62	see B.8, language is parameter	+0.022	+0.041
Random Word Deletion	B.79	delete random words	+0.011	+0.034
Replace Abbreviations and Acronyms	B.82	replace acronyms with full length expression and v.v	+0.020	+0.042
Sentence Reordering	B.88	reorder sentences	+0.024	+0.034
Shuffle Within Segments	B.90	shuffle tokens in mentions	+0.021	+0.041
Synonym Insertion	B.100	insert synonym before word	+0.019	**+0.043**
Synonym Substitution	B.101	substitute word with synonym	+0.023	+0.040
Subsequence Substitution for Sequence Tagging	B.103	replace sequence with another sequence with same POS tags	+0.019	+0.033
Transformer Fill	B.106	replace tokens using language model	+0.022	+0.041
Random Insert		insert random tokens	+0.020	**+0.043**
Random Swap		swap position of tokens	**+0.029**	+0.033

extraction approaches we used. Back-translation techniques, such as *B.8*, *B.62*, and especially *B.26* do not provide benefits in the MD and RE tasks, that would warrant their additional needs in hardware (GPUs), and runtime, which was several orders of magnitude higher, compared to simpler augmentation techniques. We therefore have to answer RQ2 with "No".

To answer research question RQ3, we defined three characteristics of textual data in Sect. 4 that are changed by the data augmentation techniques we selected. These characteristics are visualized in Figs. 6a and 6b. Figure 6a shows the "landscape" of data augmentation techniques evaluated in this paper. Three groups of techniques emerge. The first one is a group of techniques that only marginally increase the number of tokens in mentions, and keep the size of the

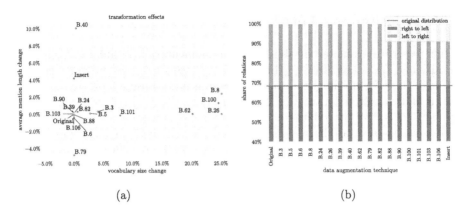

(a)   (b)

Fig. 6. *(a)*: Effects on vocabulary size and the average length of mentions in tokens. *(b)*: Effects of techniques on relation direction.

vocabulary roughly the same. These techniques mainly change the context (i.e., the text that does not contain immediately process relevant information), or the structure of the text (i.e., modify punctuation, or change the order of tokens). Techniques in the second group do not modify the vocabulary, but have a significant impact on the number of tokens in a given mention. These augmentations can theoretically be useful for the robustness of MD extraction models, but only have a moderate impact in our experiments, using the PET dataset. We count *Random Insertion, Filler Word Augmentation*, but also *Random Word Deletion* towards this group, see Fig. 2 for an example taken from the augmented data. The final group of techniques increases the size of the vocabulary, while keeping mention lengths roughly the same. These techniques are paraphrasing, aimed at preserving semantics and the structure of textual data. Techniques using WordNet to insert or substitute synonyms (*B.100, B.101*, as well as back translation methods (*B.62, B.26*) fall in this group. Figure 2 shows a sentence that is augmented with the back translation method *B.26*.

Figure 6b shows the changes in directionality certain data augmentation techniques have. Most techniques preserve the direction of relation examples in the data, with the exception of techniques *B.88* (Sentence Reordering) and *B.24* (Concatenate Random Sentences). Based on our experiments, this change seems to be less useful than other augmentations. The improvement of B.88 is among the worst ones of all techniques. In future work it could be interesting to investigate, if selectively augmenting only certain types of relations can be helpful. Also, having a more diverse test set, i.e., texts from different sources, like employee notes, handbooks, and interview notes, might change the usefulness of directionality changing data augmentation techniques.

6   Conclusion and Future Work

In this paper we evaluated established data augmentation techniques for use in the MD and RE steps of extracting process relevant information from natural language texts for use in the automated generation of business process models. To this end we selected a total of 19 distinct methods from related work, which are suitable for the given data.

We discuss several characteristics these selected data augmentation techniques change in the original data and how they relate to differences in usefulness of certain techniques for either the MD or RE task. We found that many of them are useful for improving the accuracy of the current state of the art machine learning models on the PET dataset for automated business process model generation from natural language text. For the RE model the F_1 score could be improved by up to 4.5% points, the MD model was improved by up to 2.9% points. Our findings enable researchers in the field of process model generation from natural language text to make more efficient use of the limited data available to them, enabling more precise and robust machine learning methods for extracting business process relevant information.

In future work, we want to analyze how targeted data augmentation can be used to improve extraction of certain types of mentions or relations, tackling the problem of data imbalance. Additionally we want to explore adaptive data augmentation, where samples are selected for augmentation by their value for model training, e.g., measured by the number of wrong predictions.

References

1. van der Aa, H., Di Ciccio, C., Leopold, H., Reijers, H.A.: Extracting declarative process models from natural language. In: Giorgini, P., Weber, B. (eds.) CAiSE 2019. LNCS, vol. 11483, pp. 365–382. Springer, Cham (2019). https://doi.org/10.1007/978-3-030-21290-2_23
2. Ackermann, L., Neuberger, J., Jablonski, S.: Data-driven annotation of textual process descriptions based on formal meaning representations. In: La Rosa, M., Sadiq, S., Teniente, E. (eds.) CAiSE 2021. LNCS, vol. 12751, pp. 75–90. Springer, Cham (2021). https://doi.org/10.1007/978-3-030-79382-1_5
3. Akiba, T., Sano, S., Yanase, T., Ohta, T., Koyama, M.: Optuna: a next-generation hyperparameter optimization framework. In: SIGKDD International Conference on Knowledge Discovery & Data Mining (2019)
4. Bellan, P., Dragoni, M., Ghidini, C.: Assisted process knowledge graph building using pre-trained language models. In: Dovier, A., Montanari, A., Orlandini, A. (eds.) AIxIA 2022. LNCS, vol. 13796, pp. 60–74. Springer, Cham (2022). https://doi.org/10.1007/978-3-031-27181-6_5
5. Bellan, P., Dragoni, M., Ghidini, C.: Extracting business process entities and relations from text using pre-trained language models and in-context learning. In: Almeida, J.P.A., Karastoyanova, D., Guizzardi, G., Montali, M., Maggi, F.M., Fonseca, C.M. (eds.) EDOC 2022. LNCS, vol. 13585, pp. 182–199. Springer, Cham (2022). https://doi.org/10.1007/978-3-031-17604-3_11

6. Bellan, P., Ghidini, C., Dragoni, M., Ponzetto, S.P., van der Aa, H.: Process extraction from natural language text: the pet dataset and annotation guidelines. In: NL4AI (2022)
7. Bergstra, J., Bardenet, R., Bengio, Y., Kégl, B.: Algorithms for hyper-parameter optimization. In: Advances in Neural Information Processing Systems, vol. 24 (2011)
8. Bordes, A., Usunier, N., Garcia-Duran, A., Weston, J., Yakhnenko, O.: Translating embeddings for modeling multi-relational data. In: Advances in Neural Information Processing Systems, vol. 26 (2013)
9. Devlin, J., Chang, M.W., Lee, K., Toutanova, K.: BERT: pre-training of deep bidirectional transformers for language understanding. arXiv preprint (2018)
10. Dhole, K.D., et al.: NL-Augmenter: a framework for task-sensitive natural language augmentation. arXiv preprint (2021)
11. Erdengasileng, A., et al.: Pre-trained models, data augmentation, and ensemble learning for biomedical information extraction and document classification. Database **2022**, baac066 (2022)
12. Feng, S.Y., et al.: A survey of data augmentation approaches for NLP (2021)
13. Ferreira, R.C.B., Thom, L.H., Fantinato, M.: A semi-automatic approach to identify business process elements in natural language texts. In: ICEIS (2017)
14. Friedrich, F., Mendling, J., Puhlmann, F.: Process model generation from natural language text. In: Mouratidis, H., Rolland, C. (eds.) CAiSE 2011. LNCS, vol. 6741, pp. 482–496. Springer, Heidelberg (2011). https://doi.org/10.1007/978-3-642-21640-4_36
15. Jiang, Z., Han, J., Sisman, B., Dong, X.L.: CoRI: collective relation integration with data augmentation for open information extraction. arXiv preprint (2021)
16. Kampik, T., et al.: Large process models: business process management in the age of generative AI. arXiv preprint arXiv:2309.00900 (2023)
17. Käppel, M., Jablonski, S.: Model-agnostic event log augmentation for predictive process monitoring. In: Indulska, M., Reinhartz-Berger, I., Cetina, C., Pastor, O. (eds.) CAiSE 2023. LNCS, vol. 13901, pp. 381–397. Springer, Cham (2023). https://doi.org/10.1007/978-3-031-34560-9_23
18. Käppel, M., Jablonski, S., Schönig, S.: Evaluating predictive business process monitoring approaches on small event logs. In: Paiva, A.C.R., Cavalli, A.R., Ventura Martins, P., Pérez-Castillo, R. (eds.) QUATIC 2021. CCIS, vol. 1439, pp. 167–182. Springer, Cham (2021). https://doi.org/10.1007/978-3-030-85347-1_13
19. Käppel, M., Schönig, S., Jablonski, S.: Leveraging small sample learning for business process management. Inf. Softw. Technol. **132**, 106472 (2021)
20. Klievtsova, N., Benzin, J.V., Kampik, T., Mangler, J., Rinderle-Ma, S.: Conversational process modelling: state of the art, applications, and implications in practice. In: Di Francescomarino, C., Burattin, A., Janiesch, C., Sadiq, S. (eds.) BPM 2023. LNBIP, vol. 490, pp. 319–336. Springer, Cham (2023). https://doi.org/10.1007/978-3-031-41623-1_19
21. Liu, J., Chen, Y., Xu, J.: Machine reading comprehension as data augmentation: a case study on implicit event argument extraction. In: EMNLP (2021)
22. Miller, G.A.: WordNet: a lexical database for English. CACM **38**(11), 39–41 (1995)
23. Neuberger, J., Ackermann, L., Jablonski, S.: Beyond rule-based named entity recognition and relation extraction for process model generation from natural language text. In: Sellami, M., Vidal, M.E., van Dongen, B., Gaaloul, W., Panetto, H. (eds.) CoopIS 2023. LNCS, vol. 14353, pp. 179–197. Springer, Cham (2023). https://doi.org/10.1007/978-3-031-46846-9_10

24. Quishpi, L., Carmona, J., Padró, L.: Extracting annotations from textual descriptions of processes. In: Fahland, D., Ghidini, C., Becker, J., Dumas, M. (eds.) BPM 2020. LNCS, vol. 12168, pp. 184–201. Springer, Cham (2020). https://doi.org/10.1007/978-3-030-58666-9_11
25. Shorten, C., Khoshgoftaar, T.M., Furht, B.: Text data augmentation for deep learning. J. Big Data **8**, 1–34 (2021)
26. Srivastava, N., Hinton, G., Krizhevsky, A., Sutskever, I., Salakhutdinov, R.: Dropout: a simple way to prevent neural networks from overfitting. J. Mach. Learn. Res. **15**(1), 1929–1958 (2014)
27. Yao, Y., et al.: DocRED: a large-scale document-level relation extraction dataset. arXiv preprint (2019)
28. Zoran, D., Weiss, Y.: Scale invariance and noise in natural images. In: ICCV (2009)

User Preferences and Agile Processes (BPMDS 2024)

A Generic Approach Towards Adapting User Preferences in Business Process Execution

Sebastian Petter$^{(\boxtimes)}$ and Stefan Jablonski

University of Bayreuth, Bayreuth, Germany
{sebastian.petter,stefan.jablonski}@uni-bayreuth.de

Abstract. Business Process Management (BPM) plays a vital role in modern businesses, assisting them in organizing their operational procedures. There are multiple methods to improve these processes. Process optimization often overlooks human resources as crucial parts of business processes. By focusing on individual user preferences process executions can be improved. Approaches pursuing this idea are subsumed under the term human-centric BPM. One way to achieve this kind of optimization is to integrate recommender systems into BPM. Integrated recommender systems consider user preferences during process execution and therefore enhance user experience and thus overall process efficiency. Our proposed framework offers an adaptable solution for integrating arbitrary recommendation strategies. The practicability of the framework is demonstrated through a real-world example.

Keywords: Business process management · Recommender systems · User-centered process improvement

1 Motivation

Nowadays, Business Process Management (BPM) is widely adopted in companies to achieve specific business objectives [13,25]. With its emphasis on optimizing processes and improving efficiency, BPM has become an integral part of modern business operations. At its core, BPM involves the orchestration of a sequence of activities known as business processes which are systematically structured organizational operations. The formal representation of these sequences is known as business process model. It contains the tasks that must be executed in a process and covers information on process entities involved, such as process participants and data objects. These models are essential for visualizing and understanding the flow of activities within a process, and serve as a basis for analysis, improvement, and automation of business processes. Process Aware Information Systems (PAIS) support users by guiding them through the execution of business process models [21]. These systems determine which activities can be executed by which users and provide personalized worklists containing tasks ready for execution.

H. van der Aa et al. (Eds.): BPMDS 2024/EMMSAD 2024, LNBIP 511, pp. 73–86, 2024.
https://doi.org/10.1007/978-3-031-61007-3_7

Explicate Problem. Besides process execution one of the further fundamental goals of BPM is process improvement. Most approaches are activity-centered, focusing on control flow [22]. This entails analyzing and optimizing the sequence of activities within a process to streamline operations, reduce inefficiencies, and enhance overall performance [15,17].

However, it is also important to consider the role of human resources in processes as many depend on their involvement. For this reason, it is essential to take into account the role of human resources within these processes. So, besides optimizing control flow it's equally important to ensure that people participating in process execution are well regarded. Content and engaged employees significantly contribute to business process success [6,9]; therefore, optimizing participants' satisfaction can boost productivity and efficiency.

Incorporating human preferences into BPM can be achieved through the use of recommender systems [19]. These systems enhance user experience and decision-making by providing personalized recommendations based on individual preferences [2]. Organizations can utilize recommender systems to gather and analyze user preferences, including those of human resources during business process execution. This information then can be used to tailor future process executions to employees' individual preferences, ultimately improving their satisfaction and thus overall process performance. We call this tailored form of process execution *human-centric BPM*.

Concluding the above discussion we intend to combine BPM with recommender systems to foster human-centric BPM. However, before we are able to concretize our goal both research domains, BPM and recommender systems, must be introduced (Sect. 2) and the current state of their integration must be discussed (Sect. 3). Section 4 presents requirements towards and relevance of our novel solution for the integration of recommendations into BPM. Its design and development is depicted in Sect. 5. Its practical application and its evaluation are presented in Sect. 6. Finally, the paper concludes by summarizing our findings and suggesting future research directions (Sect. 7).

2   Background

Business Process Management. BPM integrates insights from information systems and management sciences to improve operational business processes. It involves methods, techniques, and tools for managing, modeling, implementing, executing, and analyzing business processes [13].

Modeling in BPM involves creating a formal representation of a business process, known as a business process model. This model comprises data about the sequence of activities, data, and resources involved in a process. It serves as a blueprint for the actual implementation and execution of processes and is essential for understanding and optimizing the process flow [13,25].

Executing business processes means to implement the activities of the corresponding business process models in a PAIS. The latter interprets a business process model by determining the activities to be executed next, and putting these activities as tasks into the worklists of users eligible for executing them

[21]. A worklist is the main interface for a user to a PAIS. It contains all tasks that can be performed by them. By the way, user preferences must be mostly reflected in a worklist (see Sect. 5).

When a user completes a task from their worklist, it generates an event with data about process execution. These events are systematically recorded in an event log - serving as a comprehensive repository capturing every significant occurrence during process execution. Event logs play a crucial role in providing insights into process execution and performance [1].

Analyzing business processes and especially event logs enables organizations to gain valuable insights into process performance, to identify operational bottlenecks, and to make improvements for enhanced efficiency.

Recommender Systems. Recommender systems are a subfield of information filtering systems that aim to predict user preferences or rating for an item to be processed [2]. These systems are designed to provide personalized recommendations based on user behavior and preferences, helping individuals navigate vast amounts of available information while assisting service providers in enhancing user satisfaction and engagement [2].

Recommender systems are widely used in various fields such as e-commerce platforms, social media platforms, and streaming services to enhance user experience [2]. These systems suggest products, movies, music, and other items based on user preferences, aiming to boost satisfaction and loyalty. Therefore, domain specific data are exploited to personalize recommendations. For instance, in e-commerce, previous purchase patterns are frequently taken into account.

Fundamentally, recommender systems operate by collecting implicit and explicit user feedback, which is then used to generate recommendations [12]. Implicit feedback encompasses user actions, such as purchases, clicks, and views, while explicit feedback may include user ratings and reviews. These data are analyzed to create a personalized recommendation model for an user.

There are diverse methods for generating recommendations, each with its unique characteristics and suitability for particular contexts. These methods differ in their application domain and efficacy. We are going to present the four main types of filtering methods, namely collaborative filtering, content-based filtering, knowledge-based filtering, and hybrid filtering methods [2]. We reduce the following discussion to the identification of input and output of each method class and to a short outline of their logic. Refer to cited literature for further insights into these recommendation methods.

Collaborative filtering methods take user feedback to generate recommendation by identifying similarities between users or items[1]. They encounter challenges with new users or items that have minimal or no historical data available - this makes them less effective in scenarios involving niche or sparse data [11]. Content-based filtering, on the other hand, uses characteristics of items as input, providing recommendations that closely match previous interest of users.

---

[1] Items are the subject of a recommendation methods, for instance, recommended articles in a web shop or similar movies for a streaming service. In the context of BPM task of a worklist are considered as items.

However, this method entails limited variety of recommendations, as it does not allow recommendations for diverse or unexpected content [11]. Knowledge-based filtering approaches leverage explicit knowledge, offering highly personalized recommendations as output, but can be limited by a user's inability to articulate preferences or a poor knowledge base. They may not be as efficient as other filtering methods since they do not excel in uncovering unforeseen items [2]. Hybrid filtering techniques merge various recommendation strategies to address the drawbacks of singular methods [10].

3   Related Work

Existing studies have investigated the incorporation of recommendation techniques into BPM through various methods. In particular, Setiwan, Branchi and Pika explored the use of collaborative filtering algorithms in BPM [8,20,23]. However, these research works predominantly centered on enhancing processes to minimize throughput time rather than emphasizing human resource considerations. Content-based filtering algorithms, as outlined in several studies, were included in the further examination of process improvement [3,18]. The papers by Arias and Petter specifically investigated incorporating user preferences to revise worklists [3,18]. Additionally, implicit user feedback [7] is analyzed as well as explicit feedback through user ratings [18]. Knowledge-based filtering algorithms have been investigated in several papers [4,5,24]. Some of them focused on improving throughput times [4,5], while others took a different approach by emphasizing roles, skills, and contextual information to generate personalized recommendations [24].

Overall, the existing literature demonstrates that recommendation techniques are already incorporated into BPM. However, the studies also show that each approach does statically integrate exactly one filter method. An extension to or combination with further methods is not possible. Since in real-world settings it is often not clear which filter methods performs best, this static approach is not practical. In application domains beyond BPM this is the reason to introduce hybrid filtering techniques that combine multiple recommendation strategies to overcome the limitations of singular methods. However, so far there are no approaches for integrating hybrid methods into BPM.

4   Research Contribution

Define Requirements. To support users during process execution, it is essential to capture user preferences. Expressed user preferences lead to (system) requirements a recommender system must facilitate. It must work up these requirements to adjust the various aspects of process execution for satisfying user preferences. User preferences must be captured and analyzed in real-time. Furthermore, recommendations must continuously be aligned to changing process execution conditions and user feedback. Considering the diverse range of recommendation methods, it is essential for the framework to accommodate various filtering techniques and algorithms that cater to different application needs and characteristics. Often, it cannot be anticipated which recommendation method fits best to a certain problem. Thus, it is highly advantageous when filtering methods can be exchanged without having to re-implement the whole application. This adaptability to new or newly detected demands is key in catering to a variety of use cases and operational conditions. Consequently, it is important to ensure the interchangeability and customizability of various recommendation algorithms within the framework.

Altogether, the integration of a recommendation module and a BPM tool is mandatory, since this is the only way to implement all the requirements discussed above. Based on these observations the following research questions are derived:

RQ_1: How can user preferences be identified and captured during business process execution?

RQ_2: How can recommendation capability conceptually and technically be integrated with BPM?

RQ_3: How can the outcome of a recommendation system be returned to a BPM system and how does that outcome affect process execution?

RQ_1 addresses the methodical and technical considerations required for capturing and analyzing user preferences in real-time during process execution. The integration of recommendation capability into a BPM system (RQ_2) demands continuous and simultaneous processing of user requirements and user preferences. RQ_3 deals with the incorporation and reflection of outcome from a recommendation system by a BPM system for achieving human-centric BPM.

Contribution. In our research, we analyze how recommender systems can be tailored for their use in the field of BPM. In Sect. 2 we see that for different recommendation purposes, specialized recommendation systems are built. Based on examining and analyzing their recommendation methods, we constitute a novel framework for the integration of arbitrary recommendation systems supporting different types of recommendation into BPM systems. Thus, it is facilitated to tie arbitrary recommendation systems – depending on the individual needs of an application with respect to recommendation support – to a BPM system without extensive conceptual and technical adjustments. To the best of our knowledge, our approach is the first one enabling this and therefore provides a powerful platform for supporting individual human-centric BPM.

Project Relevance. Our research is inspired by a collaborative project called PRIME (Process-based integration of human expectations in digitalized work environments)[2], which involves three research and three application partners. It focused on integrating human aspects into BPM. In this paper, we use a real-world process from that project as an example process.

Research Methodology. The paper adopts the Design Science Research Methodology (DSRM), aiming to create practical artifacts [14]. The current procedure model by Johannesson and Perjson [16] consists of five iterative phases:

---

[2] https://prime-interaktionsarbeit.de.

(i) explicate problem, (ii) define requirements, (iii) design and develop artifact, (iv) demonstrate artifact, and (v) evaluate artifact. The first section already outlines the problem, while this section outlines its requirements for a solution. Design and development of the artifact are covered in Sect. 5, while Sect. 6 cover demonstration and evaluation.

5   Design and Development of Artifact

According to the DSRM research method we design a framework as artifact and problem solution. Our framework aims at enhancing business process execution by including personalization and recommendation capabilities. It includes three main elements, as depicted in Fig. 1: (i) an input module that collects data from PAIS and recommender systems; (ii) a recommendation generation module which employs various recommendation algorithms to create personalized recommendations for users based on their ratings, actions, worklist, and the current context of the business processes; (iii) an output module that transfers and incorporates the generated recommendations into business process execution. These recommendations support users during process execution. For instance, users are assisted when next activities have to be selected from the worklist. These three modules will be discussed in the following.

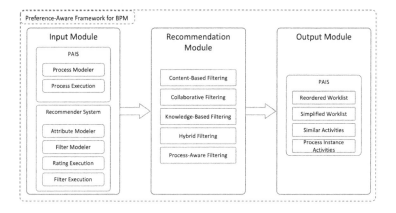

Fig. 1. Conceptual Structure of Framework

Input Module. The input module gathers and combines information from two primary sources: the PAIS and the recommendation system. Both sources consist of various modules for generating and collecting data during modeling or execution. The PAIS supplies data concerning business process execution, including worklists and event logs, as well as data related to modeling such as the process model. On the other hand, the recommendation system consists of modeling modules related to attributes and filters as well as execution modules related to ratings and filters. The attribute modeling module enriches a provided process model with context attributes required for content-based filters, while the filter modeler assists in creating custom filters. Meanwhile, the rating execution module offers different types of ratings (e.g., continuous, interval-based) to be utilized by a PAIS. Additionally, the filter execution module provides a mechanism to capture user preferences during process execution.

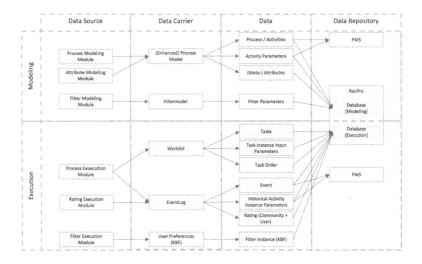

Fig. 2. Organization of input data.

Figure 2 illustrates the conceptual data architecture for integrating recommendation systems with BPM systems. It comprises four key spaces, each serving a distinct role in the data life cycle. The input data represented here are not exhaustive and can be expanded to include additional data sources and types. This enables adaption and evolution of the framework in response to new insights and requirements. The leftmost column is labeled as *Data Source*, outlining the modules responsible for generating raw data for the framework. Adjacent to this is the *Data Carrier* column, detailing intermediaries that hold the data coming from the source modules such as process models, worklists, event logs, filter models, and user preferences. The central column, labeled as *Data*, provides a comprehensive overview of all the data elements required by recommendation algorithms within process execution. This includes familiar data from a PAIS as well as data relevant for recommendation algorithms like meta attributes, filter parameters, ratings, and specific values provided by the user in a knowledge-based filter. This essential information serves as input for generating personalized recommendations that drive actionable insights. These data are sufficient to feed any recommendation algorithm with relevant input data. Finally, on the far right, the *Data Repository* column indicates the systems where data is stored. Traditionally, a PAIS stores information about processes and event logs while worklists are dynamically generated and presented to users but are not persisted. This presents a significant limitation, as the combination of worklists and event logs holds valuable implicit user feedback. To address this limitation we retain worklist data (along with all other applicable data) within our system called RecPro (RECommendations for PROcess Management). Thus, we not only keep tasks including their ordering as they appear to the user, but we also capture recommendations calculated for these tasks. This method enriches our dataset, and therefore enables a deeper analysis of user behavior and allows to refine recommendation algorithms.

Regarding the information flow into the data repository, the apparent data duplication is intentional. It is needed to preserve a historical record of raw data and to store recommendations for both current and future use. Our framework synchronizes these replicated data ensuring reliable and current recommendations.

Recommendation Module. The *Recommendation Module* is the core component of our framework, responsible for generating personalized recommendations based on user preferences and past behavior. In Table 1, we explore various recommendation strategies, including (process-aware) knowledge-based filtering, (process-aware) content-based filtering, (process-aware) collaborative filtering, (process-aware) hybrid filtering, and process-aware filtering. These strategies are applied to the data collected by the *Input Module* and leverage recommendation algorithms to generate accurate and relevant recommendations. They primarily differ in terms of the input data utilized: standard input data (denoted by solid dots (●)) are commonly used in traditional recommendation methods; while process-specific input data (represented by hollowed dots (○)) are derived from the domain of BPM and catered to the intricacies of process-aware environments. Additionally, meta data about filter initiator's identity, filter execution type, and output provided by each filter approach are included. The *Initiator* column specifies the entity responsible for configuring a filter, distinguishing between the process owner and the current user. *Filter Execution* outlines whether the recommendation is generated automatically by the system or requires manual intervention by a user, thus indicating the operational mode of the filter. Lastly, the *Output* column details the type of response produced by each filter, such as a concrete value, or a boolean value indicating whether or not a task complies with the preferences.

Table 1. Analyzed recommendation methods.

Filter Method	Process model			Filter-model	Worklist		Eventlog				Preferences	Initiator	Filter execution	Output
	Process/Activities	Activity Parameters	(Meta-) Attributes	Filter Parameters	Tasks	Task Order	Event	Activity Parameters	Rating (Community)	Rating (User)	Filter Instance (KBF)			
Knowledge-based Filter	●	○	●	○	●			○			●	User	manual	true/false
Content-based Filter	●	○	●	○	●			○		●		Process Owner	automatically	Value, true/false
Collaborative Filter	●	○	○	○	●			○	●	●		Process Owner	automatically	Value, true/false
Hybrid Filter	●	○	●	○	●			○	●	●	●	Process Owner	automatically	Value, true/false
Process Aware Filter	●	○	●	○	●	○	○	○	●	●		Process Owner	automatically	Value, true/false

The knowledge-based filtering strategy uses constraints provided by users to produce recommendations. This implies that users must specify their preferences during process execution. The content-based filtering technique determines whether a task on the worklist aligns with user preferences. In addition to conventional knowledge-based filtering approaches, process-aware knowledge-based filtering can also take into account activities, activity parameters, and task input parameters. The content-based filtering approach and the collaborative filtering approach both utilize data from the users' past behavior to generate recommendations based on derived preferences. These approaches are set up by a process owner and operate in the background without direct user involvement. The outcome of these methods determines whether each task is recommended, using similarities with other users (collaborative filtering) or similarities with a users' past actions (content-based filtering). The hybrid filtering approach combines multiple recommendation strategies to improve accuracy and relevance of recommendations. It leverages a combination of knowledge-based, content-based, and collaborative filtering techniques. The process-aware filtering method incorporates all the previously mentioned recommendation strategies and is specifically designed to consider the context of process execution as well as additional events or traces. Unlike traditional recommendation methods that might solely focus on user behavior or item attributes, process-aware filtering can consider process-specific data like task sequences or execution states. This integration ensures that recommendations are not only considering user preferences but also the process context.

These different approaches allow for a comprehensive and flexible recommendation module that can cater to various user preferences and contextual factors. While we have focused on the mentioned methods, the framework is designed to accommodate expansions and integration of additional filtering techniques seamlessly. Thus, arbitrary filtering method from any contributor can be incorporated into our system. This design choice ensures that our framework remains versatile and can be tailored to a wide range of applications and evolving needs.

Output Module. The Output Module is essential for interpreting the output data from the recommendation methods to derive recommendations for process execution. It serves as the interface between the recommendation generation module and a BPM system. This module aims at transforming output data of a filter method into practical insights that improves task execution within BPM.

Depending on the results from filter methods, users can be presented with different sets of data. For instance, using knowledge-based filtering allows for querying which task within a worklist aligns with the user preferences. Subsequently, tasks that do not match the user preferences can be concealed. Additionally, knowledge-based filtering can also show tasks belonging to the process instance that was executed by the user at last. Using collaborative filtering, the output module has the ability to suggest recommendations by analyzing tasks completed by users with comparable preferences or behaviors. Additionally, the output module can leverage the results of content-based filtering methods to recommend tasks that are similar to those previously carried out by the user.

Since the central interface between a user and process execution is the worklist, the output module directly manipulates entries of a worklist according to the results of the recommendation methods. For instance, tasks in a worklist are rearranged. Furthermore, tasks can even be hidden if they don't match with user preferences. Customizing a worklist ensures a personalized user experience, aligning presented tasks closely with user preferences. This not only enhances user satisfaction but also improves efficiency of task execution.

6   Demonstration and Evaluation

To demonstrate the feasibility of the developed artifact, we carried out a proof-of-concept implementation[3]. This implementation utilizes Camunda 7 as BPM component.[4] It is integrated with our RecPro system that takes over the recommendation part in this collaboration. The prototype is capable of collecting all the input data needed for various recommendation methods (cf. Fig. 2). It offers a user interface that allows end-users to execute processes and also provides options to rate completed tasks or set constraints for knowledge-based filters. The prototype aims to highlight the modularity of the framework by enabling smooth integration of various filters. As an example, we have incorporated two fundamental filtering methods, knowledge-based and collaborative filtering, and adapted a content-based filter documented in [18]. This integration demonstrates the flexibility and scalability of the framework in supporting arbitrary filtering methods without enforcing a (partial) re-programming of the framework.

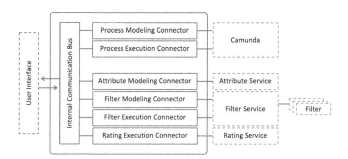

Fig. 3. Conceptual architecture of the implemented artefact.

The project is implemented as a Spring Boot 3[5] application with an Angular 16[6] front-end. Its base architecture is shown in Fig. 3. Each module is designed as a library to simplify integration of new filters. By decoupling the user interface from the core logic, we ensure that the system remains both user-friendly and resilient in case of evolving process management and recommendation services.

---

[3] https://gitlab.com/2024-BPMDS.
[4] https://camunda.com/.
[5] https://spring.io/projects/spring-boot/.
[6] https://angular.io/.

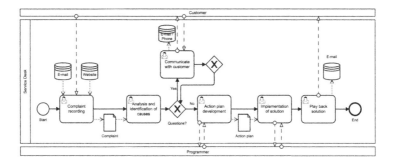

Fig. 4. Example process.

To evaluate the prototype we consider a simplified customer complaints management process (Fig. 4). This process comprises three different roles: customer,
service desk, and programmer. A customer submits a complaint via e-mail or
a company's website. A service desk employee records the complaint and then
analyzes it. If there are any unanswered questions, the service desk needs to
request more information from the customer. Next, an action plan is developed
in collaboration with the responsible programmers. The service desk receives
support from programmers during the implementation of a solution. Once completed, the customer is finally notified about the solution through email. The
recommender system can assist the service desk employees in selecting the best-
suited complaints based on their preferences. The evaluation of this tool involved
simulating different scenarios where diverse complaints are assigned to various
employees. Using our prototype's knowledge-based filtering method, employees
could efficiently sort their worklist according to preferred customers, ensuring
that it only includes requests from favoured customers.

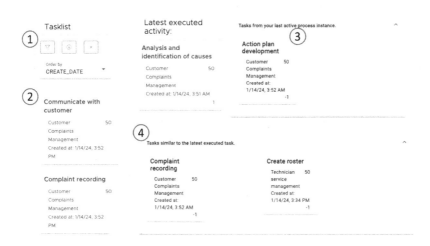

Fig. 5. User interface of developed prototype.

The prototype application proves that service desk employees could easily incorporate their preferences in real-time when managing complaints. This leads to more personalized and efficient complaint handling. The user interface (Fig. 5) demonstrates how this system integrates with the Camunda business process management tool. Specifically, it displays a worklist on the left panel where tasks not meeting explicit employee preferences are excluded and reordered according to user preferences (2). To calculate these preferences, we implemented a user-based collaborative filtering method. Users can manually define task execution preferences through a knowledge-based recommender (1). Additionally, recommendations for similar tasks within a process instance are displayed on panel (3) and tasks similar to the last executed task are shown on panel (4) (recommendations are produced by a content-based recommendation algorithm). These recommendations are grounded on a meticulous analysis of user interactions, preferences, and the contextual relevance of tasks, ensuring that recommended tasks are suited to user profiles and process context.

Task assignment within RecPro is focused on task level, enabling precise matching between individual tasks and user preferences. This task-level consideration facilitates a more granular approach to personalization, since recommendations are tailored to optimize user engagement with respect to tasks. The approach does not necessarily require a single user to complete all tasks of a process. Allowing different users to work on tasks based on their preferences and expertise supports a collaborative and flexible process execution model. The implementation thus contributes towards human-centric BPM based on the integration of recommendation methods into business process processing.

7   Conclusion and Future Work

In summary, our framework forms a significant step towards combining the capabilities of a PAIS with the analytical power of recommender systems. Through this combination we are able to provide personalized and context-aware recommendations during business process execution. The integration of new input data and alternative recommendation algorithms is easily achievable. This integration holds the promise of creating new opportunities for process optimization, enabling BPM to better cater to the preferences and requirements of its human resources. Our research approach is driven by the goal not only to understand the theoretical underpinnings of BPM and recommender systems but also to develop a tangible and practical solution that can be applied in real-world business contexts. The findings of the evaluation demonstrate that it is easily possible to effectively integrate different recommendation methods and algorithms.

Further investigation might involve expanding input data through surveys to gather more user preference details. Additionally, providing explanations with output data can help users understand why a particular task is being recommended. It is also important to study how personalized recommendations impact user satisfaction and process efficiency - our tool serves as a foundation for this research. Lastly, there is an opportunity to explore diverse recommendation algorithms in order to find best fitting recommendations for certain application.

References

1. van der Aalst, W.M.P.: Process Mining - Data Science in Action, 2nd edn. Springer, Heidelberg (2016). https://doi.org/10.1007/978-3-662-49851-4
2. Aggarwal, C.C.: Recommender Systems - The Textbook. Springer, Cham (2016). https://doi.org/10.1007/978-3-319-29659-3
3. Arias, M., Munoz-Gama, J., Sepúlveda, M.: A multi-criteria approach for team recommendation. In: Dumas, M., Fantinato, M. (eds.) BPM 2016. LNBIP, vol. 281, pp. 384–396. Springer, Cham (2016). https://doi.org/10.1007/978-3-319-58457-7_28
4. Barba, I., Weber, B., Del Valle, C.: Supporting the optimized execution of business processes through recommendations. In: Daniel, F., Barkaoui, K., Dustdar, S. (eds.) BPM 2011. LNBIP, vol. 99, pp. 135–140. Springer, Heidelberg (2012). https://doi.org/10.1007/978-3-642-28108-2_12
5. Barba, I., Weber, B., Valle, C.D., Ramirez, A.J.: User recommendations for the optimized execution of business processes. Data Knowl. Eng. **86**, 61–84 (2013)
6. Bellet, C.S., De Neve, J.-E., Ward, G.: Does employee happiness have an impact on productivity? Manag. Sci. **70**(3), 1656–1679 (2024). https://doi.org/10.1287/mnsc.2023.4766
7. Bidar, R., ter Hofstede, A., Sindhgatta, R., Ouyang, C.: Preference-based resource and task allocation in business process automation. In: Panetto, H., Debruyne, C., Hepp, M., Lewis, D., Ardagna, C., Meersman, R. (eds.) OTM 2019. LNCS, vol. 11877, pp. 404–421. Springer, Cham (2019). https://doi.org/10.1007/978-3-030-33246-4_26
8. Branchi, S., Di Francescomarino, C., Ghidini, C., Massimo, D., Ricci, F., Ronzani, M.: Learning to act: a reinforcement learning approach to recommend the best next activities. In: Di Ciccio, C., Dijkman, R., del Río Ortega, A., Rinderle-Ma, S. (eds.) BPM 2022. LNBIP, vol. 458, pp. 137–154. Springer, Cham (2022). https://doi.org/10.1007/978-3-031-16171-1_9
9. Bryson, A., Forth, J., Stokes, L.: Does worker wellbeing affect workplace performance? Technical report 9096, Bonn (2015). http://hdl.handle.net/10419/111548
10. Burke, R.: Hybrid recommender systems: survey and experiments. User Model. User-Adap. Inter. **12**, 331–370 (2002)
11. Desrosiers, C., Karypis, G.: A comprehensive survey of neighborhood-based recommendation methods. In: Ricci, F., Rokach, L., Shapira, B., Kantor, P. (eds.) Recommender Systems Handbook, pp. 107–144. Springer, Cham (2011). https://doi.org/10.1007/978-0-387-85820-3_4
12. Douglas, W.O., Jinmook, K.: Implicit feedback for recommender systems. Technical report (1998)
13. Dumas, M., Rosa, M.L., Mendling, J., Reijers, H.A.: Fundamentals of Business Process Management. Springer, Heidelberg (2013)
14. Hevner, A.R., March, S.T., Park, J., Ram, S.: Design science in information systems research. MIS Q. **28**(1), 75–105 (2004)
15. Jablonski, S., Bussler, C.: Workflow management - modeling concepts, architecture and implementation. International Thomson (1996)
16. Johannesson, P., Perjons, E.: An Introduction to Design Science. Springer, Cham (2021). https://doi.org/10.1007/978-3-030-78132-3
17. Lawrence, P. (ed.): Workflow Handbook 1997, Workflow Management Coalition. John, New York (1997)
18. Petter, S., Fichtner, M., Jablonski, S.: Considering user preferences during business process execution using content-based filtering. In: Filipe, J., Śmiałek, M., Brodsky,

A., Hammoudi, S. (eds.) ICEIS 2022. LNBIP, vol. 487, pp. 415–429. Springer, Cham (2023). https://doi.org/10.1007/978-3-031-39386-0_20

19. Petter, S., Jablonski, S.: Recommender systems in business process management: a systematic literature review. In: Proceedings of the 25th International Conference on Enterprise Information Systems - Volume 2: ICEIS, pp. 431–442. INSTICC, SciTePress (2023). https://doi.org/10.5220/0012039500003467. ISBN 978-989-758-648-4, ISSN 2184-4992

20. Pika, A., Wynn, M.T.: Workforce upskilling: a history-based approach for recommending unfamiliar process activities. In: Dustdar, S., Yu, E., Salinesi, C., Rieu, D., Pant, V. (eds.) CAiSE 2020. LNCS, vol. 12127, pp. 334–349. Springer, Cham (2020). https://doi.org/10.1007/978-3-030-49435-3_21

21. Reichert, M., Weber, B.: Enabling Flexibility in Process-Aware Information Systems - Challenges, Methods, Technologies. Springer, Heidelberg (2012). https://doi.org/10.1007/978-3-642-30409-5

22. Schonenberg, H., Weber, B., van Dongen, B., van der Aalst, W.: Supporting flexible processes through recommendations based on history. In: Dumas, M., Reichert, M., Shan, M.C. (eds.) BPM 2008. LNCS, vol. 5240, pp. 51–66. Springer, Heidelberg (2008). https://doi.org/10.1007/978-3-540-85758-7_7

23. Setiawan, M.A., Sadiq, S.W., Kirkman, R.: Facilitating business process improvement through personalized recommendation. In: Abramowicz, W. (ed.) BIS 2011. LNBIP, vol. 87, pp. 136–147. Springer, Heidelberg (2011). https://doi.org/10.1007/978-3-642-21863-7_12

24. Valentin, C.D., Emrich, A., Werth, D., Loos, P.: Context-sensitive and individualized support of employees in business processes: conceptual design of a semantic-based recommender system. IEEE (2014)

25. Weske, M.: Business Process Management: Concepts, Languages, Architectures. Springer, Heidelberg (2007). https://doi.org/10.1007/978-3-662-59432-2

Introducing Agile Controllability
in Temporal Business Processes

Roberto Posenato[1(✉)], Marco Franceschetti[2], Carlo Combi[1], and Johann Eder[3]

[1] Department of Computer Science, University of Verona, Verona, Italy
{roberto.posenato,carlo.combi}@univr.it
[2] Institute of Computer Science, University of St. Gallen, St. Gallen, Switzerland
marco.franceschetti@unisg.ch
[3] Department Informatics-Systems, University of Klagenfurt, Klagenfurt, Austria
johann.eder@aau.at

Abstract. Dynamic controllability is currently regarded as the most adequate notion for checking the temporal correctness of business processes with temporal constraints when a process model includes uncontrollable activities whose duration is revealed at the time of activity completion. However, dynamic controllability cannot take advantage when an actual duration is revealed earlier, leading to unnecessary strict checks for temporal correctness. We propose a novel notion of *agile controllability*, which takes into account that uncontrollable durations are revealed earlier and that in a viable execution strategy, a time point may depend on time points whose value is known earlier. We formalize the notion of agile controllability and present an effective checking procedure evaluated by a software implementation within a publicly available modeling and checking software tool.

Keywords: business processes · temporal constraints · agile controllability · oracles

1 Introduction

Temporal business process models are subject to requirements stating constraints on the durations and execution times of activities [12]. Durations state the minimum or maximum permissible duration of activities, as well as whether an agent may be responsible for deciding an activity duration within a predetermined interval [17] or may only be able to observe the actual duration of an activity that is controlled elsewhere. Temporal constraints restrict the permissible time windows between the occurrence of events –start and end times of activities– or temporal parameters [4].

Temporal process models are typically checked at design-time for temporal correctness to ensure that compliance with these temporal requirements can be achieved at run time, i.e., no temporal constraints violated [6]. For processes entirely under the control of an agent, the *satisfiability* of temporal constraints

H. van der Aa et al. (Eds.): BPMDS 2024/EMMSAD 2024, LNBIP 511, pp. 87–99, 2024.
https://doi.org/10.1007/978-3-031-61007-3_8

is accepted as an adequate notion for temporal correctness [3]. However, for processes in which some activity durations, known as *contingent* durations, are not controllable by the agent, satisfiability is insufficient [2]. Here, more sophisticated notions such as *dynamic controllability* are required [13,17]. These notions account for the fact that the actual duration of a contingent activity is only known when it completes: for instance, the actual duration of a Web service call is uncontrollable and known only when a value is returned, although Service Level Agreements guarantee that this will happen within a specified interval.

Dynamic controllability requires that a viable execution strategy for a process with contingent activities exists, in which later (greater) timepoints may depend on earlier (smaller) time points but not vice versa. However, the assumption that a contingent duration is only revealed at the time of activity completion is frequently too restrictive. Indeed, although an activity duration might be uncontrollable, the exact duration could be known *before* the activity completes. For example, the shipment of an order whose duration is specified to be within an uncontrollable (by the buyer) range of 6 to 10 days at the time of order placement; however, within 2 days after placing an order, the actual duration of the shipment is communicated - e.g., the shipment will take precisely seven days. In such cases, knowing the exact duration in advance allows for more flexible process scheduling since uncertainty for the agent is reduced earlier, and the agent may use this information for scheduling activities that are after the information time point but before the receipt of the ordered item. In the example, the buyer can schedule an activity that has to be executed exactly 2 days *before* the delivery since she already knows the delivery date.

Current state-of-the-art procedures for checking the dynamic controllability of a process model are based on mapping the model into a Simple Temporal Network with Uncertainty (STNU) [2,9]. However, the STNU lacks constructs for modeling contingent durations that are revealed in advance. Hence, current STNU procedures return potentially overly restrictive results for process models where contingent durations are known earlier. Specifically, these models are classified as not dynamically controllable, while in reality, they can be scheduled to avoid constraint violations thanks to duration information communicated in advance. This misclassification leads to unnecessary and costly model redesign. This shortcoming calls for a new representation of process models where contingent durations are revealed before their completion, allowing an effective design-time check for temporal correctness–the challenge we take on here.

The contribution of this paper is a conservative extension of the STNU that overcomes the limitation of not being able to represent information on contingent durations in advance. We introduce the concept of *contingent oracle* to represent the point in time in which a contingent duration is revealed, allowing checking the temporal correctness of such process models where contingent durations are revealed in advance. We define *agile controllability* as the temporal correctness of an STNU with contingent oracle nodes where an execution strategy is viable if timepoints may depend only on time points, which are known earlier. We discuss an algorithm to check agile controllability and, as proof of concept, an open-source implementation.

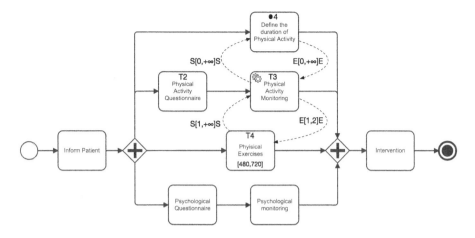

Fig. 1. BPMN diagram for the process for the patient pre-intervention period.

2   Motivating Example

Figure 1 represents a motivating example, which we will briefly discuss here. The example refers to managing patients' activities before a surgical intervention. It is becoming widely acknowledged that patients reaching some planned intervention in an (as much as possible) good health state have a better recovery [11].

The process in the figure starts with the usual information to patients, who must be aware of the following activities. Then, different threads of activities are initiated. Two threads are related to the Physical and Psychological parts, respectively. The proposed physical exercises depend on and can be refined with respect to the results of different questionnaires the patient has to answer. After the end of these activities, the intervention is performed. Focusing on the process fragment related to the physical exercise activity and the related monitoring, these activities are connected through some temporal constraints, representing the allowed delays between their start and endpoints, respectively. Moreover, activities are enriched with their allowed time duration. In the figure, only the temporal duration and the temporal constraints relevant to our discussion are reported. The notation for task durations and inter-task constraints is relatively standard in the literature [1]. Tasks have a duration attribute represented as a range $[x, y]$, with $0 < x \leq y < \infty$, where x/y is the minimum/maximum allowed time span for an activity to go from state "started" to "completed" [12]. Inter-task constraints limit the time distance between the starting/ending instants of two tasks and have the form $I_S[u, v]I_F$, where I_S is the starting (S)/ending (E) instant of the first task, while I_F is the starting/ending instant of the second one [1].

Task T4 "Physical Exercises" (PE) activity has to be performed for a period from 20 to 30 days (480 to 720 h). Task T3 "Physical Activity Monitoring" (PAM) has to start (at least) 1 h after the start of physical exercises and end

1 to 2 h before the exercises end to avoid noisy information during the initial and final phases of physical activities. As the contingent duration of PE is not determined by the system, it can only be observed when the task ends; hence PAM cannot be set to end according to the required time distance before PE. This observation holds both if we consider PAM a contingent task, having a duration only observable by the system, and if we consider it a *controllable* task, for which the system can set the duration. Indeed, in any case, the ending instant of PAM, even if controllable, should be set with respect to the ending instant of PE, which has to occur afterward. Thus, the PAM ending instant cannot be adequately set unless there is some kind of early specification/knowledge about the (contingent) duration of PE.

Let us now explicitly specify that the duration of PE is set by the activity O4 "Define the duration of Physical Activity" (DDPA). Let us also assume, for the sake of simplicity, that the system can decide when the PAM has to end. From this perspective, how do we derive when it is required to execute DDPA to make the overall process model controllable? It is straightforward to verify that if the system knows the overall duration of PE at least two hours before the effective end of PE, then the end of PAM can be set, satisfying the given constraints.

To ensure that all temporal constraints specified in the process can be satisfied in any execution, no matter how long contingent durations take, we want to be able to check (at design time) the dynamic controllability of the process model. This check is typically done by mapping the model into a proper temporal constraint network (like Simple Temporal Network with Uncertainty).

3   STNUs and Oracles

The Simple Temporal Network with Uncertainty (STNU) [13] is a data structure that models temporal problems, such as time-constrained process models, in which the execution of some events cannot be controlled. The STNU comprises a set of timepoints and a set of temporal constraints. The timepoint set is partitioned into controllable (executable) timepoints and uncontrollable (contingent) ones; the constraint set is partitioned into regular and contingent ones.

To the best of our knowledge, in the current temporal business process models and/or in the related temporal constraint networks, it is not possible to represent the possibility that a contingent duration is known before the occurrence of the corresponding contingent timepoint. Here, we consider the following issues:

- how to extend STNUs to represent contingent temporal constraints having their duration acquired/known possibly before their occurrences?
- How to derive when such extended STNUs are controllable, i.e., how early do we need to acquire/know the duration of some contingent link?

As the STNU does not allow decoupling the value of a contingent duration and the time of occurrence of the associated timepoint, we introduce a new kind of timepoint called *(contingent) oracle*. An oracle O_C is a timepoint associated bi-univocally with a contingent link (A, C). When O_C is executed, it reveals the duration of the associated contingent link. In other words, O_C can reveal the duration of the contingent link before the contingent timepoint C occurs. We extend the formal definition of an STNU in [7] with oracles as follows:

Definition 1 (STNU with Oracles). *An STNU with Oracles (STNUO) is a tuple* $(\mathcal{T}, \mathcal{C}, \mathcal{L}, \mathcal{O})$, *where:*

- $\mathcal{T}$ *is a finite, non-empty set of real-valued variables called timepoints.* $\mathcal{T}$ *is partitioned into* $\mathcal{T}_X$, *the set of executable timepoints and* $\mathcal{T}_C$, *the set of contingent timepoints.* $\mathcal{T}_O \subseteq \mathcal{T}_X$, *is the set of oracle timepoints.*
- $\mathcal{C}$ *is a set of binary (ordinary) constraints, each of the form* $Y - X \leq \delta$ *for some* $X, Y \in \mathcal{T}$ *and* $\delta \in \mathbf{R}$.
- $\mathcal{L}$ *is a set of contingent links, each of the form* (A, x, y, C), *where* $A \in \mathcal{T}_X, C \in \mathcal{T}_C$ *and* $0 < x < y < \infty$. *A is called the* activation *timepoint; C* contingent *timepoint. If* (A_1, x_1, y_1, C_1) *and* (A_2, x_2, y_2, C_2) *are distinct contingent links, then* $C_1 \neq C_2$.
- $\mathcal{O} \colon \mathcal{T}_O \to \mathcal{T}_C$ *is an injective function that associates an oracle with its corresponding contingent timepoint. For each pair* (O_C, C) *such that* $\mathcal{O}(O_C) = C$, *there must exist the constraint* $O_C - C \leq 0$ *in* $\mathcal{C}$.

We say that a controller *executes an STNUO* when it schedules its timepoints, i.e., it assigns a value to each timepoint (for contingent ones, the assignment is derived once the relative contingent duration is revealed).

An important property of the STNU is the *dynamic controllability*. An STNU is *dynamically controllable* (DC) if there exists a dynamic execution strategy (called *viable execution strategy*) that assigns the timepoints with the guarantee that all constraints will be satisfied, irrespectively from the values (within the specified bounds) of the contingent durations [7].

In the literature, there are several proposals to check dynamic controllability based on constraint propagation techniques, defined on the *distance graph* corresponding to a given STNU $(\mathcal{T}, \mathcal{C}, \mathcal{L})$ [8,13]. A distance graph associated with an STNUO is the graph $(\mathcal{T}, \mathcal{E} = \mathcal{E}_{\mathcal{C}} \cup \mathcal{E}_{\mathcal{L}})$, where the timepoints in $\mathcal{T}$ serve as the graph's nodes and the constraints in $\mathcal{C}$ and $\mathcal{L}$ correspond to labeled, directed edges in $\mathcal{E}$. In particular: $\mathcal{E}_{\mathcal{C}} = \{X \xrightarrow{\delta} Y \mid (Y - X \leq \delta) \in \mathcal{C}\}$ while for $\mathcal{E}_{\mathcal{L}}$ there are two edges for each $(A, x, y, C) \in \mathcal{L}$: the *lower-case* (LC) edge $A \xrightarrow{c:x} C$ in $\mathcal{E}_{\mathcal{L}}$ represents the *uncontrollable possibility* that the duration $C - A$ may be as low as x; the *upper-case* (UC) edge $C \xrightarrow{C:-y} A$ in $\mathcal{E}_{\mathcal{L}}$ represents the *uncontrollable possibility* that the duration $C - A$ may be as high as y.

A constraint propagation technique consists of applying constraint propagation rules in the distance graph to make explicit derived constraints from the existing ones in the STNU. The process terminates when either reaching quiescence, i.e., no new constraints can be derived (the network is dynamically controllable), or a negative circuit is found (the network is not dynamically controllable).

Now, let us consider the more structured case of Fig. 1. Using some transformation rules like the ones presented in [16], it is possible to represent the process as an STNUO instance. Figure 2 represents an excerpt of the STNUO, focused only on three activities of the process: T2, T3, O4, and T4. Each activity is

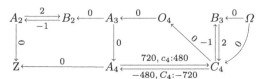

A_2, B_2 represent the starting/ending event of T2 'Physical Activity Questionnaire'
A_3, B_3 represent the starting/ending event of T3 'Physical Activity Monitoring'
A_4, C_4 represent the starting/ending event of T4 'Physical Exercises'
O_4 represents the end of O4 'Define the duration of Physical Activity'

Fig. 2. STNU distance graph representing a possible conversion of a part of the BPMN model in Fig. 1

represented by two timepoints, one representing the starting instant, the other the ending one, and one or two constraints on its duration. According to the kind of duration (controllable or not), the duration constraints can be ordinary or contingent.

Let us consider each activity.

- T2 is a controllable activity. The execution agent can fix its duration. Therefore, it is represented by the two timepoints A_2 and B_2 and by two ordinary constraints between A_2 and B_2 that impose that the duration must be in the range $[1, 2]$. Without loss of generality, we assume that the time granularity is *hours* and that all constraint values are integers.
- T4 is a contingent activity since it is possible to fix when it must start, but given a possible duration, the end of the activity can only be observed when it occurs. Therefore, it is represented as two timepoints A_4 and C_4, and by two constraints representing the upper-case and lower-case of the contingent link associated with the activity. The duration of such an activity must be in the range of 20 to 30 days, i.e., $[480, 720]$ using the time unit of hours.
- T3 is an activity that depends on T4. Therefore, its timepoints are A_3 and B_3, which are constrained to be just after A_4 and one hour before C_4 at least, respectively.
- Last, O4 is an activity represented just by one timepoint, O_4. We assume that such activity is instantaneous since it represents just the instant in which the duration of T4 is decided. In the original BPMN process, such activity is constrained to be after the start of T3, which must start after T4. O4 reveals a piece of information that can be crucial to executing the process without violating any temporal constraint. Thus, it is the oracle associated with the activity T4.

In [15], we proposed the definition of oracle dependency, and we extended the ones of viable execution strategy and dynamic execution strategy when oracle timepoints are present. Here, we recall the definition of agile controllability: *an STNU with contingent oracles (STNUO) is agilely controllable if it admits a viable dynamic execution strategy with contingent oracles. We refer to agile controllability (AC) as the property of being agilely controllable.*

Table 1. Propagation rules for checking Agile Controllability of STNUO.

Rule	Conditions	Pre-existing and generated edges
No Case (NC)		$W \xleftarrow{v} Y \xleftarrow{u} X$, $\quad u+v$
Cross Case (CC)	$D \not\equiv C;\ v < 0$	$X \xleftarrow{D:v} C \xleftarrow{c:u} A$, $\quad D:u+v$
Label Removal (LR)	$v \geq -x$	$C \xleftarrow{c:x} A \xleftarrow{C:v} X$, $\quad v$
New Lower Case (nLC)	$-u \leq 0;\ O_C$ does not exists or $v - u \geq y - x$	$X \xrightleftharpoons[-u]{v} C \xrightleftharpoons[c:x]{C:-y} A$, $\quad x-u$
New Upper Case (nUC)	O_C does not exist or $v - u \geq y - x$	$X \xrightleftharpoons[-u]{v} C \xrightleftharpoons[c:x]{C:-y} A$, $\quad C:v-y$
UC*	$Y \not\equiv C$	$X \xrightarrow{u} Y \xrightarrow{C:v} A$, $\quad C:x+v$
Oracle (ORC)	X is **not** a contingent node; O_C exists; $v - u < y - x$.	$X \xrightleftharpoons[-u]{v} C \xrightleftharpoons[c:x]{C:-y} A$, $v-x$; $0 \to O_C$, $y-u$, $x-u$

Two different issues arise with the agile controllability of temporal BPM models: (i) checking whether a given temporal BPM model with oracles is agilely controllable and (ii) determining a schedule for the given model. In the following, we discuss how to check the agile controllability of an STNUO.

4   Checking Agile Controllability

One possibility for checking the agile controllability is to exploit and expand the approach proposed by Morris-Muscettola (MM) for checking the dynamic controllability of STNUs, based on the constraint propagation [13].

In Table 1, we propose the set of MM rules modified for checking the agile controllability. In particular, the first three rules in the table are original, while rules nLC, nUC, and UC* are a restriction of the corresponding original rules LC and UC in [13], while ORC rule is a new one specific for considering oracles.

The rules were designed assuming the following properties:

- *instantaneous reaction semantics;* i.e., *"when the environment decides the duration of a contingent link, the agent can react at the same time executing one or more other timepoints".*
- *early-execution strategy;* i.e., timepoints are executed at the first possible instant. Rules are able to determine such an instant, but they do not determine the latest possible execution instant for each timepoint.

The MM DC-checking algorithm applies the rules in at most n^2 rounds, with a cost of $O(n^3)$ each round, for a global execution time of $O(n^5)$, where n is the number of network nodes.

The original rules allow us to determine a correct lower bound to the execution time of an executable X with respect to all possible durations of a contingent link (A, x, y, C). When an executable X has to be "strictly" scheduled with respect to the duration of a contingent link (A, x, y, C) with oracle, LC, and UC determine a *false* negative cycle. For example, if there is a pattern like $X \overset{2}{\underset{-1}{\rightleftarrows}} C \overset{C:-10}{\underset{c:1}{\rightleftarrows}} A$, applying LC and UC, the resulting constraints would be $X \overset{C:-8}{\underset{0}{\rightleftarrows}} A$ that represent a negative cycle. Since there are oracles in STNUOs that can help to schedule such X, it is necessary to limit the application of the original LC and UC rules (when oracles are available) to avoid a network being classified as not controllable while it is agilely controllable.

A timepoint X is "strictly" scheduled with respect to a contingent link (A, x, y, C) when: (i) X must occur before C (there is an edge between C and X with a negative value), (ii) the distance range between X and C is smaller than the contingent allowed duration. In other words, if there is a pattern like $X \overset{v}{\underset{-u}{\rightleftarrows}} C \overset{C:-y}{\underset{c:x}{\rightleftarrows}} A$, where $-u \leq 0$, $v - u < y - x$, and there is an oracle O_C for contingent link (A, x, y, C).

Therefore, the nLC rule replaces LC. It must be applied only when there is no oracle for the contingent link, or the span $v - u$ is greater than or equal to the span $y - x$. Indeed, when $v - u \geq y - x$, X can be scheduled for any possible duration of the contingent link without the necessity of an oracle.

nUC and UC* rules replace UC. In the case of the propagation of the upper-case labeled value of a contingent link, rule nUC must be considered, and it must be applied only when the contingent link (A, x, y, C) does not have its oracle node O_C, or when $v - u \geq y - x$. When an upper-case labeled value has been propagated, then the following propagations must be done by using rule UC* (in [13] such a rule was included in the UC rule).

When nLC and nUC cannot be applied, it is necessary to verify if it is possible to exploit the presence of a possible oracle associated with the contingent link to check whether X can be scheduled correctly. A possible rule that properly constrains an oracle O_C of a contingent C and a node X that has to be "strictly" scheduled is rule ORC in Table 1. Given a pattern $X \overset{v}{\underset{-u}{\rightleftarrows}} C \overset{C:-y}{\underset{c:x}{\rightleftarrows}} A$, where $-u \leq 0$, $v - u < y - x$, and an oracle O_C for contingent link (A, x, y, C), it is necessary to require that O_C must before both C and X with a proper distance for verifying whether it is possible to schedule X correctly w.r.t. any possible duration of contingent link. Therefore, constraints $C \overset{-u}{\rightarrow} O_C$ and $X \overset{0}{\rightarrow} O_C$ are added. Constraints $A \overset{x-u}{\rightarrow} O_C$, $A \overset{y-u}{\rightarrow} X$, and $X \overset{v-x}{\rightarrow} A$ are then determined by applying the NC rule; we propose to add such values directly to understand the rule better.

The soundness of the rules in Table 1 and the completeness of the general algorithm have been presented in [15].

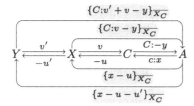

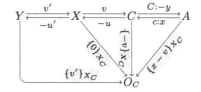

(a) Sample STNUO having labeled values generated by nLC and nUC.

(b) Sample STNUO having labeled values generated by ORC.

Fig. 3. Approach for managing values produced by two complementary rules.

Rules nLC and nUC are alternatives to rule ORC. Moreover, their application to a specific timepoint may change during the propagation of constraints. Indeed, it may be that a timepoint X becomes "strictly" scheduled w.r.t. a contingent link (A, x, y, C) during the constraint propagation. In this case, all the values determined by rules nLC and nUC and propagated by the other rules considering X and the contingent link (A, x, y, C) must be removed, and the values determined by ORC rule must be propagated. Thus, backtracking is required.

5   An Alternative Approach to Avoid Backtracking

Backtracking can slow down the actual computation of checking since it requires considering backtracking for different nodes in different phases of the constraint propagation.

Accepting the cost of more memory, it seems straightforward to properly label some derived values (the ones derived by nLC/nUC and ORC when the involved contingent link has an oracle) and use them only while they are valid.

In more detail, let us denote by $\{v\}_{\overline{X_C}}$ a value derived by using the nLC or nUC rules involving a timepoint X and a contingent link (A, x, y, C). Figure 3a shows an example of an STNUO where values determined by nLC and nUC rules and then propagated to Y are labeled.

Then, let us denote by $\{v\}_{X_C}$ a value derived by the rule ORC considering a node X and a contingent link (A, x, y, C). Figure 3b shows an example of an STNUO where values determined by ORC and then propagated are labeled.

It is also possible to have constraints that require combining different labeled values such as $X \xrightarrow{\{v\}_{\overline{X_C}}} A \xrightarrow{\{u\}_{\overline{Y_D}}} F$. In this case, we combine the values concatenating the labels $X \xrightarrow{\{v + u\}_{\overline{X_C Y_D}}} F$. Such a concatenation occurs only when the labels do not contain opposite components. For example, the two constraint values $X \xrightarrow{\{v\}_{X_C}} A \xrightarrow{\{u\}_{\overline{X_C}}} F$ cannot be combined by the NC rule. Indeed, if $X \xrightarrow{\{v\}_{\overline{X_C}}} A$ was derived by the nUC rule on contingent link (A, x, y, C), while $A \xrightarrow{\{u\}_{X_C}} F$ was derived by the ORC rule on the same contingent link, then the two values are mutually exclusive and, therefore, cannot be combined in the constraint $X \rightarrow F$.

Now, let us consider a case in which a negative cycle is detected. A negative cycle is detected when there is a loop on a node having a negative value v. The label ℓ associated with v can be one of the following:

- ℓ is empty. It occurs when the negative cycle does not depend on any contingent link having its oracle. The network is not AC.
- ℓ has only one component, e.g., $\{v\}_{\overline{X_C}}$. The negative cycle depends on the values the nLC/nUC rule determines involving X and C. All values having label $\overline{X_C}$ must be ignored from now on. We say that $\overline{X_C}$ is *blocked*. If the label X_C was blocked in a previous phase of the constraint propagation, then it is impossible to have a schedule for X satisfying all constraints. The network is not AC.
- ℓ has two or more components; e.g., $\{v\}_{X_C\overline{Y_D}}$. In this case, label $X_C\overline{Y_D}$ is blocked. All values having a label containing any other combinations of X_C and Y_D ($X_CY_D, \overline{X_C}Y_D$, or $\overline{X_C Y_D}$) are still valid and they can be propagated. If all other labels obtained by the combinations of X_C, Y_D have been blocked in the previous propagations; then it is impossible to find a configuration for timepoints X, C, D that is agilely controllable. Hence, the network is not AC.

The AC-checking algorithm based on this technique made the same maximum number of rule applications, $O(n^5)$, of the MM DC-checking one because it applies a set of rules that work like MM rules. The difference in the AC-checking algorithm is that each rule application can manage more labeled values instead of just 3 like in an MM rule. A simple (gross) upper bound to the number of values that could be present on each edge is $2^{|\mathcal{T}_X||\mathcal{T}_C|}$. Therefore, the complexity is limited by $O(n^5 2^{|\mathcal{T}_X||\mathcal{T}_C|}) = O(2^{n^2})$, where n is the number of network nodes.

6   Proof of Concept

The presented approach was implemented as a proof-of-concept prototype in the (freely available) CSTNU Tool, v. 1.42 [14]. It enables users to create different kinds of temporal constraint networks and to verify automatically some properties like dynamic controllability or consistency (for some kinds of networks). In particular, it allows one to verify the agile controllability of an STNUO by the labeling technique. In case a network is agilely controllable, it returns the minimal agilely controllable network and the information of which oracles are necessary.

The screenshot from Fig. 4 shows the CSTNU Tool after the checking of the STNUO associated with the process in Fig. 1.   On the left side, there is the initial network that can be edited. On the right side, there is the checked network with minimal derived constraints (edges) and the auxiliary information about the check (on the green status bar, here indicating that the process model derived from the motivating example is agilely controllable).

Currently, the tool can only manage networks having a limited number (26) of pairs of "(contingent, strictly scheduled external node)" for efficiency reasons.

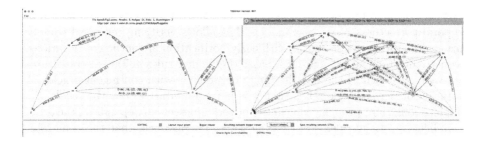

Fig. 4. Determining Agile Controllability of an STNUO in CSTNU Tool. (Color figure online)

We conducted some experiments considering the STNU benchmarks made available in [14]. In particular, we considered 30 random instances of the sub-benchmark "DC 500", which consists of DC STNU instances of 500 nodes (50 contingent ones) representing random temporal business processes. We reduced them to STNUO instances of 30 nodes (5 contingent and 2 oracles) and we verified that the average AC checking time results to be around 3 s. The benchmark is available at http://profs.scienze.univr.it/~posenato/software/cstnu/benchmarkWrapper.html. The Java program to view/edit/test such instances is `TNEditor` [14].

7 Discussion and Conclusion

Verifying the possibility of achieving compliance of executions with process models is typically a design-time activity [6]. Specifically for temporal processes [12,16], dynamic controllability is the most advanced property that ensures the satisfaction of all temporal requirements, irrespective of uncontrollable execution aspects [2]. Dynamic controllability has been studied in several works such as [7,8,10,17]. However, since it is not possible to take advantage of early notification of the actual duration of contingent activities for scheduling the executions, processes relying on such a possibility cannot be represented (hence verified) adequately [15].

The proposed STNU with oracles increases the modeling expressiveness for the temporal perspective of real-world processes that, until now, could not be formalized, in particular with respect to the early specification of contingent tasks. The proposed contingent durations with an associated contingent oracle resemble parameter nodes, which were introduced for the STNU in [4] and the Conditional STNU in [5]. Like contingent links, they are not under the control of the system. However, their value is revealed when the network execution starts, i.e., at time *zero*, before any other activity; additionally, parameter nodes are not associated with a duration. Conversely, an oracle node may reveal the associated contingent duration any time after the start of network execution. Therefore, existing algorithms to check the dynamic controllability of parameterized (C)STNUs are not applicable in the presence of contingent oracles.

With the introduction of Agile Controllability, we propose a new notion of temporal correctness of process models that allows verifying temporal compliance at design time for scenarios with early notification of contingent durations. A constraint propagation algorithm based on the new rules in Table 1 constitutes a possible approach to the AC-checking of an STNU with contingent oracles. A limitation of the new rule set is that it is not commutative, i.e., the result of a complete constraint propagation (until network quiescence) depends on the order of application of the rules [15]. It is possible, for instance, that the constraint propagation algorithm initially applies rules nLC and nUC, but later on, the conditions for applying such rules do not hold anymore due to the application of other rules, making the application of the initial rules overconstraining. The approach proposed in Sect. 5 based on labeling constraints makes it sufficient, during the constraint propagation, to ignore constraints with specific labels without having to delete any derived constraints that should not have been derived. While this has the benefit of avoiding backtracking and the resulting slowdown in the AC-checking, the price to pay is in terms of memory, as more complex labels have to be managed. We plan to design more sophisticated and efficient AC-checking approaches using the proposed rule set in future work.

References

1. Combi, C., Gambini, M., Migliorini, S., Posenato, R.: Representing business processes through a temporal data-centric workflow modeling language. IEEE Trans. Syst. Man Cybern. Syst. **44**(9), 1182–1203 (2014). https://doi.org/10.1109/TSMC.2014.2300055
2. Combi, C., Posenato, R.: Controllability in temporal conceptual workflow schemata. In: Dayal, U., Eder, J., Koehler, J., Reijers, H.A. (eds.) BPM 2009. LNCS, vol. 5701, pp. 64–79. Springer, Heidelberg (2009). https://doi.org/10.1007/978-3-642-03848-8_6
3. Dechter, R., Meiri, I., Pearl, J.: Temporal constraint networks. Artif. Intell. **49**(1–3), 61–95 (1991)
4. Eder, J., Franceschetti, M., Köpke, J.: Controllability of business processes with temporal variables. In: ACM SAC 2019, pp. 40–47 (2019). https://doi.org/10.1145/3297280.3297286
5. Franceschetti, M., Posenato, R., Combi, C., Eder, J.: Dynamic controllability of parameterized CSTNUs. In: ACM SAC 2023, pp. 965–973 (2023). https://doi.org/10.1145/3555776.3577618
6. Hashmi, M., Governatori, G., Lam, H.P., Wynn, M.T.: Are we done with business process compliance: state of the art and challenges ahead. Knowl. Inf. Syst. **57**(1), 79–133 (2018). https://doi.org/10.1007/s10115-017-1142-1
7. Hunsberger, L.: Efficient execution of dynamically controllable simple temporal networks with uncertainty. Acta Inform. **53**, 89–147 (2016)
8. Hunsberger, L., Posenato, R.: A faster algorithm for converting simple temporal networks with uncertainty into dispatchable form. Inf. Comput. **293**, 105063 (2023). https://doi.org/10.1016/j.ic.2023.105063
9. Hunsberger, L., Posenato, R., Combi, C.: The dynamic controllability of conditional STNs with uncertainty. In: Workshop PlanEx@ICAPS-2012 (2012). http://arxiv.org/abs/1212.2005

10. Hunsberger, L., Posenato, R., Combi, C.: A sound-and-complete propagation-based algorithm for checking the dynamic consistency of conditional simple temporal networks. In: 22nd International Symposium on Temporal Representation and Reasoning (TIME 2015) (2015). https://doi.org/10.1109/TIME.2015.26
11. Kagedan, D., Ahmed, M., Devitt, K., Wei, A.: Enhanced recovery after pancreatic surgery: a systematic review of the evidence. HPB **17**, 11–16 (2015)
12. Lanz, A., Reichert, M., Weber, B.: Process time patterns: a formal foundation. Inf. Syst. **57**, 38–68 (2016). https://doi.org/10.1016/J.IS.2015.10.002
13. Morris, P.H., Muscettola, N.: Temporal dynamic controllability revisited. In: 20th National Conference on Artificial Intelligence (AAAI-2005) (2005). https://cdn.aaai.org/AAAI/2005/AAAI05-189.pdf
14. Posenato, R.: CSTNU tool: a Java library for checking temporal networks. SoftwareX **17**, 100905 (2022). https://doi.org/10.1016/j.softx.2021.100905
15. Posenato, R., Franceschetti, M., Combi, C., Eder, J.: Some results and challenges Extending Dynamic Controllability to Agile Controllability in Simple Temporal Networks with Uncertainties. Technical report 1/2023, Dip. Informatica-Univ. di Verona (2023). https://iris.univr.it/handle/11562/1116013
16. Posenato, R., Zerbato, F., Combi, C.: Managing decision tasks and events in time-aware business process models. In: Weske, M., Montali, M., Weber, I., vom Brocke, J. (eds.) BPM 2018. LNCS, vol. 11080, pp. 102–118. Springer, Cham (2018). https://doi.org/10.1007/978-3-319-98648-7_7
17. Vidal, T., Fargier, H.: Handling contingency in temporal constraint networks: from consistency to controllabilities. J. Exp. Theor. Artif. Intell. **11**(1), 23–45 (1999)

Reviewing Conformance Checking Uses for Run-Time Regulatory Compliance

Finn Klessascheck[1,2](✉)[iD], Tom Knoche[3], and Luise Pufahl[1,2]

[1] School of CIT, Technical University of Munich, Heilbronn, Germany
{finn.klessascheck,luise.pufahl}@tum.de
[2] Weizenbaum Institute for the Networked Society, Berlin, Germany
[3] Technische Universität Berlin, Berlin, Germany

Abstract. Organizations manage numerous business processes to deliver their products and services to customers effectively while adhering to laws, industry standards, or guidelines, summarized here as regulations. Compliance checking involves verifying whether these processes align with the relevant regulations. There has been an increase in the availability of process execution data within IT systems that support these business processes. One valuable operation of process mining – *conformance checking* – enables a comparison between the actual execution behaviour, represented as event logs, and the desired behaviour outlined in a process model. As a result, conformance checking can be employed for run-time compliance checking, a concept that has been explored and enhanced through various research studies. This work presents a systematic literature review on regulatory compliance checking with conformance checking that offers insights into different domains, the operationalization of regulations, applied conformance checking techniques, and visualizations. Our analysis reveals that several steps are still performed manually, but we anticipate that future advancements in automation can significantly support the goals of run-time compliance checking.

Keywords: Conformance Checking · Regulations · Process Compliance · Literature Review

1 Introduction

Organizations must effectively manage a diverse range of business processes in order to deliver their services and products to their customers [7]. A *business process* is a structured and repeatable set of activities designed to achieve specific business objectives [26]. Business processes are usually subject to a set of laws, industry standards, or guidelines [9], summarized here as *regulations*, stemming from their environment and governing their execution.

Funded by the Deutsche Forschungsgemeinschaft (DFG, German Research Foundation) - 465904964.

H. van der Aa et al. (Eds.): BPMDS 2024/EMMSAD 2024, LNBIP 511, pp. 100–113, 2024.
https://doi.org/10.1007/978-3-031-61007-3_9

To guarantee organizational success, it is important for businesses to ensure that their processes comply with relevant regulations [14], e.g., to avoid legal and financial penalties or reputational damage. For this, organizations conduct compliance checking [11]. Compliance checking is an operation that can be conducted when the business processes are designed, at run-time [11], or after the fact [10]. In the area of business process management and *process mining*, the technique of *conformance checking* has been established [3], aiming at providing data-driven solutions for assessing the conformance of the real-world execution behaviour of a business process to a desired process behaviour.

Given the range of research that utilizes conformance checking for evidence-based compliance checking (e.g., case studies [13] or new approaches [14]), it seems to be a useful approach. However, there currently is no overview of works that apply conformance checking for run-time regulatory compliance checking. To this end, so that practitioners are aware of existing solutions and researchers of the potential for further contributions, this work conducts a systematic literature review to answer the following research questions:

RQ1: What are existing contributions that practically apply conformance checking techniques to business processes for regulatory compliance checking?

RQ2: What characterizes the concrete conformance checking mechanisms used in the contributions for regulatory compliance checking?

RQ3: What are, based on the characterization of existing works, potential areas of further investigation for the use of conformance checking for regulatory compliance checking?

In Sect. 2, we provide background on conformance and compliance checking, and related work. Section 3 presents the approach utilized for identifying and synthesizing relevant works. In Sect. 4, we analyse the synthesis and present results. Section 5 discusses our results and the contribution, which is finally concluded in Sect. 6, where we also present potential for future work.

2   Background and Related Work

2.1   Conformance Checking

Central to the execution of business processes are information systems, which capture information about the processes and their execution. These so-called *event logs* contain ordered records of individual process instances and the events that record what activity has happened when [24].

A common consideration is, whether the behaviour captured in the event log corresponds to normative, i.e., prescribed, behaviour given through a *prescriptive* process model [3,10]. Process models are – usually graphical – representations of business processes, describing the actives and their ordering [26]. The technique of *conformance checking* can be used to analyse the relation between recorded and prescribed process behaviour. Usually, the results of such an analysis are expressed in the form of fitness values, expressing the degree of conformance between event log and process model, and lists of deviations, i.e., recorded process instances that deviate from the process model. Different approaches exist to facilitate conformance checking, mainly differentiated by the type of prescriptive model used [8]. *Imperative* approaches use imperative models, such as BPMN or Petri nets, which describe only allowed behaviour. *Declarative* approaches apply declarative models, such as Declare, which only express constraints on process behaviour, instead of explicitly specifying it. Further, *hybrid* approaches use a mixture of imperative and declarative elements to prescribe the behaviour of business processes [6]. Prescriptive models formalize constraints towards one or more *process perspectives*, which are characteristics of processes relevant for conformance checking. These perspectives include the ordering of activities, temporal aspects, data and documents, and resources that execute the process [20].

2.2 Compliance Checking

As discussed above, it is necessary for businesses to assess whether their behaviour complies with the regulations to which they are subject. These regulations are usually available in the form of textual documents. Hence, for checking regulatory process compliance, an interpretation, or operationalization, becomes necessary to relate the regulation to the process under investigation.

This act of ensuring that business processes do not violate the regulations relevant for them is called *regulatory compliance checking* [10]. One existing approach, the so-called *run-time regulatory compliance checking*, aims at monitoring process executions to assess their compliance with regulations [2,10]. This contrasts with traditional *design-time regulatory compliance checking* [10], in which the process model itself is analysed for violations of and compliance with regulations. However, processes are usually executed in ways that differ from the process model, thus giving relevancy to run-time compliance checking [11].

In practice, conformance checking has been identified as a suitable technical approach for run-time regulatory compliance checking [3]. Here, regulations relevant for a business process are interpreted and operationalized into prescriptive models, which are then used to assess the regulatory compliance of recorded process executions in the form of event logs, with the help of conformance checking techniques. This is done either based on event logs (offline and ex-post, similar to auditing), or based on event streams (online, during run-time). According to [10], the main issue with using conformance checking for run-time regulatory compliance checking lies in the fact that the prescriptive model being used must *also* be proven to be regulatory compliant with regulatory compliance checking. However, given that conformance checking *is* indeed applied for run-time regulatory compliance checking, a systematic investigation is warranted.

2.3 Related Work

Some contributions have already aimed at systematically assessing the capabilities of existing conformance checking approaches. In [8], conformance checking approaches are analysed for the modelling language and the type of algorithm being used, the kind of metric with which conformance is expressed, and the process perspective that is considered (e.g., the ordering of activities or temporal aspects). However, the work does not focus on compliance checking with regulations in particular, nor is the creation of the prescriptive models analysed. Further, in [16], approaches that exclusively assess clinical guidelines are investigated. Concretely, the guidelines that are used by existing works are analysed per disease, their complexity is assessed, as well as the prescriptive model in terms of e.g., nodes in the process model or number of declarative constraints. However, there is no further consideration of how these prescriptive models are created, nor what the results are or how the techniques are applied. Thus, we see a need for investigating how conformance checking approaches for run-time regulatory compliance checking utilize regulations in a practical sense, how they are applied, and what results they provide.

3   Research Method

To address the research questions above, we conduct a *systematic literature review* (SLR) to identify scientific works that apply conformance checking techniques for run-time regulatory compliance checking of business processes with *concrete* regulations. For this, we follow the eight-step method of Okoli [15]. These steps are: (1) purpose of the literature review, (2) protocol and training, (3) searching for the literature, (4) practical screen, (5) quality appraisal, (6) data extraction, (7) synthesis of studies, and finally (8) writing the review. Additionally, we use a concept matrix as a framework for presenting the results [25]. Figure 1 illustrates our search process.

The *purpose* of this SLR is stated above, and detailed upon in Sect. 1. For the *protocol and training* step, we set up a shared document in which we documented all identified articles and reasons for their inclusion, respective exclusion. The *search* is conducted using four scientific databases (ACM, IEEE Explore, Science Direct, Web of Science), up to and including December 2023. We explicitly include conformance checking as the technique for run-time regulatory compliance checking. Moreover, we include terms commonly associated with regulations. The complete search term (*"conformance checking" AND ("law", "guideline", "manual", "reference", "quality", "compliance", "regulation")*) is applied to the title, abstract, and keyword search, where applicable.

Aiming to investigate the scientific support for practical regulatory compliance checking with conformance checking (i.e., run-time checking, both online and offline), we exclude EX1) all works that assess this topic in an abstract manner, such as literature reviews, EX2) works that provide general techniques or metrics for conformance checking without application, and EX3) works where conformance checking is not applied to a *concrete* business process and regulation. We explicitly include IN1) works that apply conformance checking to business processes against specific guidelines, laws, regulations, manuals, etc., IN2) which are peer-reviewed and written in English. This constitutes the *practical screen.*

An initial search with the databases and search term described above produces, after deduplication, 215 candidates for analysis. Afterwards, we conduct the *quality appraisal* by deciding first based on the title and abstract, and then on the full text, whether the found works meet our criteria. In total, 41 remain after the title and abstract screening and 22 after the full-text screening. We add 8 papers through the authors' expert knowledge and identify 6 additional works via a "forward-backward-search" we conduct to find potentially missing works. This leads to 36 papers we consider relevant for our analysis.

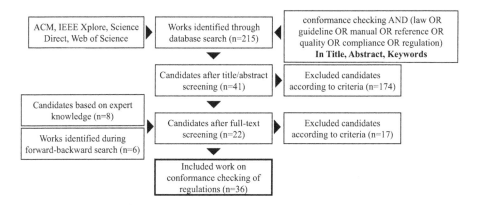

Fig. 1. Search process for relevant literature

After having identified 36 relevant works, we continue with *data extraction* and *synthesis* of the extracted information. In relation to our research questions, we define a set of categories and corresponding characteristics to capture the distinctions within the conformance checking approach of each work. We first extract highly detailed information as raw material for each category. Subsequently, we analyse the extracted information for similarities in their characteristics. Finally, as the synthesis step, we identify potential levels of abstraction that accurately reflect the essential information content while avoiding excessive specificity.

We identify characteristics in relation to the lifecycle model of conformance checking projects, as discussed in [3], which divides the application of conformance checking into three phases: *preparation* (where a prescriptive model is formalized, an event log created, and the two related), *action* (where a conformance checking algorithm is applied), and *reflection* (where results are interpreted and insights derived). An excerpt of these results, in the form of a concept matrix following [25], can be found in Table 1. For the preparation phase, we capture the process *domain*, the *goal* with which conformance checking is applied (to improve conformance checking techniques, to improve the business process compliance, or to demonstrate conformance checking techniques), as well as whether the prescriptive model is *created* manually or automatically, and whether it is explicitly *validated* through e.g., process experts or stakeholders. For the action phase, we identify whether *expert knowledge* is necessary for applying conformance checking techniques, whether imperative, declarative, or hybrid conformance checking *techniques* are used (see [3,5]), which *process perspectives* are assessed (control flow, temporal, data, or resource, see [20]), and whether the conformance checking techniques are *applied* manually, in a tool-supported manner, automatically, or in real-time (i.e., *online*). For the reflection phase, we capture the different *types of results* and their representation (i.e., whether conformance is *qualified*, *quantified*, *broken down and compared*, or *explained and diagnosed*, following a classification of representations identified from current process mining tools [17]).

All data extraction and synthesis steps are performed independently by one of three authors for a subset of the relevant works and validated by all three.

Table 1. Excerpt of a concept matrix [25] displaying the synthesis results. *PM* refers to *prescriptive model*; the domains and results are abbreviated.

Work Reference	Domain	Goal — Technique Improv.	Goal — Process Improv.	Goal — Demonstration	PM Creation — manual	PM Creation — automated	PM validated — yes	Exp. Knowl. — yes	Technique — Imperative	Technique — Declarative	Technique — Hybrid	Process Perspective — Control Flow	Process Perspective — Temporal	Process Perspective — Data	Process Perspective — Resources	Application — Manual	Application — Tool-supported	Application — Automated	Application — Real-Time	Results — Quality conf.	Results — Quantify conf.	Results — BD & Comp.	Results — Loc. & Show	Results — Expl. & Diagn.
[1]	Fin	•		•			•	•	•			•	•	•	•		•				•	•	•	•
[4]	PS	•		•						•		•					•			•		•		
[12]	HC	•	•		•		•	•	•			•	•	•	•			•	•	•				•
[13]	SW		•	•	•		•		•			•					•			•	•	•	•	•
[14]	Data	•		•			•	•		•		•	•			•				•				
[18]	HC		•	•	•		•	•				•	•				•			•	•	•	•	•
[22]	HC	•	•	•	•		•	•				•					•			•	•			
[23]	Man	•	•	•	•		•	•	•			•	•	•	•			•	•	•				•
[27]	HC	•		•	•		•	•			•	•	•	•	•		•			•			•	•

Due to limitations in length, we provide the entire concept matrix and a bibliography in a separate document online.[1] In the following, we analyse the resulting synthesis along its dimensions, thereby *writing the review*.

---

[1] See https://doi.org/10.6084/m9.figshare.25118849 [Accessed: 03/04/2024].

4   Results

After inductively coding and synthesizing the 36 relevant works, we analyse the resulting data, in order to characterize their conformance checking mechanisms. This is done along the three phases of conformance checking projects, being preparation, action, and reflection [3].

4.1   Preparation

Domain. The majority of works focusses on the area of healthcare (17 works), with finance being second (6 works). Other areas, such as public services (4 works) or data processing (3 works), are also present. The prevalence of health-care and finance seems to indicate that regulations in these areas are well-suited to be assessed with conformance checking.

Goals. Regarding the explicitly stated goals of the works for applying confor-mance checking, we see that those in the area of healthcare mainly aim to improve the conformance checking technique and its application (11 of 17) or to demonstrate the applicability of conformance checking (11 of 17), whereas only half of the works utilizing healthcare-related regulations aim to improve the process itself. Similarly, no finance-related contribution aims to provide actual process improvement, but all of them aim to improve conformance checking tech-niques, and two out of six explicitly intend to demonstrate them. This tendency is noticeably present across all domains we identified, with more than two thirds (25) aiming to improve techniques, more than half aiming to demonstrate them (19), and less than half of the works (14) aiming to investigate actual process improvement.

Prescriptive Model Creation. Considering how prescriptive models are created in the relevant works, we see that no contribution out of the 36 identified studies automatically creates them based on the relevant regulations. In fact, all works rely on manual input for creation of the required prescriptive model. Notably, the exact operationalization that led to the model is not described, and instead, only descriptions or visualizations of them are provided. For example, in [1], a BPMN model is created manually with and validated by process experts (in this case, bank managers), and further requirements are provided informally by bank managers and auditors, and manually translated into LTL formulae by the authors.

Prescriptive Model Validation. Additionally, we note that in less than half of the works (14 of 36), the prescriptive model is explicitly validated by the authors in conjunction with stakeholders or process experts.[2] Interestingly, half (7 out of 14) of those works in which a validation is reported are in the healthcare

---

[2] The remaining works did not mention whether the prescriptive model was evaluated or not. Hence, we only capture whether an explicit evaluation took place.

domain. We assume that this may be because of the need for expert involvement in healthcare settings to even operationalize the treatment guidelines, so that validation is a comparatively trivial addition.

4.2   Action

Technique. The techniques utilized in the investigated contributions, are largely imperative, with a third declarative and only three hybrid techniques. The largest share of declarative techniques is present in the healthcare domain (9 of 12), underlining that the nature of clinical guidelines may be especially suited for declarative techniques.

Process Perspective. As to the process perspective, we observe that control-flow constraints are always assessed. All other perspectives, being temporal (15 times), data (22 times), and resource (13 times), are used in various combinations in around half of the approaches, with a prevalence of data constraints. Notable is that all hybrid approaches assess both data and resource perspectives. Hence, relevant process perspectives seem to have some importance for the choice of technique.

Application. We identify that the majority of approaches are applied with tools, but not in an automated or real-time fashion. More concretely, we only note three approaches that are automated and two that are real-time. One of these real-time works proposes an automated approach, where clinical events created during patient treatment of unstable clinical angina are pre-processed using i.a. NLP techniques, constructed into traces, and checked against compliance rules describing the treatment process. Potential violations are sent directly as feedback to the clinical information system, allowing clinicians to react and remedy or accept compliance violations [12]. Only one approach is truly manual, where no tool is utilized to check for conformance, but instead a new technique is defined formally and applied for illustration purposes by manually considering the formal definitions [14]. Finally, all other approaches rely on tool support for conformance checking. For example, in [27] ProM is used for checking conformance to a Declare-based prescriptive model. From this, we conclude that existing tools, especially ProM, have been disseminated widely and reached acceptance in the scientific community. Notably, the automated/real-time approaches are limited to the healthcare and manufacturing domain, potentially due to the presence of information systems in hospitals and production chains allowing for detailed event log recording and automatic application of conformance checking techniques.

Expert Knowledge. Of all the contributions, around two thirds (25 of 36) explicitly reference the need for expert knowledge, either in operationalizing the regulations into a prescriptive model for conformance checking, in the application

of conformance checking, or in interpreting the results.[3] For example, [27] relies
on clinical experts for interpreting the conformance checking results. Further,
how expert knowledge concretely contributes is often not mentioned in detail,
but instead only the resulting prescriptive model or interpretation are presented
(e.g., in [22], the use of expert knowledge in the form of a medical specialist for
definition of the case study is mentioned, but the exact input of the expert and
to what end remain not known). Notably, we see that 16 out of 17 approaches in
healthcare and 4 out of 6 approaches in finance explicitly require expert knowledge throughout the application, a higher ratio than in any other application
domain we identified. This might be explained by the difficulty of operationalizing these regulations and deriving prescriptive models for conformance checking
compared to other domains. A potential reason might lie in the language and
wording specific to these domains, or the implicit domain knowledge required
for interpreting the regulations correctly.

4.3 Reflection

Finally, regarding the results and their visualization, we see that most contributions (28 of 36) use *quantitative measures*, i.e., numerical representations, to
present the conformance checking results. One example for this is [19], where a
table detailing the counts of conformance violations and fulfilments is provided.

Few works (8 in total) employ a *qualification*, such as [4], where a differentiation is made between strong compliance, conditional compliance, and noncompliance. Further, less than half of the works (i.e., 14) elaborate further on
those measures by *break-down and comparison*, for example [13] compares the
most frequent variants and their conformity. 15 of 36 works *localize and show*
deviations or further results in, e.g., a process model. One example of this is [18],
where individual traces and occurring violations are considered and related to the
general fitness value. However, almost two thirds (i.e., 23) *explain and diagnose*
the observed deviations in context and discuss potential causes and remedies,
such as [23], where deviations are explained by confirmed measurement errors
and a previously undetected collision of robotic arms in a manufacturing process. Additionally, it should be noted that works are not limited to one way of
presenting the results, but usually use multiple representations throughout.

Moreover, we see that all the works relying on imperative techniques use
quantitative measures for representing results and no qualification. In contrast,
half of the declarative approaches employ qualitative measures, and the other
half quantitative ones. Additionally, both imperative and declarative techniques
(9 of 21, respective 5 of 12) localize and show deviations in, e.g., a process
model less often. However, explanations and diagnoses appear to be relatively
frequent (12 of 21, respective 9 of 12 times) in declarative approaches. As to
hybrid approaches, it is notable that all types of results are covered, and a focus

---

[3] Similar to the model validation, the remaining works made no explicit reference to
such a requirement; therefore we only differentiate between explicit needs for expert
knowledge and no reference to such a need.

seems to lie on qualifying and explaining diagnoses. Thus, it appears that the conformance checking technique chosen in the approaches is related to the results and their contextualization by them, and therefore should be chosen with care.

5   Discussion

Following the analysis of the works that apply conformance checking techniques for run-time regulatory compliance checking, we discuss and contextualize our findings along our research questions.

5.1   RQ1—Identification of Existing Contributions

The SLR has identified existing contributions that check business processes for their run-time regulatory compliance and has underlined that the majority of works are focused on the domain of healthcare, finance, and public services. Notably, we observe that a large share of works focuses on demonstrating and improving conformance checking techniques, especially in healthcare and finance.

5.2   RQ2—Characteristics of Existing Contributions

Next, we look at the steps necessary for run-time regulatory compliance checking of business processes with conformance checking. As to the characteristics of the identified mechanisms, we have underlined that the operationalization of regulations into prescriptive models is, so far, a manual process, that often is in need of expert knowledge for interpreting the regulations. There also seems to be a lack of reporting regarding the validation of prescriptive models, either due to a lack of access to expert knowledge, or due to the general difficulty in deriving them from the relevant regulations in a sound way. This ties back to the point raised above, where, when using conformance checking techniques for run-time regulatory compliance checking, the prescriptive model must also be proven to be regulatory compliant [10], which is not reported upon in more than half of the approaches. Contributions that aim at automatically creating prescriptive models and incorporate expert knowledge in a more explicit manner could provide a benefit here, and some research in this direction has already been started [21]. We see, in contrast to the literature review by [8], a wide range of process perspectives being assessed together. This illustrates the importance placed on data, time, and resource perspectives for regulatory compliance checking with conformance checking. Further, a noticeable focus on imperative and declarative techniques exists in the investigated works, with only 3 out of 36 utilizing hybrid conformance checking approaches. Almost all approaches are tool-supported, meaning they employ established conformance checking tooling for the analysis of regulation conformance, and only three are applied in an automated or real-time fashion. Moreover, we see that the choice of the conformance checking technique seems to be related to the overall results and visualization of insights. However, there appears to be no general guidance or reasoning provided

by the works on when to choose what technique, and why. Additionally, regarding
the results offered by the primary studies, we observe a general focus on quantitative analyses and less often on explanations and qualifications in imperative
approaches, with declarative approaches focussing additionally on qualitative
analyses, as well as explanations and diagnoses. Localizations of deviations and
break-downs are less common.

5.3   RQ3—Research Opportunities

Analysing existing contributions, we see the following *research opportunities*
(ROs) for future work, summarized in Table 2: First, the prevalent use of imperative and declarative techniques hints at a potential for further investigation
of hybrid techniques and their utilization for run-time regulatory compliance
checking (RO1). This is underlined by the fact that hybrid approaches produce a
wide range of results, and utilize multiple process perspectives, which may prove
advantageous. Second, in terms of automatization (RO2), we see a small number
of contributions that go beyond utilizing existing conformance checking tooling.
This illustrates a potential for further research in the area of truly automated or
real-time regulatory compliance checking with conformance checking. We additionally expect to see a benefit for the creation and validation of prescriptive
models. Third, we also determine potential for research of automated conformance checking for run-time regulatory compliance checking in other domains
and processes beyond healthcare and manufacturing, which are not yet considered in great numbers by existing contributions (RO3). Moreover, we identify a
need for approaches and techniques that help in deriving regulatory compliant
prescriptive models for conformance checking, which are applicable across a wide
range of domains (RO4).

Table 2. Research opportunities of conformance checking for run-time regulatory compliance checking identified

Research Opportunity	Description
RO1	Uses of hybrid conformance checking techniques for run-time regulatory compliance checking
RO2	Automated/real-time conformance checking tooling; Automated creation and validation of prescriptive models
RO3	Automated conformance checking in domains besides healthcare and manufacturing
RO4	Generalizable techniques for supporting the creation of regulatory compliant prescriptive models for conformance checking

Generally, we observe that the role of expert knowledge is under-illustrated
and not detailed upon. To derive a clear procedure for a more automatic opera-

tionalization of regulations, including the creation and validation of prescriptive models, more details are needed. Existing works rather analyse and demonstrate the potential of conformance checking for regulatory compliance checking, and it is unclear from individual contributions where the actual challenges and tasks to solve are. To develop useful conformance checking tools for run-time regulatory compliance checking, we therefore suggest a structured requirement analysis of these.

5.4   Threats to Validity

Notably, our work underlies some limitations which pose threats to its validity. Arguably, the search terms and criteria for our SLR limit the relevant contributions we were able to identify. However, by incorporating a forward-backward search and adding works through prior knowledge, we sought to limit the influence of this on our findings. Moreover, the inductive coding we applied to the studies is subjective, due to the judgement and careful reading required of the authors. We addressed this threat by following a thorough protocol when analysing the works, by taking detailed notes during analysis, and by clarifying uncertainties through discussions.

6   Conclusion and Future Work

To conclude, we identified relevant contributions that practically apply conformance checking to business processes for run-time regulatory compliance checking. We investigated properties to characterize them, and noted that existing approaches are, generally, reliant on expert knowledge and largely only tool-assisted. This underlines a potential for research in approaches that aid in the knowledge-intense operationalization of regulations, assess their compliance in an automated fashion, and provide detailed results beyond numeric assessments. In the future, we plan to investigate novel ways of visualizing deviations in a way that is actionable and contextualizes deviations with the corresponding regulations. Based on the SLR, we observe that supporting experts in the derivation of prescriptive models from regulations is a valuable field for future research.

References

1. Accorsi, R., Stocker, T.: On the exploitation of process mining for security audits: the conformance checking case. In: Proceedings of the ACM Symposium on Applied Computing, pp. 1709–1716. ACM (2012)
2. van Beest, N., Groefsema, H., Cryer, A., Governatori, G., Tosatto, S.C., Burke, H.: Cross-instance regulatory compliance checking of business process event logs. IIEEE Trans. Softw. Eng. **49**(11), 4917–4931 (2023)
3. Carmona, J., Van Dongen, B., Solti, A., Weidlich, M.: Conformance Checking: Relating Processes and Models. Springer, Cham (2018). https://doi.org/10.1007/978-3-319-99414-7

4. Chesani, F., et al.: Abducing compliance of incomplete event logs. In: Adorni, G., Cagnoni, S., Gori, M., Maratea, M. (eds.) AI*IA 2016. LNCS (LNAI), vol. 10037, pp. 208–222. Springer, Cham (2016). https://doi.org/10.1007/978-3-319-49130-1_16

5. De Leoni, M., Maggi, F.M., van der Aalst, W.M.P.: An alignment-based framework to check the conformance of declarative process models and to preprocess event-log data. Inf. Syst. **47**, 258–277 (2015)

6. van Dongen, B.F., De Smedt, J., Di Ciccio, C., Mendling, J.: Conformance checking of mixed-paradigm process models. Inf. Syst. **102**, 101685 (2021)

7. Dumas, M., La Rosa, M., Mendling, J., Reijers, H.A., et al.: Fundamentals of Business Process Management, vol. 1. Springer, Heidelberg (2013)

8. Dunzer, S., Stierle, M., Matzner, M., Baier, S.: Conformance checking: a state-of-the-art literature review. In: S-BPM ONE. ACM (2019)

9. Governatori, G., Sadiq, S.: The journey to business process compliance. In: Handbook of Research on Business Process Modeling, pp. 426–454. IGI Global (2009)

10. Groefsema, H., van Beest, N., Governatori, G.: On the use of the conformance and compliance keywords during verification of business processes. In: Di Ciccio, C., Dijkman, R., del Río Ortega, A., Rinderle-Ma, S. (eds.) BPM 2022. LNBIP, vol. 458, pp. 21–37. Springer, Cham (2022). https://doi.org/10.1007/978-3-031-16171-1_2

11. Hashmi, M., Governatori, G., Lam, H.P., Wynn, M.T.: Are we done with business process compliance: state of the art and challenges ahead. Knowl. Inf. Syst. **57**(1), 79–133 (2018)

12. Huang, Z., Bao, Y., Dong, W., Lu, X., Duan, H.: Online treatment compliance checking for clinical pathways. J. Med. Syst. **38**(10), 123 (2014)

13. Lemos, A.M., Sabino, C.C., Lima, R.M.F., Oliveira, C.A.L.: Using process mining in software development process management: a case study. In: 2011 SMC, pp. 1181–1186. IEEE (2011)

14. López, H.A., Debois, S., Slaats, T., Hildebrandt, T.T.: Business process compliance using reference models of law. In: FASE 2020. LNCS, vol. 12076, pp. 378–399. Springer, Cham (2020). https://doi.org/10.1007/978-3-030-45234-6_19

15. Okoli, C.: A guide to conducting a standalone systematic literature review. Commun. Assoc. Inf. Syst. **37** (2015)

16. Oliart, E., Rojas, E., Capurro, D.: Are we ready for conformance checking in healthcare? Measuring adherence to clinical guidelines: a scoping systematic literature review. J. Biomed. Inform. **130**, 104076 (2022)

17. Rehse, J.R., Pufahl, L., Grohs, M., Klein, L.M.: Process mining meets visual analytics: the case of conformance checking. In: HICSS, pp. 5452–5461 (2023)

18. Rinner, C., Helm, E., Dunkl, R., Kittler, H., Rinderle-Ma, S.: Process mining and conformance checking of long running processes in the context of melanoma surveillance. Int. J. Environ. Res. Public Health **15**(12), 2809 (2018)

19. Rovani, M., Maggi, F.M., de Leoni, M., van der Aalst, W.M.P.: Declarative process mining in healthcare. Expert Syst. Appl. **42**(23), 9236–9251 (2015)

20. Russell, N., van der Aalst, W.M.P., ter Hofstede, A.: Workflow Patterns: The Definitive Guide. MIT Press, Cambridge (2016)

21. Sai, C., Winter, K., Fernanda, E., Rinderle-Ma, S.: Detecting deviations between external and internal regulatory requirements for improved process compliance assessment. In: Indulska, M., Reinhartz-Berger, I., Cetina, C., Pastor, O. (eds.) Advanced Information Systems Engineering. Lecture Notes in Computer Science, vol. 13901, pp. 401–416. Springer, Cham (2023)

22. Sato, D.M.V., de Freitas, S.C., Dallagassa, M.R., Scalabrin, E.E., Portela, E.A.P., Carvalho, D.R.: Conformance checking with different levels of granularity: a case study on bariatric surgery. In: 2020 13th CISP-BMEI, pp. 820–826. IEEE (2020)
23. Stertz, F., Mangler, J., Rinderle-Ma, S.: The role of time and data: online conformance checking in the manufacturing domain (2021)
24. van der Aalst, W.M.P.: Process mining: overview and opportunities. ACM TMIS **3**, 1–17 (2012)
25. Webster, J., Watson, R.T.: Analyzing the past to prepare for the future: writing a literature review. MIS Q. **26**(2), xiii–xxiii (2002)
26. Weske, M.: Business Process Management - Concepts, Languages, Architectures. Springer (2019). https://doi.org/10.1007/978-3-662-59432-2
27. Xu, H., Pang, J., Yang, X., Ma, L., Mao, H., Zhao, D.: Applying clinical guidelines to conformance checking for diagnosis and treatment: a case study of ischemic stroke. In: 2020 IEEE International Conference on Bioinformatics and Biomedicine (BIBM), pp. 2125–2130. IEEE (2020)

Process Discovery and Analysis (BPMDS 2024)

Visual Representation of Resource Analysis Insights for Process Mining

Alana Hoogmoed[1], Maxim Vidgof[1(✉)] ⓘ, Djordje Djurica[3,4] ⓘ,
Christoffer Rubensson[2,3] ⓘ, and Jan Mendling[1,2,3] ⓘ

[1] Wirtschaftsuniversität Wien, Vienna, Austria
{alana.hoogmoed,maxim.vidgof}@wu.ac.at
[2] Humboldt-Universität zu Berlin, Berlin, Germany
{christoffer.rubensson,jan.mendling}@hu-berlin.de
[3] Weizenbaum Institute, Berlin, Germany
[4] BOC Group, Vienna, Austria
djordje.djurica@boc-group.com

Abstract. Resource analysis is an area of process mining concerned with the behavior and performance of resources within business processes. Recent contributions in this field have predominantly focused on gaining specific insights, less so on their visual representation. In this paper, we propose a resource analytics technique that focuses on effective visualization of the analysis. Our technique allows us to analyze the allocation and performance of single resource units and roles within a business process. We evaluate our technique using a prototypical implementation.

Keywords: Process mining · Resource analysis · Performance analysis · Visual analytics

1 Introduction

Resource analysis is a subfield of process mining focusing on the performance of human and non-human actors in business processes [1]. Information retrieved from event data using process mining methods provides analysts with contextual insights about *how* and by *whom* processes were performed. These insights are valuable for in-depth analysis to support managerial decision-making [9,18,27] such as in resource assignment [15] or process simulations [11].

In recent years, an increasing number of contributions to resource analysis can be acknowledged from the mining of organizational and social structures (e.g., [2,6,9,12,22]) to the discovery of resource behavioral patterns (e.g., [18,23,27]).

J. Mendling—The research of the authors was supported by the Einstein Foundation Berlin under grant EPP-2019-524, by the German Federal Ministry of Education and Research under grant 16DII133, and by Deutsche Forschungsgemeinschaft under grant ME 3711/2-1.

H. van der Aa et al. (Eds.): BPMDS 2024/EMMSAD 2024, LNBIP 511, pp. 117–128, 2024.
https://doi.org/10.1007/978-3-031-61007-3_10

However, compared to other areas in process mining, such as performance analysis of process variants [13,24], the research landscape on resource analysis is fragmented with no adequate solution for unifying multiple behavioral measures. A few exceptions are works on *resource profiling* [18,27]. Similarly, most contributions are driven by developing and improving algorithmic design with little emphasis on effectively communicating the results to analysts using visual means. To this end, the research question of how to effectively combine and display multiple performance metrics from the resource perspective remains.

In this paper, we take these observations as a starting point. More specifically, we develop visualizations for key categories of resource analysis techniques. These techniques were implemented in a research prototype and subject to a user evaluation study. We applied the *Technology Acceptance Model* (TAM) [8] in the evaluation to demonstrate the effectiveness of our visualizations.

The paper is structured as follows. Section 2 describes the background of our research. Section 3 defines the concepts of our visualization technique. Section 4 presents our study for evaluating the technique. Section 4.3 discusses our findings before Sect. 5 concludes the paper.

2 Background

In this section, we provide a brief overview of resource analysis in process mining (Sect. 2.1) and discuss the role of visualization within this context (Sect. 2.2).

2.1 Resource Analysis in Process Mining

Process mining is an interdisciplinary field in computer science and information systems that applies data mining techniques to derive process insights from event data [1]. The data can be analyzed from various perspectives, such as the control-flow, organizational, case, or time perspective [1, p. 34], where control-flow is the most dominant one. Resource analysis in process mining is part of the organizational perspective, as it aims to understand the behavioral patterns of resources in the data. Resources can be workers, roles, machines, or other units that perform activities in a process. The insights gained from resource analysis can be utilized to support managerial decision-making or enhance the realism of process simulations, among other applications.

Resource analysis in process mining comprises multiple streams of research addressing different aspects of resource behavior. These streams can be broadly divided into *organizational mining* and *resource behavior mining*. Organizational mining is the most common stream, which aims to discover organizational structures in the data. The primary focus is discovering organizational models as relational networks by combining data mining metrics such as *handover of work* or *working together* [2] with concepts from *social network analysis* (e.g., [2,12,22]). Other authors emphasize the modeling aspect to discover new resource entities. Burattin et al. [6] propose a technique to mine *roles*, inter alia, to support the partition of process activities into swimlanes in business process diagrams. Schönig et al. [19] presented a declarative approach to mining team compositions from event data. Lastly, Deokar & Tao [9] proposed the framework *OrgMiner*, which allows analysts to define and select relational patterns to mine organizational models more flexibly.

The other stream of research investigates resources' ability to execute work. Often, the concept of *resource profiling* is used where multiple behavior metrics are combined. Pika et al. [18] were one of the first to address this topic by proposing five categories of resource behavior indicators, *skills*, *utilization*, *preferences*, *productivity*, and *collaboration* [18, p. 1:8], all integrated into one framework for mining, analyzing and evaluating different behavioral patterns. Yang et al. [27] provided a similar framework, which combined group-level and within-group analysis, each with three classes of resource indicators, respectively, to identify and analyze work profiles of resource groups. In another work by some of the same authors, Yang et al. [26] proposed *OrdinoR*, a hybrid framework that merges organizational modeling with group behavior evaluation metrics based on execution contexts, i.e., a multidimensional view of process executions.

2.2   Visualization of Resource-Related Indicators

Visualization is the process of transforming raw data to a visual abstraction [20, p.3] to leverage human comprehension in identifying meaningful insights [17,25]. In process mining, process graphs such as Petri nets or Directly-follows graphs are the primary means to visually represent processes (cf., [4]). Although rare, some authors utilize other types of visual representations or enhance process models with additional information. An example is the *Dotted chart* by Bose et al. [5], who aligned process instances along a time axis, where each event is characterized by a colored dot depicting a property. Another example is Kaur et al. [14], who proposed a method to align Directly-follows graphs along a time axis without deviating from the typical process semantics. An extensive survey of visual representations of event sequence data, including process mining, was conducted by Yeshchenko & Mendling [28].

The type of visual representations used to depict the resource perspective partially depends on the type of analysis. In organizational mining, *sociograms* [21] are commonly employed to depict resource relations (e.g., [12,22]). On the other hand, resource behavior mining utilizes standard graphs from statistics such as line graphs and bar charts (e.g., [18,23,27]) to display miscellaneous metrics. Beyond this, some works provide conceptual illustrations for visualizing resource behavior phenomena -yet lack an adequate implementation. Two examples of this are Martin et al. [16], who illustrate Gantt-like charts to depict resource availability calendars, and Burattin et al. [6], who exemplified swimlanes in BPMN diagrams for their role discovery method.

To the best of our knowledge, no study explicitly addresses the need for an adequate visualization representation to support analysts when exploring resource-related phenomena in event data. Hence, this is the purpose of our work.

2.3   Requirements

Against this background, we define the following requirements for a resource analytics technique.

   Requirement 1 (Organizational mining). A resource analytics technique must offer basic functionality of analyzing connections between resources, roles and tasks.

   Requirement 2 (Behavior mining). A resource analytics technique must offer techniques to analyze the performance of resources and roles.

   Requirement 3 (Effective visualization). A resource analytics technique must present the analysis in an understandable way.

3   Approach

In this section, we propose our resource analytics technique. It takes an event log as input and allows the user to select the desired analysis. Then, the relevant statistics are computed and visualized using interactive plots. We support two directions of analysis: resource allocation analysis and resource performance analysis. The former aims to understand the organizational structure and allocation between resources, roles and tasks. The latter focuses on investigating the efficiency of resources in a process. Within the scope of this technique, the focus is on time-related performance metrics, specifically the *service time* (also referred to as *processing time* [10, p. 60]). This dual approach aims to unravel the complexity of resource distribution and activity durations, providing insights into potential bottlenecks and avenues for enhancing operational efficiency. In the remainder of this section, we provide the necessary definitions and describe the implementation of our technique in detail.

3.1   Preliminaries

Definition 1 (Event, event attributes). *Let $\mathcal{E}$ be the universe of events. Each event has attributes. Let AN be the set of attribute names. For any event $e \in \mathcal{E}$ and name $n \in AN$, $\#_n(e)$ is the value of the attribute n for event e.*

   An activity is a specific attribute of an event, i.e., $\#_{activity}(e)$ is the activity associated to the event. We further define role and resource event attributes as $\#_{role}(e)$ and $\#_{resource}(e)$, respectively. Finally, each event has a start ($\#_{start}(e)$) and an end ($\#_{end}(e)$) timestamp.

   Note that we define the *event* such that it contains the information about both start and end timestamps of an activity, in contrast to having separate events for the start and end of an activity. In subsequent sections of the paper, we will use the terms *event* and *activity* interchangeably.

Definition 2 (Trace, event log). *A trace $\sigma = \langle e_1, \ldots, e_n \rangle$ is a finite sequence of events. An event log $L \subseteq \{\sigma\}^*$ is a multi-set of traces.*

A *trace* contains events related to one *case*, and in the remainder of the paper we will use these two terms interchangeably.

Definition 3 (Duration, average case duration). *Duration of an event is trivially defined as* $\#_{duration}(e) = \#_{end}(e) - \#_{start}(e)$.

Average Case Duration (ACD) of an activity is the average amount of the total time spent on a specific activity within a case. Importantly, if an activity is repeated multiple times in one case, the sum of all these durations is used for computing ACD. ACD can also be computed with respect to a role or a resource, i.e. how much time a specific resource spends on a specific activity within a case. ACD is computed as follows:

$$ACD = \text{average}(\sum_{\substack{\sigma \in L \\ e' \in \{e \in \sigma | condition\}}} \#_{duration}(e'))$$

where condition is $\#_{role}(e) = role$ *or* $\#_{resource}(e) = resource$ *for a specific role or resource.*

3.2   Implementation

We implement our technique with a web application. The source code is available on Github[1]. Our implementation consists of four steps: *i)* importing and preprocessing; *ii)* metric selection; *iii)* metric computation; and *iv)* metric visualization.

In the first step, the event log is imported. It has to have at least the attributes provided in Definition 1. As the only preprocessing step, event duration is computed as $\#_{duration}(e) = \#_{end}(e) - \#_{start}(e)$ for each event. In the second step, the user selects the desired analysis.

The third step involves computation of the selected metrics. We demonstrate it with one algorithm from resource allocation analysis and one algorithm from resource performance analysis, respectively. Within the scope of the resource allocation analysis, we determine the distribution and utilization of resources across different roles, as well as the allocation of resources and roles to various activities. A crucial aspect of this analysis includes calculating the number of unique resources per role, which can be achieved by applying Algorithm 1 to the preprocessed event log. The algorithm groups the event log by roles and counts the unique resources for each role, shedding light on the organizational structure and resource distribution.

Conversely, the resource performance analysis focuses on investigating the efficiency of resources by scrutinizing how long different resources take to complete their assigned tasks. This type of analysis allows us to pinpoint process bottlenecks and highlight opportunities for efficiency improvements. Our performance analyses are structured to determine the average case duration (ACD) across different roles, resources and activities. We commence with an examination of ACD per role, progressing to more detailed analyses of resource performance within roles, that is how well resources perform compared to others within

---

[1] https://github.com/MaxVidgof/resource-analytics

Algorithm 1: Resources per Role

Input: Preprocessed event log L
Result: Table (Role, Resource Count)

1 $roles\_resources \leftarrow \{\}$;
2 **forall the** $event \in L$ **do**
3 | **if** $\#_{role}(event) \notin roles\_resources$ **then**
4 | | $roles\_resources[\#_{role}(event)] \leftarrow \{\#_{resource}(event)\}$;
5 | **else**
6 | | $roles\_resources[\#_{role}(event)] \leftarrow$
   | | $roles\_resources[\#_{role}(event)] \cup \{\#_{resource}(event)\}$
7 | **end**
8 **end**
9 $table \leftarrow []$;
10 **forall the** $role \in roles\_resources.keys()$ **do**
11 | $resource\_count \leftarrow |roles\_resources[role]|$;
12 | $table \leftarrow table \cup (role, resource\_count)$;
13 **end**
14 **return** $table$

---

the same role. To further improve the analysis, we also consider the activities involved in the process. We examine every pairing of activity and role to offer insights on the amount of time different roles dedicate to various activities. The same approach can be applied to activity-resource combinations, using Algorithm 2, to enable a detailed comparison of resource performance across various activities.

The algorithm starts by grouping the event log by activities and resources. Subsequently, it computes the average case duration for each activity-resource combination and performs min-max normalization on these average durations within each group of activities. This normalization process adjusts the average durations using the formula $\frac{x - min(x)}{max(x) - min(x)}$, where x represents the average time a resource spends on a particular activity. Finally, the algorithm records the findings in a table, listing the activity-resource pairs along with their average and normalized case durations.

In the fourth step, we developed visualizations to enable a comprehensive analysis. On the one hand, we employed conventional statistical graphs such as bar plots, known to be leveraged in resource behaviour mining, but made them interactive to enhance the user experience. On the other hand, we created interactive heatmaps to facilitate an effortless comparison of the performance of roles and resources across various activities.

Algorithm 2: Normalized Average Case Duration per Activity and Resource

---

Input: Preprocessed event log L

Result: Table (Activity, Resource, Average Case Duration, Normalized Duration)

1 $activities\_resources \leftarrow \{\}$;

2 **forall the** $(activity, resource) \in$ $\{\#_{activity}(event)|event \in L\} \times \{\#_{resource}(event)|event \in L\}$ **do**

3 $\quad$ $key \leftarrow (activity, resource)$;

4 $\quad$ **forall the** $\{\#_{case}(event)|event \in L\}$ **do**

5 $\quad\quad$ $activities\_resources[(key, case)] = \sum \#_{duration}(e)$ for $e \in \{event \in L|\#_{activity}(event) = activity \wedge \#_{resource}(event) = resource \wedge \#_{case}(event) = case\}$;

6 $\quad$ **end**

7 **end**

8 $average\_case\_duration \leftarrow \{\}$;

9 **forall the** $(key, case) \in activities\_resources$ **do**

10 $\quad$ $average\_case\_duration[key] \leftarrow \text{average}\,(activities\_resources[(key, case)]$ for $case \in activities\_resources[key]$;

11 **end**

12 $table \leftarrow []$;

13 $min\_duration \leftarrow min(average\_case\_duration)$;

14 $max\_duration \leftarrow max(average\_case\_duration)$;

15 **forall the** $(activity, resource) \in average\_case\_duration$ **do**

16 $\quad$ $avg\_duration \leftarrow average\_case\_duration[(activity, resource)]$;

17 $\quad$ $normalized\_duration \leftarrow (avg\_duration - min\_duration)/(max\_duration - min\_duration)$;

18 $\quad$ $table \leftarrow table \cup (activity, resource, avg\_duration, normalized\_duration)$;

19 **end**

20 **return** $table$

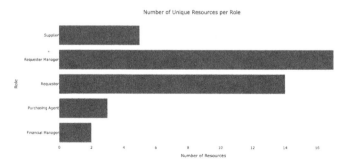

Fig. 1. Number of Unique Resources per Role

The visualizations were developed with the Plotly[2] graphing library, making the charts interactive through hover-over effects on the bars or cells. Figure 1

---

2 https://plotly.com/python/.

depicts a visual analysis from our collection of resource allocation analyses. The figure shows a horizontal bar chart illustrating the number of unique resources linked to each role within the organization, as calculated by Algorithm 1. The length of the bar indicates the diversity of resources utilized by each role, with a longer bar representing a wider variety of resources.

The heatmap presented in Fig. 2 provides a systematic visualization of resource performance by depicting the normalized average case duration for each activity and resource pairing. Utilizing a color gradient that transitions from blue to red, with blue indicating the fastest resource and red the slowest resource, this visualization facilitates an objective assessment of each resource's performance relative to their counterparts. Resources characterized predominantly by dark red cells are identified as the least efficient, indicating longer average case duration times overall. Conversely, those with primarily dark blue cells are recognized as the most efficient, completing tasks with the shortest average case duration. This differentiation aids in pinpointing both bottlenecks and areas of exceptional performance within the process. By taking advantage of the plot's interactive elements, which showcase the calculated average case duration for a specific activity-resource pair, users can benefit from a more in-depth analysis.

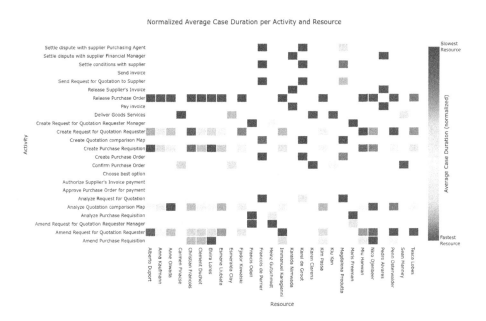

Fig. 2. Normalized Average Case Duration per Activity and Resource

4   Evaluation

This section presents the evaluation of our technique. First, we describe the event log used to evaluate our technique. Then, we describe the setup and results of user evaluation. Finally, we discuss the results.

4.1   Event Log

For our evaluation study, we used an event log provided by Fluxicon[3], containing events of a procurement process that covered the processing of purchase orders from the creation of purchase requisitions through to final invoice payment. The log encapsulates 608 cases, summing up to a total of 9,119 events, and spans a period of ten months. Every event captures six data attributes, including case ID, start and end timestamps, activity names, as well as the assigned resources and roles. Each activity within the process is presumed to be completed by a distinct role, indicating a streamlined sequence of operations with dedicated responsibilities for each step.

4.2   User Evaluation

This section discusses our user study evaluating our prototype through qualitative and quantitative feedback. The study involved three parts: the first tested participants with seven tasks, aiming to assess their ability to find and interpret correct visualizations. The second part of the study employed the Technology Acceptance Model (TAM) [8] to gauge perceived usefulness and ease of use – crucial determinants of technology adoption and usage. Participants were asked to rate their agreement on a 7-point Likert scale, ranging from 1 ('I fully disagree') to 7 ('I fully agree'), with six statements focusing on the prototype's potential to enhance job performance (perceived usefulness) and its user-friendliness, based on their direct interaction and experience with the system (perceived ease of use). Lastly, participants provided open-ended feedback on the prototype's strengths and areas for improvement.

As prior research demonstrated that there are no significant differences between the cognitive processes of IT professionals and students [7], we decided to recruit final semester bachelor students who previously successfully completed a course related to process mining. In accordance with the recommendations of AlRoobaea and Mayhew [3], who advocate for a sample size of 16 ± 4 participants for effective usability testing, our study involved 13 students. However, due to one submission being invalid, the actual count of participants concluded at 12.

The average number of correctly given answers on the tasks was 5.33 indicating that participants had no troubles identifying the visualization needed to answer the question and finding a correct answer on it. Further, the results of TAM assessment, suggest that participants rated our tool highly both in terms

---

[3] https://fluxicon.com/disco/files/Disco-Demo-Logs.zip.

of perceived usefulness and ease of use. The average score for perceived usefulness is 5.69 and 5.83 for ease of use, respectively, indicating that the participants consider the tool to be both useful and easy to use for their purposes. Finally, the qualitative feedback provided by participants suggests that the tool provides simple and understandable visualizations, with only one participant calling it overly complicated. Regarding further improvements, participants suggested that having grid lines on the graphs, the ability to zoom, select multiple diagrams simultaneously, and a tutorial to guide first-time users would be beneficial.

4.3   Discussion

This section discusses how the proposed resource analytics technique fulfills the requirements specified in Sect. 2.3.

Addressing **Requirement 1**, we proposed and implemented various analyses of the resource allocation. Our technique allows us to study the allocation of resources and roles to tasks as well as the assignment of resources to roles.

Addressing **Requirement 2**, our technique incorporates a variety of performance analyses, allowing the potential user to study task duration for selected roles or resources as well as directly compare resources' performance or find bottlenecks presented by specific activities, roles or resources.

Addressing **Requirement 3**, our technique provides visualizations tailored to each specific analysis. It utilizes simple bar plots for discrete values, e.g. resources per role, or duration of an activity in minutes, as well as heatmaps for comparing normalized durations and spotting bottlenecks. Importantly, the results of the evaluation confirm that the visualizations are understandable to the potential users.

4.4   Limitations

Our technique comes with limitations. First, the technique's reliance on specific data attributes, such as start and end timestamps, resources, and roles, may limit its applicability across diverse organizational contexts where such data might not be at hand or consistently recorded. Moreover, handling of sensitive data introduces privacy concerns that further constrain its deployment. Second, assessments of resource performance must account for the fact that process logs may only offer a fragment of the resources' engagements. The technique presented here depends on specific data attributes which, if not fully available, may obscure the complete spectrum of a resource's activities across various processes. Lastly, its performance and scalability in handling exceedingly large event logs remain to be explored.

5   Conclusion

Resource analysis is concerned with the behavior and performance of resources within business processes. Existing approaches primarily focused on acquiring specific insights but often overlooked the critical aspect of visualization. To bridge this gap, we introduced a new resource analytics technique aimed at analyzing the allocation and performance of resources with an emphasis on visualizing the outcomes. By providing a tool that simplifies the visualization and analysis of resource-related data, organizations can better pinpoint process inefficiencies and areas for enhancement. This is particularly crucial in today's context, where operational efficiency and resource optimization are paramount for securing competitive advantages. A user study validated the effectiveness and user-friendly nature of our technique. Looking ahead, future work should focus on expanding the technique's scope by integrating a wider array of analyses that leverage various event log attributes. Additionally, incorporating machine learning algorithms into this framework could yield predictive insights, which would significantly enhance analytical depth.

References

1. van der Aalst, W.M.P.: Process Mining - Data Science in Action, 2nd edn. Springer, Heidelberg (2016). https://doi.org/10.1007/978-3-662-49851-4
2. van der Aalst, W.M.P., Reijers, H.A., Song, M.: Discovering social networks from event logs. Comput. Support. Coop. Work **14**(6), 549–593 (2005)
3. Alroobaea, R., Mayhew, P.J.: How many participants are really enough for usability studies? In: 2014 Proceedings of the Science and Information Conference, London, UK, 27–29 August 2014, pp. 48–56 (2014)
4. Augusto, A., et al.: Automated discovery of process models from event logs: Review and benchmark. IEEE Trans. Knowl. Data Eng. **31**(4), 686–705 (2019)
5. Bose, R.P.J.C., van der Aalst, W.M.P.: Process diagnostics using trace alignment: opportunities, issues, and challenges. Inf. Syst. **37**(2), 117–141 (2012)
6. Burattin, A., Sperduti, A., Veluscek, M.: Business models enhancement through discovery of roles. In: IEEE Symposium on Computational Intelligence and Data Mining, CIDM 2013, Singapore, 16–19 April 2013, pp. 103–110. IEEE (2013)
7. Compeau, D., Marcolin, B., Kelley, H., Higgins, C.: Research commentary-generalizability of information systems research using student subjects-a reflection on our practices and recommendations for future research. Inf. Syst. Res. **23**(4), 1093–1109 (2012)
8. Davis, F.D.: Perceived usefulness, perceived ease of use, and user acceptance of information technology. MIS Q. 319–340 (1989)
9. Deokar, A.V., Tao, J.: OrgMiner: a framework for discovering user-related process intelligence from event logs. Inf. Syst. Front. **23**(3), 753–772 (2021)
10. Dumas, M., Rosa, M.L., Mendling, J., Reijers, H.A.: Fundamentals of Business Process Management. Springer, Heidelberg (2013)
11. Estrada-Torres, B., Camargo, M., Dumas, M., García-Bañuelos, L., Mahdy, I., Yerokhin, M.: Discovering business process simulation models in the presence of multitasking and availability constraints. Data Knowl. Eng. **134**, 101897 (2021)
12. Ferreira, D.R., Alves, C.: Discovering user communities in large event logs. In: Daniel, F., Barkaoui, K., Dustdar, S. (eds.) BPM 2011, Part I. LNBIP, vol. 99, pp. 123–134. Springer, Heidelberg (2012). https://doi.org/10.1007/978-3-642-28108-2_11

13. Ingh, L.V.D., Eshuis, R., Gelper, S.: Assessing performance of mined business process variants. Enterp. Inf. Syst. **15**(5), 676–693 (2021)
14. Kaur, H., Mendling, J., Rubensson, C., Kampik, T.: Timeline-based process discovery. CoRR abs/2401.04114 (2024)
15. Kumar, A., Dijkman, R., Song, M.: Optimal resource assignment in workflows for maximizing cooperation. In: Daniel, F., Wang, J., Weber, B. (eds.) BPM 2013. LNCS, vol. 8094, pp. 235–250. Springer, Heidelberg (2013). https://doi.org/10.1007/978-3-642-40176-3_20
16. Martin, N., Depaire, B., Caris, A., Schepers, D.: Retrieving the resource availability calendars of a process from an event log. Inf. Syst. **88** (2020)
17. Moody, D.L.: The "physics" of notations: toward a scientific basis for constructing visual notations in software engineering. IEEE Trans. Softw. Eng. **35**(6), 756–779 (2009)
18. Pika, A., Leyer, M., Wynn, M.T., Fidge, C.J., ter Hofstede, A.H.M., van der Aalst, W.M.P.: Mining resource profiles from event logs. ACM Trans. Manag. Inf. Syst. **8**(1), 1:1–1:30 (2017)
19. Schönig, S., Cabanillas, C., Ciccio, C.D., Jablonski, S., Mendling, J.: Mining team compositions for collaborative work in business processes. Softw. Syst. Model. **17**(2), 675–693 (2018)
20. Schroeder, W.J., Martin, K.M.: 1 - overview of visualization. In: Hansen, C.D., Johnson, C.R. (eds.) Visualization Handbook, pp. 3–35. Butterworth-Heinemann, Burlington (2005)
21. Scott, J.: What is Social Network Analysis? Bloomsbury Academic (2012)
22. Song, M., van der Aalst, W.M.P.: Towards comprehensive support for organizational mining. Decis. Support Syst. **46**(1), 300–317 (2008)
23. Suriadi, S., Wynn, M.T., Xu, J., van der Aalst, W.M.P., ter Hofstede, A.H.M.: Discovering work prioritisation patterns from event logs. Decis. Support Syst. **100**, 77–92 (2017)
24. Taymouri, F., Rosa, M.L., Dumas, M., Maggi, F.M.: Business process variant analysis: survey and classification. Knowl. Based Syst. **211**, 106557 (2021)
25. Thomas, J.J., Cook, K.A. (eds.): Illuminating the Path: The Research and Development Agenda for Visual Analytics. National Visualization and Analytics Center (2005). ISBN 0-7695-2323-4
26. Yang, J., Ouyang, C., van der Aalst, W.M.P., ter Hofstede, A.H.M., Yu, Y.: OrdinoR: a framework for discovering, evaluating, and analyzing organizational models using event logs. Decis. Support Syst. **158**, 113771 (2022)
27. Yang, J., Ouyang, C., ter Hofstede, A.H.M., van der Aalst, W.M.P., Leyer, M.: Seeing the forest for the trees: group-oriented workforce analytics. In: Polyvyanyy, A., Wynn, M.T., Van Looy, A., Reichert, M. (eds.) BPM 2021. LNCS, vol. 12875, pp. 345–362. Springer, Cham (2021). https://doi.org/10.1007/978-3-030-85469-0_22
28. Yeshchenko, A., Mendling, J.: A survey of approaches for event sequence analysis and visualization using the ESeVis framework. CoRR abs/2202.07941 (2022)

Process Variant Analysis Across Continuous Features: A Novel Framework

Ali Norouzifar[1]([✉])[iD], Majid Rafiei[1][iD], Marcus Dees[2][iD],
and Wil van der Aalst[1][iD]

[1] RWTH University, Aachen, Germany
{ali.norouzifar,majid.rafiei,wvdaalst}@pads.rwth-aachen.de
[2] UWV Employee Insurance Agency, Amsterdam, The Netherlands
Marcus.Dees@uwv.nl

Abstract. Extracted event data from information systems often contain a variety of process executions making the data complex and difficult to comprehend. Unlike current research which only identifies the variability over time, we focus on other dimensions that may play a role in the performance of the process. This research addresses the challenge of effectively segmenting cases within operational processes based on continuous features, such as duration of cases, and evaluated risk score of cases, which are often overlooked in traditional process analysis. We present a novel approach employing a sliding window technique combined with the earth mover's distance to detect changes in control flow behavior over continuous dimensions. This approach enables case segmentation, hierarchical merging of similar segments, and pairwise comparison of them, providing a comprehensive perspective on process behavior. We validate our methodology through a real-life case study in collaboration with UWV, the Dutch employee insurance agency, demonstrating its practical applicability. This research contributes to the field by aiding organizations in improving process efficiency, pinpointing abnormal behaviors, and providing valuable inputs for process comparison, and outcome prediction.

Keywords: process mining · process comparison · business process improvement

1 Introduction

Process mining techniques are used to analyze event data generated by different types of information systems. For instance, performance analysis using process mining techniques has provided a range of new opportunities for business owners to analyze and improve their processes. From the performance point of view, we often observe that the execution policies may vary significantly for different groups of process instances based on their characteristics.

This research was supported by the research training group "Dataninja" (Trustworthy AI for Seamless Problem Solving: Next Generation Intelligence Joins Robust Data Analysis) funded by the German federal state of North Rhine-Westphalia.

H. van der Aa et al. (Eds.): BPMDS 2024/EMMSAD 2024, LNBIP 511, pp. 129–142, 2024.
https://doi.org/10.1007/978-3-031-61007-3_11

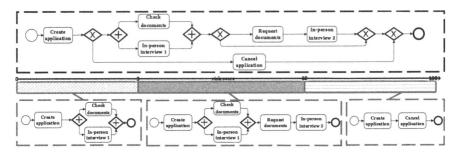

(a) The BPMN on top shows a claim handling process in which each case has a risk score and may have a different handling procedure based on the risk score.

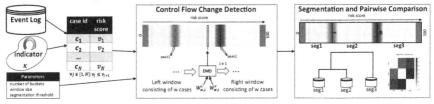

(b) The proposed framework for process variant analysis based on the risk score.

Fig. 1. A claim handling process as a motivating example.

For example, in the claim handling process shown in Fig. 1a, a risk score assigned to the cases affects the handling procedure. On top, the business process explaining the whole process is shown without giving any clue that the process could be different for cases in different ranges of the risk score. After creating an application, cases with a risk score higher than 10 are canceled. The remaining cases go through the check documents step and require an in-person interview, then there is an exclusive choice that decides whether the cases are required to submit more documents and have another interview, or they can skip these two steps if the risk score is lower than 3.

Using the available data in information systems and process analysis tools, different dimensions for each case in the event log can be extracted. The introduced approach in Fig. 1b considers risk score as an example of a continuous dimension and has two main parts. First, the *control flow change detection* is designed by using a sliding window shifting over the dimension range. Then, local peaks are used for *segmentation and pairwise comparison*.

In this paper, we have the following goals: 1) Motivating the problem of finding process variants over the range of a continuous dimension, e.g., risk score or case duration. 2) Introducing a sliding window approach using the earth mover's distance to find the changes in control flow. 3) Case segmentation based on continuous dimensions and control flow, and pairwise comparison of the segments. 4) Testing the usability of the framework with a real-life case study.

The output of the framework is an automated segmentation of cases based on key dimensions influencing the control-flow behavior which can be used as input for other types of analysis, such as process comparison [13], outcome prediction [14], or labeling the traces as desirable or undesirable in order to use them in process discovery algorithms working with desirable and undesirable traces [5,11].

2   Related Work

Extracted event logs from information systems often consist of a variety of process executions containing deviating behaviors, manual interventions, infrequent patterns, process drift over time, and many other inconsistencies resulting in high complexity [6]. While filtering out infrequent behavior can mitigate data complexity [4], it is important to note that infrequent behavior may sometimes include significant deviations that need further investigation. In [8], the earth mover's distance is used to identify distinct cohorts of traces based on trace attributes, offering a framework that explores all trace attributes to uncover combinations leading to the most diverse control-flow behavior. Unlike this paper, we do not need the assumption that the dimensions are discretized in advance.

Trace clustering can also be considered as related work to our research. Different trace clustering approaches may use a control-flow perspective, other available attributes, or a combination of both [7]. In [1], different similarity measures to cluster the traces based on the control flow are introduced and compared. In [17], an event log is divided into sub-event logs considering an attribute value, then hierarchical clustering is used to merge similar clusters. However, choosing a distinctive attribute is not straightforward. In addition, when considering continuous attributes it is even more challenging to set distinctive thresholds. In [15], the active trace clustering framework is introduced which takes process models explaining the clusters into account while doing trace clustering. The trace clustering methods cannot directly provide solutions for our problem, i.e., considering the performance perspective.

Considering time as an important dimension in event data analysis, the identification of concept drift is an interesting research question [12]. These methods usually use a feature space to characterize the control flow and use some techniques to pinpoint the changes. If a change is not observable using the selected feature space, these algorithms fail to detect it. In [16], a concept drift detection algorithm is introduced which leverages declarative constraints to represent control-flow behavior. A multi-variate change point detection algorithm is implemented to find the changes over time. In [10], another method is proposed which is based on the statistical tests applied to the distribution of partially ordered runs in two consecutive time windows. In [2], the earth mover's distance is used to find drifts in the control flow. The mentioned approaches only focus on changes in control flow behavior over time and not on different continuous dimensions. Similar to the framework proposed in [2], we employ a window-based approach using the earth mover's distance function to identify the changes across continuous features. Our framework works effectively without a large feature space, which might struggle to capture all potential changes in control flow. Additionally, it does not use statistical tests that often rely on some assumptions.

3   Preliminaries

$\mathcal{B}(A)$ is the set of all multisets over some set A. Considering $B \in \mathcal{B}(A)$, $B(a)$ denotes the frequency of element $a \in A$. We write $x \in B$ if $B(x) > 0$. The event log is an important concept in our work, therefore we formally introduce it.

Definition 1 (Event Log). *Let $\mathcal{C}$, $\mathcal{A}$, and $\mathcal{T}$ be the universe of case identifiers, the universe of activities, and the universe of timestamps respectively. $e = (c, a, t)$ is a tuple representing an event where $\pi_{\mathcal{C}}(e) = c \in \mathcal{C}$, $\pi_{\mathcal{A}}(e) = a \in \mathcal{A}$, and $\pi_{\mathcal{T}}(e) = t \in \mathcal{T}$. $\mathcal{E} = \mathcal{C} \times \mathcal{A} \times \mathcal{T}$ is the universe of events. A trace is a finite sequence of events $\sigma = \langle e_1, e_2, ..., e_n \rangle \in \mathcal{E}^*$ with size $n \in \mathbb{N}$ such that for each $1 \le i < n$, $\pi_{\mathcal{C}}(e_i) = \pi_{\mathcal{C}}(e_{i+1}) \wedge \pi_{\mathcal{T}}(e_i) \le \pi_{\mathcal{T}}(e_{i+1})$. An event log L is a set of traces such that each trace belongs to a different case. $\mathcal{L}$ is the universe of event logs. $|L|$ is the number of traces in event log L. In addition, we define $cf : \mathcal{L} \to \mathcal{B}(\mathcal{A}^*)$ as a function that extracts the control flow of L, i.e., the multiset of traces projected on activities such that $cf(L) = [\langle \pi_{\mathcal{A}}(e_1), ..., \pi_{\mathcal{A}}(e_n) \rangle | \langle e_1, e_2, ..., e_n \rangle \in L]$.*

In addition to the control flow and time dimension, other dimensions could be assigned to cases from other sources of information. We use $\kappa_L : L \to \mathbb{R}$ to show a case-level indicator. Case-level indicators assign a numerical value $\kappa_L(\sigma)$ to each trace $\sigma \in L \in \mathcal{L}$. If the context is clear, we drop L from the notation $\kappa_L(\sigma)$.

Definition 2 *(Ordering function). Let $L \in \mathcal{L}$ be an event log and κ be a case-level indicator that assigns a value to each case in L. We define $rank_\kappa(L) = \langle \sigma_1, \sigma_2, ..., \sigma_{|L|} \rangle$ such that $L = \{\sigma_1, \sigma_2, ..., \sigma_{|L|}\}$ and for $1 \le i < j \le |L| : \kappa(\sigma_i) \le \kappa(\sigma_j)$.*

For example, $L = \{\langle (c_1, a, 13), (c_1, b, 23) \rangle, \langle (c_2, a, 14), (c_2, b, 16), (c_2, c, 20) \rangle, \langle (c_3, a, 17), (c_3, b, 20), (c_3, c, 35) \rangle\}$ is an event log with $cf(L) = [\langle a, b, c \rangle^2, \langle a, b \rangle^1]$. Consider κ as a function that calculates the duration of cases, therefore, $\kappa = \{(\sigma_{c_1}, 10), (\sigma_{c_2}, 6), (\sigma_{c_3}, 18)\}$ and $rank_\kappa(L) = \langle \sigma_{c_2}, \sigma_{c_1}, \sigma_{c_3} \rangle$.

Definition 3 *(Stochastic Language). Given the universe on activities $\mathcal{A}$, $f : \mathcal{A}^* \to [0, 1]$ is a stochastic language iff $\sum_{s \in \mathcal{A}^*} f(s) = 1$. $\mathcal{F}$ is the universe of stochastic languages.*

Definition 4 *(Stochastic Language of an Event Log). Let $L \in \mathcal{L}$ be an event log. $stoch : \mathcal{L} \to \mathcal{F}$ is a function that extracts the stochastic language of an event log such that $stoch(L) = \{(s, p) | s \in cf(L) \wedge p = \frac{cf(L)(s)}{|L|}\}$.*

The earth mover's distance calculates the distance between two stochastic languages. We use this distance to compare the control flow in two event logs.

Definition 5 *(The earth mover's distance). Let $L \in \mathcal{L}$, and $L' \in \mathcal{L}$ be two event logs, $\delta : \mathcal{A}^* \times \mathcal{A}^* \to [0, 1]$ be a trace distance function, and $r : L \times L' \to [0, 1]$ be a function that indicates the movement of frequency between two event logs. $\mathcal{R}$ is the universe of all reallocation functions. The earth mover's distance between L and L' is defined by $EMD(L, L') = \min_{r \in \mathcal{R}} \sum_{s \in cf(L)} \sum_{t \in cf(L')} r(s, t) . \delta(s, t)$ such that $\forall s \in cf(L) : \sum_{t \in cf(L')} r(s, t) = stoch(L)(s)$, $\forall t \in cf(L') : \sum_{s \in cf(L)} r(s, t) = stoch(L')(t)$, and $\forall s \in cf(L), \forall t \in cf(L') : r(s, t) \ge 0$.*

We use the Levenshtein distance δ to calculate the distance between the traces. The calculation of the efficient reallocation amounts, i.e., r in Definition 5 is solved as a linear programming problem. For more details, we refer to [9].

4   Process Variant Identification Framework

As illustrated in Fig. 1b, the framework proposed in this paper consists of two main parts, a control flow change detection over the range of a case-level indicator and a segmentation and comparison framework. Unlike concept drift frameworks which focus on time dimension, we identify changes in control flow across continuous dimensions. Our framework does not generate a large feature set that might overlook certain types of changes. Instead, it leverages the earth mover's distance to effectively capture the variability in control flow.

4.1   Control Flow Change Detection

Our proposed method consists of a bucketing step and then moving a sliding window. In Fig. 2a, three different event logs, i.e., L_1, L_2, and L_3 are illustrated. Each of the event logs has 150 cases and the cases are ordered based on a case-level indicator. A bucketing strategy is used to divide the event logs into 15 buckets each containing 10 traces. The buckets are shown as patterned boxes such that different patterns show that the traces are different. In this example, two different window sizes $w_1 = 1$ and $w_2 = 3$ are used. Considering event log L_1 and window size w_1, we start from $i = 1$ and each time we move the central point one unit to the right up to $i = 14$ and compare w_1 bucket on the left-hand side of the central point to w_1 bucket on the right-hand side of it using the earth mover's distance. Comparative results for some combinations of the event logs and time windows are illustrated in Fig. 2b using a color range proportional to the difference level. Next, we formally define buckets and sliding windows.

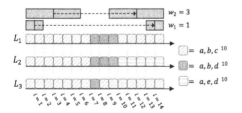

(a) Event logs L_1, L_2, and L_3 with different types of changes in the control flow.

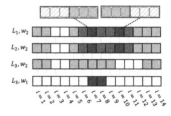

(b) Visualised *ldist* value with moving the sliding window.

Fig. 2. Some examples illustrating how the framework works considering three different event logs, $b = 15$, and two time windows $w_1 = 1$ and $w_2 = 3$.

Definition 6 *(Buckets).* *Let* $L \in \mathcal{L}$ *be an event log,* κ *be a case-level indicator,* $\sigma_i = rank_\kappa(L)(i)$, *and* $b \in \mathbb{N}^{[2,|L|]}$ *be the number of buckets given by the user. For the sake of simplicity, we assume that* $|L|$ *is divisible by* b. *Then,* $l = \frac{|L|}{b}$ *is the number of cases in each bucket such that* $B_i = \langle \sigma_{(i-1).l+1}, ..., \sigma_{i.l} \rangle$ *for* $1 \leq i \leq b$.

Definition 7 *(Left and Right Windows).* *Let* $L \in \mathcal{L}$ *be an event log,* κ *be a case-level indicator,* $\sigma_i = rank_\kappa(L)(i)$, $b \in \mathbb{N}^{[2,|L|]}$ *be the number of buckets given by the user, and* $w \in \mathbb{N}^{[1,\frac{b}{2}]}$ *be a window size parameter. Considering a window size* w *and* $i \in \{w, ..., b-w\}$, *we can create a left window* $W^l_{w,i} = \{\sigma \in B_j | i-w < j \leq i\}$ *and a right window* $W^r_{w,i} = \{\sigma \in B_j | i < j \leq i+w\}$.

To perform a comparative analysis, we move the sliding window over the whole range of κ. We need at least w buckets on the left window. Therefore, we start from $i = w$ and each time move the sliding window for one bucket. We repetitively continue until we reach a point where the number of buckets on the right window is equal to the window size, i.e., $i = b - w$.

Definition 8 *(Local Distance Function).* *Let* $L \in \mathcal{L}$ *be an event log,* κ *be a case-level indicator,* $b \in \mathbb{N}^{[2,|L|]}$ *be the number of buckets given by the user, and* $w \in \mathbb{N}^{[1,\frac{b}{2}]}$ *be a window size parameter. We define the local distance function* $ldist_{L,\kappa,w,b} : \{w, ..., b-w\} \rightarrow [0,1]$ *such that* $ldist_{L,\kappa,w,b}(i) = EMD(W^l_{w,i}, W^r_{w,i})$. *If the context is clear, we show* $ldist_{L,\kappa,w,b}$ *as* $ldist$.

In Fig. 2b, some analysis is performed based on different event logs and different window sizes. Using the event log L_1 and the window size w_2, from $i = 5$ the change in behavior is detectable by calculating the earth mover's distance between the left and right windows. The earth mover's distance value is visualized with colors, i.e., darker color shows a higher distance. After shifting the sliding window, the maximum difference between the left and right windows is observed at $i = 7$ and $i = 10$. A similar pattern in changing $ldist$ value is observed using L_2 and w_2. However, the introduced framework does not give us any clue whether the control flow behavior before $i = 7$ and after $i = 10$ are similar or different. Using L_3 and the smaller window w_1, it is observed that the change in behavior is only observed sharply at $i = 7$ and $i = 10$. Using the larger window w_2, the change in behavior started to affect $ldist$ from $i = 5$ but with shifting the sliding window, it cannot exactly identify the point in which the behavior is changed. Therefore, the larger window size is more robust against noise but may miss some important change points.

The running example introduced in Fig. 1a is simulated using the CPN tools and the generated event log is used to explain how the framework works. This event log consists of 10,000 cases and 31 trace variants[1]. The cases are ordered based on their risk score value. In Fig. 3a, the results using $b = 100$, i.e., 1 % of the cases in each bucket and different window sizes $w \in \{2, 5, 10, 15\}$ are shown.

---

[1] https://github.com/aliNorouzifar/process-variants-identification/blob/main/event %20logs/test.xes.

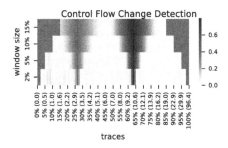
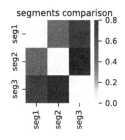

(a) Results of applying the introduced framework using the simulated event log with $b=100$ and $w \in \{2, 5, 10, 15\}$.

(b) Pairwise comparison between the segments.

Fig. 3. Process variant identification framework for the claim handling process.

The numbers in the parenthesis show the raw risk score values. The experiment is repeated for different window sizes. The colors show how high the earth mover's distance is between the left and right windows.

4.2 Segmentation and Pairwise Comparison

Based on the visualizations shown in Fig. 2, the control flow behavior may change several times through the range of the indicator but with each change, we only know that w buckets on the left are different from the w buckets on the right. Therefore, we extend the proposed framework to make it more applicable to obtain global insights. The idea is to use the peaks in the *ldist* values based on specific b and w parameters to perform a segmentation. Each time we observe a peak in *ldist*, we generate a segment consisting of the cases from the previous change point to the current change point. Then, it is possible to compare non-adjacent segments with the earth mover's distance measure.

Definition 9 *(Change Point in Control Flow).* Let $L \in \mathcal{L}$ be an event log, κ be a case-level indicator, $b \in \mathbb{N}^{[2, |L|]}$ be the number of buckets given by the user, and $w \in \mathbb{N}^{[1, \frac{b}{2}]}$ be a window size parameter. $\theta \in [0, 1]$ is a user-defined threshold to check whether a high value of ldist is significant. $p \in [w, b-w]$ is a change point in the control flow behavior if $ldist(p) \geq \theta$, $ldist(p-1) \leq ldist(p)$ if $p \in (w, b-w]$, and $ldist(p+1) \leq ldist(p)$ if $p \in [w, b-w)$.

Definition 10 *(Segments).* Let $P = \langle p_1, ..., p_{|P|} \rangle$ be the ordered sequence of change points in ldist function such that $\forall i, j \in \{1, ..., |P|\} : p_i \leq p_j$ iff $i < j$. Considering $|P|$ as the number of peaks, we can generate $|P|+1$ segments which we refer to as seg_1 to $seg_{|P|+1}$ such that $seg_1 = \{\sigma \in B_x | x \leq p_1\}$, $seg_i = \{\sigma \in B_x | p_{i-1} < x \leq p_i\}$ for $i \in [2, |P|]$, and $seg_{|P|+1} = \{\sigma \in B_x | p_{|P|} < x\}$.

Considering $w = 10$ in Fig. 3a and $\theta = 0.1$, *ldist* has two peaks in $i = 26$ (*risk score* $= 3$) and $i = 63$ (*risk score* $= 10$). We can use heatmaps to compare the resulting segments pairwise to check if non-adjacent segments have similar control flows. Using the identified peaks, the whole event log is divided into three segments, and the segments are compared in Fig. 3b.

Next, we can hierarchically merge similar segments in case the control flow is not significantly different with regard to the user-defined difference threshold θ. We recursively merge two segments with the minimum *ldist* if this minimum distance is lower than θ, i.e., a user-defined threshold to check whether the distance is significant.

5   Case Study

The introduced framework is implemented and is publicly available[2]. To assess the effectiveness of our framework, we conducted a comprehensive case study in collaboration with UWV, the employee insurance agency of the Netherlands responsible for executing social security in case of unemployment and disability. UWV provided real-life event data for this case study. We worked closely with experts from the agency, who provided invaluable guidance and insights. Their expertise enabled us to align our research with practical, real-world scenarios, ensuring that our algorithms are usable in real business contexts.

5.1   UWV Event Log

UWV has over 18000 employees and several branches all over the Netherlands. One of the main processes of this governmental sector is investigated in this paper. The duration of the cases in this process has been of particular interest. UWV wants to know how the process is changed concerning the duration of the cases and whether we can find the change points in the duration. The duration of cases varies in the range of 1 day to 575 days. The event log has 144,096 cases, 1,026 variants, 29 activities, and 1,316,128 events. Among all the cases, 5,449 cases (3.8% of the cases) are rejected and 138,647 cases (96.2% of the cases) are accepted.

The normative BPMN model shown in Fig. 4 represents a claim-handling process at UWV. First, a claim from a customer is received. Then, either the claim is accepted or blocked. A blocked claim indicates either some information needs to be checked or corrected after which the claim is accepted, or the claim is blocked and then immediately rejected. After a rejected claim, an objection can be received by customers if they do not agree with the decision. The handling of this objection is out of the scope of this process model. After an accepted claim, which has received one or at most three payments, an objection can be received. This is due to customers who in hindsight find that they do not need the payments. A claim withdrawal process is started that results in repayment of the total sum of received benefits. In case the customer is still entitled to one or more payments, the *Block Claim* activity is executed. This prevents any new payments from being automatically made. This normative model has an alignment fitness of 99.3% with respect to the event log [3].

---

[2] https://github.com/aliNorouzifar/process-variants-identification.

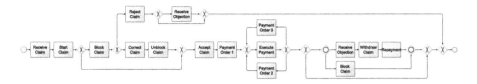

Fig. 4. The normative BPMN model representing the investigated UWV claim handling process.

5.2 Process Variant Analysis Using UWV Event Log

The first experiment is performed using the complete event log and the results are shown in Fig. 5. In this experiment, $b = 100$ and the window sizes 2, 5, 10, and 15 are considered. The comparative results are illustrated in Fig. 5a which shows that the cases with a very short duration or very long duration are different from other cases. Considering $\theta = 0.1$, $w = 5$, and i referring to the central point of the sliding window, two peaks are observed at $i = 3$ (17 days) and $i = 95$ (78 days) which can be used to generate three segments, i.e., $[0, 17]$ days, $[18, 77]$ days and $[78, 575]$ days. In Fig. 5b, the three generated segments are compared to each other using the earth mover's distance.

The number of cases in each segment and their alignment fitness with respect to the normative model is reported in Table. 1. All the segments have a high fitness value implying that the observed behavior in the segments fits the normative model. According to the replay results, Fig. 6 shows the normative BPMN model where the parts of the model that cover each of the segments are highlighted. The colors are proportional to the frequencies and the transition labels are colored as gray if the frequency is lower than 5%. For segment 1 in Fig. 6a, the activities *Receive Claim*, *Start Claim*, *Block Claim*, *Reject Claim* and *Receive Objection* are highlighted. *Segment 1* represents the claims that are rejected and optionally UWV receives an objection to the decision. *Segment 2* shows claims that are accepted, i.e., the customer receives three payments and then the pro-

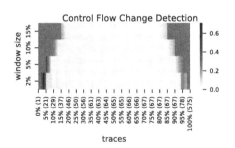

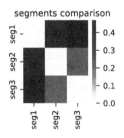

(a) Control flow change detection with b=100 and $w \in \{2, 5, 10, 15\}$.

(b) Segmentation and pairwise comparison.

Fig. 5. Applying the introduced framework to the complete UWV event log.

Table 1. Using alignment fitness as a conformance checking metric to check whether the event logs fit the process model or not.

Event log		Number of traces		Alignment fitness	
UWV complete log	segment 1: [0, 17] days	144096	4323	99.3%	99.6%
	segment 2: [18, 77] days		132572		99.7%
	segment 3: [78, 575] days		7201		93.4%
UWV rejected claims	segment 1: [0, 15] days	5449	3888	98.4%	99.7%
	segment 2: [16, 83] days		1350		97.3%
	segment 3: [84, 550] days		211		81.7%

cess finishes. Finally, *segment 3* represents again accepted cases. However, after the payments an objection is received, and optionally a block is executed. For these claims, the customer withdraws the claim. The customer then pays the received sum back to UWV. Blocking is done to prevent new payments from being made while the claim withdrawal process has not finished yet.

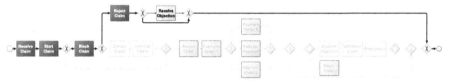

(a) Segment 1 in the complete event log with duration in the range [0,17] days.

(b) Segment 2 in the complete event log with duration in the range [18,77] days.

(c) Segment 3 in the complete event log with duration in the range [78,575] days.

Fig. 6. The normative BPMN model is highlighted based on the frequency of the transitions in replaying the segments from the complete event log experiment.

5.3   A Deeper Analysis Considering Rejected Cases

The extracted segments are highly correlated with the process outcome, i.e., the rejection or acceptance of a claim. However, the correlation between the extracted segments with specific duration is less clear. Another experiment using the 5,449 rejected cases is performed to get more understanding of the relation between duration ranges and specific process variants[3]. The alignment fitness of the rejected cases is 98.04% with respect to the normative model.

An overview of the results for the rejected cases is shown in Fig. 7. Based on Fig. 7a considering $w = 2$ and $\theta = 0.1$, four segments are found, with duration periods of $[0, 13]$ days, $[14, 15]$ days, $[16, 83]$ days, and $[84, 550]$ days respectively. Segments 1 and 2 are merged into one segment, with a duration period of $[0, 15]$ days, since the distance between them is lower than $\theta = 0.1$. This can be observed in the heatmap in Fig. 7b. Segments 1 and 2 have very similar colors when compared to each other in comparison to the other segments.

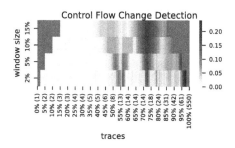 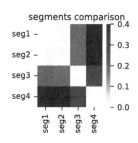

(a) Control flow change detection with b=100 and $w \in \{2, 5, 10, 15\}$.

(b) Segmentation and pairwise comparison.

Fig. 7. Applying our framework to the rejected cases in the UWV event log.

The number of cases in each segment and alignment fitness values of the identified segments are shown in Table 1. These results show that segment 3 does not fit the normative model well with an alignment fitness value of 81.7%. Figure 8 contains the highlighted normative model for each of the three segments. Figure 8a shows the first segment with a duration period of $[0,15]$ days and contains cases that are rejected and no objection is received. This segment represents customers who file a claim even though they know that they most likely will not be entitled. In the second segment, with a duration period $[16,83]$ days, in Fig. 8b cases are described that are rejected and some also have an objection. Finally, the third segment, with a duration period of $[84,550]$ days, in Fig. 8c consists of claims that are first accepted and end as rejection with a full repayment, or claims that are first rejected and are accepted after an objection is received and granted.

---

[3] The analysis of accepted cases is explained in the supplementary material https://github.com/aliNorouzifar/process-variants-identification/blob/main/supplementary%20material/supplementary%20material.pdf.

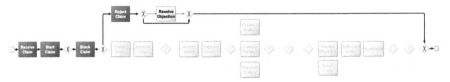

(a) Segment 1 in the rejected cases event log with duration in the range [0,15] days.

(b) Segment 2 in the rejected cases event log with duration in the range [16,83] days.

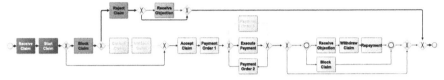

(c) Segment 3 in the rejected cases event log with duration in the range [84,550] days.

Fig. 8. The normative BPMN model highlighted based on the frequency of the transitions in replaying the segments from the rejected event log experiment.

6   Conclusion

In this study, we delved into the concept of segmenting a continuous dimension concerning changes in control flow. While our framework primarily focuses on identifying segments with differing control flows, it may not directly imply the desirability or undesirability of individual cases. For instance, with a dimension like duration, cases within segments featuring either very short or very long duration could be associated with undesirability or efficiency. This approach holds promise for extension, particularly in identifying and labeling cases as undesirable, taking the broader process context into account. The interconnections between different dimensions may also play a role in the changes in behavior which is highly relevant for future investigations. Considering them may lead to some interesting analyses. For instance, the duration of cases could correlate with the workload of the process, potentially generating delayed yet normal cases during high workload periods. Considering only one dimension may not show whether cases are normal or problematic. The output of our framework can be used as input for various process mining tasks like process comparison, outcome prediction, and process discovery using desirable and undesirable cases.

References

1. Back, C.O., Simonsen, J.G.: Comparing trace similarity metrics across logs and evaluation measures. In: Indulska, M., Reinhartz-Berger, I., Cetina, C., Pastor, O. (eds.) CAiSE 2023. LNCS, vol. 13901, pp. 226–242. Springer, Cham (2023)
2. Brockhoff, T., Uysal, M.S., van der Aalst, W.M.P.: Time-aware concept drift detection using the earth mover's distance. In: 2020 2nd International Conference on Process Mining (ICPM), pp. 33–40. IEEE (2020)
3. Carmona, J., van Dongen, B.F., Solti, A., Weidlich, M.: Conformance Checking - Relating Processes and Models. Springer, Cham (2018). https://doi.org/10.1007/978-3-319-99414-7
4. Chapela-Campa, D., Mucientes, M., Lama, M.: Understanding complex process models by abstracting infrequent behavior. Future Gener. Comput. Syst. **113**, 428–440 (2020)
5. Chesani, F., et al.: Shape your process: discovering declarative business processes from positive and negative traces taking into account user preferences. In: Almeida, J.P.A., Karastoyanova, D., Guizzardi, G., Montali, M., Maggi, F.M., Fonseca, C.M. (eds.) EDOC 2022. LNCS, vol. 13585, pp. 217–234. Springer, Cham (2022). https://doi.org/10.1007/978-3-031-17604-3_13
6. De Leoni, M., van der Aalst, W.M.P., Dees, M.: A general process mining framework for correlating, predicting and clustering dynamic behavior based on event logs. Inf. Syst. **56**, 235–257 (2016)
7. Hompes, B., Buijs, J., van der Aalst, W.M.P., Dixit, P., Buurman, J.: Discovering deviating cases and process variants using trace clustering. In: Proceedings of the 27th Benelux Conference on Artificial Intelligence (BNAIC), pp. 5–6 (2015)
8. Leemans, S.J.J., Shabaninejad, S., Goel, K., Khosravi, H., Sadiq, S., Wynn, M.T.: Identifying cohorts: recommending drill-downs based on differences in behaviour for process mining. In: Dobbie, G., Frank, U., Kappel, G., Liddle, S.W., Mayr, H.C. (eds.) ER 2020. LNCS, vol. 12400, pp. 92–102. Springer, Cham (2020). https://doi.org/10.1007/978-3-030-62522-1_7
9. Leemans, S.J.J., Syring, A.F., van der Aalst, W.M.P.: Earth movers' stochastic conformance checking. In: Hildebrandt, T., van Dongen, B.F., Röglinger, M., Mendling, J. (eds.) BPM 2019. LNBIP, vol. 360, pp. 127–143. Springer, Cham (2019). https://doi.org/10.1007/978-3-030-26643-1_8
10. Maaradji, A., Dumas, M., Rosa, M.L., Ostovar, A.: Detecting sudden and gradual drifts in business processes from execution traces. IEEE Trans. Knowl. Data Eng. **29**(10), 2140–2154 (2017)
11. Norouzifar, A., van der Aalst, W.M.P.: Discovering process models that support desired behavior and avoid undesired behavior. In: SAC 2023: The 38th ACM/SIGAPP Symposium on Applied Computing (2023)
12. Sato, D.M.V., Freitas, S.C.D., Barddal, J.P., Scalabrin, E.E.: A survey on concept drift in process mining. ACM Comput. Surv. **54**(9), 189:1–189:38 (2022)
13. Taymouri, F., La Rosa, M., Dumas, M., Maggi, F.M.: Business process variant analysis: survey and classification. Knowl.-Based Syst. **211**, 106557 (2021)
14. Teinemaa, I., Dumas, M., Rosa, M.L., Maggi, F.M.: Outcome-oriented predictive process monitoring: review and benchmark. ACM Trans. Knowl. Discov. Data **13**(2), 17:1–17:57 (2019)
15. Weerdt, J.D., vanden Broucke, S.K.L.M., Vanthienen, J., Baesens, B.: Active trace clustering for improved process discovery. IEEE Trans. Knowl. Data Eng. **25**(12), 2708–2720 (2013)

16. Yeshchenko, A., Ciccio, C.D., Mendling, J., Polyvyanyy, A.: Visual drift detection for event sequence data of business processes. IEEE Trans. Vis. Comput. Graph. **28**(8), 3050–3068 (2022)
17. van Zelst, S.J., Cao, Y.: A generic framework for attribute-driven hierarchical trace clustering. In: Del Río Ortega, A., Leopold, H., Santoro, F.M. (eds.) BPM 2020. LNBIP, vol. 397, pp. 308–320. Springer, Cham (2020). https://doi.org/10.1007/978-3-030-66498-5_23

A Novel Contextualization Method for Process Discovery Using Activity Specialization Hierarchies

Zahra Ahmadi[(✉)][iD], Jochen De Weerdt[iD], and Estefanía Serral Asensio[iD]

Research Centre for Information Systems Engineering (LIRIS), KU Leuven,
Warmoesberg 26, 1000 Brussels, Belgium
{zahra.ahmadi,jochen.deweerdt,estefania.serralasensio}@kuleuven.be

Abstract. While context information has been demonstrated to be essential in understanding processes, the use of context in process discovery techniques is still very limited. This paper proposes a novel process discovery method that improves process analysis through the definition and exploitation of activity specialization hierarchies. Our method includes strategies for extracting process models by flexibly incorporating contextual information into process activities, allowing for seamless transitions across different levels of contextual detail. We use a real case study on bees' foraging to show how activity specialization hierarchies can help in contextualizing the discovered processes. This integrated method provides a comprehensive framework for contextualized process analysis, offering practical insights for both researchers and practitioners seeking to analyze processes whose execution varies depending on their context.

Keywords: Process mining · Process discovery · Contextualization · Activity specialization hierarchies

1 Introduction

Process discovery entails the automated creation of visual process models from event logs, providing detailed insights into how processes are executed, such as activity paths, their frequency, and duration.

With the aim of more accurate and informative process mining results, contextualization emerges as a powerful way to leverage information about the real-world environment in which a process is executed, commonly referred to as contextual data [7]. By incorporating contextual data, analysts can discern connections between the process and real-world dynamics, thereby elucidating variations or deviations in process executions. While various techniques have been proposed in the literature to incorporate contextual information into process mining [2,4,10,13], existing approaches do not directly integrate contextual details into the control-flow of discovered process models.

This paper addresses this research gap by introducing a novel process discovery method that adopts a flexible strategy to exploit contextual information

© The Author(s), under exclusive license to Springer Nature Switzerland AG 2024
H. van der Aa et al. (Eds.): BPMDS 2024/EMMSAD 2024, LNBIP 511, pp. 143–155, 2024.
https://doi.org/10.1007/978-3-031-61007-3_12

through activity specialization hierarchies. Specifically, our core contribution is a new context-aware process discovery method that leverages activity-related context data to refine activity labels, thereby creating activity specialization hierarchies. By utilizing context variables, activities can be systematically specialized, ranging from generic to more contextualized. This hierarchical structuring facilitates the creation of contextually rich process models at varying levels of detail, enabling analysts to navigate between complexity and interpretability effectively. To demonstrate the efficacy of our method, we implement it in a real-world scenario focusing on the monitoring of bees to discern behavior patterns. We demonstrate the capability of the method to distil meaningful insights from intricate process data while ensuring the resulting models remain comprehensible and actionable.

In summary, our paper contributes to advancing process mining by introducing a novel method of contextualization through activity specialization hierarchies. By affording analysts the flexibility to tailor process models to specific contextual nuances, our method promises to enhance the relevance, accuracy, and interpretability of process discovery endeavors.

The remainder of this paper is structured as follows: Sect. 2 reviews the related work, Sect. 3 presents the definitions necessary to understand the method, Sect. 4 illustrates the running case study, Sect. 5 outlines our method, Sect. 6 explores important discussion points, and finally, Sect. 7 concludes the paper.

2   Related Work

This section offers an extensive review of previous research on contextualization and hierarchical process mining techniques, aiming to establish the foundation for our proposed method.

2.1   Contextualization in Process Mining

In [6], context is "any information that can be used to characterize the situation of an entity", with an entity encompassing persons, places, or objects relevant to user-application interactions. In [1], the importance of considering the context of the events in business processes analysis was emphasized. The authors advocate for incorporating context-specific event data to enrich process mining and improve analysis accuracy. The paper [7] aims to increase the quality of event-activity mappings by considering contextual factors to improve process mining results in scenarios with low-level events by a framework that includes four context dimensions: personal and social, task, environmental, and spatial-temporal. Another context classification system is created in [4] to be used in process monitoring and prediction. We specifically focus on this research on task dimension, i.e., specific details and circumstances surrounding the execution of a particular task within a business process, including task rules, goals, causality, history, application, and property.

Numerous scholarly contributions have incorporated the utilization of context within the domain of process mining. For instance, [9] proposes the Guided Process Discovery method, grouping low-level events based on behavioral activity patterns, and capturing domain knowledge on the relation between high-level activities and low-level events. [11] introduces a framework for context-aware process mining, automatically capturing contexts from business process execution environments to enhance process flexibility. A framework is proposed in [14] for generating label refinements based on the time attribute of events. The authors of [10] introduce the CAP3 approach that makes use of context-specific domain knowledge and input from experts to identify relevant contextual information. The paper [13] presents a new technique that merges the control flow and data perspectives into a single approach by expanding inductive process discovery. The technique establishes criteria that prioritize context data over control flow. The TROPIC approach in [2] exploits contextual information in a multi-perspective trace clustering technique that takes into account the control flow, the trace attribute data, and the time series sensor data perspective.

Although previous research has not fully explored the use of contextual information to derive process insights, we leverage task-related contexts to develop a new process discovery approach capable of flexibly exploiting context information through activity specialization hierarchies. By comprehensively exploring the context, our research aims to significantly contribute to understanding and optimizing processes at different granularity levels.

2.2 Hierarchical Process Mining

Hierarchical structuring in process mining involves organizing activities in a hierarchical manner, through the creation of sub-activities and nested relationships. Several studies propose hierarchical approaches for discovering process models.

In [3] a methodology is presented for discovering hierarchical process models using a sequence of plugins in the ProM framework. The authors use Simple Filter(s), Pattern Abstractions, and Fuzzy Miner plugins to facilitate the systematic discovery of hierarchical process models. Moreover, [12] proposes an incremental algorithm for extending hierarchical process models by integrating new behavior trace by trace. a Multi-Level Miner framework for the process discovery of hierarchical models, providing a comprehensive solution to balancing behavioral quality and model complexity in process mining. Lastly, in [8], a technique is presented in four steps for discovering hierarchical multi-instance business process models from event logs with sub-process multi-instantiation information.

While hierarchical process mining aids in understanding complex processes, sub-activities represent subprocesses, not specialized activities as in our approach. Additionally, hierarchies are the output of the mining algorithm, whereas we consider them as input. Finally, none of the hierarchical process mining approaches exploit context information.

3   Preliminaries

In process mining, event logs document the executions of activities. In this work, we assume our event log contains the activity and the timestamp, as well as variables that represent contextual information related to that activity execution (task context). Specifically, we define an event log as follows:

Definition 1. Event Log. Let the event log E represent the set of events in the process P. Each event e_i, has a case id, an activity identifier, a timestamp and additional task context variables: $e_i = \{caseid, activity, t, c_1, c_2, ..., c_m\}$, where each *activity* is an element of set A, which contains all activities in the process P. A context variable can take different values. Here, we assume these values to be categorical. Let C_x represent the set of values for the x-th context variable, the set of values is defined as $C_x = \{C_{x,1}, C_{x,2}, \ldots, C_{x,k_x}\}$.

Definition 2 (Activity Specialization Hierarchy). A specialization hierarchy describes how an activity is specialized using the activity context variables. At the top of the hierarchy, we find the most general activity (level 0). This top activity is then specialized using one context variable (level 1), the level 1 activities are then specialized using another context variable (level 2), and so on. We denote each level as L_i, where i is the index of the level and indicates the number of context variables that have been used to form that specialized activity. The hierarchical structure is defined by the relation $L_0 \prec L_1 \prec \ldots \prec L_n$, signifying that each level L_i is a specialization of an activity at level L_{i-1}. The label of the activities at L_{i+1} is formed by the label at L_i plus a context variable value.

4   Running Case Study

To illustrate our approach, we use a real case study tracking the behavior of bees using Internet of Things (IoT) technology. This study provides valuable insights into the foraging behavior of bees, a topic of significant ecological importance. During foraging, bees visit flowers for varying duration, corresponding to specific activities. Various factors including flower color, content or food type, and location or distance from the hive, influence foraging behavior.

   Four experiments were conducted to collect data on colony behavior, two involving healthy bees and two involving sick bees. Each experiment utilized two identical greenhouse tents, each housing a colony of approximately 30 worker bees, one queen, and eight robotic flowers. In [5], robotic flowers were developed to provide sugar water simulating natural nectar and to measure flower visit rates and duration. Half of the flowers in this experiment provided regular sugar water (untreated), while the other half contained sugar water that acted as a medicine (treated) to treat the illness affecting sick bees. Additionally, the flowers were either blue or yellow. Our focus was on studying colony behavior as a unified entity, rather than individual bees, with each colony treated as a distinct case. Bee activities were categorized based on flower visit duration as eating, probing, resting, and sleeping.

By applying our contextualization process mining method to colony data, we aim to address the following questions:

1. *Foraging patterns:* What constitutes the foraging pattern exhibited by colonies of bees?
2. *Floral preferences:* What types of flowers do the colonies exhibit a preference for during their foraging activities?
3. *Temporal allocation:* How is the temporal duration allocated by colonies to each flower, and what patterns emerge based on the color of the flowers?
4. *Influential factors on flower choice:* To what extent do various factors, such as the content or location of the flowers, influence the colonies' choices regarding the flowers they forage?

The process contextualization using activity specialization hierarchies in the analysis of colonies' data holds the promise of unravelling intricate insights into answering the previous questions. These questions form the foundation of our investigation to gain a comprehensive understanding of the behaviors exhibited by bee colonies during their foraging activities.

5 Process Discovery with Activity Specialization Hierarchies

Our method introduces a novel approach for generating more relevant discovered process models by utilizing activity specialization hierarchies. Activity specialization hierarchies enable the exploration of different levels of contextualization, facilitating detailed analyses of particular process activities executed in specific contexts while also offering a holistic view of the entire process with efficient navigation between different levels of detail. Figure 1 shows the three phases of our method, each of them consisting of one or more steps which are either executed manually or in an automated manner. The proposed method explains step by step how activity specialization hierarchies are created using the task context variables, and how these hierarchies are exploited in process mining.

5.1 Create Activity Specialization Hierarchies (Phase 1)

The initial phase of the method involves a series of steps aimed at creating the necessary activity specialization hierarchies. The steps in this phase, as outlined in Algorithm 1, are as follows:

1.1 Select activities for specialization: In this step, it is determined which process activities can be specialized based on contextual variables. Let $Act = \{a_1, \ldots, a_n\}$ be a subset of A ($Act \subset A$), representing the activities that can be specialized (line 3). In our example, only eating and probing are selected to be specialized as their contextualization is fundamental to understand the bees' behavioral patterns.

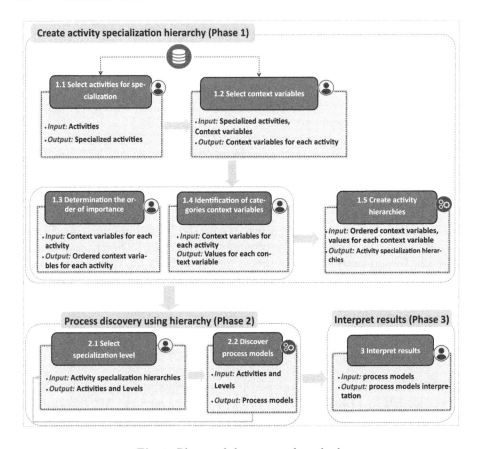

Fig. 1. Phases of the proposed method

1.2 Select context variables: For every activity to be specialized, the corresponding contextual variables from the event log are chosen (lines 4–5). Let $C = \{C_1, \ldots, C_m\}$ be the set of context variables in E, where $a_i \in Act$ can be specialized using Cntx (a subset of C ($Cntx \subset C$)). Note that the context variables can be different for each activity. For instance, in our case study, we consider the following categorical context variables for both eating and probing activities: food type, flower color, and distance from the hive.

1.3 Determine the order of context variables' importance: For every activity, priorities must be assigned to contextual variables indicating their order of importance. The context variable with the highest priority (the most important for the specific study) will be used to create the first specialization level. The second context variable will be added to the first level to create the second specialization level, and so on and so forth (line 6). In our running case, we assign the following priorities based on the defined questions in Sect. 4: food type with priority $= 1$, color with priority $= 2$, and distance with priority $= 3$.

Algorithm 1. Create activity specialization hierarchies (Phase 1)

```
1: Input: activities, context_variables
2: Output: activity_specialization_hierarchies
3: specialized_activities ← select_specialized_activities(activities)              ▷ Step 1.1
4: for each activity in specialized_activities do
5:     activity_context_variables ← select_context_variables(context_variables)    ▷ Step 1.2
6:     ordered_variables ← order_variables(activity_context_variables)             ▷ Step 1.3
7:     for each variable in activity_context_variables do
8:         variable_values ← identify_values()                                     ▷ Step 1.4
9:     end for
10:    activity_hierarchy ← create_hierarchy(ordered_variables, variable_values)   ▷ Step 1.5
11:    activity_specialization_hierarchies ← add(activity_hierarchy)
12: end for
```

1.4 Identify values of context variables: In this step, the different values C_{x,k_x} that each context variable can take should be determined (lines 7–8). Currently, we assume that these values are categories. In our case study, we have the following categories: treated and untreated for food type, blue and yellow for color, and closest and farthest for distance.

1.5 Create activity specialization hierarchies: The activity specialization hierarchies are automatically created from the information captured in the previous steps as defined in Definition 2 (line 10).

As an example, in our case study, Fig. 2 shows the specialization hierarchy for the eating activity.

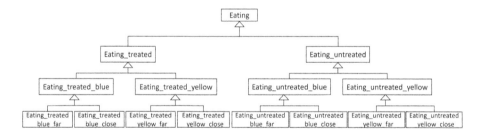

Fig. 2. Specialization hierarchy for the eating activity

5.2 Process Discovery Using Hierarchies (Phase 2)

In this phase, processes are discovered through a systematic exploration utilizing the activity specialization hierarchies created in Phase 1. These hierarchies enable the analysis to focus on contextual levels that are most relevant for each case. This phase is composed of two steps, executed iteratively to transition between a higher-level process view and contextualized views.

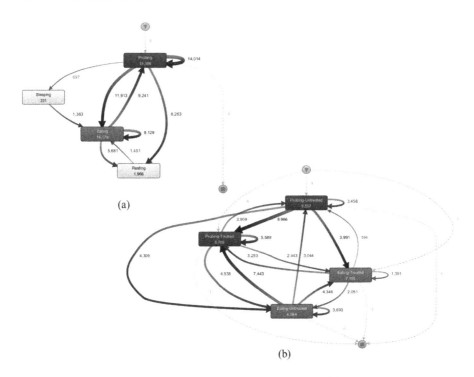

Fig. 3. Process maps with (a) main biological activities and (b) contextualized activity specialization in the first level

2.1 Select specialization levels: The only manual step in discovering the underlying processes using the created activity specialization hierarchies is to specify the activities we wish to focus our analysis on at which specialization level (l). Note that l could vary for different activities. To showcase the approach's potential within our case study, we conduct three iterations: 1) selecting all activities at L_0 ($l = 0$, i.e., without contextualization); 2) choosing probing and eating both at L_1 ($l = 1$); 3) selecting probing and eating both at L_2 ($l = 2$).

2.2 Discover process models: This step involves discovering the processes using the information selected in the previous step, i.e., using the selected activities as the indicated levels. To accomplish this, we utilize the capabilities of process mining tools. The process models obtained in iterations 1) and 2) are shown in Fig. 3. Figure 3(a) shows the most general model with the most frequent paths (100% of Activities and 40% of Paths). The activities are represented by boxes and the process flow between these activities is visualized by arrows. Moreover, the numbers placed on the transition arrows denote the count or frequency of transitions occurring between two activities. The thickness of the arrows and the coloring of the activities visually support these numbers (higher values are demonstrated with thicker arrows or in darker colors). Figure 3(b) provides a more detailed representation of the eating and probing patterns according to the food type (100% of Activities and Paths with filtering Eating and Probing).

The process model obtained in iteration 3) is shown in Fig. 4 (100% of Activities and Paths while retaining the Eating and Probing activities). This model shows not only the patterns according to the food type, but also according to the flower color.

Notice how this method facilitates the gradual revelation of nuanced patterns and insights into the colonies' behavior.

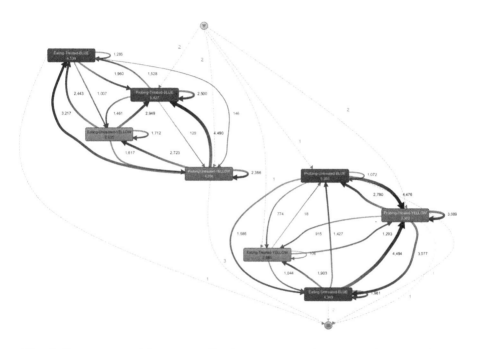

Fig. 4. Process map with contextualized activity specialization in the second level

5.3 Interpret Results (Phase 3)

Our aim is to thoroughly examine the process models obtained in Phase 2 to gain a comprehensive understanding of colonies' behaviour. By carefully examining the process maps, we can uncover the nuances crucial to effectively answer our research questions.

1. Foraging Patterns: After examining the most general process map (iteration 1), it becomes apparent that the most common activities among bee colonies are probing and eating. Through systematic investigation of these activities, we found the different behaviors of probing and eating of bees on different types of flowers. By taking into account color, content, and distance as context variables, we can gain a deeper understanding of ecological dynamics, assist in conservation efforts, clarify pollination dynamics, and glean insights into resource allocation strategies. Failing to consider these contexts may lead to oversimplified models that overlook nuances in the intricate relationships between bees and their surroundings.

2. Floral Preferences: Upon careful examination of context variables, it has been observed that there is a distinct behavioral pattern among bee colonies. The colonies tend to probe untreated flowers more frequently, while they consume treated flowers more often. This difference in behavior highlights a noticeable preference and divergence in the foraging strategies employed by the colonies. It reveals a complex interplay between their probing and eating behavior, particularly in the context of treated and untreated flowers (Fig. 3(b).

3. Temporal Allocation: Our analysis showed a clear trend that bee colonies spend more time eating and probing blue flowers than yellow ones (Fig. 4. By using the performance feature, we were able to quantitatively evaluate this trend and provide strong evidence for the difference in time allocation towards the flowers of different colors. This empirical observation improves our understanding of the colonies' preferences about specific flower color variables, thereby enhancing our understanding of their foraging behaviors.

4. Influential Factors on Flower Choice: The behavior of colonies is influenced by the content and color of flowers they encounter. However, when flowers are placed too close, it becomes difficult to analyze their behavior based on location. In such cases, it can be deduced that the colonies do not show a significant preference for flowers based on their location. Due to the close proximity of the flowers, the colonies tend to forage in a similar pattern, regardless of the spatial arrangement of the flowers. This observation highlights the impact of spatial constraints on the decision-making processes of colonies.

Note that focusing on general activities without contextualization does not give the necessary information to answer the research questions. Similarly, going to a deeper level for all activities would render models that are no longer understandable or useful.

6   Discussion

The presented method provides a systematic approach to exploit contextualization in the process discovery. It enables a more comprehensive analysis leading to better insights.

In this paper, the analysis is done manually using filtering options on activities and context variables. This requires going back and forth modifying all the options to discover the necessary models. We plan to develop an implementation of our method through a more user-friendly and interactive interface, e.g., by implementing a slider tool on the process maps that allows zooming in/out on the specialization levels for each activity.

Also, throughout the analysis, there are several decisions that could be further supported. One of such decisions is determining the optimal number of contextualization levels. The hierarchical nature of our method requires a critical examination of how deeply we should delve into the contextual layers. While a more detailed analysis can provide a complete picture, it can also result in complex models (e.g., considering the deepest level of all the activities in the same model will create an unnecessary complex process model). Therefore, it is essential to strike a balance between the level of detail and the clarity of the analysis to ensure that the insights obtained are both comprehensive and understandable. While there is no predefined guideline for the appropriate number of levels, our future research will focus on the development of a complexity hyperparameter that would allow to dynamically configure levels and values of contextual variables, resulting in a kind of map-metaphor inspired exploration tool.

In addition, our experiment currently focuses on addressing categorical contexts. Managing numerical contexts is a distinct challenge. A simple solution would be to convert them into categoricals, e.g., assigning categories to distinct value ranges. In the future, we will consider extensions or adaptations that can seamlessly incorporate numerical data, ensuring a more inclusive and versatile application in diverse process mining scenarios.

Our proposed method provides a structured approach to creating hierarchies. However, it's important to note that the interpretation of the results may vary depending on the specific characteristics and complexities of each domain. To address this concern, we have planned future work to incorporate more standardized criteria for decision-making and explore automated or semi-automated approaches to result interpretation.

The purpose of this paper is to improve process analysis through activity specialization hierarchies. The number of activities is not important, and the method is adaptable to different scenarios with varying degrees of activities and features. The model's complexity is directly related to the number of features chosen, and there is a trade-off between the model's complexity and the amount of detail required by the user or experts. Moreover, a high number of context variables and/or a high number of categories for some variables may quickly make our method too complex to apply. In future work, we will consider potential strategies for reducing complexity to enhance scalability and interpretability, such as aggregation techniques or context-specific transformations.

Whether analyzing business processes like supply chain management and customer relationship management or non-business processes like natural processes, consultation with an expert in that domain is essential. In this article, we have used an expert to check the importance of activities. We acknowledge that practical implementation challenges exist, particularly regarding the manual effort required for activity specialization and context definition. Addressing these challenges is necessary for broader applicability. However, we believe that by collaborating with domain experts and data analysts, we can effectively address these challenges. To reduce the potential complexity of process models resulting from specialization, we propose prioritizing activities based on their significance to analysis purposes. For example, identifying and specializing activities that are identified as critical by experts, allows for more focused analysis and actionable insights. In future research, we plan to diversify our case studies to showcase the versatility and applicability of our approach across a broader range of process mining contexts. We also intend to investigate automated techniques and algorithmic approaches to streamline the process of activity specialization and context enrichment. Finally, although the method has been shown using a real case study, it should be applied to other case studies to demonstrate its generalized applicability.

7   Conclusion

We have presented a novel contextualization method for process discovery using activity specialization hierarchies. This method enables a systematic and comprehensive analysis, spanning from macroscopic overviews to microscopic details, showing promising results in a better understanding of processes. The insights derived through contextualized analysis and hierarchy features empower organizations to continually make data-driven improvements, fostering a dynamic and responsive approach to process optimization.

Our future work will focus on transforming this method into a fully functional tool, engaging in collaborative development efforts to ensure its robustness, scalability, and applicability across diverse scenarios. Note that currently no tool explicitly features the implementation of the presented method. Several manual steps can be taken to apply the method in widely used process discovery tools, like Disco; but this is not ideal. To improve the user experience of the method, we plan to implement a slider mechanism that will allow users to dynamically adjust and explore different specialization levels for each process activity, enhancing the user experience and providing flexibility in adapting the model's behavior to specific requirements. Furthermore, we also plan to extend our method to explore the creation/usage of temporal context variables as well as environmental variables within the activity specialization hierarchies.

References

1. van der Aalst, W., Dustdar, S.: Process mining put into context. IEEE Internet Comput. **16**(1), 82–86 (2012)
2. Bertrand, Y., De Weerdt, J., Serral, E.: A novel multi-perspective trace clustering technique for IoT-enhanced processes: a case study in smart manufacturing. In: Di Francescomarino, C., Burattin, A., Janiesch, C., Sadiq, S. (eds.) BPM 2023. LNCS, vol. 14159, pp. 395–412. Springer, Cham (2023). https://doi.org/10.1007/978-3-031-41620-0_23
3. Bose, R.P.J.C., Verbeek, E.H.M.W., van der Aalst, W.M.P.: Discovering hierarchical process models using ProM. In: Nurcan, S. (ed.) CAiSE Forum 2011. LNBIP, vol. 107, pp. 33–48. Springer, Heidelberg (2012). https://doi.org/10.1007/978-3-642-29749-6_3
4. Brunk, J.: Structuring business process context information for process monitoring and prediction. In: 2020 IEEE 22nd CBI, vol. 1, pp. 39–48. IEEE (2020)

5. Debeuckelaere, K., Janssens, D., Asensio, E.S., Jacquemyn, H., Pozo, M.I.: A wireless, user-friendly, and unattended robotic flower system to assess pollinator foraging behaviour. bioRxiv, pp. 2022–06 (2022)
6. Dey, A.K.: Understanding and using context. Pers. Ubiquit. Comput. **5**, 4–7 (2001)
7. Koschmider, A., Mannhardt, F., Heuser, T.: On the contextualization of event-activity mappings. In: Daniel, F., Sheng, Q.Z., Motahari, H. (eds.) BPM 2018. LNBIP, vol. 342, pp. 445–457. Springer, Cham (2019). https://doi.org/10.1007/978-3-030-11641-5_35
8. Liu, C., Wang, Y., Wen, L., Cheng, J., Cheng, L., Zeng, Q.: Discovering hierarchical multi-instance business processes from event logs. IEEE Trans. Serv. Comput. (2023)
9. Mannhardt, F., de Leoni, M., Reijers, H.A., van der Aalst, W.M., Toussaint, P.J.: Guided process discovery-a pattern-based approach. IS **76**, 1–18 (2018)
10. Márquez-Chamorro, A.E., Revoredo, K., Resinas, M., Del-Rio-Ortega, A., Santoro, F.M., Ruiz-Cortes, A.: Context-aware process performance indicator prediction. IEEE Access **8**, 222050–222063 (2020)
11. Mounira, Z., Mahmoud, B.: Context-aware process mining framework for business process flexibility. In: Proceedings of the 12th IIWAS, pp. 421–426 (2010)
12. Schuster, D., van Zelst, S.J., van der Aalst, W.M.P.: Incremental discovery of hierarchical process models. In: Dalpiaz, F., Zdravkovic, J., Loucopoulos, P. (eds.) RCIS 2020. LNBIP, vol. 385, pp. 417–433. Springer, Cham (2020). https://doi.org/10.1007/978-3-030-50316-1_25
13. Shraga, R., Gal, A., Schumacher, D., Senderovich, A., Weidlich, M.: Inductive context-aware process discovery. In: 2019 ICPM, pp. 33–40. IEEE (2019)
14. Tax, N., Alasgarov, E., Sidorova, N., Haakma, R.: On generation of time-based label refinements. arXiv preprint arXiv:1609.03333 (2016)

Evaluation of Modeling Methods (EMMSAD 2024)

Enhancing Our Understanding of Business Process Model Comprehension Using Biometric Data

John Krogstie$^{(\boxtimes)}$ ⓘ and Kshitij Sharma ⓘ

Norwegian University of Science and Technology (NTNU), Trondheim, Norway
{John.Krogstie,Kshitij.Sharma}@ntnu.no

Abstract. Much research has been done on the comprehension and development of conceptual models. In related areas such as linguistics and software engineering one has taken techniques from neuroscience into use, to study the biological and neurological processes when working with textual knowledge representations in tasks such as program code debugging. The use of such techniques has only to a limited degree been used to improve our understanding of visual conceptual models so far.

We will in this paper present ongoing research on the use of techniques collecting biometric data to investigate how we work with visual conceptual models. The approach, which are based on techniques used in multi-modal learning analytics (MMLA), investigates how performance on modeling tasks is correlated with biometric data, collecting data in parallel from EEG, eye-tracking, wristbands, and facial expression (through cameras). We find that good understanding of performance of modeling tasks can be achieved by using biometric data in a natural usage situation. We have just scratched the surface of this topic, and we present the start of a larger research program in this area in the concluding remarks.

Keywords: Business Process Modeling · BPMN · Multi-modal biometric data · Neuro-conceptualization

1 Introduction

Visual conceptual modeling is a central activity in information systems analysis and design. Comprehension of visual models e.g. process models is an important activity when working with models. The main parts of model comprehension are described in detail in [27] and has been investigated with a number of techniques.

Modeling involves the construction of abstract visual representation that capture the structure, behavior, and relationships of real-world entities or phenomena, and the two-dimensional layout allows to play with both the primary and secondary notation [50] to create knowledge and convey meaning. Using techniques from multi-modal learning analytics (MMLA) in conceptual modeling opens new opportunities for understanding how we processes and represents complex information, which can, in turn, inform and enhance the development of more effective modeling approaches, support modeling and

H. van der Aa et al. (Eds.): BPMDS 2024/EMMSAD 2024, LNBIP 511, pp. 159–174, 2024.
https://doi.org/10.1007/978-3-031-61007-3_13

make it more probable that modelling is used in the most appropriate way. MMLA combines two major theoretical frameworks, the Cognitive Load Theory (CLT) [38] and second, the Affective Learning Framework (ALF) [11], and we will combine techniques investigating both areas.

NeuroIS is a research field in which neuroscience theories and tools are used to better understand information systems (IS) phenomena. Existing research areas in NeuroIS is summarized in [66], where it appears that the focus is on the use of IS and not so much on the of the development of the IS. Lately also software development tasks such as programming has been intensively studied [28, 63], whereas other tasks often linked to IS-development such as visual conceptual modeling has so far to a very limited degree been studied using techniques from neuroscience, although certain techniques such as the use of eye-tracking and wristband for capturing physiological data have a been done by some researchers [1, 35, 62, 64].

The use of neuroscience and biometric data in conceptual modeling focuses on understanding the neural and physiological mechanisms underlying concept formation, representation, comprehension, validation, and manipulation as part of model development and use. By leveraging advanced neuroimaging techniques such as functional magnetic resonance imaging (fMRI), and electroencephalography (EEG), researchers can potentially examine brain activation patterns and connectivity while participants engage in tasks that require conceptual reasoning. A challenge with some of the more advanced techniques such as fMRI is that the accuracy of results comes at a cost, particularly on the ecological validity of the trial situation and the cost-benefit of the technique used. We present in this paper an experiment illustrating that the use of simpler biometric techniques can provide results in understanding performance of modeling activities, and thus enable the use of biometrics on modeling situations closer to how they would be done without the collection of biometric data than you would have e.g. laying in an MR-machine.

In the next section, we will provide background from multi-modal learning analytics and how biometric data has been used for understanding the modeling process so far. In Sect. 3 we describe the experiment and highlight in Sect. 4 results on how data from the different sensors can improve our understanding of model comprehension performance. In Sect. 5 we discuss the results, whereas Sect. 6 provides a conclusion and points out future work.

2 Background and Related Work

Multi-modal data (MMD) have been used to capture, analyze, and predict learners' behavior [2], task-performance [12] and learning gains [7]. Most of the research carried out for instance to provide feedback to learners is based on measurements rooted in unimodal data streams such as, emotions [5], content (log data, [48]), and attention (gaze data, [54]). The feedback systems using MMD depend heavily on the subjective judgement of human experts and are deeply contextualized in informal learning settings [36]. This makes the transfer of existing knowledge into formal settings difficult. In process modeling, we see for instance that the effect of models in variants of BPMN can have large effect on organizational performance, if one is able to have these models learnt and understood by those that use the models to guide work [24].

MMLA combines two major theoretical frameworks. First, the Cognitive Load Theory (CLT) [38] and second, the Affective Learning Framework (ALF) [11]. MMLA looks at these in concert with traditional methods to in our case understand processes in process modeling [23, 27]. CLT considers the cognitive processes of learning and retention to explain the learner's behavior. The working principle of CLT is that humans have a limited information processing capacity when they engage with a task. CLT defines three types of cognitive loads: intrinsic (inherent difficulty associated with the topic), extraneous (generated by how information is presented), and germane (generated by processing, construction, and automation of knowledge schemas such as the BPMN language in process modeling based on the information presented).

To model the learner's behavior using the principles of CLT, one can use EEG and eye-tracking (ET) data streams. EEG and ET are two main data sources that reveal various mental processes involved in the comprehension, construction, and organization of schemas including models. For example, on the one hand, EEG can be used to compute constructs such as, divergent [57] and convergent [45] thinking, working memory load [21], cognitive load [3], engagement [43] and distraction patterns [59]. ET can be used to measure different aspects of behavior such as, cognitive load [17], fatigue [58], attention [54], information processing behavior [49] and anticipatory patterns [39]. Eye-tracking has also been used extensively in collaborative learning scenarios to assess both the quality of collaboration [22] and collaborative learning outcome [52]. Combining EEG with ET can provide us a holistic view of how learners process the given information to create knowledge and understanding.

The second theoretical framework supporting our work is the Affective Learning Framework (ALF). ALF is mostly concerned with how learners feel while they are processing the information presented. ALF is also concerned with how learning experiences are internalized. These learning experiences, once internalized, later guide the learners' attitudes and behavior in future and in turn, affect the learning outcome.

To incorporate ALF in the methodology, we use facial and physiological (Heart rate variability (HRV), electrodermal activity (EDA), blood volume pulse (BVP), temperature (TMP)) data. Using facial data, one can capture several sets of emotions. The two widely used sets are 1) based on the Control Value theory (anger, happiness, sadness, surprise, fear, disgust, [41]) and 2) based on the educational expressions (confusion, boredom, frustration, delight, engagement, [9]). Both sets have been used in learning contexts, however, the educational emotional experiences have been more used in affective feedback learning systems. When learners face an error or uncertainty, they show confusion [11]. If learners cannot resolve the issues, they experience frustration, which if it is persistent, can easily transition into boredom [11]. Furthermore, using physiological data (i.e., HRV, BVP, EDA, TMP) one can also detect the emotional states of the learners as well as their stress and arousal levels. Recently, with the developments in wearable technology, researchers have employed "smartwatch-like" devices (e.g., Empatica E4 and Shimmer 3GSR+) to leverage the notion of "quantified-self" and to compute physiological arousal and stress in various learning settings [14, 18].

Early use of eye-tracking for researching model comprehension is found in [35, 62], but these works mainly focus on capturing area of interest (i.e. what the modeler is looking at). Later, eye-tracking is also used for capturing other parameters such as cognitive load in process model comprehension [6, 64]. The toolset has lately been extended to include wristbands for capturing for instance EDA [1, 65]. Papers in the area primarily mention that a more extensive treatment with other neuroscience and biometric techniques is to be tried as the next step [67]. So far techniques have not been used in a combined fashion for investigating model comprehension as we have done in the work presented in this paper.

A lot of work is done on model comprehension more generally [27] but note that it is primarily cognitive aspects that are investigated. [31] list specifically as one of limitation of existing work that one has not looked at emotional aspects. [1, 47] also reminds on the use of other ways of collecting data, including video and sound of the modeler while talking aloud on how he/she thinks when modeling, combined with tracking the activities done on screen and retrospectives of activities done.

3   Method

We have in the work presented in this paper collected data from an experiment investigating the comprehension of visual models and textual representations of the same settings. The main research question pursued in this paper is:

RQ1: What are the differences in affective and cognitive processes across different levels of process model comprehension?

We use Cognitive Load Theory (CLT) [38] to investigate the cognitive processes and the Affective Learning Framework (ALF) [11] to investigate the affective processes. Level of comprehension is judged based on the performance in answering comprehension question based on using information from the process model.

The set-up of the experiment is illustrated in Fig. 1 (from [28]).

The sensors used were like those used in [28], since we already were experienced with using this set-up in similar tasks (code comprehension and debugging). In addition, we included the use of a wristband. We briefly describe the sensors below:

1. EEG data: The EEG signals were recorded with a 20-channel ENOBIO device following the international 10–20 system, as shown in Fig. 1. The raw EEG signal data were recorded at a 500 Hz using a portable EEG cap and divided into the following band powers: delta (below 4 Hz), theta $- \theta$ (4–7 Hz), alpha $- \alpha$ (8–12 Hz), and beta $- \beta$ (18–30 Hz). The Fz electrode in the middle of the skull was used as a signal reference electrode, two channels were used for Electrooculography (EOG) correction, one channel for electric reference, and three Channels Accelerometer with sampling rate at 100 Hz.
2. Gaze data: To record gaze, we used a Tobii X3–12 eye-tracking device at a 120 Hz sampling rate and using a 5-point calibration. The device is non-invasive and mounted at the bottom of a computer screen. The screen resolution was 1920 x 1080 and participants were 50–70 cm away from the screen. All sat on a non-wheeled chair.
3. Facial expression data: To capture face expressions we used LogiTech web camera, pointed straight at the subject from the screen, capturing video at 30 frames-per-second (FPS). The web camera focus zoomed at 150% onto the faces of the participants. During the tasks, the students exhibited a minimal body and gesture interaction;

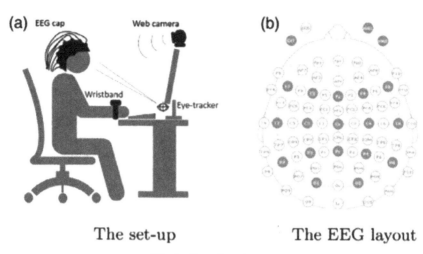

Fig. 1. Experiment setup.

hence, the video recordings hold high quality data from students' facial expressions. The video resolution was 640 x 480.

4. The Wristband was positioned at the left wrist (unless the tester was left-handed in case it was put on the right wrist). The device was an Empatica E4. We extracted the following features: mean, median, variance, skewness, maximum, minimum of (1) Blood volume pressure, (2) Electrodermal activity (EDA), (3) heart rate and (4) Temperature.

All sensors' data was synchronized by having all devices' clocks synchronized with the computers that participants were using in the experiment.

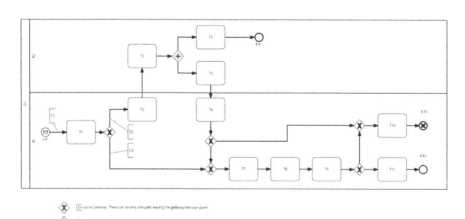

Fig. 2. Illustrating the type of model.

The experiment tasks redo parts of the experiment of [46] which focused on the comprehension of different models and texts for different task types. A focus in [46] was to investigate different business process models task types as for appropriateness of textual or BPMN – models. This is not the focus in the current paper, due to the experiment setup, we chose a somewhat limited coverage of the tasks used in [46], primarily including comprehension for search and recognition and inference tasks.

The experimental tasks refer to two separate cases of typical business processes: a Goods Receipt Handling Process (GHP) and a Procure-to-Pay Process (PPP). The structure of the GHP process is seen in Fig. 2. The models provided in the experiment had meaningful textual labels. The models were the same as used in [46] reimplemented in the modeling tool Signavio. We used existing models from another experiment from colleagues to be able to do certain comparisons on differences in comprehension levels on the different models and representation formats. In [46] they first created a BPMN diagram for each case and then constructed a corresponding text according to the formally defined transformation rules of [26]. We also reused the texts from [46]. The PPP case is regarded as more complex than the GHP, because it had more activities, organizational units, and business objects. For the GHP case, the total number of elements (pools, lanes, events, gateways, and activities) in the BPMN model is 24. The text has 136 words. For the PPP case, the BPMN model contains 31 elements, whereas the PPP text is expressed in 255 words. Subjects were randomly assigned and counterbalanced on if they first answered questions related to the text of one of the cases and a BPMN-model of the other or vice versa. For each case, the participants had to work on two of the four task types in [46]:

- Search and recognition tasks: First, participants worked on a set of schema-based search and recognition tasks with multiple-choice answers adapted from process model comprehension experiments. An example of a question in the search part included "What is the next task after setting invoice as payable?" These questions required participants to scan or locate a piece of information. Recognition questions were formulated in an open way such as "List only six activities which are observable… When a delivery note without purchase order is approved from the point when the delivery is identified until the goods are placed in stock." Here, participants had to recognize the sequence of activities in the process description.
- Inference tasks: Participants were required to integrate prior knowledge with the process description to provide the right answer to a multiple-choice question as "Yes," "No," and "Unknown." There were questions for which "Unknown" was the correct answer when essential information to answer the question was missing in the material.

The same sequence of tasks was presented afterwards for the second case. After each of the two cases, a NASA TLX [60] form was filled with self-reporting of the subjective experience of the difficulty of the previous tasks. Before the tasks the informants also gave an indication of their prior knowledge of text-based, model-based, and BPMN-based representation formats, knowledge of English, and of the two domains. The datasets presented in this article are not readily available because due to the ethics regulations we cannot share the data in full. Test material is available on request from the first author.

After getting permission from the national ethics board, the experiment took place. After signing a consent form, a total of 68 persons (primarily students and employees at NTNU) took part in the experiment that was done in the Autumn and Winter of 2023–2024.

3.1 Data Preprocessing

Before usage, the data had to be pre-processed, which entailed also discarding some of the experiments due to errors in readings.

EEG Data. First, an Independent Component Analysis (ICA) was used to remove the noise from the jaw movements. We also applied an EOG filter (in-build function in the ENOBIO software for neural data processing) to remove the noise from the blinks and the eye-brow movements, and an additional filter to remove the noise from the tongue movements. A 60 Hz line filter was also used to remove any noise coming from the interference within the EEG wires.

Wristband Data. There were four data streams originating from the E4 wristband. These four data streams, HRV, EDA, Skin Temperature, and blood volume pulse (BVP), were analyzed using a simple smoothing function to remove any unwanted spikes in the time series. We used a moving window of 100 samples and overlapping windows of 50 samples between two consecutive windows for the analysis. HRV, BVP, and skin temperature are some of the physiological response data that are susceptible to a wide range of subjective and contextual biases. Time of day, physical health condition, gender, ageing, overnight sleep, and a variety of other factors can contribute to these biases. To remove the subjective and contextual biases from the data, the first 30 seconds of all four streams of data were used to normalize the remainder of the time series for everyone, to remove the subjective and contextual biases from the data.

Gaze Data. Tobii's default algorithm (i.e., in-build function in the Tobii software for gaze data processing) was used to identify fixations and saccades[1] (for details please see [37]). A filter (i.e., in-build function in the Tobii software) was used to remove the raw gaze points that were classified as blinks.

Facial Expression Data. In most of the frames in the video recordings only one face was visible. However, sometimes the experimenter appeared in the view of the camera. Due to the settings of the experimental space, the experimenter could only appear to the right side of the student. Moreover, the algorithm in the OpenFace recognition software gave each face in the frame an ID from left to right. This means that in the frames where both the experimenter and the participant were present, the participant's face ID was always zero. For frames with two faces (as this was the highest number of faces in any frame) the experimenter's face that had an ID value of one was systematically removed.

After pre-processing we had data from 57 persons to be used for further analysis.

---

[1] A saccade is a quick, simultaneous movement of both eyes between two or more phases of fixation.

4   Results

The survey started with a self-assessment on skills in working with text, diagrams in general and BPMN in particular for documenting business processes using four questions on a 1-5 scale (coded 1-5, 5 being the highest). Descriptive statistics for these variables are found in Table 1. Text expertise is found to be significantly higher than the BPMN expertise (t (53) = 7.5, p < .00001).

Table 1. Descriptive data on skill assessment

	N	Min	Max	Mean	STD
Text expertise	57	4	20	13,91	4,189
Diagram expertise	57	4	20	13,19	3,676
BPMN expertise	53	4	20	7,94	4,189

The results on comprehension tasks related to the two models (GHP and PPP, presented in the previous section is found in Table 2). Maximum score is 1 (all questions answered correctly). There is a significant task based difference between the GHP and PPP (t(55) = 8.38, p = .00001). The scores for GHP are significantly higher than the scores for PPP (the more complex model). There is no order effect on the GHP score (t(55) = −0.9, p = .37) or the PPP Score (t(55) = −0.6, p = .52). This means that when looking on all tasks done, there was no significance difference between the performance on text comprehension and model comprehension, which might have been expected based on the results from [46]. One thing that might influence this is the significantly lower (self-reported) expertise on BPMN than on text.

Table 2. Descriptive data on comprehension performance

	N	Min	Max	Mean	STD
GHP score	57	,47	1	,83	,10
PPP Score	57	,39	,91	,65	,12

In the experiment, data on many features were collected from the sensors. We wanted to look on areas also found significant in [28], all of which was backed in literature as potentially significant for performance of cognitive tasks as will be described below. In addition, we included a test for drowsiness since most experiments were done in the afternoon.

The areas which correlated with a significant difference in performance (using Pearson correlation) are described below, and the results are found in Table 3. Below, we describe each measurement. We will discuss the results in the next section.

Backtracks. A backtrack is defined as a saccade that went to the part of the screen which is not in the usual forward reading direction and had already been visited by the participant. Backtracks would represent rereading behavior while getting the information from the BPMN-model. The notion of term rereading in the present study was slightly different than what is used in existing research (for example, [16, 32, 40]). The difference comes from that in the present study, the participants did not reread the whole text/model completely, but they can refer to the previously seen content on the screen. We counted the number of backtracks on the screen as a scan-path variable.

Information Processing Index is the ratio of the global to local processing. Global processing is defined as a series of short fixations and long saccades in each time window. While the local processing is defined by the series of long fixations and short saccades in each time window. A high value of this index indicates a large area of screen explored per unit time. This index shows how much information is received by the modeller in each period [42, 56].

Average Attention. This is the average fixation duration of the participants in each time-window, indicating the average attention exerted by them on the task.

Saccade Velocity. This is the velocity of the saccades. This measurement has been found to be associated with the perceived difficulty of the problem-solving task. Higher velocity indicates lower perceived difficulty [13].

Frustration, Boredom, Confusion. These are captured using the action units from the faces in the recorded facial videos. An overview of action units is found in Fig. 3. For example, detecting frustration is based on AU12, AU43; confusion is based on AU1, AU4, AU7, AU12; and boredom is based on AU4, AU7, AU12. The combinations of action units that can be used to calculate different facial expressions is inspired by [30].

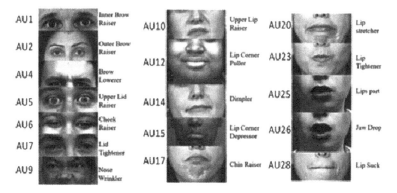

Fig. 3. Action units.

Stress. The heart rate variability (HRV) has been used to measure stress in educational [55] and problem-solving [33] contexts. In several recent contributions (independent studies, meta-analysis, and systematic literature reviews), HRV-based measurements have been shown to be an appropriate measure [4, 8, 53, 61].

Engagement. This is captured by wristband using EDA as the data source. This is a combination of two measurements: Number of EDA peaks and phasic EDA levels. The number of EDA peaks is computed using the same method as described by [14] and is associated with physiological arousal and engagement [20, 25]. Furthermore, the EDA signal is comprised of two parts: the tonic and phasic components. The tonic component of the EDA signal is the one with slow-evolving patterns. The phasic component of the EDA signal is the one with rapid changes and is found to be related to physiological arousal. In this paper, we consider only the mean phasic EDA component as a measure of physiological arousal and engagement.

Convergent Thinking. To compute convergent thinking from EEG signals, the following steps were followed: (a) compute the discrete Fourier transform (DFT) of the signal; (b) apply two band pass filters for computing the delta (1–3 Hz), theta (3–7 Hz) alpha (8–13 Hz), beta (13–30 Hz); (c) extract the signal from the outputs of the filters by using an inverse DFT; (d) compute the power per second for the beta signals (power = root mean square of the amplitude); (e) compute the mean of all the positive slopes for beta waves. Beta activity (13–30 Hz), which is an irregular pattern occurs mostly during alertness and active thinking [15]. The band frequency has been associated with decision making, problem solving, and information processing [44], and concentration and intense mental activity [57].

Table 3. Overview of correlations between measurements and comprehension performance

Modality	Measurement	Sensor measure	GHP score		PPP Score	
			R	P	R	P
Eye-tracking	Backtracks	Scanpath	–		−0.64	.000001
	Information processing index	Scanpath - ratio of the global to local processing	0.45	.0003	–	–
	Average attention	Fixation duration	0.39	.002	0.33	.01
	Familiarity/expertise (Perceived difficulty)	Saccadic velocity	0.36	.005	0.50	.00005
Face	Frustration	AU12, AU43 (facial action units)	−0.48	.0001	−0.47	.0001
	Boredom	AU4, AU7, AU12	−0.26	.04	−0.33	.009
	Confusion	AU1, AU4, AU7, AU12	−0.38	.002	−0.27	.03
Wristband	Stress	Heart rate variability (HRV)	−0.28	.03	−0.29	.02
	Engagement	Number of EDA peaks and phasic EDA levels	0.42	.001	0.45	.0004
EEG	Convergent thinking	Upper beta-band power	0.38	.003	0.43	.0006
	Memory load	Theta band power	0.31	.01	0.26	.04
	Drowsiness	Delta band power	−0.49	.00008	−0.51	.00003

Memory Load. To compute the memory load from EEG signals, the first four steps (a–d) from the computation of convergent thinking were followed. Then, the mean theta band power was calculated as the measurement of memory load [34].

Drowsiness. To compute the drowsiness from EEG signals, the first four steps (a–d) from the computation of convergent thinking were followed. Then, the mean delta band power was calculated as the measurement of drowsiness [10].

5 Discussion

The findings from our experiment demonstrate that particular cognitive-affective states are relevant and influential to both the cognitive process of model comprehension and the performance of model interpreters, and in this way are part of answering RQ1.

First of all, we find that all of the modalities provide information on the performance of the people doing the comprehension tasks. The experiments were for practical purposes done in the afternoon, and due to this we investigated the effect of drowsiness (and area not investigated in [28]), finding this to strongly negatively correlated to the performance of the comprehension of both the models. Apart from that we found many similar results as in the study on code comprehension, with some marked differences. In [28], frustration was positively correlated with performance, whereas in our study it was the opposite. The tasks done in [28] were not only on comprehension though, but also included debugging, thus active problem-solving, where the situation that one through a phase of frustration\can solve a problem might be positive (if one is able to solve it). When the task is just comprehension, the frustration is negative. As in [28] boredom and confusion were negatively correlated to the performance.

The other area where we differed was on memory load, which was positively correlated with performance, in contrast to in the code debugging task in [28]. Those already familiar with BPMN were probably using their knowledge on the notation in the comprehension of the model. Those not familiar with the notation would have less memory load, but also would perform poorly.

Convergent thinking and attention were as expected positively correlated with performance. Another area which not surprisingly correlated positively with performance was expertise.

Use of wristband, being new compared to [28] illustrate the negative correlation of stress, and positive correlation of engagement on comprehension performance.

The implications from our method articulate the benefits of using MMLA as a sufficiently sensitive technique to capture the complexities of cognitive engagement (compared to the long-standing self-report measures [19]), utilizing process-related data generated with sensors from the moment-to-moment heart rate, EDA, facial expressions, gaze, and EEG activity of the brain.

Model comprehension is an important aspect of modeling, since often a lot of model interpreters are involved, not themselves having developed the model, both in the modeling process [27] and having to relate to models for guidance of work [23, 24].

Considering the effects from the affective, cognitive, and behavioral dimension of model comprehension on the performance of model interpreters, our method has implications for those communicating knowledge through model representations in the struggle to overcome the one-size-fits-all approach. Our method provides researchers and practitioners with a set of multimodal data measures which have been extracted from related works and allows them to account for model interpreters cognitive, affective, and behavioral processes. We agree that this list is not exhaustive but provides a set of measures that are widely accepted in the learning technology literature.

6   Concluding Remarks

We have in this paper presented initial results from the use of biometric techniques in Multi-modal learning analytics for the understanding of aspects influencing modeling performance. In the current experiment, we have focused on model comprehension, in particular because it is easier to do model comprehension tasks in a close to natural way, at the same time as one is gathering biometric data along all modalities. Thus, if we had not been able to collect data on model comprehension, it would not be worthwhile to attempt to collect data on modeling tasks that need more movement, e.g. model validation and correction tasks, and modeling from scratch. In particular, extensive movement strongly influences the possibility to collect EEG-data, which is why this is just another paper on model comprehension. In later research we plan to collect data both in connection to other comprehension tasks, but also in connection to individual and pair-wise model validation and modeling activities. Some areas we plan to investigate (some using the current collected data) are:

1. Investigate the usage of the brain when working with conceptual/visual models in more detail, looking not only on the main brainwaves, but on where the brain activity is situated.
2. Investigate the usage of the brain when working with conceptual/visual models as compared to how it operates when using a text expressing the same information, and how combined models including both text and diagrams with overlapping information can be beneficial.
3. Investigate the usage of the brain when using different modeling languages (BPMN vs. UML AD for process modeling for instance, or OntoUML vs. UML for information and ontology modeling).
4. Investigate the use of abstraction mechanisms and model decomposition when representing larger models that do not fit on a single diagram.
5. How do layout and other aspects of secondary notation (influencing empirical quality [23]) influence model comprehension?
6. Investigate the usage of the brain when interpreting models with syntactic errors, compared to models without syntactic errors. As seen in [24] different syntactic quality errors seem to have different influence on model comprehension.
7. Investigate the usage of the brain when interpreting models with semantic errors, compared to models without semantic errors.
8. How can detected information on e.g., frustration, confusion and cognitive load be used to provide feedback tools and other scaffolding to support the modeler, for instance to reduce cognitive load in future tasks?
   a. Support of peer review of models and other model validation tasks.
   b. Support modeling processes (facilitated, pair modeling, individual modeling).

9. Support of learning modeling languages enabling a richer palette to be used (scaffolding of modeling language learning). In most cases [23, 24] a very small part of BPMN for instance is used, making it harder to make precise models, and thus increasing the chance of errors in later interpretations.

10. Leaps of abstraction. Seamless movement between abstraction levels: What happens when humans go from type to meta-type/meta-meta-type and back, when we are representing knowledge, for instance as conceptual models.

Whereas most work on using biometrics in the way we have described here is done in a controlled laboratory setting, we plan to also use biometrics in the understanding of the use of models in an organizational setting, similar to [29]. We also will study the data in parallel to other ways of getting understanding of the process of modeling through logs, use of talk-aloud protocols, video-analysis and doing retrospectives.

Acknowledgements. We would like to thank all the participants in the experiment. Special thanks to Lea Marie Braun and Alevtina Roshchina for assisting in running the experiment.

References

1. Abbad-Andaloussi, A., Burattin, A., Slaats, T., Kindler, E., Weber, B.: Complexity in declarative process models: metrics and multi-modal assessment of cognitive load. Expert Syst. Appl. **233** (2023)

2. Andrade, A., Danish, J.A., Maltese, A.V.: A measurement model of gestures in an embodied learning environment: accounting for temporal dependencies. J. Learn. Anal. **4**(3), 18–46 (2017)

3. Antonenko, P., Paas, F., Grabner, R., Van Gog, T.: Using electroencephalography to measure cognitive load. Educ. Psychol. Rev. **22**(4), 425–438 (2010)

4. Antoun, M., Edwards, K.M., Sweeting, J., Ding, D.: The acute physiological stress response to driving: a systematic review. PLoS ONE **12**(10), e0185517 (2017)

5. Baker, R., D'Mello, S.K., Rodrigo, M.M.T., Graesser, A.C.: Better to be frustrated than bored: the incidence, persistence, and impact of learners' cognitive–affective states during interactions with three different computer-based learning environments. Int. J. Hum. Comput. Stud. **68**(4), 223–241 (2010)

6. Batista Duarte, R., Silva da Silveira, D., de Albuquerque Brito, V., Lopes, C.S.: A systematic literature review on the usage of eye-tracking in understanding process models. Bus. Process Manag. J. **27**(1), 346 (2021)

7. Blikstein, P., Worsley, M.: Multimodal learning analytics and education data mining: using computational technologies to measure complex learning tasks. J. Learn. Anal. **3**(2), 220–238 (2016)

8. Bravi, A., et al.: Do physiological and pathological stresses produce different changes in heart rate variability? Front. Physiol. **4**, 197 (2013)

9. Calvo, R.A., D'Mello, S.: Affect detection: an interdisciplinary review of models, methods, and their applications. IEEE Trans. Affect. Comput. **1**, 18–37 (2010)

10. Craig, A., Tran, Y., Wijesuriya, N., Nguyen, H.: Regional brain wave activity changes associated with fatigue. Psychophysiology **49**(4), 574–582 (2012)

11. D'Mello, S., Graesser, A.: Dynamics of affective states during complex learning. Learn. Instr. **22**, 145–157 (2012)

12. Di Lascio, E., Gashi, S., Santini, S.: Unobtrusive assessment of students' emotional engagement during lectures using electrodermal activity sensors. Proc. ACM Interact. Mob. Wearable Ubiquit. Technol. **2**(3), 1–21 (2018)
13. Di Mitri, D., Scheffel, M., Drachsler, H., Börner, D., Ternier, S., Specht, M.: Learning pulse: a machine learning approach for predicting performance in self-regulated learning using multimodal data. In: Proceedings of the Seventh International Learning Analytics & Knowledge Conference, pp. 188–197. ACM (2017)
14. Di Stasi, L.L., Catena, A., Cañas, J.J., Macknik, S.L., Martinez-Conde, S.: Saccadic velocity as an arousal index in naturalistic tasks. Neurosci. Biobehav. Rev. **37**(5), 968–975 (2013)
15. Dietrich, A., Kanso, R.: A review of EEG, ERP, and neuroimaging studies of creativity and insight. Psychol. Bull. **136**(5), 822 (2010)
16. Dowhower, S.L.: Effects of repeated reading on second-grade transitional readers' fluency and comprehension. Reading Res. Q. 389–406 (1987)
17. Duchowski, A.T., et al.: The index of pupillary activity: measuring cognitive load vis-à-vis task difficulty with pupil oscillation. In: Proceedings of the 2018 CHI Conference on Human Factors in Computing Systems, pp. 1–13 (2018)
18. Giannakos, M.N., Sharma, K., Papavlasopoulou, S., Pappas, I.O., Kostakos, V.: Fitbit for learning: towards capturing the learning experience using wearable sensing. Int. J. Hum. Comput. Stud. **136**, 102384 (2020)
19. Greene, B.A.: Measuring cognitive engagement with self-report scales: reflections from over 20 years of research. Educ. Psychol. **50**(1), 14–30 (2015)
20. Hasson, U., et al.: Enhanced intersubject correlations during movie viewing correlate with successful episodic encoding. Neuron **57**(3), 452–462 (2008). https://doi.org/10.1016/j.neuron.2007.12.009
21. Jensen, O., Tesche, C.D.: Frontal theta activity in humans increases with memory load in a working memory task. Eur. J. Neurosci. **15**, 1395–1399 (2002)
22. Jermann, P., Nüssli, M.A.: Effects of sharing text selections on gaze cross-recurrence and interaction quality in a pair programming task. In: Proceedings of the ACM 2012 Conference on Computer Supported Cooperative Work, pp. 1125–1134 (2012)
23. Krogstie, J.: Quality in Business Process Modeling. Springer, Cham (2016)
24. Krogstie, J., Heggset, M., Wesenberg, H.: Business process modeling of a quality system in a petroleum industry company. In: vom Brocke, J., Mendling, J. (eds.) Business Process Management Cases, pp. 557–575. Springer, Cham (2018). https://doi.org/10.1007/978-3-319-58307-5_30
25. Leiner, D., et al.: EDA positive change: a simple algorithm for electrodermal activity to measure general audience arousal during media exposure. Commun. Methods Measur. **6**(4), 237–250 (2012). https://doi.org/10.1080/19312458.2012.732627
26. Leopold, H., Mendling, J., Polyvyanyy, A.: Supporting process model validation through natural language generation. IEEE Trans. Software Eng. **40**(8), 818–840 (2014)
27. Malinova, M., Mendling, J.: Cognitive diagram understanding and task performance in system analysis and design. Manag. Inf. Syst. Q. **46** (2022)
28. Mangaroska, K., Sharma, K., Gašević, D., Giannakos, M.: Exploring students' cognitive and affective states during problem solving through multimodal data: lessons learned from a programming activity J. Comput. Assisted Learn. (2022)
29. Martinez-Maldonado, R., et al.: Lessons learnt from a multimodal learning analytics deployment in-the-wild. ACM Trans. Comput.-Hum. Interact. **31**, 1 (2023)
30. McDaniel, B., et al.: Facial features for affective state detection in learning environments. In: Proceedings of the Annual Meeting of the Cognitive Science Society, vol. 29, no. 29 (2007)
31. Mendling, J., Malinova, M.: Experimental evidence on the cognitive effectiveness of diagrams. Procedia Comput. Sci. **197**, 10–15 (2022)

32. Millis, K.K., King, A.: Rereading strategically: the influences of comprehension ability and a prior reading on the memory for expository text. Read. Psychol. **22**(1), 41–65 (2001)
33. Mirjafari, S., et al.: Differentiating higher and lower job performers in the workplace using mobile sensing. Proc. ACM Interact. Mob. Wearable Ubiquitous Technol. **3**(2), 1–24 (2019)
34. Missonnier, P., et al.: Frontal theta event-related synchronization: comparison of directed attention and working memory load effects. J. Neural Transm. **113**, 1477–1486 (2006)
35. Nordbotten, J.C., Crosby, M.E.: The effect of graphic style on data model interpretation. Inf. Syst. J. **9**, 139–155 (1999)
36. Ochoa, X., Domínguez, F., Guamán, B., Maya, R., Falcones, G., Castells, J.: The rap system: automatic feedback of oral presentation skills using multimodal analysis and low-cost sensors. In: Proceedings of the 8th International Conference on Learning Analytics and Knowledge, pp. 360–364. ACM (2018)
37. Olsen, A.: The Tobii I-VT Fixation Filter, Algorithm description. Tobii Technology (2012)
38. Paas, F., Van Merriënboer, J.J.: Instructional control of cognitive load in the training of complex cognitive tasks. Edu. Psych. Rev. **6**, 351–371 (1994)
39. Pappas, I., Sharma, K., Mikalef, P., Giannakos, M.: Visual aesthetics of E-commerce websites: an eye-tracking approach (2018)
40. Paris, S.G., Jacobs, J.E.: The benefits of informed instruction for children's reading awareness and comprehension skills. Child Dev. 2083–2093 (1984)
41. Pekrun, R.: The control-value theory of achievement emotions: assumptions, corollaries, and implications for educational research and practice. Educ. Psychol. Rev. **18**(4), 315–341 (2006)
42. Poole, A., Ball, L.J.: Eye tracking in HCI and usability research. In: Encyclopedia of Human Computer Interaction, pp. 211–219. IGI Global (2006)
43. Pope, A.T., Bogart, E.H., Bartolome, D.S.: Biocybernetic system evaluates indices of operator engagement in automated task. Biol. Psychol. **40**(1–2), 187–195 (1995)
44. Ray, W.J., Cole, H.W.: EEG alpha activity reflects attentional demands, and beta activity reflects emotional and cognitive processes. Science **228**(4700), 750–752 (1985)
45. Razoumnikova, O.M.: Functional organization of different brain areas during convergent and divergent thinking: an EEG investigation. Cogn. Brain Res. **10**(1–2), 11–18 (2000)
46. Ritchi, H., Jans, M., Mendling, J., Reijers, H.A.: The influence of business process representation on performance of different task types. J. Inf. Syst. **34**(1), 167–194 (2020)
47. Rosenthal, K., Strecker, S., Snoeck, M.: Modeling difficulties in creating conceptual data models. SOSYM **22**, 1005–1030 (2023)
48. Rus, V., D'Mello, S., Hu, X., Graesser, A.: Recent advances in conversational intelligent tutoring systems. AI Mag. **34**(3), 42–54 (2013)
49. Schmid, P.C., Mast, M.S., Bombari, D., Mast, F.W., Lobmaier, J.S.: How mood states affect information processing during facial emotion recognition: an eye tracking study. Swiss J. Psychol. (2011)
50. Schrepfer, M., Wolf, J., Mendling, J., Reijers, H.A.: The impact of secondary notation on process model understanding. In: Persson, A., Stirna, J. (eds.) PoEM 2009. LNBIP, vol. 39, pp. 161–175. Springer, Heidelberg (2009). https://doi.org/10.1007/978-3-642-05352-8_13
51. Seipajarvi, S.M., et al.: Measuring psychosocial stress with heart rate variability-based methods in different health and age groups. Physiol. Measur. **43**(5), 055002 (2022)
52. Sharma, K., Leftheriotis, I., Giannakos, M.: Utilizing interactive surfaces to enhance learning, collaboration and engagement: insights from learners' gaze and speech. Sensors **20**(7), 1964 (2020)
53. Sharma, K., Papavlasopoulou, S., Giannakos, M.: Joint emotional state of children and perceived collaborative experience in coding activities. In: Proceedings of the 18th ACM International Conference on Interaction Design and Children, pp. 133–145. ACM (2019)

54. Sharma, K., Caballero, D., Verma, H., Jermann, P., Dillenbourg, P.: Looking AT versus looking THROUGH: a dual eye-tracking study in MOOC context. International Society of the Learning Sciences. Inc. [ISLS] (2015)
55. Sharma, K., Papamitsiou, Z., Giannakos, M.: Building pipelines for educational data using AI and multimodal analytics: a "grey-box" approach. Br. J. Edu. Technol. **50**(6), 3004–3031 (2019)
56. Sharma, K., Lee-Cultura, S., Giannakos, M.: Keep calm and do not carry-forward: toward sensor-data driven AI agent to enhance human learning. Front. Artif. Intell. **4**, 713176 (2022)
57. Shemyakina, N., Dan'ko, S.: Changes in the power and coherence of the beta EEG band in subjects performing creative tasks using emotionally significant and emotionally neutral words. Hum. Physiol. **33**, 20–26 (2007)
58. Stern, J.A., Brown, T.B.: Bio-behavior analysis systems LLC St Louis MO. Detection of Human Fatigue (2005)
59. Thiruchselvam, R., Blechert, J., Sheppes, G., Rydstrom, A., Gross, J.J.: The temporal dynamics of emotion regulation: an EEG study of distraction and reappraisal. Biol. Psychol. **87**(1), 84–92 (2011)
60. TLX. https://humansystems.arc.nasa.gov/groups/TLX/. Accessed 16 Mar 2023
61. van Loon, A.W., et al.: The effects of school-based interventions on physiological stress in adolescents: a meta-analysis. Stress. Health **38**(2), 187–209 (2022)
62. Weber, B., et al.: Fixation patterns during process model creation: initial steps toward neuro-adaptive process modeling environments. In: 49th Hawaii International Conference on System Sciences (HICSS), Koloa, HI, USA (2016)
63. Weber, B., Fischer, T., Riedl, R.: Brain and autonomic nervous system activity measurement in software engineering: a systematic literature review. J. Syst. Softw. **178** (2021)
64. Winter, M., Neumann, H., Pryss, R., Probst, T., Reichert, M.: Defining gaze patterns for process model literacy – exploring visual routines in process models with diverse mappings. Expert Syst. Appl. **213** (2023)
65. Winter, M., Bredemeyer, C., Reichert, M., Neumann, H., Pryss, R.: A Comparative Cross-Sectional Study on Process Model Comprehension driven by Eye Tracking and Electrodermal Activity Research Square (2023). https://doi.org/10.21203/rs.3.rs-3705553/v1
66. Xiong, J., Zuo, M.: What does existing NeuroIS research focus on? Inf. Syst. **89** (2020)
67. Zimoch, M., Mohring, T., Pryss, R., Probst, T., Schlee, W., Reichert, M.: Using insights from cognitive neuroscience to investigate the effects of event-driven process chains on process model comprehension. In: Teniente, E., Weidlich, M. (eds.) BPM 2017. LNBIP, vol. 308, pp. 446–459. Springer, Cham (2018). https://doi.org/10.1007/978-3-319-74030-0_35

A Method for Digital Business Ecosystem Design: Evaluation of Two Cases in the Maritime Dataspaces

Chen Hsi Tsai[1]([envelope]) [iD], Ben Hellmanzik[2] [iD], Jelena Zdravkovic[1] [iD], Janis Stirna[1] [iD], and Kurt Sandkuhl[2] [iD]

[1] Stockholm University, Kista, Sweden
{chenhsi.tsai,jelenaz,js}@dsv.su.se
[2] University of Rostock, Rostock, Germany
{ben.hellmanzik,kurt.sandkuhl}@uni-rostock.de

Abstract. In contrast to traditional business models, Digital Business Ecosystems (DBE) have several distinctive features - heterogeneity of involved actors, symbiosis in the exchange of resources, co-evolution of their interactions, and self-organisation. Designing DBEs is a task demanding a well-defined DBE's scope, roles and responsibilities of the actors, their interactions and dependencies, as well as versatile technologies and data. The study focuses on two DBEs – Marispace-X and Skippo in the maritime domain to capture the tenets of the blue economy with dataspaces. Because the design approaches to DBE are scarce due to the paradigm's novelty, the study aims to evaluate a model-based design method, DBEmap. The evaluation results concerning practitioners' perceived usefulness of the DBEmap and its support for integrating DBE-related perspectives and designing and managing DBE resilience are presented.

Keywords: Digital Business Ecosystem · Dataspace · Method Evaluation

1 Introduction

Digital Business Ecosystems (DBE) are interconnected networks of organisations, individuals, and technologies that collaborate, interact, and transact within the digital setting [1, 2]. They are characterised by their complex and evolving nature due to the involvement of diverse actors each having unique interests, responsibilities, and requirements while interacting through a wide range of digital assets and activities, including online platforms, digital services, and data exchanges that need to be interoperable and continuously integrated. These characteristics, in turn, boost the magnitude of the involved entities and tasks, leading to various challenges and difficulties in efficient DBE management [3]. Yet, [4] finds that studies of DBE with different kind of actors are few, while well-designed industry ecosystem architectures are not many.

Enterprise modelling is useful for analysis of complex problems related to ICT in organisations. In [5], we have, following the requirements of industry and practitioners

H. van der Aa et al. (Eds.): BPMDS 2024/EMMSAD 2024, LNBIP 511, pp. 175–190, 2024.
https://doi.org/10.1007/978-3-031-61007-3_14

and by conducting action research in a real DBE setting, proposed a model-based method for the DBE design. This method, called DBEmap, has undergone several development iterations and is being evaluated in practice to ensure that the method is viable, effective, aligned with the needs and goals of all the roles and actors being engaged in the business of an ecosystem, as well as supporting the system's resilience. To this end, the goals of this paper are to *elaborate and present an evaluation of the DBE design method proposed in [5] using two DBE cases in the maritime domain, namely, - Marispace-X in Germany and Skippo in Sweden.*

The context in which the method is evaluated is that of the maritime data management where multiple organisations need to collaborate in the same domain. This domain has challenges as pointed out in [6]. First, there is a "wide diversity" of different sensor formats. This variety leads to higher costs: searching, understanding and using the right data for the right application is (in terms of invested time) expensive. While standard-isation in some areas is low, it is questionable if solutions in this domain can benefit from more advanced automatisation techniques. Another problem is the multitude of different data structures. Data is not stored conveniently in one place, but in a lot of different places. Sometimes, meta-data is missing, while other times, data is duplicated or delayed. This, especially in the absence of data standardisation, leads to different issues with data interoperability.

One challenge is also the increased volume of data: through new technologies, e.g., autonomous platforms, it is now possible to produce yearlong accurate data. This increased volume, seen as significant in [7], is a challenge for most data management systems (being well-organised or not). On top of that comes the fact that a lot of newer sensors create new sensor formats. These need to be mapped to existing standards.

Another challenge that are especially important in a business context [6] is the gap between scientists and data users. Sharing of data is at the moment not a common practice because the feeling of "data ownership" by scientists is strong. The last problem the authors mention is the missing application of best practices in data management. The V of "Value" in the 5V of Big Data represents this issue: poor documented data may have no value without access to the team that collected the data.

Solutions to these problems need (i) utilising the concept of a *dataspace* [8] for managing the large-scale heterogeneous collections of data distributed over various data sources, and (ii) accompanying with the ecosystem design approach for getting different company actors together to jointly develop a DBE of the maritime domain.

The maritime domain has a significant innovation potential, e.g., the building of offshore windfarms, earning new resources, optimising of shipping routes, fisheries provide business opportunities for different stakeholders [9]. In this light, they propose Multi-Use or Multi-Purpose Platforms offshore. To realise such concepts, the building of new business models and accessing real data are unavoidable.

The challenges mentioned here are not unique to just the maritime sector. Similarly, in the manufacturing sector, data about various aspects of production needs to be shared among suppliers and business partners. This is nowadays referred to as co-production. While theoretical principles of co-production are straightforward, the design and man-agement of large and diverse suppliers' networks, their roles, offerings and performance need ecosystem thinking to be successful in practice.

The rest of the paper is structured as follows. Section 2 presents a background to DBEs and DBEmap. Section 3 describes the research design. Section 4 presents the application of DBEmap to the Marispace-X and Skippo cases, and the quantitative and qualitative evaluation results. In Sect. 5, a discussion and conclusions are provided.

2   Background to DBEs and the DBEmap Method

A DBE is defined as: "a socio-technical environment, enabled by shared digital platforms and ICTs, where loosely-coupled interdependent organisations and individuals in an economic community deliver, consume, or exchange resources and co-evolve their capabilities and roles. [10]" The unique characteristics, namely, the digital environment, heterogeneity, symbiosis, co-evolution, and self-organisation, stand out and contribute to the novel DBE theory focusing on resilience.

A DBE can be in three different phases [10] - *design phase* is the initiation phase of a DBE focusing on designing of the structure, such as architectures or platforms, and how the structure supports the integration of capabilities, core services or products, and DBE actors. A DBE becomes more stable during *deployment phase* when improvements are supported by analysis of its different aspects. During *management phase*, a stabilised DBE is continuously monitored and actively managed to facilitate changes leading to a more resilient system.

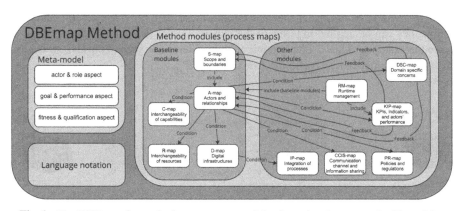

Fig. 1. The DBEmap, its method components, and the dependencies among its 11 modules

DBEmap is a method for DBE modelling proposed in [5]. DBEmap is engineered based on the needs and requirements elicited from various industries [10]. It is a modular method for design of new DBEs, or analysis and management of existing ones. It consists of the method components (Fig. 1): i) the meta-model with three aspects, ii) the 11 modules as method process maps, and iii) the language notation. To encourage the understanding of DBEmap, these components are made openly available via the study's website on the Open Science Framework (https://osf.io/zbdph/?view_only=6a1ff6d9e 9ec4361929179f35f3bf301).

The DBEmap method aims to support industrial practitioners and DBE researchers in designing, analysing, and managing DBEs. Thanks to its modularised feature, the method modules can be chosen and used in different order or simultaneously, depending on the needs of individual projects. The application of these modules allows the possibility of reusing existing enterprise architecture and enterprise modelling approaches. As analogues to polarised lenses, these modules are used for highlighting and investigating specific aspects or parts of multi-actor socio-technical constellations. For example, the lenses focusing on capability facilitate the identification and the understanding of the capabilities and their interchangeability (Fig. 2).

The method uses Situational Method Engineering as the underlying methodology and its Map approach [11], which facilitated modular DBE design that resolves the development of individual DBE's components: i) each having a work intention, ii) being applicable in a situation, and iii) in relation and dependencies with some other components. The method modules rely on underlying meta-models that define concepts and relationships valid for the module. The importance of DBE resilience is incorporated in the method in terms of the supporting goal structure with *resilience goals*, the analysis enabled by *resilience indicators*, and the *DBE roles* (driver, aggregator, modular producer, complementor, customer, end-user, governor, reputation guardian) ensuring resistant functioning.

Each method module, as a process map, targets a design and structural concern of a DBE. The five modules, namely *S-map, A-map, C-map, R-map, and D-map* are the baseline modules for design. The others are: *IP-map, PR-map, DSR-map, CCIS-map, KIP-map, and RM-map*. The dependencies among these maps provide a general guidance on how they can be applied in terms of the temporal order (shown in Fig. 1). Figure 2 shows the example of the C-map module with its intentions (green ellipses), strategies (arrows) and its dependency with the A-map module.

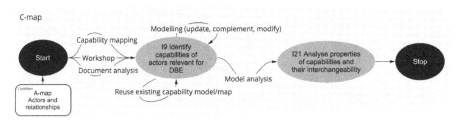

Fig. 2. The *Interchangeability of Capabilities* module (C-map) of the DBE method [5]

The actors are individuals and organisations that engage an DBE by taking specific *DBE roles* according to their capabilities, and accepting the corresponding responsibilities. These DBE roles are of vital significance for the DBE's design as they define specific responsibilities of the actors involved and provide underlying knowledge for the capabilities relevant to a DBE [10]. The interactions among the DBE actors are supported by the DBE's digital platform and its services, smart devices, cloud storage, etc. Note the difference between a *role* (or *generic role*) and a *DBE role* – a *role* concern actors' functions in business contexts, e.g., sea chart maker or healthcare provider, and is domain specific. *A DBE role* is a generalisation of the eight significant DBE roles with their corresponding responsibilities which are DBE specific.

3 Research Design

Adopting case study design, the DBEmap method established by a PhD design science research [12] project was applied to two DBEs – the Marispace-X and Skippo to evaluate the method as well as to facilitate the design and analysis of these DBEs.

The Maritime Smart Sensor Dataspace (Marispace-X) is a project of the German Gaia-X initiative. Based on the values of sovereignty, security, interoperability, and modularity, the goal is to improve data processing and the analysis of sensor data in the maritime domain. New opportunities to process data and create value are planned to be tested in different use cases (ammunition in the sea, critical infrastructure, biological climate protection, offshore-wind and a maritime test field). Among the expected benefits are increases in efficiency and cost reductions in data related problems, cross industry bundling of data, and a broader data availability. As we pointed out in the introduction, the need for a scalable and interoperable data platform in the maritime domain exists. However, according to [13], one of the main issues in the research of platforms is a bias towards successful cases, which are studied ex-post. The Marispace-X and the envisioned DBE is still in its design phase which provides an opportunity to apply the DBEmap method to help the actors in the DBE to reach a joint understanding of the emerging platform design, to steer the project in the right strategic direction, and to help with governance issues. While some of the issues of realising a dataspace in the industry and analyses of the different stakeholders in the dataspace have been conducted [14, 15], there is still a conceptual gap of the alignment in the DBE.

Skippo AB is a Swedish company aiming to simplify boat life in the Nordics through its DBE. By aggregating assets in the DBE and integrating various data layers in sea charts, Skippo has created and now provides innovative boating products and services related to boat navigation. Skippo's main challenges are integrating and packaging data into sea charts, sea charts data caching, and identifying erroneous data in sea charts. Skippo also needs to collaborate with other business actors to address these challenges.

This study presents a formative evaluation of the use of the method in both naturalistic and artificial settings. As part of the iterative evaluation process, this evaluation is one of the initial applications of the entirety of the method. The DBEmap method has been applied in workshop sessions with stakeholders in both Marispace-X and Skippo cases for designing and analysing their DBEs. A workshop protocol has been developed and pilot-tested for feasibility and quality improvement. After these workshop sessions, semi-structured interviews and a web-based questionnaire have been used to gather evaluation feedback. The questionnaire statements and the interview structure are available via the study's OSF website (c.f. link in Sect. 2).

4   Method Application and Evaluation

4.1   Modelling the Marispace-X DBE

Since the Marispace-X DBE was in its design phase, the workshop sessions focused on the design concerns – the scope of the Marispace-X DBE and onboarding of the relevant actors when applying the method (the sessions took place in November 2023 at the headquarters of North.io and in February 2024 via Teams). Following the workshop protocol and guidelines, hands-on approaches digital whiteboard and index-cards were used. The approaches were combined with modelling on a Miro Board where the DBE method language notation was defined (see Fig. 3) when applying the method modules – *S-map, A-map, C-map, and R-map* to the Marispace-X DBE.

While designing the actor structure using the *A-map*, it was understood that there were no existing actor models of the DBE. Hence, it was designed from scratch based on a study from the IEDS project [16] connected to the Gaia-X initiative. The study defines the relevant archetypes in already functioning ecosystems of the dataspace service kind. These archetypes, including *Service Provider, Data Provider, Cloud-Platform Provider, Data-Infrastructure Provider*, etc., were used for the discussion concerning the needed (generic) roles as the part of the initial Marispace-X DBE actor structure.

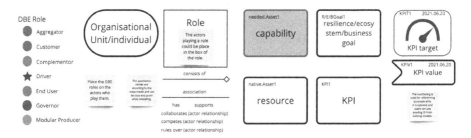

Fig. 3. The DBE method language notation

Figure 4 shows the actors who play, or need to play, generic and DBE roles. They were identified together with the needed (i.e., necessary in the DBE) and native (owned by an actor) capabilities and resources (*C-map* and *R-map* modules). E.g., the data-infrastructure provider generic role was considered necessary despite not knowing all the actors who could play this role. In this case, the participants agreed that Marispace-X needs an additional company (with a pseudo-name *Federator*) with all the partners as shareholders, to provide the central data infrastructure as suggested by needed capabilities related to dataspace and data integration and processing. The company Stackable would play this generic role to provide a critical software and Kubernetes operators as the resources for the data infrastructure.

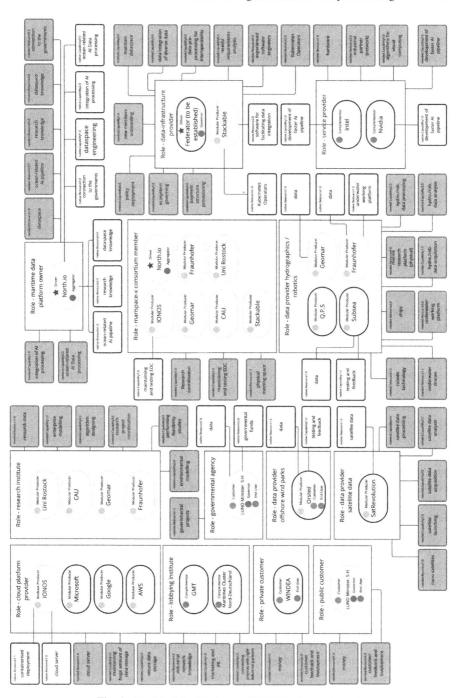

Fig. 4. Model of the Marispace-X DBE actors and assets

Based on the DBE roles' responsibilities, the participants suggested that the DBE role *Driver* is currently played by North.io but could be taken over by Federator once this actor would be established. North.io also plays the DBE role *Aggregator, meaning that* it would be packaging end-products or services aiming for customers and end-users through the dataspace, a digital platform, as suggested by the native assets, e.g., dataspace knowledge, dataspace engineering, integration of AI processing. The actor Federator (with the data-infrastructure provider generic role) will also have the responsibilities of ensuring the development and adherence of the Gaia compliance (sovereignty, security, interoperability and modularity) and the FAIR-Data principles, which means the actor would also play the DBE role *Governor*. The needed capabilities, such as policy deployment and ecosystem governing, suggested the importance of the actor Federator being able to ensure the compliance through its role and DBE role. The development and adherence of the Gaia compliance was acknowledged as a vital goal of the Marispace-X DBE. LUND Minsiter. S-H will be another actor playing the DBE role *Governor* as they govern the funds and projects and define regulations related to the maritime industry.

The DBE role *Modular Producer* was identified as being played by all the actors with the cloud platform provider generic role (IONOS, Microsoft, Google, AWS) providing needed assets cloud server and data storage; the research institute generic role (CAU, Uni Rostock, Geomar, Fraunhofer) supporting research related assets, e.g., research data and performing feasibility studies; the data provider generic roles with offshore wind parks, satellite data, and hydrographics/robotics (Orsted, SatRevolution, Q.P.S., Subsea, Geomar, Fraunhofer) bringing in related hardware and various data; and the data-infrastructure provider Stackable providing relevant critical resources.

The DBE role *Customer* and *End-User* are played by LUND Minsiter. S-H, WINDEA, and Orsted because they will be the ones using the Marispace-X dataspace and consuming services and products offered there.

The DBE role *Complementor* is played by GMT and Maritimes Cluster Nord-Deutschland with the lobbying institute generic role. As suggested by the needed assets, they will promote the Marispace-X project and ecosystem to other interested entities, meaning the lobbying services would complement the core products/services of the Marispace-X ecosystem. Furthermore, Intel and Nvidia with the service provider generic role take focus on the possibility of improving data visualisation and AI pipeline as ways to complement the core products/services.

The DBE role – *Reputation Guardian* was not incorporated in the design of the actor structure. For the Marispace-X ecosystem case, we identified the actors we have foreseen. This actor structure could change, meaning that the ecosystem could grow and stabilise with time and its actors may evolve and take on different roles. We argued that the maturity level of a DBE as a factor was a major reason for the reputation guardian DBE role not being able to be incorporated in this early design. More time is needed to allow the growth of the ecosystem, which could stimulate conversations among the actors to reach consensus on who would take the responsibilities of the *Reputation Guardian* in the Marispace-X ecosystem and thus cover the surveillance of actors' conditions.

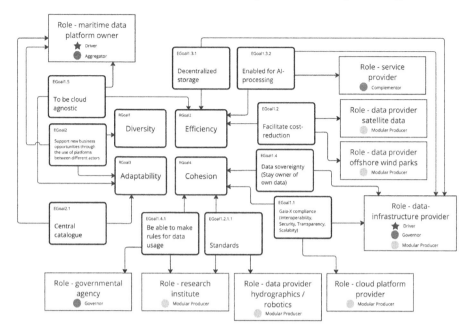

Fig. 5. Resilience goals supporting model for the design phase Marispace-X DBE

The design and analysis of resilience of the design phase Marispace-X DBE is conducted using the resilience goals supporting model (Fig. 5) and the resilience indicators [17]. The four resilience goals are: *Diversity* meaning the variety of DBE actors and the collection and variety of resources and capabilities they offer; *Efficiency* referring to resource productivity and utilisation with enabling capabilities among DBE actors; *Adaptability* in terms of the transparency - adaptation and flexibility for a DBE to evolve; and *Cohesion* concerning the alignment and closeness among DBE actors and their capabilities toward a DBE's mission [10].

Resilience goal support indicator I_{rg} is calculated by dividing the number of supporting relationships from ecosystem goals to each of the four resilience goals by the total number of supporting relationships (arrows from EGoals to RGoals in Fig. 5). The I_{rg} highlights the resilience goals having the largest relative support. The I_{rg} for the current design phase are – *Diversity* 0.084; *Efficiency* 0.333; *Adaptability* 0.250; and *Cohesion* 0.333. This indication that *Efficiency* and *Cohesion* have relatively higher support is in line with the aim of creating an efficient dataspace where compliance and standards are enforced in the Marispace-X DBE.

DBE role fulfilment index I_{rr} shows whether the DBE roles are supported by generic roles and the amount. Currently, the I_{rr} for the DBE roles are – *Driver* 2; *Aggregator* 1; *Modular Producer* 7; *Complementor* 2; *Customer* 3; *End User* 3; *Governor* 2; *Reputation Guardian* 0.

Resilience goal-role mutual supporting indicator $I_{(rr,rg)}$ identifies relationships among the DBE roles and the resilience goals. The indicator represents a count of paths leading from DBE roles to resilience goals - unique paths leading from a resilience role to a resilience goal via roles and ecosystem goals. The $I_{(rr,rg)}$ of the design phase Marispace-X DBE are shown in Table 1.

Table 1. Relations among the resilience goals and the DBE roles in the Marispace-X DBE

Resilience goal	Driver	Aggregator	Modular Producer	Complementor	Customer	End user	Governor	Reputation guardian	$I_{(rr,rg)}$ (design)
Diversity	1	1	0	0	0	0	0	0	0.067
Efficiency	3	1	4	1	0	0	2	0	0.367
Adaptability	3	3	0	0	0	0	0	0	0.200
Cohesion	2	0	6	0	0	0	3	0	0.366

4.2 Modelling the Skippo DBE

The Skippo DBE is in its deployment phase. Applying the method modules – *S-map, A-map, C-map, R-map, and KIP-map*, the workshop sessions focused on not only the relevant actors and assets but also the KPIs and resilience indicators (the physical sessions took place in July 2023 and in January 2024; and in February 2024 via Zoom).

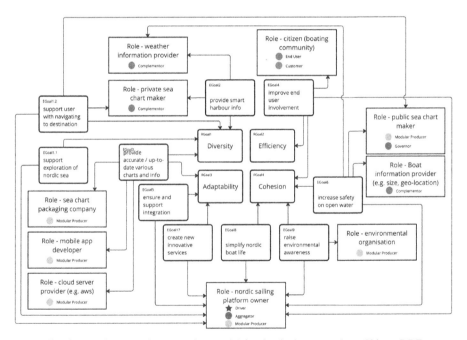

Fig. 6. Resilience goals supporting model for the deployment phase Skippo DBE

Figure 6 shows the analysis of resilience of the deployment phase Skippo DBE using the resilience goals supporting model. The I_{rg} for current deployment phase are – *Diversity* 0.333; *Efficiency* 0.084; *Adaptability* 0.250; and *Cohesion* 0.333. This indication that

Diversity and *Cohesion* have relatively higher support is in line with the aim of providing new boating products and services but still ensuring simplicity and safety in the Skippo DBE. The relatively low supported resilience goal efficiency suggests improvement in related ecosystem goals, which reflects the challenges of how to efficiently integrate and package various data into sea chart layers and identify and address errors in them. Currently, the I_{rr} for the DBE roles are – *Driver* 1; *Aggregator* 1; *Modular Producer* 6; *Complementor* 3; *Customer* 1; *End User* 1; *Governor* 1; *Reputation Guardian* 0. The $I_{(rr,rg)}$ of the deployment phase Skippo DBE are shown in Table 2.

Table 2. Relations among the resilience goals and the DBE roles in the Skippo DBE

Resilience goal	Driver	Aggregator	Modular Producer	Complementor	Customer	End user	Governor	Reputation guardian	$I_{(rr,rg)}$ (deploy)
Diversity	2	2	6	3	0	0	1	0	0.318
Efficiency	1	1	1	0	1	1	0	0	0.114
Adaptability	2	2	5	0	0	0	0	0	0.205
Cohesion	3	3	5	2	1	1	1	0	0.363

Figure 7 shows the current actors with their generic roles, DBE roles, needed and native assets, and KPIs. The DBE role *Driver* is played by Skippo. The company also plays the DBE role *Aggregator,* packaging end-products or services through the mobile app; and the DBE role *Modular Producer,* providing capability of developing basic harbour information. The maritime agencies from the Nordic countries are public agencies providing capabilities of developing essential sea charts as the DBE role *Modular Producer.* These public maritime agencies also play the DBE role *Governor* by defining regulations for boating and sailing. Other actors in the DBE role *Modular Producer* are Eniro and Mapbox owning the sea chart packaging technology, map tiling services, and chart rendering; AWS providing cloud servers and map tiles caching; the Stockholm University Baltic Sea Centre and the Swedish boat union monitoring and supplying environmental data about the Baltic Sea; and the mobile app development company.

The DBE role *Complementor* is played by Hydro and Hamnguiden providing detailed sea chart or maps and harbour information; and ECC and MET.no providing transient data, such as boat location and weather information.

These capabilities can create added values complementing core products and services for premium subscribers in the Skippo DBE. The boating community (as the DBE role *Customer* and *End-User*) play an active role in the DBE by populating information, such as uploading pictures of harbours and updating real-time gas prices. These user interaction parameters are KPIs monitored and analysed in the DBE. Some other KPIs are the cost and availability metrics for servers, user consumption for map tiles caching and map tiling services. The values of these KPIs are kept confidential, hence not shown in the model (Fig. 7). The KPI1 discrepancy (error and error addressing) can be implemented in order to track the errors in the detailed maps and harbour information and how fast they are addressed, which reflects one of the challenges in the Skippo DBE.

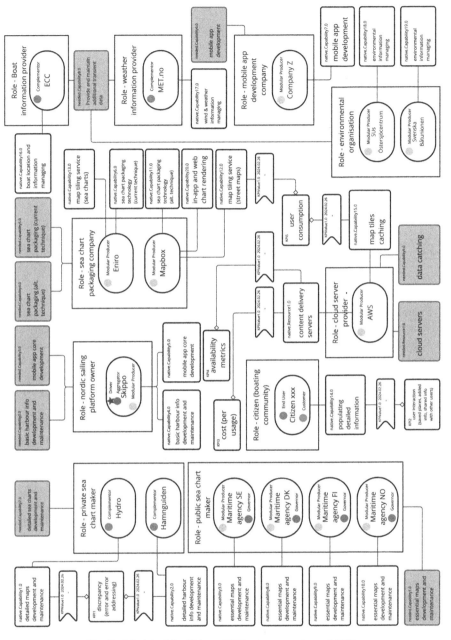

Fig. 7. Model of the Skippo DBE actors, assets, and KPIs

4.3 Evaluation

Based on the synthesis in a systematic literature review investigating the conceptual modelling methods applied to DBEs [10], we aimed to address the lack of methodological guidance in integrating different DBE-related concepts and supporting resilience by developing the DBEmap method. Requirements were gathered for the method [10]. For the evaluation of the method, the 30 requirements were rephrased as 27 simple statements in a web-based questionnaire to understand participants' perceived usefulness. A 5-point Likert scale with the option of "n/a" – not applicable was used for the participants to rate how much they agreed with the statements.

Participants were instructed to only answer "n/a" when they considered not having applied the method for the purposes described in the statements. A pilot was conducted to test the readability of the 27 statements. We engaged 8 participants – 4 in a naturalistic setting (group N) and 4 in an artificial setting (group A) for the questionnaire following the presented evaluation design (Sect. 3). The participants in group N were those who have substantial experience and currently work in a DBE. In contrast, those in group A were modelling experts presented with the DBEmap method and how it was applied to the Skippo case. The complete list of the 27 questionnaire statements and the aggregated responses can be accessed via the study's website (c.f. link in Sect. 2).

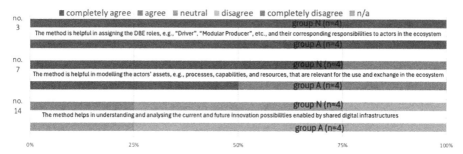

Fig. 8. Participants' perceptions of example statements related to baseline modules of DBEmap

75% to 100% of participants in both groups agreed or completely agreed with most statements related to the baseline modules (*S-map, A-map, C-map, R-map, and D-map*) of the DBEmap method (see examples in Fig. 8). There were some statements where more participants gave neutral answers or considered them as not applicable. These statements reflected the modules (or parts of the modules) which were not applied to the cases, for example, the statement no.14 related to *D-map*.

For the statements related to the other modules (*IP-map, PR-map, DSC-map, CCIS-map, KIP-map, RM-map*), the results suggested a generally higher percentage in "neutral", "disagree", and "n/a" responses (see examples in Fig. 9) in both groups. This trend could also be explained by the fact that these modules were not applied to the two cases, which reflects in participants' answers. These modules were not applied because they are primarily applicable to DBEs in their management phase and because of the time and resources the participants could dedicate to the project. For the statements related to the general principles of the DBEmap method, 75% to 100% of the participants in both groups agreed or completely agreed with most of them. The statement no.25 was an exception, where 50% of the participants in group N perceived it as not applicable.

Semi-structured interviews took place with three participants in group N without time constraints after the workshop sessions. In line with the needs suggested in [10] as the

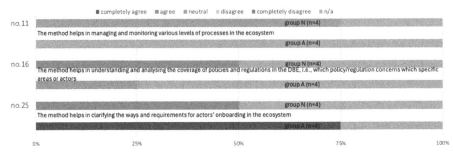

Fig. 9. Perceptions of example statements related to other modules and principles of DBEmap

motivation of developing the DBEmap method, the interview questions were designed to understand if DBEmap has supported: (i) the integration of different DBE-related perspectives, i.e., concepts and constructs, and (ii) the design and management of DBE resilience. The participants were asked to rate how well DBEmap supports these two aspects during the interview. Table 3 shows the questions and their responses.

Table 3. Participants' perceptions about perspectives and designing/managing resilience

Interview question/Participant no	P1	P2	P3
On a scale of 1–5, how well does the method help with integration of the perspectives?	3.5	4	4
On a scale of 1–5, how well does the method help with designing and managing of your ecosystem's resilience?	4	4	5

Based on the analysis of the qualitative data, three themes emerged.

Understanding the concepts and constructs used in the DBEmap method was improved after instantiating examples in models. Further working with applying the method to the two cases made the concepts and constructs self-explanatory as suggested by *P2*. Dividing assets in needed and native ones was helpful, especially looking into the needed assets in an DBE was an intuitive way of working *(P2)*. Two participants *(P1, P2)* said that these concepts and constructs in DBEmap are important. But explanation is need for users to understand them *(P1)*. E.g., some DBE roles defined in this method and the mapping between them and other frameworks were confusing *(P2, P3)*.

Visualising the complexity and connections among concepts in DBEs with DBEmap was appreciated by the participants. A visualised overview of an DBE could facilitate universal understanding of the DBE in its current stage and support joint discussions about relevant issues in the ecosystems *(P2)*. This aggregated visualisation of an ecosystem helped clarify the connections between actors' responsibilities and their assets *(P2)*. Furthermore, it supported identifying the need and aspects of DBE monitoring by establishing connections between simple concepts, such as actors and assets, and the more advanced concepts, e.g., process, cost, performances *(P3)*. There was, however, different opinions on the timing of applying the DBEmap method. *P1* suggested *"it could* *really help in the beginning stage – visualise and map (model) the different concepts and integrate and incorporate all that in the ecosystem."* In contrast, *P3* expressed concern in the willingness for users to invest time and resource in applying DBEmap during design phase (beginning stage), *"but it is useful for something (a DBE) that is running (operating) – it is like reverse engineering."*

Finding the balance and gaps was considered an advantage of applying the DBE-map method, especially because the method incorporated resilience concern. All three participants suggested that the resilience goals and DBE role supporting structure are valuable and helpful in showing how to shift focuses in DBEs to find the necessary balance for better resilience. The applying of the method and the visualising/modelling process engaged stakeholders in honest and open dialogue and acknowledge the gaps, e.g., having a single source of needed core resources; and the urgency of bringing in new actors *(P3)*. This could stimulate conversations about strategic measures and operational procedures related to "how" in DBEs *(P2)*.

5   Discussion and Conclusions

We have presented an application and evaluation of the DBEmap method in its entirety using the Marispace-X project and Skippo DBEs as cases. We have aimed to facilitate the alleviation of the challenges related to the development of dataspaces in the maritime domain by assisting the establishment and analysis of these DBEs with DBEmap. The evaluation participants agreed that the method is useful concerning its general principles and those modules that have been applied. They have also suggested that the method application supports connecting various concepts in a DBE and striving towards a balance in DBE resilience by facilitating visualisation and communication.

However, continual studies with even larger scales and longer timeframes would be beneficial to generate more elaborated outcome on how the method modules support the connection and integration of DBE-related perspectives. This is considered one of the limitations of this study. Another limitation concerns the research design of the evalua-tion where not all method modules could be applied to the chosen cases. Even though this limitation suggests that the evaluation results provide fragmented understanding of the usefulness of the DBEmap method, we still consider the application in this study successful owing to the modularisation of the method. The modularisation enables an advantage of the DBEmap method regarding its applicability since the method does not need to be applied in its entirety. That is, the applicability conditions of the method depend on the phase of a DBE and the users' needs and available resources.

At the moment, we are unable to assert how resilience will improve over time with the use of the method. Long-term evaluation and follow-ups combining with continuous measurement of the resilience indicators and control of the network effects are therefore necessary.

As one of the initial studies for the iterative evaluation process of the entire method, the results presented in this study are crucial for the continual work on evaluating and improving the method. Future work will focus on the further design of the Marispace-X DBE using the method in order to observe how the integration of the various concerns focusing in different module can be realised and supported in a natural DBE setting as well as how resilience changes over time when the method is in used.

References

1. Moore, J.F.: Predators and prey: a new ecology of competition. Harv. Bus. Rev. **71**, 75–86 (1993)
2. Senyo, P.K., Liu, K., Effah, J.: Digital business ecosystem: literature review and a framework for future research. Int. J. Inf. Manag. **47**, 52–64 (2019)
3. Senyo, P.K., Liu, K., Effah, J.: Towards a methodology for modelling interdependencies between partners in digital business ecosystems. In: LISS 2017, pp. 1165–1170. IEEE (2017)
4. Coskun-Setirek, A., Carmela Annosi, M., Hurst, W., Dolfsma, W., Tekinerdogan, B.: Architecture and governance of digital business ecosystems: a systematic literature review. Inf. Syst. Manag. **9**(11), 1–33 (2023)
5. Tsai, C.H., Zdravkovic, J., Söder, F.: A method for digital business ecosystem design: situational method engineering in an action research project. Softw. Syst. Model. **22**(2), 573–598 (2023)
6. Tanhua, T., Pouliquen, S., Hausman, J., O'Brien, et al.: Ocean fair data services. Front. Marine Sci. **6**, 92 (2019)
7. Lytra, I., Vidal, M.E., Orlandi, F., Attard, J.: A big data architecture for managing oceans of data and maritime applications. In: ICE/ITMC 2017, pp. 1216–1226. IEEE (2017)
8. Curry, E.: Dataspaces: fundamentals, principles, and techniques. In: Curry, E. (ed.) Real-time Linked Dataspaces, pp. 45–62. Springer, Cham (2020). https://doi.org/10.1007/978-3-030-29665-0_3
9. Dalton, G., et al.: Feasibility of investment in blue growth multiple-use of space and multi-use platform projects; results of a novel assessment approach and case studies. Renew. Sustain. Energy Rev. **107**, 338–359 (2019)
10. Tsai, C.H.: A method for designing resilient digital business ecosystems. Licentiate dissertation, Department of Computer and Systems Sciences, Stockholm University (2023)
11. Henderson-Sellers, B., Ralyté, J., Ågerfalk, P.J., Rossi, M.: Situational Method Engineering, 1st edn. Springer, Heidelberg (2014)
12. Hevner, A., March, S.T., Park, J., Ram, S.: Design science in information systems research. Manag. Inf. Syst. Q. **28**(1), 75–105 (2004)
13. De Reuver, M., Sørensen, C., Basole, R.C.: The digital platform: a research agenda. J. Inf. Technol. **33**(2), 124–135 (2018)
14. Hellmanzik, B., Sandkuhl, K.: Towards a FAIR-ready data value chain for dataspaces. In: Griffo, C., Guerreiro, S., Iacob, M.E. (eds.) EEWC 2022. LNBIP, vol. 473, pp. 90–105. Springer, Cham (2023). https://doi.org/10.1007/978-3-031-34175-5_6
15. Hellmanzik, B., Sandkuhl, K.: A data value matrix: linking FAIR data with business models. In: Nurcan, S., Opdahl, A.L., Mouratidis, H., Tsohou, A. (eds.) RCIS 2023. LNBIP, vol. 476, pp. 585–592. Springer, Cham (2023). https://doi.org/10.1007/978-3-031-33080-3_41
16. Azkan, C., et al.: Anreizsysteme und Ökonomie des Data Sharings. Fraunhofer-Gesellschaft (2022)
17. Grabis, J., Tsai, C.H., Zdravkovic, J., Stirna, J.: Endurant ecosystems: model-based assessment of resilience of digital business ecosystems. In: Nazaruka, Ē, Sandkuhl, K., Seigerroth, U. (eds.) BIR 2022. LNBIP, vol. 462, pp. 53–68. Springer, Cham (2022). https://doi.org/10.1007/978-3-031-16947-2_4

Technology for Automatic Usability Evaluation Using Model Driven Engineering

Susel Matos Claro[1]([✉]) [iD], Jenny Ruiz de la Peña[1] [iD], Leydis Lamoth Borrero[1] [iD], and Monique Snoeck[2] [iD]

[1] University of Holguin, XX Anniversary, 80100 Holguin, Cuba
{smatosc,jruizp,llamothb}@uho.edu.cu
[2] KU Leuven, Naamsestraat 69, 3000 Leuven, Belgium
monique.snoeck@kuleuven.be

Abstract. User interfaces are key to application quality and acceptance. Manual usability evaluation the final stages of development is time consuming and resource intensive. Model Driven Engineering streamlines development by relying on models and transformations, facilitating early systematic usability evaluation. MERODE, an object-oriented Model Driven Engineering-based analysis methodology, abstracts domain modeling from technological specifications. FENIkS, a MERODE-associated tool, enables co-designing application and user interface models. This paper presents a procedure and tool leveraging FENIkS's presentation model to automatically evaluate usability, shortening development time and enhancing application quality. The tool allows correcting usability issues in user interfaces during the modelling step and feedback is provided on detected errors.

Keywords: User Interfaces · Usability · Model Driven Engineering · Automatic Usability Evaluation

1 Introduction

The advancement of technologies leads to a greater demand for software development that meets the needs of users without sacrificing quality and security. User Interfaces (UIs) are fundamental in computer systems, since they facilitate the interaction between users and software and significantly influence the quality and acceptance of applications. The importance of creating usable UIs is increasing, taking almost half of the time in the software development process [1, 2].

The quality of a product is key when creating it or providing a service. For a software, quality is often a subjective factor, determined by appearance, functionality, learnability and ease of use. Sometimes, developers focus on functional requirements of a computer system and neglect non-functional requirements that guarantee decisive aspects for its quality [3]. UIs are often designed without considering the application behind them, leading to a mismatch between the UI and the application architecture [4].

It is essential to evaluate the usability of the UIs, even though it is costly in terms of resources and time: it requires the participation of experts, potential or real users,

H. van der Aa et al. (Eds.): BPMDS 2024/EMMSAD 2024, LNBIP 511, pp. 191–200, 2024.
https://doi.org/10.1007/978-3-031-61007-3_15

laboratories, cameras, etc. Usability means that computing products are easy for users, allowing to complete their goals and tasks efficiently and successfully [5]. Its evaluation typically occurs late in software development, often when UIs are almost finalized. The absence of usability evaluation across all stages is a major flaw, as late detection of usability problems requires backtracking, wasting time and resources [2].

Since the 1970s, various authors have addressed software usability. Among the most prominent are Nielsen's heuristics [6], the design principles of Hansen [7], and Shneider-man's golden rules [8]. Most agree that usability cannot be defined by a single parameter, but implies a set of rules that guarantee the usability of software. The emergence of Model Driven Engineering (MDE) offered a new perspective on how requirements are considered. MDE streamlines development through the use of models and transformations, enhancing efficiency and maintenance [9]. UI-related models can be integrated into MDE, enabling early usability issue detection, saving time and resources. Addressing problems before implementation stage is feasible with MDE [10].

Taking advantages of the MDE approach, there are many modeling tools, such as, Mendix[1], Eclipse Modeling Framework[2], among others. These tools allow modeling a problem and generating the corresponding code. Other tools such as SilabUI [11], focus on the automatic generation of UIs without generating the code for a functional application. However, they are not optimal for communicating the importance of conceptual modeling to users and its impact on the final result. These tools also do not allow users to get feedback on the generated UI or the design principles reflected in it, or whether they are correctly applied or not.

MERODE is a MDE approach to developing enterprise information systems [12] that was extended with FENIkS for the design of UIs and the development of interactive systems. It uses the conceptual model to capture the functional logic of the application to provide a basis for the UI design, and incorporates a new model called presentation model to capture characteristics of the UI components and user preferences [13]. The aim of our paper is the automatic usability evaluation of applications by using models in MDE. To achieve this, we extend previous work [14] and develop a procedure and a tool to support usability evaluation either automatically, by experts or in a hybrid way.

The remainder of the paper is structured as follows. Section 2 presents related work. Section 3, explains previous work and the main contribution: the extended presentation model, the evaluation procedure and the evaluation tool. Section 4 presents the evaluation of the proposed procedure and tool by experts. Section 5 concludes the paper.

2 Related Work

Over the past decades, the literature and studies on automated or semi-automated usability evaluation show significant progress. Most of the existing studies are applicable to very specific types of interfaces. Various techniques have been proposed for the automatic evaluation of usability. Among the most popular are Aspect-Oriented Programming, Trace Analysis, Data Mining, Model-Based Approach and MDE [14].

---

[1] www.mendix.com.

[2] Www.eclipse.dev/modeling/emf/.

The model-based approach used in [15] identifies potential usability problems by analyzing interaction traces specifically in mobile and web applications. Data mining is used in [1] and proposes opinion mining to evaluate subjective usability. The model extracts knowledge from user opinions to improve the usability of the analyzed systems. Aspect-oriented programming is used by the AJMU tool [16] for evaluating user tasks in desktop applications. MDE is used in [17], where quality failures are detected by evaluating quality attributes in early stages of the development process.

To automate the usability evaluation process, the most commonly used inspection methods were those performed by experts rather than by users. Metrics are associated with these inspection methods so that the result is less subjective. Examples are Web-Tango [18], which offers quantitative measures based on empirical metrics for UIs to create predictive models to check other UIs, and WebQEM [19], which performs a quantitative evaluation of the usability aspects proposed in ISO 9126-1 and aggregates these quantitative measures to provide usability indicators. PROKUS is a software that measures the usability of a system based on ergonomics as a quality criterion, based on the ISO 9241-10 standard [20]. SIRIUS is a web usability evaluation system that is based on heuristic evaluation that offers its application in any type of website and a percentage value of the usability level of the evaluated site [21]. WebSAT is a tool that detects errors in the HTML of web pages through usability guidelines. It performs inspections using a set of usability rules or those of the IEEE Std 2001-1999 [22]. The WUEP tool automates activities within the software development process using Model-Driven Web Development, especially the intermediate artefacts [2].

The approach presented in this paper differs from prior works in several ways. Most of the case studies focus on web platforms, leaving a gap when it comes to other applications. This approach does not evaluate an specific kind of application but the models used for a further generation of an application. Furthermore, most of the works perform the evaluation in the last stages of software development. The most significant difference is that FENIkS allows evaluating the usability at early stages by testing the compliancy of UI design principles in an actual UI that is designed through the specification of domain and presentation models. The analyzed approaches do not provide feedback related to a real design, something possible in FENIkS evaluating UI design principles.

3   Model-Driven Usability Evaluation Process and Tool

MERODE is a model-driven approach to enterprise information systems engineering that fosters domain-driven development, and separates the domain layer (inner layer) from the IS service layer (middle layer) and the user interface layer (outer layer) [12]. Two modelling tools support the development of domain models according to MERODE: MERLIN, a web-based tool, and JMermaid, a Java-based tool. JMermaid includes a code generator and allows you to do the conceptual modeling and turn it into a fully functional desktop application in a few clicks. It is also a didactic tool that can be used as a teaching method that promotes the understanding of the importance of implementing the conceptual design of the resulting application [10].

3.1 FENIkS

The extension of JMermaid called FENIkS [13] is an approach for the design of UIs and the development of interactive systems. In addition to the domain model used by MERODE that captures the functional logic of the application, FENIkS incorporates the presentation model that captures the characteristics of the interface components and user preferences. This presentation model captures code generation options that define how the generated prototype will show the information and how the interaction will be.

The presentation model defines input aspects and window aspects defined by the presentation meta-model [10]. These aspects contain the information that the user specifies regarding the organization, layout and appearance of the UI. The characteristics contained in the presentation model are associated with design principles and guidelines, which in turn allow measuring the usability of the interfaces generated from the model [10]. Window aspects capture the preferences related to the static layout of the top level containers of the generated prototype and how the information is displayed (e.g. how the pagination will be). The preferences for input services are captured by Input aspect. They are related to the way users will input the information into the generated prototype. (e.g. what kind of widgets are needed for inputting the information).

The presentation model of FENIkS has options to support UI design based on design principles that allows automatic usability evaluation: *Prevent errors, Provide good error messages, Allow users to use the keyboard or mouse, Provide visual cues, Offer informative feedback, Strive for consistency, Make things visible* and *Structure the UI.*

3.2 Extended Presentation Model

The options configured by the presentation model can be visualized in a feature model that defines the window and input aspects. In previous work, the FENIkS presentation model contained a set of 18 features. We extended the presentation model to include new parameters that allow the storage of additional UI characteristics. An analysis was made of the aspects already included in the presentation model and the usability evaluation needs not yet covered by it. Adding new features would make it possible to test other UI usability parameters. Based on this assessment it was decided to add four new features to the window aspects. These new features were considered because they support other design principles that can be tested automatically. Figure 1 shows the UI Feature Model included in the FENIkS presentation model. Shown in blue are the new features that extend the original FENIkS model, to evaluate a larger number of UI principles.

'Option to cancel in forms or windows' is one of the added features. This allows to evaluate principles related to *explicit control*. 'Alerts before closing or canceling a process' makes it possible to check if the system handles well the principle related to *design dialogs to produce closure*. 'Progress bar on buttons' allows the user to *estimate the remaining processing time*. The 'User manual or online help' feature allows to check the compliance with the principle *Help and system documentation*.

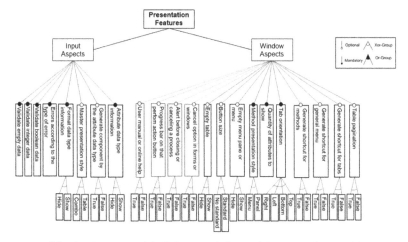

Fig. 1. Feature model of the extended FENIkS presentation model

3.3 Usability Evaluation Procedure

The usability evaluation procedure has 9 steps organized in 4 phases. In each of these phases, objectives and techniques to be used are stated. Through the procedure, usability evaluation can be carried out in different ways: automatically by the tool by evaluating the characteristics of the presentation model; by an expert evaluating the same characteristics; or hybrid by combining both types of evaluation. Figure 2 shows the entire process with all the phases and steps, the blue steps being automated by the tool.

The main goal of the diagnostic phase is to test the metrics and ways to evaluate usability in the development process. In this phase the proposal is presented to the development group and the focus is on avoiding resistance to change by explaining the benefits of the procedure. First the tool, its goals and advantages in achieving high usability standards are presented. Step 2 focuses on characterizing the development process of the development group or company that intends to use the tool. This allows the need for early usability evaluation to be assessed. Once the conditions of use are clear, Step 3 presents the tool adapted to the needs of each particular group. Then FENIkS is then introduced as the modeling tool to be used to export the models.

In the planning phase, the developers must prepare for the use of the tool and define the parameters that must be achieved to complete the usability evaluation. In step 4, the metrics for usability evaluation must be defined, how the tool measures each parameter, and the stop condition must be set. Step 5 is performed to set the score that must be achieved to end the evaluation, that is, the stop condition. The developers choose whether to perform the automatic evaluation or the hybrid evaluation. If only the automatic evaluation is performed, they proceed directly to step 7. If the hybrid evaluation is to be carried out, the experts who will perform the evaluation must be selected. The selection is based on a knowledge questionnaire about usability and good UI design practices, which must be completed successfully.

In the evaluation phase the tool is used to automatically evaluate the usability given a FENIkS model. Step 6 is only performed if the hybrid evaluation is performed. In this

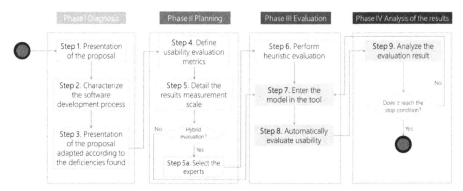

Fig. 2. Procedure for usability evaluation

step, the evaluation is performed by experts using a form that describes the characteristics saved in the presentation model. The experts give their ratings and judgments according to their usability evaluation. In step 7, the model exported from FENIkS is uploaded in the tool to be evaluated. In step 8, the automatic usability evaluation is performed to conclude the evaluation phase. Finally, the results analysis phase determines whether the system meets the parameters established in the planning phase. The developers must also analyze the information provided by the tool about which design principles are correctly or incorrectly implemented. If the system does not meet the expected values, the identified problems must be corrected and the evaluation must be repeated by returning to step 7 until the UI usability errors are resolved.

3.4   Usability Evaluation Tool

In the process described above, step 8 uses a tool for the automatic usability evaluation. The main purpose of this tool is to facilitate software development by measuring usability in the early stages. It provides a score for each design principle evaluated and an overall score. At the same time, it provides feedback on possible solutions to the identified usability problems. It also allows a comparison of the evaluation history of the same model, as well as a comparison between automatic and expert evaluation.

The evaluation performed by the tool is based on rules and design principles that have been paradigms in usability studies for years. These principles are formulated in such a way that they can be applied to any type of UI, which is why they have been chosen as the basis for the evaluation performed by the tool. From this set of design principles and roles, those that can be automatically verified by the tool were selected, leaving aside those with more subjective values or depending on human criteria: Hansen's Principles [7], Norman's Principles [23], Shneiderman's Golden Rules [8], Nielsen Heuristics [6].

The tool evaluates 10 guidelines, each of which has one or more ergonomic criteria that allow the evaluation to be performed. The guidelines evaluated are: *Actions must be reversible, Helps users recognize, diagnose and recover from errors, Allow the user to change the focus, Help and documentation, Allow the user to abort lengthy operations, Minimize user memory load, Simple and natural dialogues, Give control to the user, Design dialogues to produce closures and Allow the user to estimate how long.*

To begin the evaluation, the tool receives as input a model exported from the FENIkS tool in which, in addition to the modeling of the business logic, the characteristics of the user interface are specified in the presentation model.

When the model to be evaluated is introduced into the tool, you can choose the type of evaluation you want to perform, either automatic or expert, as shown in Fig. 3.

Fig. 3. Evaluation method selection in the tool and Part of the expert questionnaire

Fig. 4. Example of Evaluation result

In the case of automatic evaluation, the system is responsible for verifying compliance with the UI design principles in the presentation model, and provides grades according to the correct or incorrect application of the guidelines.

Each ergonomic criteria evaluated by the tool is then linked to a natural language text string previously defined corresponding to what each principle evaluates. These are presented to the experts by means of a questionnaire to give their evaluation and criteria for the application of the design principles and guidelines. The results are displayed in a text box where an overall score is given based on a maximum of 100 points. The guidelines applied correctly and incorrectly are indicated (see Fig. 4). The tool shows a history of the evaluations carried out on a model so the user can see if the detected usability errors have improved. It is important to clarify that, until now, the usability evaluation tool can only be used with a model exported from FENIkS as a starting point.

4   Evaluation by Experts

To determine the level of satisfaction and compliance, the procedure and tool were evaluated by experts, in particular people with expertise in software engineering and development of procedures. Two surveys were conducted. The first was used to determine the level of competence of the experts. The second survey was applied to those experts with higher level of competence.

In total, 21 experts with no experience using the tool filled the survey after analyzing the procedure and interacting with the tool. Figure 5 shows the results of the 8 aspects included in the survey. None of the aspects of the tool or the procedure were deemed little or not appropriate. The three aspects that are directly related to the tool (bottom 3, right), are found to be very appropriate. The procedure (left) is deemed very or quite appropriate by the large majority (80%). Even though the tool is tightly coupled with the use of FENIkS, the experts agree that is contextualizable.

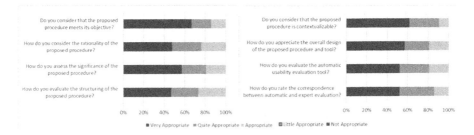

Fig. 5. Expert evaluation result

The experts agree that the use of the procedure and tool for automatic usability evaluation implies significant savings in time and resources. Thanks to the advantages of the MDE and the use of the presentation model, it can be integrated into different phases of the software development process from early stages, without necessarily involving an expert as in traditional methods. This favors early detection of usability problems. A report with feedback on the usability problems with suggestions to solve them is obtained. Suggestions on improvements to the procedure were found through the open questions, e.g. the use of other operation than the average to evaluate each criterion.

5 Conclusion and Further Work

The quality and usability of UIs can be decisive in the success of a computer application. Special attention must be paid to UI development. Usability evaluation in the traditional way has been the way to ensure the quality of UIs, but it requires waiting for the full coding of the UI and going back to the initial stages of development to correct the problems found. This is usually costly and frustrating for the developers. In addition, it can delay product delivery and cause dissatisfaction on the part of the customer.

The procedure and tool created for the automatic evaluation of usability through MDE saves time and human resources in the detection of usability problems. The evaluation can be integrated into the development process from the beginning, resulting in computer products with higher levels of usability in less time. Using the tool, not only a list of usability problems is presented, but also recommendations to solve them.

Future research is planned to improve the tool. The suggested improvement on alternative methods for aggregating scores is already in process with the introduction of artificial intelligence techniques. Specifically, by introducing supervised machine learning methods, it will be possible to predict the values of the criteria by learning from previous cases. The aim is to test the procedure in a business production environment to verify its goals in other real work and software development environments.

A major limitation of the tool is its strong connection to the presentation model used in the FENIkS-tool. This limits generalizing its use to software development teams using other MDE tools. While this environment has already proven its usefulness for teaching UI design [13], ideally it should also be usable in a professional context. Future research will investigate to what extent a presentation model can be reverse engineered from other MDE environments, which would broaden the applicability of the tool.

References

1. El-Halees, A.M.: Software usability evaluation using opinion mining. J. Softw. **9**(2), 343–349 (2014)
2. Fernandez, A., Insfran, E., Abrahão, S.: Usability evaluation methods for the web: a systematic mapping study. Inf. Softw. Technol. **53**(8), 789–817 (2011)
3. Jarzębowicz, A., Weichbroth, P.: A qualitative study on non-functional requirements in agile software development. IEEE Access **9**, 40458–40475 (2021)
4. Moreno, J.C., Marciszack, M.M.: Validación de especificaciones no funcionales de aplicaciones web a través de técnicas de testing de usabilidad. In: XV Workshop de Investigadores en Ciencias de la Computación (2013)
5. Martin, C., Braune, A.: Integration of a template system into model-based user interface development workflows. In: Kurosu, M. (ed.) HCI 2017. LNCS, vol. 10271, pp. 480–495. Springer, Cham (2017). https://doi.org/10.1007/978-3-319-58071-5_36
6. Nielsen, J.: Usability Engineering. Morgan Kaufmann (1994)
7. Hansen, W.J.: User engineering principles for interactive systems. In: Proceedings of the November 16–18, 1971, Fall Joint Computer Conference, pp. 523–532 (1972)
8. Shneiderman, B.: Designing The User Interface: Strategies for Effective Human-Computer Interaction, 4/e (New Edition). Pearson Education India (1987)
9. Whittle, J., Hutchinson, J., Rouncefield, M.: The state of practice in model-driven engineering. IEEE Softw. **31**(3), 79–85 (2013)

10. Ruiz, J., Serral, E., Snoeck, M.: Technology enhanced support for learning interactive software systems. In: Hammoudi, S., Pires, L.F., Selic, B. (eds.) MODELSWARD 2018. CCIS, vol. 991, pp. 185–210. Springer, Cham (2019). https://doi.org/10.1007/978-3-030-11030-7_9
11. Antović, I., Vlajić, S., Milić, M., Savić, D., Stanojević, V.: Model and software tool for automatic generation of user interface based on use case and data model. IET Softw. **6**(6), 1–15 (2012). https://doi.org/10.1049/iet-sen.2011.0060
12. Snoeck, M.: Enterprise information systems engineering. The MERODE Approach (2014)
13. Ruiz, J., Asensio, E.S., Snoeck, M.: Learning UI functional design principles through simulation with feedback. IEEE Trans. Learn. Technol. **13**(4), 833–846 (2020)
14. de la Peña, J.R., Claro, S.M.M.: El estado del arte de la evaluación automática de Interfaces de Usuario. In: 9na Edición de la Conferencia Científica Internacional de la Universidad de Holguín (2019)
15. Paternò, F., Schiavone, A.G., Conti, A.: Customizable automatic detection of bad usability smells in mobile accessed web applications. In: Proceedings of the 19th International Conference on Human-Computer Interaction with Mobile Devices and Services, pp. 1–11 (2017)
16. Casas, S., Trejo, N., Farias, R.: AJMU: an aspect-oriented framework for evaluating the usability of wimp applications. J. Softw. Eng. **10**, 1–15 (2016)
17. Molina, F., Toval, A.: Integrating usability requirements that can be evaluated in design time into model driven engineering of web information systems. Adv. Eng. Softw. **40**(12), 1306–1317 (2009)
18. Ivory, M.Y.: Web TANGO: towards automated comparison of information-centric web site designs. In: CHI 2000 Extended Abstracts on Human Factors in Computing Systems, pp. 329–330 (2000)
19. Olsina, L., Rossi, G.: Measuring web application quality with WebQEM. IEEE Multimedia **9**(4), 20–29 (2002)
20. Zülch, G., Stowasser, S.: Usability evaluation of user interfaces with the computer-aided evaluation tool PROKUS. MMI-Interaktiv **3**, 1–17 (2000)
21. Chamba-Eras, L., Jacome-Galarza, L., Guaman-Quinche, R., Coronel-Romero, E., Labanda-Jaramillo, M.: Analysis of usability of universities web portals using the prometheus tool – SIRIUS. In: 2017 4th International Conference on eDemocracy and eGovernment, ICEDEG 2017, Institute of Electrical and Electronics Engineers Inc., pp. 195–199 (2017). https://doi.org/10.1109/ICEDEG.2017.7962533
22. Martins, W.S., Lucas, D.C.S., de Souza Neves, K.F., Bertioli, D.J.: WebSat-a web software for microsatellite marker development. Bioinformation **3**(6), 282 (2009)
23. Norman, D.: The Design of Everyday Things: Revised and Expanded Edition. Basic Books (2013)

Model-driven Engineering & AI 1
(EMMSAD 2024)

Building BESSER: An Open-Source Low-Code Platform

Iván Alfonso[1([✉])], Aaron Conrardy[1], Armen Sulejmani[1], Atefeh Nirumand[1],
Fitash Ul Haq[1], Marcos Gomez-Vazquez[1], Jean-Sébastien Sottet[1],
and Jordi Cabot[1,2]

[1] Luxembourg Institute of Science and Technology, Esch-sur-Alzette, Luxembourg
{ivan.alfonso,aaron.conrardy,armen.sulejmani,atefeh.nirumand,
fitash.ulhaq,marcos.gomez,jean-sebastien.sottet,jordi.cabot}@list.lu
[2] University of Luxembourg, Esch-sur-Alzette, Luxembourg

Abstract. Low-code platforms (latest reincarnation of the long tradition of model-driven engineering approaches) have the potential of saving us countless hours of repetitive boilerplate coding tasks. However, as software systems grow in complexity, low-code platforms need to adapt as well. Notably, nowadays this implies adapting to the modeling and generation of smart software. At the same time, if we want to broaden the userbase of this type of tools, we should also be able to provide more open source alternatives that help potential users avoid vendor lock-ins and give them the freedom to explore low-code development approaches (even adapting the tool to better fit their needs). To fulfil these needs, we are building BESSER, an open source low-code platform for developing (smart) software. BESSER offers various forms (i.e., notations) for system and domain specification (e.g. UML for technical users and chatbots for business users) together with a number of generators. Both types of components can be extended and are open to contributions from the community.

Keywords: low-code · AI · Model-driven · DSL · code generation

1 Introduction

Low-code platforms are designed to accelerate software delivery by minimizing hand-coding efforts [15]. Low-code platforms can be regarded as a style of Model-Driven Engineering (MDE) [2,16] with an emphasis on software development.

Low-code platforms hold significant promise, especially in today's software landscape where complexity is on the rise, and software requirements are becoming increasingly demanding. This includes the growing need to develop/deploy/integrate Artificial Intelligence (AI) components to support and provide advanced features. For instance, the adoption of new user interfaces (such as

---

This project is supported by the Luxembourg National Research Fund (FNR) PEARL program, grant agreement 16544475.

augmented/virtual reality, chat, and voice interfaces), the implementation of intelligent behavior to classify, predict, or recommend information based on user input, and the need to address emerging security and sustainability concerns. These AI-enhanced systems are commonly referred to as *smart software* [4].

We have witnessed an explosion of low-code tools, mostly targeting Enterprise software [14], with Gartner defining Mendix, OutSystems, Microsoft, ServiceNow, Appian and Salesforce as leaders in this space [11]. Nevertheless, all these tools excel at "classical" data-intensive web applications while presenting severe limitations for more complex scenarios. An example would be the definition of AI-enhanced interfaces, that, if done, usually only consists of adding endpoints to third party applications (e.g. integration of third party chatbots or Appian's OpenAI plugin), acting rather as an add-on than an actual integral component of the application. Moreover, they are proprietary ecosystems where modelers usually do not even have access to the code generated from their models as applications are transparently deployed in the vendor's cloud. This is convenient but at the same time generates a clear vendor lock-in.

Given the increasing complexity of software development, we argue there is a need for powerful open source low-code platforms that facilitate the adoption of low-code approaches while offering an extensible environment enabling companies to adapt and tailor the tool to their specific needs, but also tackling applications beyond Enterprise software, such as AR/VR interfaces or digital twins.

To address these needs, we are developing BESSER, short for BEtter Smart Software FastER, an open-source low-code platform for smart software development. BESSER is available in our project repository [1]. The platform development is a core element in a 5-year funded project on this same topic, guaranteeing the evolution of the platform over the next years.

The rest of this paper is as follows: in Sect. 2, we introduce BESSER, detailing its architecture, languages and generators. Section 3 showcases some practical applications of BESSER through case studies. Section 4 delves into the primary insights gained from our experiences, and finally, Sect. 5 concludes the paper.

2   Overview of the BESSER Platform

Figure 1 illustrates the architecture of the BESSER platform. At the core of this architecture we have B-UML (short for BESSER's Universal Modeling Language), the foundational language of the BESSER platform used for specifying domain models. B-UML models are then transformed to other models or to software artefacts via model transformations.

The next sections describe the B-UML language and the code generators provided with it, implemented as model-to-text transformations.

2.1   B-UML Language

B-UML, the BESSER Universal Modeling Language, is the base language of the BESSER low-code platform. This language is heavily inspired by UML [7]

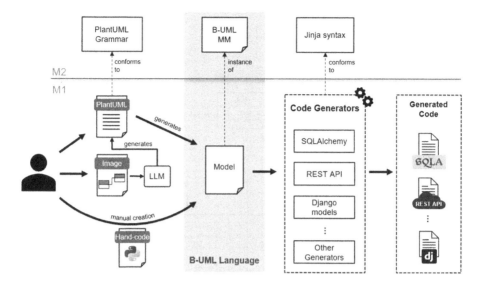

Fig. 1. BESSER low-code platform architecture

but does not aim to be fully compliant with it. Instead, the goal is to have the freedom to integrate other types of (meta)models while benefitting from parts of the UML that we find interesting for our approach. It is up to the designer to decide which of these sublanguages to 'activate' for a given project based on their specific modeling requirements.

Figure 2 depicts an excerpt of the B-UML language divided into submodules. For the sake of brevity and space, this metamodel omits various concepts and relationships, focusing on the most relevant ones. The complete metamodel is available in the project repository [1]. Note that these are the submodules or sublanguages currently defined in BUML. However, we have a list of additional sublanguages outlined in our immediate roadmap (Sect. 2.4) that we plan to design and develop to further support BESSER's objectives (e.g., AI component modeling).

Structural metamodel: it enables the specification of a domain model using the typical concepts of a class diagram. Elements such as *Classes*, *Properties*, *Associations*, and *Generalizations* can be instantiated to define the static structure of a system. While this metamodel is rooted in the UML specification, certain modifications and additions have been implemented to provide additional modeling capabilities. For instance, the *is_id* attribute has been introduced in the Property class to specify whether a property serves as an identifier for the instances of that class, a common need in many code generation scenarios.

Object diagram metamodel: while the structural metamodel centers on classes and their static structures, the object diagram metamodel enables the representation of how these classes are instantiated into objects and interact with each other. The *Object* class in the metamodel represents the instances of a

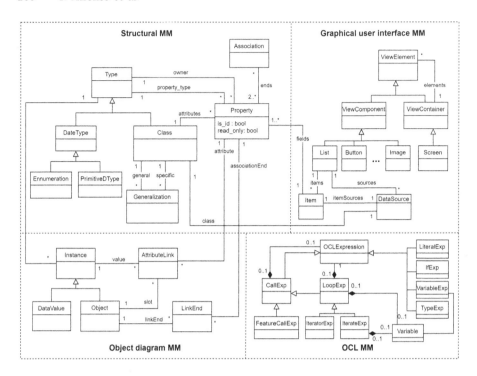

Fig. 2. Excerpt of the B-UML language metamodel

Class from the structural metamodel. Its object attributes are defined using the *AttributeLink* class, and associations with other classes are established using the *LinkEnd* class. In BESSER, the object diagram metamodel is primarily utilized for conducting validations or tests on the model. For instance, validating OCL rules over instances of the B-UML model.

OCL metamodel: it adds support for defining OCL constraints (e.g. to specify invariants or business rules) on the B-UML models. OCL expressions can be written in plain text and then automatically parsed to create the abstract syntax tree (AST) for expression according to the OCL metamodel [12].

Graphical user interface metamodel: it focuses on the specification of graphical user interfaces (GUIs) and draws inspiration from the Interaction Flow Modeling Language (IFML) [13], which is widely recognized and adopted in the field of UI modeling. By leveraging IFML, we ensure compatibility and interoperability with existing UI modeling tools and frameworks. This abstract syntax also enables the definition of GUI components that read and modify elements from a diversity of data sources, including B-UML model elements.

Concrete Syntax. B-UML models can be created using three types of concrete syntaxes (i.e., notations for the metamodel):

1. Textual models conforming to a grammar developed using ANTLR to facilitate the modeling of class diagrams following the syntax of PlantUML[1]. This also facilitates importing existing PlantUML models into BESSER. Moreover, ChatGPT and other LLMs are familiar with the PlantUML notation and can generate PlantUML models, which is convenient for experimenting in the intersection of modeling and LLMs (see next point).
2. Models in an image (for example, a photo of a diagram drawn on a whiteboard) can also be processed and transformed into a B-UML model.
   To achieve this, BESSER employs a LLM to transform the image into a PlantUML model to then generate the B-UML model. A discussion on the quality and accuracy of the recognized models is available here[2]
3. Using the B-UML python library, a model can be easily created by instantiating the B-UML metaclasses. Several helpers facilitate this task.

2.2   Code Generators

BESSER implements Model-to-Text(M2T) transformations to support code generation. More specifically, it offers a collection of code generators based on the Jinja template engine[3]. These generators read a B-UML model and produce executable code for various technologies and tools such as Django, REST APIs backends or SQLAlchemy for database support. A predefined interface facilitates the addition of new generators.

Listing 1 shows a glimpse of the Jinja template for generating plain Python classes from B-UML models. At the core of this (and many other) generators you can see a set of nested loops to traverse the different model elements and the properties of every element.

Listing 1. Example Jinja Template for Python Generation

```
{% for class in classes %}
class {{ class.name }}:
    def __init__(self{% for attribute in class.attributes
        %}, {{ attribute.name }}{% endfor %}):
        {% for attribute in class.attributes %}
        self.{{ attribute.name }} = {{ attribute.name }}
        {% endfor %}
{% endfor %}
```

2.3   Running Example

As an illustrative case study, we draw inspiration from the Digital Product Passport (DPP) initiative [17], an initiative within the European region aimed at enhancing the circular economy and improving product traceability by collecting

---

[1] https://plantuml.com/.

[2] https://modeling-languages.com/image-to-uml-with-llm/.

[3] https://palletsprojects.com/p/jinja/.

data throughout their lifecycle. Illustrated in Fig. 3, we present a reduced model designed using PlantUML, showcasing key components within this domain, including the *ProductPassport* and its lifecycle stages (*Design*, *Use*, *Manufacture*, etc.). Leveraging the capabilities of BESSER, we utilize the Django code generator to automatically generate a portion of the executable code required for a web application tailored to manage digital passport registrations for products.

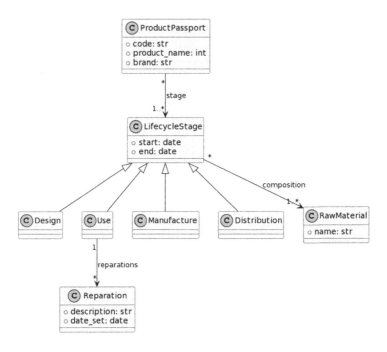

Fig. 3. DPP model domain

The Django code generator uses the DPP domain model as input to generate the model layer code. This code defines model classes that represent the database tables and establishes relationships between them. Figure 4 showcases the user interface of the web application's administration panel that utilizes the generated code. This interface enables the management of database information structured according to the DPP domain model. For instance, the attributes (*code*, *product_name*, and *brand*) of the *ProductPassport* class are represented as input fields in the creation form in Fig. 4.

The source code and detailed guide of this running example is available in the BESSER examples repository[4].

----
[4] https://github.com/BESSER-PEARL/BESSER-examples.git.

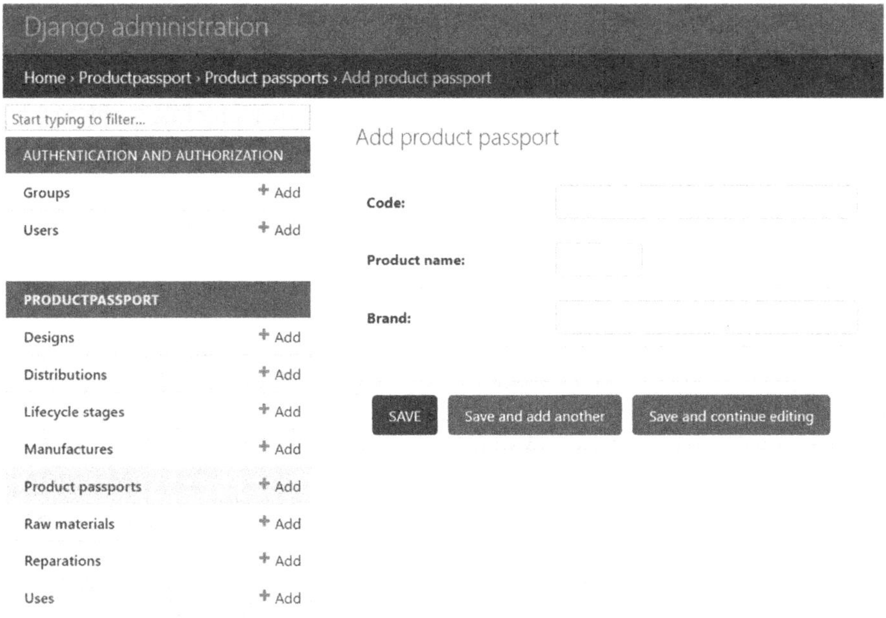

Fig. 4. Django web application user interface

2.4   Roadmap

In this section, we briefly describe only a few items, due to space limit, in our roadmap.

Modeling Smart Software. As discussed in previous sections, we want BESSER to be useful to model smart software systems. This implies being able to model AI components both for the front-end (e.g. chatbots) and the back-end (e.g. recommender systems). While this depends on having a strong core set of modeling components (our core focus at the moment) we have already experimented with the modeling and generation of chatbots (see the next roadmap item) as a concrete first step in this direction.

Finite-State Machines Modeling. The BESSER Bot Framework (BBF)[5] implements finite-state machines (FSM) as a key element in the definition of expressive (chat)bots. In BBF, bot is defined as a FSM where transitions can be triggered by external events such as matching a user input text with one of the bot's intents. Every state has an associated body (a custom Python function) that can run any arbitrary action (e.g., default actions such as replying to the user). As FSMs can be useful in many other modeling scenarios we will "promote" the corresponding metaclasses to the main low-code platform.

---

[5] https://github.com/BESSER-PEARL/BESSER-Bot-Framework.

Fully-Fledged Web and Mobile Generators. While we include a sublanguage for User Interface design and a sample generator for Django, we are aware that to interest a broader user base we should also provide more complete generators, including also generators targeting popular web and mobile development framework such as Flutter or React Native. In the mid-term we would even like to generate a first version (CRUD-like) of the User Interface models from structural models to go from a domain definition to a fully operational mobile application.

OCL Interpreter. Beyond its current support for the definition of OCL expressions, we want as well to provide an OCL interpreter that can, for instance, be used to validate the constraints on top of scenarios modeled with our object diagram support (kind of what USE does [10]). Given the lack of OCL interpreters, especially outside the Java world, we believe this will be a useful contribution. A partial interpreter is already available.

Flexible Modeling. Traditional definition of domain specific languages (DSL) follows a top-down approach, where both abstract (metamodel) and concrete syntaxes are formulated to specify precisely the model shape and structure. However, in some context (e.g., early design phase) this rigid approach does no longer fit. In order to avoid conflicting situations, the conformance relation that links models and metamodels should be relaxed [8]. BESSER will ultimately embed flexibility as a mean to support design changes or natural evolution. However, flexibility should be managed: some part of the model should remain rigid (e.g., for security, regulatory concerns). A mechanism to go from a flexible situation to a rigid one and vice versa will be implemented where, according to a given strategy i) it infers a new metamodel from a given instance or ii) it enforces the conformance and erases all non-conform elements in the model.

3   BESSER Verticals

BESSER provides a core set of components that can be specialized to provide tailored solutions for specific verticals. Depending on the needs of the domain, the specialization can be done via simple subtyping of BESSER concepts or via more complex strategies such as promotional transformations [9].

As an example, we are developing *BESSER for Clima* as part of the Climaborough[6] EU project. The goal by providing the necessary tools to produce a dashboard showcasing the performance of climate solutions and the progress on reaching various climate related goals such as net neutrality. Beyond using BUML and the SQL generator to produce the necessary database schema, a visualisation generator is being developed. This generator will consume models that associate data with visualisations and produce visualisations that can be directly integrated into JavaScript pages. The usage of JavaScript libraries covers a large range of visualisation possibilities and is supported by the state-of-the-art web development frameworks.

---

[6] https://climaborough.eu/.

Additional verticals (e.g. for digital twin architectures, for digital product passports in a lifecycle context, etc.) will be developed as well.

4   Discussion

This section briefly comments on three design decisions that influence the development of BESSER.

Python over Java. Most modeling tools are built in Java, and especially around the Eclipse Modeling Framework[7] ecosystem. Nevertheless, given that Python is the default language for all types of Machine Learning (ML) libraries and frameworks we decided to opt for Python as core language for BESSER. This facilitates the integration of ML components in it.

Internal DSLs over External Ones. Based on our experience building other modeling tools [5], we decided that BESSER would be better suited to be defined as an Internal DSL, i.e. a language implemented on top of an underlying programming language [6], instead of building it as a completely separated language. The key reason is that we want BESSER to cover as many scenarios as possible and this would often imply relying on general programming language, e.g. to specify complex behaviour. Defining BESSER as an internal DSL facilitates this. Similarly, we opted to choose other common language processing tools (such as Jinja and ANTLR) to implement the generators and parsers. As an additional advantage, they have both a strong and active community behind, which is important for the long-term sustainability and evolution of BESSER.

Why Not Just Fully UML Compliant? As discussed before, B-UML is inspired but not a clone of UML. This gives us the freedom to keep the parts we need but disregard those that we do not. It also allow us to integrate new languages that cover aspects that UML does not support well (e.g. UI modeling) or add new concepts or properties that are needed when modeling in the context of low-code development.

5   Conclusion

This paper presents BESSER, a new open source low-code platform targeting not only traditional software systems but also smart components. We have also presented a short-term roadmap and a discussion on the design decisions that, so far, have shaped the architecture of the tool. We hope the modeling community finds our platform useful and decides to adopt it (and even collaborate to its development) in future projects and initiatives around the world of modeling, low-code and, in general, model-driven engineering approaches.

---

[7] https://eclipse.dev/modeling/emf/.

As longer-term future work, we plan to add smart components to BESSER itself, facilitating the creation of B-UML models via low-modeling techniques [3] such as chatbots or automatic model inference from (semi)structured data.

References

1. Github repository: BESSER (2023). https://github.com/BESSER-PEARL/BESSER
2. Cabot, J.: Positioning of the low-code movement within the field of model-driven engineering. In: MODELS 2020: ACM/IEEE 23rd International Conference on Model Driven Engineering Languages and Systems, Virtual Event, Canada, 18–23 October 2020, Companion Proceedings, pp. 76:1–76:3. ACM (2020). https://doi.org/10.1145/3417990.3420210
3. Cabot, J.: Low-modeling of software systems. arXiv preprint arXiv:2402.18375 (2024)
4. Cabot, J., Clarisó, R.: Low code for smart software development. IEEE Softw. **40**(1), 89–93 (2023)
5. Daniel, G., Cabot, J.: Applying model-driven engineering to the domain of chatbots: the xatkit experience. Sci. Comput. Program. **232**, 103032 (2024). https://doi.org/10.1016/J.SCICO.2023.103032
6. Ghosh, D.: DSL for the uninitiated. Commun. ACM **54**(7), 44–50 (2011)
7. Group, O.M.: OMG unified modeling language tm (omg UML), pp. 1–754 (2017)
8. Hili, N., Sottet, J.S.: The conformance relation challenge: building flexible modelling frameworks. In: Workshop on Flexible Model Driven Engineering, FlexMDE 2017, pp. 418–423 (2017)
9. Jácome-Guerrero, S.P., de Lara, J.: *TOTEM*: reconciling multi-level modelling with standard two-level modelling. Comput. Stand. Interfaces **69**, 103390 (2020). https://doi.org/10.1016/J.CSI.2019.103390
10. Kuhlmann, M., Hamann, L., Gogolla, M.: Extensive validation of OCL models by integrating SAT solving into USE. In: Bishop, J., Vallecillo, A. (eds.) Objects, Models, Components, Patterns, TOOLS 2011. LNCS, vol. 6705, pp. 290–306. Springer, Heidelberg (2011). https://doi.org/10.1007/978-3-642-21952-8_21
11. Matvitskyy, O., Iijima, K., West, M., Davis, K., Jain, A., Vincent, P.: Magic quadrant for enterprise low-code application platforms. technical report. gartner. (2023)
12. Object constraint language (OCL), version 2.4 (2014)
13. OMG: About interaction flow modeling language specification. https://www.omg.org/spec/IFML. Accessed 26 Feb 2024
14. Pinho, D., Aguiar, A., Amaral, V.: What about the usability in low-code platforms? A systematic literature review. J. Comput. Lang. **74**, 101185 (2023). https://doi.org/10.1016/j.cola.2022.101185
15. Richardson, C., Rymer, J.R., Mines, C., Cullen, A., Whittaker, D.: New development platforms emerge for customer-facing applications. Forrester, Cambridge (2014)
16. Ruscio, D.D., Kolovos, D.S., de Lara, J., Pierantonio, A., Tisi, M., Wimmer, M.: Low-code development and model-driven engineering: Two sides of the same coin? Softw. Syst. Model. **21**(2), 437–446 (2022). https://doi.org/10.1007/S10270-021-00970-2
17. Walden, J., Steinbrecher, A., Marinkovic, M.: Digital product passports as enabler of the circular economy. Chem. Ing. Tec. **93**(11), 1717–1727 (2021)

Towards Taming Large Language Models with Prompt Templates for Legal GRL Modeling

Sybren de Kinderen[(✉)] and Karolin Winter

Department of Industrial Engineering and Innovation Sciences,
Eindhoven University of Technology, Eindhoven, The Netherlands
{s.d.kinderen,k.m.winter}@tue.nl

Abstract. The Legal Goal-oriented Requirements Language (Legal GRL) is a promising conceptual modeling approach for supporting regulatory compliance analysis. Yet, despite early attempts at automation, such Legal GRL models are still manually created, being time consuming and error prone. Recent work has demonstrated how Large Language Models can support the creation of conceptual models. Although showing promise, the application scenarios for conceptual modeling are often limited to well structured, and scoped, scenarios. Dealing with practical, less controlled, regulatory analyses, whereby often a particular actor or topic needs to be pulled into focus, is an open issue. In this paper, we propose using prompt templates to structure the process of using LLMs to create a Legal GRL model from text. The core idea is that prompt templates are created from state of the art prompt patterns, which can restrict LLM output, can manage a LLM conversation context, and can structure a LLM conversation. We report on an initial assessment of prompt templates on multiple law articles from the healthcare and energy community domains. Our initial results are promising for Legal GRL modeling, but at the same time show that caution is warranted.

Keywords: Requirements Engineering · Goal Modeling · Legal GRL · Large Language Models · Prompt Templates

1 Introduction

Background and Motivation. The recent advances in Artificial Intelligence and especially in Natural Language Processing (NLP) through Large Language Models (LLMs) give rise to exploring application opportunities that have been difficult to address with conventional NLP methods. In particular, requirements engineering and business process compliance constitute promising application areas for NLP methods and LLMs as demonstrated recently [5,8,19,31]. Companies face the challenge of a constantly evolving and changing regulatory landscape due to the vast and steadily growing amount of regulatory documents [14]. Moreover, if companies neglect business process compliance regulations they

H. van der Aa et al. (Eds.): BPMDS 2024/EMMSAD 2024, LNBIP 511, pp. 213–228, 2024.
https://doi.org/10.1007/978-3-031-61007-3_17

run the risk of being charged considerable fines and eventually reputation loss [14]. As regulatory documents are not just extensive but also often complex to understand, there exist several notations for modeling legal requirements in such a way that they can be easily understandable and usable by requirements engineers [1, 14]. Among those, the Legal Goal-oriented Requirements Language (Legal GRL) [9] is promising due to (a) its foundation being constituted by a Hohfeldian conception law, a framework for regulatory analysis that is well established in the regulatory domain [9, p.16-17], and (b) Legal GRL extends the GRL, a well established goal modeling language that is part of the standard User Requirement Notation [2] and which comes equipped with extensive software tool support. Despite its promises, creating a Legal GRL model still requires manual translation of legal texts, which is both a complex and time consuming task, especially for requirements engineers which do not have a background in law [23]. However, while [23, 24] present first steps towards automating Legal GRL modeling, to the best of our knowledge, it has not been realized. In the light of most recent work [5] demonstrating that LLMs like OpenAI's GPT-4 model [20] can be used for GRL modeling, but with caution, we want to continue exploring the possibility of automating Legal GRL modeling.

Research Gap and Challenges. While early experiences on using LLMs for modeling tasks show promise [5, 8], the modeled scenarios are often well defined and unambiguous, such as course assignments. The ability of LLMs to process real-world regulatory texts for a scenario with less straightforward implications is less well known. However, this is a relevant gap to tackle in the sense that we do not only have to deal with the real-world nature of regulatory texts, but also importantly, that for the given analysis purpose at hand we may require *additional interpretation* of the law text. This additional interpretation, then, goes beyond a prima facie, mechanistic, analysis of regulatory text. To illustrate this, consider the implication of Article 50(1) of the Dutch environmental law for a particular energy community scenario, which is documented in [15] and elaborated in Sect. 4. Article 50(1) stipulates that *"The tax is levied on the supply of natural gas or electricity via a connection to the consumer, as well as on the supply of natural gas via a connection to a CNG filling station."* (translated from Dutch [15]). In the light of the scenario what is most relevant is that the energy community member is liable to electricity taxation. Thus for the given article we need to, at the very least, pull into focus (i) electricity, and ignore the regulation on natural gas also stipulated in Article 50 (1), since in scenario of [15] we speak of electricity taxation only, and (ii) the implication of this law for the consumer of electricity, implicating that s/he is subject to electricity taxation.

The above is particularly challenging when acknowledging that LLMs are "statistical models of regularities found in language" [25, p.3] rather than that they understand natural language itself. Thus it is an open question of how a LLM deals with an (arguably) more conceptual task such as ignoring regulation on a certain topic, or pulling analysis for a certain actor into focus. Also, LLMs lack a grounding of the texts on which they are trained, meaning, that LLMs lack a notion of the (social, communicative, goal-driven) context from which these texts originate [22, p.13-14]. The aforementioned limitations of LLMs result in risks such as an inability to distinguish between factual and non factual information [25] and according hallucinations.

Additionally, as we will outline in Sect. 3, a LLM can be unfamiliar with Legal GRL. This compounds the challenges mentioned above, in the sense that it implies having to "teach" Legal GRL to a LLM prior to its use.

In light of both of the above two challenges we argue that an additional structure is needed to "tame" a LLM for translating law texts into a Legal GRL model. A promising structure is constituted by so called prompt templates. Such prompt templates, which borrow from the notion of prompt patterns [29], can restrict the output of a LLM, can be used to manage the context of a LLM conversation, and to structure a LLM dialog. For our purposes, these templates can be adapted to deal with pulling a certain actor in focus (through a persona pattern [29]), pull a topic into focus (through a context manager pattern [29]), or to "teach" novel concepts to a LLM (through a meta language pattern [29]).

Contribution and Main Results. The core idea of this paper is to capitalize on prompt templates, constructed from state-of-the-art prompt patterns [29], to add structure to LLM's use to create Legal GRL models from text. Such templates, then, are able to partly "tame", both, the interaction with and output generated by a LLM. Results from experiments with GPT-3.5, our LLM of choice (cf. Sect. 3), show promise in terms of GPT being able to retrieve relevant elements with the use of templates. Nevertheless, the results on precision are mixed, in the sense that elements are unpredictably retrieved that are either redundant, or not sensible at all. Thus, as a novelty we find that prompt patterns can help with a targeted analysis (e.g., pulling a certain actor or topic into focus), but at the same time, in line with earlier findings on translating structured scenarios into goal models [5] on the basis of our experiments we propose to exercise optimistic caution in the use of LLMs.

This paper is structured as follows. In Sect. 2 we discuss challenges to which prompt templates are a response. In Sect. 3 we present our prompt patterns and the procedure in which to use them. Subsequently we report on the evaluation in terms of experiments with multiple law articles in Sect. 4 including a report on lessons learned. Related work is outlined in Sect. 5 before the paper concludes with a summary of results and outlook on future work in Sect. 6.

2   Challenges to Motivate Legal GRL Prompt Templates

In this paper, we aim to elicit *LLM prompt templates for Legal GRL modeling*. Also, we report on a consciously selected and justified procedure for using them. The prompt templates can be considered as blueprints including variables like the law text which shall be modeled and which are to be defined by the user. Since missing out on requirements or wrongly modeling them can lead to severe consequences in terms of, e.g., compliance violations triggering high fines, it is of utmost importance to ensure that those prompt templates deliver reliable and complete results. Several conceptual and technical challenges are derived based on existing literature on i) exploring the usage of LLMs for modeling tasks, e.g., [5,8], ii) discussions on the general capabilities of LLMs, i.e., what LLMs do and do not do well, such as reported in [17,25].

First of all, briefly summarizing the arguments from the introduction on the lack of grounding of texts [22, p.13], and LLMs uncovering statistical patterns in language rather than understanding language itself [25], it can be said that LLMs tend to be limited when it comes to language in real life use. This limited competence is reflected in the inability of LLMs to distinguish properly between factual and nonfactual knowledge [25]), leading LLMs to *hallucinate*, in particular when executing complicated prompts without context. This in turn requires to ensure that the LLM is provided with **sufficient context** [29] (though we by no means want to imply that one should conflate context and LLM hallucinations). Also, the LLM should be familiar with the concepts central to executing the task at hand. In case the LLM is not familiar with the relevant concepts, it becomes vital to "teach" it these concepts. In our case this involves to break down the Legal GRL modeling into atomic tasks following [9]. Doing so gives rise to the challenge of **processing intermediate outputs** [4]. Namely, we need to design a prompt that delivers output which can be processed in successive prompts. Another challenge is dealing with the **non deterministic behaviour** of LLMs, meaning, they produce varying output when executing the same prompt [21].

Practical challenges to be considered are **character input and output limits** [4,29]. The character input limit becomes particularly relevant in our case because regulatory documents can be quite extensive. For example, the General Data Protection Regulation contains more than 300000 characters but the character limit for GPT-3.5 is below that (4096 tokens). As such, it is not feasible to process an entire document in a single prompt resulting in the necessity to split documents in a way reflecting logically connected parts, e.g., an article [9,30].

To sum up, acknowledging the real life use linguistic competence of LLMs, we agree with [17] to capitalize on the formal linguistic competence of LLMs, and to complement LLMs with additional mechanisms to alleviate their limited competence. In this paper, as stated, we do so by means of templates for prompt engineering. In particular, said templates can restrict the output of a LLM, manage the context of a LLM conversation, and structure a dialog [29].

3   Designing Legal GRL Prompt Templates

In the following we elaborate on our *Legal GRL Prompt Templates*[1], including our justification for using them, and the consciously selected procedure of their application. The procedure and prompt template design i) addresses the challenges presented in Sect. 2, ii) applies and combines prompt patterns as presented in [29], and iii) includes findings from intermediate experiments. As a representative example for a LLM, we select OpenAI's GPT-3.5 model in the form of the ChatGPT interface. It has several advantages such as being free of

---

[1] The full prompts are available at https://docs.google.com/document/d/1uktW42y KTwzLz7cl1Xg_KYJKV9BsSJ3RD4BCtQmxp1U/edit?usp=sharing.

charge, fast and easily accessible, in part because it does not need to be hosted compared to, e.g., Llama models [28]. This contributes to being reproducible, however, the transferability of the prompt templates to other LLMs might be limited [4]. Furthermore, it is not evident upfront which knowledge the selected LLM has on the concepts that are necessary for Legal GRL modeling. The latter is explored in Sect. 3.1, which constitutes the basis for developing the prompt templates for Legal GRL modeling in Sect. 3.2–3.3.

3.1 Preparations

As demonstrated by [5], GPT-4 is familiar with the concept of GRL and so is GPT-3.5 which we exemplary use in this paper. In case it is also familiar with Legal GRL modeling, our envisioned task would become rather straight-forward. However, this needs to be tested. Therefore, we first explore the LLMs' capabilities for Legal GRL modeling, through the following prompt.

Prompt 1

What do you know about Legal Goal-oriented Requirements Language?

Since GPT-3.5 responds it is not familiar with the concept of Legal GRL, we break down the overall task into smaller ones. This is a considerable difference compared to recently presented papers like [5]. For Legal GRL modeling this includes, adapted from [9], developing the Hohfeldian model of law (↦ Sect. 3.2), and then generating the corresponding Legal GRL model (↦ Sect. 3.3).

Similar to before, in order to realize the first step for Legal GRL modeling, the LLMs' capabilities in terms of Hohfeldian analysis must be determined. It turns out that GPT-3.5 is familiar with the Hohfeldian model of law. However, there exist different Hohfeldian taxonomies [9], so we must ensure the LLM can provide the analysis using the taxonomy which is required in this case [26].

Prompt 2

What do you know about the Hohfeldian taxonomy by Alberto Siena?

In summary, GPT-3.5 is familiar with the Hohfeldian model of law, however it is not familiar with the Hohfeldian taxonomy as expressed by Alberto Siena [26]. The fact that GPT-3.5 uses a different Hohfeldian taxonomy could be confirmed during the first iteration of experiments.

3.2 Develop a Hohfeldian Model of Law

Since developing the Siena interpretation of a Hohfeldian model of law consti-tutes one fundamental concept towards Legal GRL modeling, it becomes nec-essary to provide the LLM with more details on the concepts from Siena. For this, the *Meta Language Creation Pattern* [29] can be employed. During this first iteration of experiments, we could confirm that the *Cognitive Verifier Pattern* [29] has a strong effect on the results. In particular, the results improved when executing multiple prompts that divide the overall task into smaller ones. In addition, after each smaller step, users could correct intermediate results. Thus, we keep the human in the loop and enhance transparency throughout the modeling. This latter aspect is vital since we are dealing with business process compliance rules which could, in case of violation, lead to extensive fines and reputation loss. In summary, for generating a Hohfeldian model of law cf. Siena, we suggest to *successively* execute the following prompt templates. The prompt templates contain statements taken from [9].

Prompt 3

```
In the following I will ask you to perform a Hohfeldian analysis of a
law including the four fundamental legal relations which are
1) Duty means <definition as in [9]>.
2) Privilege is <definition as in [9]>.
3) Power is <definition as in [9]>.
4) Immunity is <definition as in [9]>.          The law I want you to analyze is:
< law text >.
Return the Hohfeldian analysis as a JSON file that per legal relation,
classifies the law per ''Actor'', ''Modal Verb'',''Precondition'', ''Clause''.
A ''Clause'' consists of ''Verb'' and ''Action''. Only provide ''Actor'' if it
is explicitly mentioned in the law.
```

The third prompt utilizes the *Template Pattern* [29] to enhance readability and to facilitate automated processing. The JSON format was selected because it can be easily understood by humans, thus allowing for easy error corrections. In order to control hallucinations, i.e., avoid that the LLM adds actors which are not explicitly mentioned in the law, the *Fact Check List Pattern* [29] is employed in the last sentence. Furthermore, earlier experiences with regulatory analysis teach us that, for some purposes, regulation should be analysed from the perspective of a particular actor [15]. This, then, requires a shift from a prima facie regulatory analysis, where the regulation for all actors is foregrounded equally, to an actor-centric analysis, whereby regulation for a particular actor is foregrounded. To address such actor centric foregrounding during a regulatory analysis with GPT, the *Persona Pattern* can be added in a fourth prompt.

Prompt 4

```
Return this Hohfeldian analysis as JSON file from the perspective of
the actor < Actor >.
```

Finally, regulatory texts often contain topics that are irrelevant for the analysis at hand. An example discussed in Sect. 4.1 is a law for environmental taxes, which includes regulation on both gas and electricity, but of which only electricity is relevant for the analysis. To put the focus on a particular topic, respectively to exclude a certain topic, we use the *Context Manager Pattern* [29].

Prompt 5

Ignore $< Topic >$ Regulation.

3.3 Generate a Legal GRL Model

Taking the Hohfeldian analysis as a basis, we now use GPT to create a Legal GRL model. We offer GPT the procedure from [9, p.91–92] to do so. Nevertheless, given the intricacy of said procedure (10 steps in overall, with several sub steps) next to the final Legal GRL output, we are also interested in *how* GPT arrives at the final result. Thus, we are interested in generating intermediary results as well. To produce intermediate results, we capitalize on the idea of Chain of Thought prompting by adding the phrase "Let's think step by step", in line with [16]. While originally meant to promote step-by-step reasoning [16], such Chain of Thought prompting can be equally used to offer transparency into the intermediate results of an intricate procedure, such as inherent to [9, p.91–92].

Prompt 6

Translate the above Hohfeldian analysis into a Legal GRL model using the following steps. <steps from [9, p.91--92]>
Let's think step by step.

To arrive at a Legal GRL model which can be imported and refined in JUCM-Nav, the output of Prompt 6 must be transformed into a suitable format. This is achieved through Prompt 7 which uses, similar to Prompt 3, the *Template Pattern* [29]. The output, in this case, a similar XML structure as used in [24][2], can be copied into a local file by users for later import into JUCMNav.

Prompt 7

Summarize the above Legal GRL model into one XML file.
The root of this XML file is ''<?xml version=''1.0'' ?>'' and it has a child
''grl-catalog'' with attributes ''author'' having value ''ChatGPT'',
''catalog-name'' with value ''URNspec'' and description with value ''''. The
child ''grl-catalog'' shall contain a subchild ''element-def'' containing
one or multiple subchildren of ''intentional-element''. An
''intentional-element'' thereby represents a Goal, Task or Subgoal and has an attribute
''decompositiontype'' which can be either ''And'', ''Or'' or
''Xor'', an attribute ''id'' representing the unique identifier for this
intentional element in the form of a consecutive number, an attribute
''type'' which is either Goal, Task or Subgoal and nothing else. Ignore
Permission and Obligation. Also add an attribute ''name'' which contains
the description of the intentional element. The child ''grl-catalog''
shall contain a second subchild''link-def''
<continued description of the XML structure>.

---

[2] For examples see https://github.com/aminrabinia/GDPR-GRL-Models.

4 Evaluation

As a first step towards testing the efficacy of prompt templates, we performed two experiments.[3] Note that our use the term "experiment" refers to testing the efficacy of prompt patterns for different datasets. As such, we in no means imply that we perform a formal experiment, whereby one, in a controlled setting, manipulates independent variables to observe potential causal effects on a dependent variable. The two datasets for the experiments are described in Sect. 4.1. Besides reporting on quantitative results (in Sect. 4.2) these experiments mainly inform lessons learned, as reported in Sect. 4.3.

4.1 Datasets for Scenarios

The experiments are performed on two different datasets for which we establish a baseline against which to judge the LLM experiment results. The baseline comprises, both, the Legal GRL model, but also the intermediate Hohfeldian analysis. The latter helps to identify correctness of intermediate results.

PHIPA and FIPPA. The first dataset comprises multiple articles of the Personal Health Information Act (PHIPA) [12] and the Freedom of Information and Protection of Privacy Act (FIPPA) [18]. The goal for this dataset is to establish a good understanding of the performance of Prompt 3, i.e., the Hohfeldian analysis which provides the basis for the subsequent Legal GRL modeling. The baseline is taken from [9] and the article selection covers all four statement types. For PHIPA Article 10 we expect four duty statements, for PHIPA Article 18(2) one privilege statement, for PHIPA Article 52(3) one power statement and for FIPPA Article 12(1) one immunity statement.

Energy Communities. The second dataset comprises regulations on energy communities from [15]. This dataset is selected due to familiarity with the performed analyses by one of the authors. For the energy community scenario we focus on two articles: (i) *Article 50 (1) of the Dutch environmental tax act* [3], as already articulated in the introduction. This regulation is interesting for our experimental purposes since it allows us to experiment with the capability of LLMs to focus on the *relevant* implications of a regulation. In particular, energy community members in The Netherlands have no special exemptions, and so are treated as regular electricity consumers. As such, they are subject to energy taxes conform Article 50 (1) and can even be subject to double taxation, for both electricity storage and supply [15]. Yet, in its formulation, Article 50 (1) highlights mostly electricity and gas supply. The consumer being subject to taxation is treated in the context of a connection, whereas due to its financial implications for energy community members (as per the introduction) this part is actually the most pertinent for our analysis purposes. Thus for our purposes, for Article 50 (1) GPT should be able pull the actor consumer into focus, and

---

[3] Supplementary material is available at https://tinyurl.com/ycxajsf4.

also, due to its focus on electricity GPT should be able to ignore gas regulation; (ii) *Article 4 of EU directive 2019/944* [7], on the free choice of electricity supplier, which stipulates that *"Member States shall ensure that all customers are free to purchase electricity from the supplier of their choice and shall ensure that all customers are free to have more than one electricity supply contract at the same time, provided that the required connection and metering points are established."* This regulation is interesting since it offers complexity relative to the earlier environmental tax law. It covers multiple rights and duties (the free choice of supplier, the right to have multiple suppliers), of relevance to different actors. Also, the article contains preconditions (the connection and metering points being established), which in terms of conceptual coverage is relevant for our experiments. We focus on the Legal GRL model as a final outcome, cf. [15].

4.2   Results

The quantitative evaluation measures precision and recall of intermediate results for Prompt 3 – 7. Precision corresponds to the *total number of retrieved and relevant documents* divided by the *total number of retrieved documents* [27]. Recall corresponds to the *total number of retrieved and relevant documents* divided by the *total number of relevant documents in the dataset* [27]. A document for us includes, e.g., a Hohfeldian statement type, or a goal in the Legal GRL model. To realize precision and recall calculations, we need to determine what is a correctly retrieved document. This requires manual intervention. For example, in Article 50 (1) of the Dutch environmental tax act "the consumer" has an obligation to pay electricity tax, and a (Hohfeldian, Legal GRL) analysis of this article then also yields a consumer obligation accordingly. Yet, in the baseline reported in [15] "the prosumer" is an actor having to pay electricity taxes. Nevertheless, knowing that a prosumer is a type of consumer, "consumer" is considered as a relevant document. Additionally, the case that no document is expected and also none is retrieved by GPT is considered a positive result, while if no document is expected but GPT detected one, is considered a negative result.

PHIPA and FIPPA. This dataset consists of four different articles of two regulations and the goal is to evaluate precision and recall for results of Prompt 3. We perform 5 iterations (new chat per iteration) of Prompt 3 in order to evaluate the stability of results. The scores reported in Table 1 indicate the (lowest, average, highest score) of these 5 iterations. Per Hohfeldian statement the following scenarios are conceivable: 1) the statement type is correct and all elements, i.e., actor, modal verb, precondition and clause are correct; 2) the statement type is correct but a subset of elements or none are correct; 3) the statement type is incorrect but all elements are correct; 4) the statement type is incorrect and a subset of elements or all are incorrect. To capture those scenarios, precision and recall are calculated per article, iteration and along two dimensions.

Statement Types. For precision and recall calculations for the identification of statement types we solely look at how many statements were retrieved and their

Table 1. Results for Hohfeldian Analysis PHIPA and FIPPA, P = precision, R = recall

article		statement type	actor	modal verb	clause	precondition
PHIPA 10	P	$(0.67, 0.93, 1)$	$(1, 1, 1)$	$(1, 1, 1)$	$(0.5, 0.9, 1)$	$(0.25, 0.83, 1)$
	R	$(1, 1, 1)$	$(1, 1, 1)$	$(1, 1, 1)$	$(0.5, 0.9, 1)$	$(0.25, 0.83, 1)$
PHIPA 18(2)	P	$(0.25, 0.65, 1.00)$	$(0, 0, 0)$	$(0, 0.8, 1)$	$(0, 0.8, 1)$	$(0, 0.8, 1)$
	R	$(1.00, 1.00, 1.00)$	$(0, 0, 0)$	$(0, 0.8, 1)$	$(0, 0.8, 1)$	$(0, 0.8, 1)$
PHIPA 52(3)	P	$(0.00, 0.19, 0.25)$	$(0, 0.25, 1)$	$(0, 0.13, 0.5)$	$(0, 0.5, 1)$	$(0, 0.25, 1)$
	R	$(0.00, 0.80, 1.00)$	$(0, 0.25, 1)$	$(0, 0.13, 0.5)$	$(0, 0.5, 1)$	$(0, 0.25, 1)$
FIPPA 12(1)	P	$(0.00, 0.23, 0.50)$	$(1, 1, 1)$	$(0, 0, 0)$	$(0, 0.5, 1)$	$(0, 0.3, 0.5)$
	R	$(0.00, 0.60, 1.00)$	$(0.5, 0.83, 1)$	$(0, 0, 0)$	$(0, 0.5, 1)$	$(0, 0.3, 0.5)$

type, i.e., at this stage we do not take into account if the content of the statements is correct. This will be evaluated in the next step. In terms of Hohfeldian analysis, for PHIPA Article 10 we expect four duty statements, for PHIPA 18(2) one privilege, for PHIPA Article 52(3) one power and for FIPPA Article 12(1) one immunity statement. Overall we observe that on average recall is higher than precision. However, for some cases it drops to 0.00. This is observed for the articles containing a power and an immunity statement. Looking at Prompt 3, we observe that those are types for which the modal verb consists of a combination of modal verbs for duty and privilege. It seems that this could be the cause of the drop in recall. We will elaborate on this when reporting on observations of the Hohfeldian elements. Further it can be seen the best performing statement type is Duty with an average precision of 0.93 and recall of 1.00. Since in the given setting, a high recall is very important because missing out on parts of a legislation can result in tremendous fines, the results can be assessed positive. Last we want to mention that we received results which were marked as a particular statement type but the content for each of the elements was evaluated with not available. Since content is not considered those were marked as false positives. Not doing so would however increase the scores for some articles.

Element Types. Second, we measure precision and recall per element type over all articles, only for statements for which their type was correctly identified in first place as considering incorrectly identified statement types is not meaningful because we cannot have a baseline for statements that should not be there in first place. Again, the article containing the duty statements scored very well for both precision and recall. For Article 18(2) we can observe that precision and recall for actor is 0 for all iterations. Looking at the expected baseline output which is stating that the actor is undefined, we could come up with the hypothesis that there seems to be a problem for GPT in case no actor is expected. Instead, GPT was suggesting that the actor should be "j", exactly as mentioned in the examples given in Prompt 3. A similar observation was made for modal verbs, sometimes, GPT just put the full list of modal verbs for a statement type as outlined in Prompt 3. For Article 18(2) no precondition is expected and GPT seems to handle missing preconditions better than missing actors. In the case of Article 12(1) only parts of a statement were identified, i.e., the baseline expected "Disclose a record", GPT identified "allow disclosure of a record". We scored such a case with 0.5 in our assessment of whether a document was correctly retrieved.

Energy Communities. For the Legal GRL analysis, we calculate precision and recall as a variation of the above Hohfeldian analysis. For example, for calculating the recall of actors and modalities, we judge not only if the given element is relevant, but also if the goal that the modality or actor belongs to is relevant. Only if both conditions are met, the element is considered as relevant. In terms of the recall scores in Table 2 for the two energy community articles GPT correctly identifies all relevant goals and associated to those, the relevant actors, and deontic modalities for goals. Equally GPT scores quite well on preconditions and dependencies, with those of Article 4 achieving full recall on both precondition goals and correct dependencies, whereas for Article 50(1) a relevant precondition and dependency were identified, but GPT also erroneously identified the precondition (and dependency) "The tax on the supply of electricity via a connection". For the two energy community articles of note is that GPT fails to identify the contribution links and identifies tasks not present in the baseline. These tasks introduce a measure of redundancy into the Legal GRL model. For example, the task "Pay tax on the supply of electricity via a connection" is identified for the obligation goal "Pay tax on the supply of electricity via a connection".

Table 2. Results for the Legal GRL analysis. P = Precision, R = Recall

Article		Goal	DType	Actor	Task	Precond	Depend	Contr	Decomp
Art 4	P	0.67	0.67	0.67	0	0.5	0.5	0	0
	R	1	1	1	0	1	1	0	0
Art 50(1)	P	0.67	0.67	0.67	0	0.5	0.5	0	1
	R	1	1	1	0	0.5	0.5	0	1

4.3 Lessons Learned

Lesson 1: Templates Offer Guidance in Constructing Prompts for "Taming" GPT. One of the key takeaways of our experiments is that, indeed, the use of prompt templates helps us to "tame" GPT to translate regulatory text into a Legal GRL model. As we have seen, in our prompts we have relied variously (1) on the meta language creation pattern, to prepare GPT in performing a Siena variation of a Hohfeldian analysis, (2) on the template pattern to, both, add structure to the output (e.g., in terms of identifying clauses and actions for a given Hohfeldian concept), and to enhance readability and future automated processing, and (3) on the persona pattern, to pull into focus the Hohfeldian analysis of a regulatory article for a particular actor.

To further illustrate the use of such prompt templates for analysing articles of law, consider the analysed Article 50(1). For this law, both the persona pattern and context manager have proven to be particularly useful to obtain a result from GPT that is consistent with the analyses underlying [15]. In terms of the *persona pattern*, we used the prompt "Return this Hohfeldian analysis as JSON file from the perspective of the actor Consumer." to pull the electricity consumer into focus for our analysis. Without using the persona pattern, GPT generates a Hohfeldian analysis whereby, next to the "Government" as the actor levying taxation, the "Supplier of electricity", and the "Supplier of natural gas to CNG filling stations" are in focus. Nevertheless, purely in terms of financial implications it is mostly the electricity consumer that is implicated by Article 50(1), as emphasized in our baseline in [15]. Thus, in order to gain analysis results from GPT that mimic the consumer implications of the analysis from [15], adopting a persona seems to be a necessary step in between. Additionally, for Article 50(1) we rely on the *context manager pattern* with the prompt "Ignore gas related regulation." to pull into focus electricity taxes. Without such a context manager, even when using the persona pattern, also gas related regulation will be analysed by GPT, while this is irrelevant for the given energy community scenario.

Lesson 2: Sequential Introduction of Prompts Matters. For one, the sequential use of patterns helps us to "teach" GPT a technique that becomes prominent in later prompts. In our case, to teach GPT the Siena variant of a Hohfeldian analysis. Also, sequential prompt use reduces prompt complexity, which in turn reduces the risk that GPT starts to hallucinate. Namely, early experiments indicate that creating one, encompassing, prompt, which combines all desired patterns, leads to results that are not sensible. For example, with an encompassing pattern suddenly liberty is used as a Hohfeldian type, which is not sensible, and actors are erroneously omitted as a Legal GRL concept.

Lesson 3: GPT Performs Pretty Well in Delivering Relevant Results, but Offers Mixed Results on Precision. Our experiments with multiple law articles display promise in terms of GPT's ability to retrieve relevant elements, as reflected in the consistently solid recall scores for both the Hohfeldian analysis and the Legal GRL analysis. Nevertheless, we also find that GPT tends to generate output beyond that which is provided in the baseline, as reflected in the mixed precision scores. The role of this additional output is ambivalent. On the one hand, it can inspire additional modeling ideas. On the other hand, in our experiments we found that the additional output manifested itself often in terms of either (i) redundant modeling elements, such as a task with the exact same name as a goal, or (ii) simply in terms of nonsense, such as GPT generating a Privilege with completely empty sub elements (missing a clause, actor, or action), or GPT generating a generic link concept, which simply does not exist in (Legal-)GRL. In that sense our findings are in line with [5], who used GPT 4 for supporting goal modeling tasks. While GPT offers promise for modeling tasks in terms of generating relevant results, due to its unpredictable tendency generate obsolete and nonsensical results one should be cautious in its use.

5   Related Work

An overview of NLP techniques applied to the requirements engineering domain was addressed in a recent survey [31]. One important finding was that papers have mainly focused on extracting i-Star goal models from user stories, such as [13], and apply conventional NLP methods like POS tagging and dependency parsing. A hybrid modeling approach for extracting goal models from text using BERT was presented in [32] and the application of LLMs for requirements engineering modeling tasks was recently explored by [5,8]. Similarly, to extract Decision Requirements Models (a standard operational decisions modeling language) from textual descriptions first employed a pipeline centering on BERT [11], but recently [10] focused on the use of GPT-3 for the same extraction task.

   In contrast to above papers, our input are regulatory documents and our output Legal GRL models. Our work is closest related to and can be seen as a continuation of [23,24] which envision a framework for automatic generation of Legal GRL models. Yet, full automation of the entire pipeline was not achieved, in particular legal requirements extraction remained a manual task though a concept for automation was presented. As such, our work differentiates itself (1) compared to Legal GRL model extraction work specifically [23,24], in line with the above requirements engineering advances we employ LLMs, whereas (2) generally speaking, for the use of LLMs to support modeling tasks, we propose to capitalize on combinations of prompt patterns so as to structure prompts, being crucial for the quality of the results produced by LLMs [29].

6   Conclusion and Outlook

In this paper, we propose prompt templates to structure the use of LLMs for creating Legal GRL models from law text. Results from three experiments with one LLM, GPT-3.5, show promise in terms of retrieving relevant elements. At the same time, the unpredictable tendency of GPT to generate redundant and nonsensical results indicate that optimistic caution is warranted.

   For future work we see many further directions for the use of LLMs in conceptual modeling. For one, this includes *a comprehensive coverage* of the activities required for legal modeling. The Legal GRL modeling which was explored in this paper only comprises the final step of a larger method [23]. In particular, like many other approaches, we assumed retrieval, collection and preparation of relevant documents. However, these are as well time-consuming tasks for which state-of-the-art technology, e.g., transformer models [6] have been applied successfully. Also, for Legal GRL specifically we aim to experiment with *making explicit the regional context*. This is relevant since the regional legal theory may influence the law's interpretation (e.g., common law versus civil law). At the same time, we aim to abstract from the particular application of Legal GRL *to modeling languages in general*, so that the idea of using prompt templates can become useful for other conceptual modeling tasks as well. Finally, in line with the calls from [25] it seems to us worthwhile to experiment with using the ability of LLMs to discover patterns in language for the *"bottom-up" creation of conceptual models* from a given instance population.

References

1. Akhigbe, O., Amyot, D., Richards, G.: A systematic literature mapping of goal and non-goal modelling methods for legal and regulatory compliance. Requir. Eng. **24**(4), 459–481 (2019). https://doi.org/10.1007/S00766-018-0294-1
2. Amyot, D., Mussbacher, G.: User requirements notation: the first ten years, the next ten years (invited paper). J. Softw. **6**(5), 747–768 (2011). https://doi.org/10.4304/JSW.6.5.747-768
3. Belastingdienst: Wet belastingen op milieugrondslag. https://wetten.overheid.nl/BWBR0007168/2023-02-13/#HoofdstukVI_Afdeling2_Artikel50
4. Busch, K., Rochlitzer, A., Sola, D., Leopold, H.: Just tell me: prompt engineering in business process management. In: van der Aa, H., Bork, D., Proper, H.A., Schmidt, R. (eds.) BPMDS 2023, pp. 3–11. Springer, Cham (2023). https://doi.org/10.1007/978-3-031-34241-7_1
5. Chen, B., et al.: On the use of GPT-4 for creating goal models: an exploratory study. In: RE 2023 - Workshops, Hannover, Germany, 4–5 September 2023, pp. 262–271. IEEE (2023). https://doi.org/10.1109/REW57809.2023.00052
6. Dimlioglu, T., et al.: Automatic document classification via transformers for regulations compliance management in large utility companies. Neural Comput. Appl. **35**(23), 17167–17185 (2023). https://doi.org/10.1007/S00521-023-08555-4
7. European Parl., Council of the EU: Directive (EU) 2019/944 of the European Parliament and of the Council. http://data.europa.eu/eli/dir/2019/944/oj
8. Fill, H., Fettke, P., Köpke, J.: Conceptual modeling and large language models: impressions from first experiments with ChatGPT. Enterp. Model. Inf. Syst. Archit. Int. J. Concept. Model. **18**, 3 (2023). https://doi.org/10.18417/emisa.18.3
9. Ghanavati, S.: Legal-URN framework for legal compliance of business processes. University of Ottawa (Canada) (2013)
10. Goossens, A., Smedt, J.D., Vanthienen, J.: Comparing the performance of GPT-3 with BERT for decision requirements modeling. In: Sellami, M., Vidal, ME., van Dongen, B., Gaaloul, W., Panetto, H. (eds.) CoopIS 2023. LNCS, vol. 14353, pp. 448–458. Springer, Cham (2023). https://doi.org/10.1007/978-3-031-46846-9_26
11. Goossens, A., Smedt, J.D., Vanthienen, J.: Extracting decision model and notation models from text using deep learning techniques. Expert Syst. Appl. **211**, 118667 (2023). https://doi.org/10.1016/J.ESWA.2022.118667
12. Government of Ontario: Personal health information protection act (PHIPA) (2004). http://www.e-laws.gov.on.ca/html/statutes/english/elaws_statutes_04p03_e.htm#BK39
13. Günes, T., Öz, C.A., Aydemir, F.B.: ArTu: a tool for generating goal models from user stories. In: RE 2021, Notre Dame, IN, USA, 20–24 September 2021, pp. 436–437. IEEE (2021). https://doi.org/10.1109/RE51729.2021.00058
14. Hashmi, M., Governatori, G., Lam, H., Wynn, M.T.: Are we done with business process compliance: state of the art and challenges ahead. Knowl. Inf. Syst. **57**(1), 79–133 (2018). https://doi.org/10.1007/S10115-017-1142-1
15. de Kinderen, S., Ma, Q., Kaczmarek-Heß, M., Eshuis, R.: Conceptual modeling in support of economic and regulatory viability assessment - a reality check on the example of developing an energy community. In: Proper, H.A., Pufahl, L.,

Karastoyanova, D., van Sinderen, M., Moreira, J. (eds.) EDOC 2023. LNCS, vol. 14367, pp. 206–222. Springer, Cham (2023). https://doi.org/10.1007/978-3-031-46587-1_12

16. Kojima, T., Gu, S.S., Reid, M., Matsuo, Y., Iwasawa, Y.: Large language models are zero-shot reasoners. Adv. Neural. Inf. Process. Syst. **35**, 22199–22213 (2022)

17. Mahowald, K., Ivanova, A.A., Blank, I.A., Kanwisher, N., Tenenbaum, J.B., Fedorenko, E.: Dissociating language and thought in large language models (2023)

18. Ministry of Health and Long-Term Care Ontario: Freedom of information and protection of privacy act (FIPPA) (2011). http://www.e-laws.gov.on.ca/html/statutes/english/elaws_statutes_90f31_e.htm#BK63

19. Mustroph, H., Barrientos, M., Winter, K., Rinderle-Ma, S.: Verifying resource compliance requirements from natural language text over event logs. In: Di Francescomarino, C., Burattin, A., Janiesch, C., Sadiq, S. (eds.) BPM 2023. LNCS, vol. 14159, pp. 249–265. Springer, Cham (2023). https://doi.org/10.1007/978-3-031-41620-0_15

20. OpenAI: GPT-4 technical report. CoRR **abs/2303.08774** (2023). https://doi.org/10.48550/arXiv.2303.08774

21. Ouyang, S., Zhang, J.M., Harman, M., Wang, M.: LLM is like a box of chocolates: the non-determinism of chatgpt in code generation. arXiv preprint arXiv:2308.02828 (2023)

22. Pavlick, E.: Symbols and grounding in large language models. Phil. Trans. R. Soc. A **381**(2251), 20220041 (2023)

23. Rabinia, A., Ghanavati, S.: The FOL-based legal-GRL (FLG) framework: towards an automated goal modeling approach for regulations. In: MoDRE@RE 2018, Banff, AB, Canada, 20 August 2018, pp. 58–67. IEEE Computer Society (2018). https://doi.org/10.1109/MODRE.2018.00014

24. Rabinia, A., Ghanavati, S., Humphreys, L., Hahmann, T.: A methodology for implementing the formal legal-GRL framework: a research preview. In: Madhavji, N., Pasquale, L., Ferrari, A., Gnesi, S. (eds.) REFSQ 2020. LNCS, vol. 12045, pp. 124–131. Springer, Cham (2020). https://doi.org/10.1007/978-3-030-44429-7_9

25. Saba, W.S.: Stochastic LLMs do not understand language: towards symbolic, explainable and ontologically based LLMs. In: Almeida, J.P.A., Borbinha, J., Guizzardi, G., Link, S., Zdravkovic, J. (eds.) ER 2023. LNCS, vol. 14320, pp. 3–19. Springer, Cham (2023). https://doi.org/10.1007/978-3-031-47262-6_1

26. Siena, A.: Engineering Law-Compliant Requirements: the Nomos Framework. Ph.D. thesis, University of Trento, Italy (2010). https://opac.bncf.firenze.sbn.it/bncf-prod/resource?uri=TD12025791

27. Ting, K.M.: Precision and recall. In: In: Sammut, C., Webb, G.I. (eds.) Encyclopedia of Machine Learning, pp. 781–781. Springer, Boston (2010). https://doi.org/10.1007/978-0-387-30164-8_652

28. Touvron, H., et al.: Llama 2: open foundation and fine-tuned chat models. CoRR **abs/2307.09288** (2023). https://doi.org/10.48550/ARXIV.2307.09288

29. White, J., et al.: A prompt pattern catalog to enhance prompt engineering with chatgpt. CoRR **abs/2302.11382** (2023). https://doi.org/10.48550/ARXIV.2302.11382

30. Winter, K., Rinderle-Ma, S., Grossmann, W., Feinerer, I., Ma, Z.: Characterizing regulatory documents and guidelines based on text mining. In: Panetto, H., et al. (eds.) OTM 2017, Part I. LNCS, vol. 10573, pp. 3–20. Springer, Cham (2017). https://doi.org/10.1007/978-3-319-69462-7_1

31. Zhao, L., et al.: Natural language processing for requirements engineering: a systematic mapping study. ACM Comput. Surv. **54**(3), 55:1–55:41 (2022). https://doi.org/10.1145/3444689

32. Zhou, Q., Li, T., Wang, Y.: Assisting in requirements goal modeling: a hybrid approach based on machine learning and logical reasoning. In: MODELS 2022, Montreal, Quebec, Canada, 23–28 October 2022, pp. 199–209. ACM (2022). https://doi.org/10.1145/3550355.3552415

Process Modeling with Large Language Models

Humam Kourani[1,2]([✉]) [iD], Alessandro Berti[1,2] [iD], Daniel Schuster[1,2] [iD],
and Wil M. P. van der Aalst[1,2] [iD]

[1] Fraunhofer Institute for Applied Information Technology FIT,
Sankt Augustin, Germany
{humam.kourani,alessandro.berti,daniel.schuster,
wil.van.der.aalst}@fit.fraunhofer.de
[2] RWTH Aachen University, Aachen, Germany

Abstract. In the realm of Business Process Management (BPM), process modeling plays a crucial role in translating complex process dynamics into comprehensible visual representations, facilitating the understanding, analysis, improvement, and automation of organizational processes. Traditional process modeling methods often require extensive expertise and can be time-consuming. This paper explores the integration of Large Language Models (LLMs) into process modeling to enhance the accessibility of process modeling, offering a more intuitive entry point for non-experts while augmenting the efficiency of experts. We propose a framework that leverages LLMs for the automated generation and iterative refinement of process models starting from textual descriptions. Our framework involves innovative prompting strategies for effective LLM utilization, along with a secure model generation protocol and an error-handling mechanism. Moreover, we instantiate a concrete system extending our framework. This system provides robust quality guarantees on the models generated and supports exporting them in standard modeling notations, such as the Business Process Modeling Notation (BPMN) and Petri nets. Preliminary results demonstrate the framework's ability to streamline process modeling tasks, underscoring the transformative potential of generative AI in the BPM field.

Keywords: Process Modeling · Business Process Management · Generative AI · Large Language Models

1 Introduction

Process modeling is an essential aspect of Business Process Management (BPM), serving as a comprehensive toolkit for understanding, documenting, analyzing, and improving complex business operations. Business process modeling covers several formats – from textual representations to visual diagrams and executable models – thus facilitating a multifaceted approach to capturing organizational processes.

© The Author(s), under exclusive license to Springer Nature Switzerland AG 2024
H. van der Aa et al. (Eds.): BPMDS 2024/EMMSAD 2024, LNBIP 511, pp. 229–244, 2024.
https://doi.org/10.1007/978-3-031-61007-3_18

Business process modeling encompasses several key perspectives, each focusing on different process aspects. Traditionally, these perspectives include the *control-flow perspective*, which outlines the flow of activities and their dependencies; the *data perspective*, focusing on how data is generated, manipulated, and consumed throughout the process; the *resource perspective*, detailing the human and system resources involved in the process execution; and the *operational perspective*, which describes the operational rules and execution semantics. In this paper, we focus on enhancing the control-flow perspective of process modeling as the control-flow establishes the basic structure upon which the data, resource, and operational perspectives are built.

Business process modeling traditionally involves extensive manual effort and deep knowledge of complex process modeling languages like BPMN (Business Process Model and Notation) [28] or Petri nets [25]. Additionally, process models often necessitate ongoing updates to reflect process changes. These challenges create significant barriers to entry for users without expertise in modeling languages, underscoring the need for new, streamlined process modeling methodologies.

The advent of Large Language Models (LLMs) such as GPT-4 [22] and Gemini [8] introduces a promising solution for enhancing the efficiency and accessibility of process modeling. Trained on diverse and extensive datasets, these LLMs show advanced capabilities in performing different tasks, ranging from coherent and contextually relevant text generation to solving complex problem-solving queries and generating executable code [18,26,30]. Their ability to understand and process complex textual information in natural language makes LLMs particularly well-suited for process modeling and other tasks that require generating and refining structured outputs directly from textual descriptions. Therefore, leveraging LLMs in process modeling heralds a transformative shift, potentially reducing the dependence on manual effort and specialized knowledge.

Our paper introduces a novel framework that utilizes the power of LLMs to automate the generation of process models. It incorporates advanced techniques in prompt engineering, error handling, and code generation to transform textual process descriptions into process models illustrating the described processes. Additionally, our framework features an interactive feedback loop, allowing for refining the generated models based on the user's feedback. To demonstrate the feasibility and practical application of our framework, we implement a concrete system that instantiates it. This system leverages the Partially Ordered Workflow Language (POWL) [16] for the intermediate process representation, providing robust guarantees on the quality of the generated models. The generated POWL models can then be viewed and exported in standard modeling notations such as BPMN and Petri nets. We integrate the implemented system with state-of-the-art LLMs, showing the framework's ability to streamline process modeling and underscoring the potential of generative AI in revolutionizing BPM.

The remainder of this paper is structured as follows. In Sect. 2, we discuss related work. Section 3 outlines our LLM-based process modeling framework. Section 4 evaluates the integration of our framework with state-of-the-art LLMs. In Sect. 5, we discuss the limitations of our framework and propose ideas for future work. Finally, Sect. 6 concludes the paper.

2   Related Work

An overview of various approaches for extracting process information from text is provided in [1]. While [6] leverages Natural Language Processing (NLP) and text mining techniques to derive process models from text, [11] combines NLP with computational linguistics techniques to generate BPMN models. In [23], the authors employ NLP techniques to extract structured relationship representations, termed *fact types*, from text, and the derived fact types are subsequently transformed into BPMN components. The BPMN Sketch Miner [13] leverages process mining [24] to generate BPMN models starting from text in a *domain-specific language*. Commercial vendors are integrating AI into process modeling, e.g., Process Talks (https://processtalks.com) provides an AI-powered system for creating process models starting from textual descriptions.

The integration of LLMs in BPM has been explored recently. Several studies [4,27] delve into the potential applications and challenges of employing LLMs for BPM tasks. In [21], limitations of using GPT-4 in conceptual modeling are discussed. LLMs are evaluated on various process mining tasks in [3]. The proposed approach in [5] employs BERT [7] for the classification and analysis of process execution logs, aiming to improve process monitoring and anomaly detection. In [14], the authors explore the novel concept of conversational modeling with LLMs, proposing a method for generating process models through dialogue-based interactions. The paper [12] demonstrates the capability of LLMs to translate textual descriptions into procedural and declarative process model constraints. Finally, [10] investigate the broader implications of LLMs in conceptual modeling, suggesting potential applications beyond traditional BPM tasks.

3   LLM-Based Process Modeling Framework

In this section, we detail our framework that leverages the power of LLMs for generating process models starting from process descriptions in natural language.

3.1   Framework Overview

Figure 1 provides a schematic overview of our proposed framework. First, users input a textual description of a process in natural language. Upon receiving the textual description, we incorporate additional information to craft a comprehensive prompt (the employed prompt engineering techniques are detailed in Sect. 3.3). This prompt is designed to guide the LLM to generate executable code that can be used for the generation of process models (the selection of the modeling language used for process representation is discussed in Sect. 3.2). The code generation step leverages a set of functions we designed to facilitate the creation of process models. After the prompt is generated, it is dispatched to the LLM. Note that the framework is independent of the selected LLM; it can be integrated with any advanced LLM that offers a large context window and code generation capabilities. After receiving the LLM's response, we extract the code

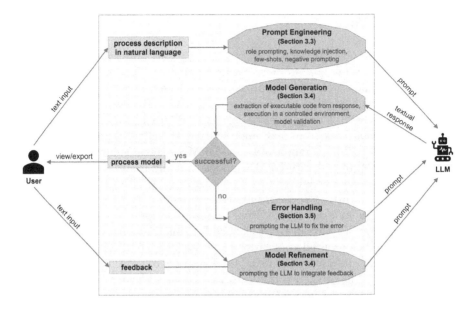

Fig. 1. LLM-based process modeling framework.

snipped from the response and try to execute it (cf. Sect. 3.4). In instances where the code extraction or execution encounters errors, we employ an error-handling mechanism that involves sending a refined prompt back to the LLM, exploiting LLMs' self-refinement capabilities to fix the error (cf. Sect. 3.5). Upon successful code execution and process model generation, users can view or export the model using established process modeling notations, such as BPMN and Petri nets. Moreover, the framework incorporates an interactive feedback loop. Users can provide feedback on the generated model, which is subsequently integrated into the model. This feature enables the continuous optimization and refinement of the generated process model.

3.2 Process Representation

To better explain the different stages within our framework, we instantiate a concrete system that utilizes the Partially Ordered Workflow Language (POWL) [16] for intermediate process representation. The foundational principles of our framework allow for the integration with other modeling languages tailored to the requirements of process modeling. In this section, we motivate our choice of the POWL language.

Our aim is to generate process models in standard notations familiar to most professionals in the business process management field, such as BPMN and Petri nets. However, such modeling languages are complex with a high potential for quality issues. For example, it is possible to generate Petri nets or BPMN models with dead parts that can never be reached. Therefore, the concept of *soundness* is introduced, and many approaches for the automated discovery of process models use process modeling languages that guarantee soundness (e.g., [15,17]). Our system for process modeling employs POWL for intermediate process representation, and the generated POWL models are then transformed into BPMN or Petri nets. A POWL model is a partially ordered graph extended with control-flow operators for modeling choice and loop structures. POWL represents a subclass of Petri nets that allow for the generation of hierarchical models where sub-models are combined to generate larger ones.

We have selected POWL as an intermediate process representation due to the following reasons:

- *Soundness Guarantees:* Unlike BPMN models or Petri nets, POWL inherently ensures soundness.
- *Simplicity:* POWL's hierarchical nature enables a simplified model generation by recursively generating models and combining them into larger ones. Moreover, POWL allows for combining sub-models as partial orders under the assumption that tasks are inherently parallel unless explicitly defined otherwise. This assumption of concurrent task execution mirrors the dynamics of numerous real-life processes, and it facilitates the generation of process models as the order of concurrent elements does not need to be specified.
- *Expressive Power:* While POWL and process trees[17] both guarantee soundness, POWL supports a broader range of process structures [16]. POWL allows for modeling intricate, non-hierarchical dependencies while maintaining the quality guarantees of hierarchical process modeling languages.

3.3   Prompt Engineering

This section discusses the prompting strategies we employ to effectively utilize LLMs for process modeling. We guide the LLM toward a precise comprehension of the provided process descriptions and the subsequent generation of the targeted process models. These strategies aim to leverage the inherent capabilities of LLMs without the need for retraining or adjustments.

The following prompting strategies are employed within our process modeling framework:

- *Role Prompting:* This strategy involves assigning a specific role to the LLM to guide its responses or behavior in a particular direction [29]. We implemented role prompting by instructing the LLM to act as an expert in process modeling, familiar with common process constructs. The LLM is also tasked to assume the role of a process owner and to use its expertise in the context of the process to fill in any gaps in the provided process description.
- *Knowledge Injection:* This strategy involves providing the LLM with new, specific information or context that it may not have been exposed to during its initial training [19]. We provide comprehensive knowledge about POWL, offering detailed insights into its hierarchical structure and the semantics of the different POWL components. Moreover, our framework leverages LLM

Listing 1.1. Injecting the LLM with knowledge about POWL. Lines that extend beyond the displayed text are abbreviated with "..." to keep it compact.

```
Use the following knowledge about the POWL modeling language: A POWL ...
Provide the Python code that recursively generates a POWL model. Save the ...
Assume the class ModelGenerator is properly implemented and can be ...
ModelGenerator provides the functions described below:
  - activity(label) generates an activity. It takes 1 string argument, ...
  - xor(*args) takes n >= 2 arguments, which are the submodels. Use it to ...
  - loop(do, redo) takes 2 arguments, which are the do and redo parts. Use ...
  - partial_order(dependencies) takes 1 argument, which is a list of ...
Note: for any powl model, you can call powl.copy() to create another ...
```

capabilities in generating executable code [26] by instructing the LLM to generate Python code that utilizes a predefined set of functions we designed for the safe generation of POWL models. We provide a detailed explanation of these predefined methods and how they can be used to generate POWL models. Listing 1.1 illustrates the injected knowledge about POWL.

– *Few-Shots Learning:* This method involves training the LLM on solving the task by providing several example pairs of input and expected output [9]. This enhances the LLM's ability to generate POWL models starting from process descriptions. For instance, Listing 1.2 shows one the examples we use for training. This example shows how to generate a POWL model for the bicycle manufacturing process from [2].

– *Negative Prompting:* Negative prompting refers to instructing the LLM by specifying what it should avoid in its response [20]. We implement negative prompting by instructing the LLM to avoid common errors that can occur using our predefined methods for generating POWL models (e.g., trying to generate partial orders that violate irreflexivity). Moreover, we extend our few-shot demonstrations with common mistakes that should be avoided during the construction of each process. For example, a common mistake for the bicycle manufacturing process (cf. Listing 1.2) is to create a local choice between two activities "reject order" and "accept order" instead of modeling a choice between the complete paths that are taken in each case.

3.4   Model Generation and Refinement

After receiving the LLM's response, the Python code snippet is extracted from the response, which might also include additional text (e.g., intermediate reasoning steps). If the code extraction is successful, then the extracted code is executed to generate the model. Executing code generated by an LLM involves multiple considerations to handle security risks and invalid results. The following strategies are implemented to ensure a safe environment for producing valid process models:

Listing 1.2. POWL model generation example used for few-shots learning, extended with instructions to avoid common errors. Lines that extend beyond the displayed text are abbreviated with "..." to keep it compact.

```
Process description for example 1:
A small company manufactures customized bicycles. Whenever the sales ...

Process model for example 1:
'''python
from utils.model_generation import ModelGenerator
gen = ModelGenerator()
create_process = gen.activity('Create process instance')
reject_order = gen.activity('Reject order')
accept_order = gen.activity('Accept order')
inform = gen.activity('Inform storehouse and engineering department')
process_part_list = gen.activity('Process part list')
check_part = gen.activity('Check required quantity of the part')
reserve = gen.activity('Reserve part')
back_order = gen.activity('Back-order part')
prepare_assembly = gen.activity('Prepare bicycle assembly')
assemble_bicycle = gen.activity('Assemble bicycle')
ship_bicycle = gen.activity('Ship bicycle')
finish_process = gen.activity('Finish process instance')

check_reserve = gen.xor(reserve, back_order)

single_part = gen.partial_order(dependencies=[(check_part, check_reserve)])
part_loop = gen.loop(do=single_part, redo=None)

accept_poset = gen.partial_order(
    dependencies=[(accept_order, inform),
                  (inform, process_part_list),
                  (inform, prepare_assembly),
                  (process_part_list, part_loop),
                  (part_loop, assemble_bicycle),
                  (prepare_assembly, assemble_bicycle),
                  (assemble_bicycle, ship_bicycle)])

choice_accept_reject = gen.xor(accept_poset, reject_order)

final_model = gen.partial_order(
    dependencies=[(create_process, choice_accept_reject),
                  (choice_accept_reject, finish_process)])
'''

Common errors to avoid for example 1:
creating a local choice between 'reject_order' and 'accept_order' instead ...
```

- In order to eliminate the risk of executing unsafe code, we restrict the LLM to use the predefined functions we designed for the generation of POWL models. We employ a strict process to verify that the code strictly complies with the prompted coding guidelines, explicitly excluding the use of external libraries or constructs that may pose security threats.
- We define validation rules to ensure that the code generates models that align with the POWL specifications and requirements. For example, we validate that all partial orders within the generated model adhere to the transitivity and irreflexivity requirements.

Our framework converts the generated POWL models into Petri nets and BPMN models. It offers functionalities for displaying and exporting the models in these established notations, which are widely acknowledged within the business process management community.

Refinement Loop. The framework supports model refinement based on user feedback. Users can provide comments on the generated model, and we prompt the LLM to update the model accordingly. These feedback prompts are sent along with the full conversation history. This interactive approach ensures continual improvement and customization of the models.

3.5 Error Handling

Despite their advanced coding capabilities, LLMs do not always generate error-free code. We employ a robust error-handling mechanism tailored to mitigate potential inaccuracies and ensure the reliability of the generated process models.

Recognizing the variability in the severity and implications of errors, we categorize them into two distinct groups:

- *Critical Errors:* This category covers errors that significantly disrupt the system's functionality or compromise security. These encompass execution failures, security risks, and major model validation violations. Given their potential impact, critical errors necessitate decisive action and cannot be overlooked.
- Adjustable Errors: This category includes errors related to the model's qualitative aspects, such as the reuse of submodels within the same POWL model. Although they affect the model's precision or quality, adjustable errors are considered less critical. They can be adjusted automatically, allowing for a degree of flexibility in their resolution. For example, the error of reusing submodels within the same POWL model can be automatically resolved by creating copies of the reused models. However, such intervention is approached with caution to prevent significant deviations from the behavior of the intended process.

Our framework incorporates an iterative error-handling loop, engaging the LLM in resolving identified errors. A new prompt that details the error and requests the LLM to address it, along with the conversation history, are submitted to the LLM. This iterative cycle facilitates dynamic correction, leveraging the LLM's capabilities to refine and improve the generated code.

For critical errors, the system persistently seeks resolution via the LLM up to a predetermined number of allowed attempts. If the LLM fails to fix the error after the allowed number of attempts, the system terminates the process and marks the model generation as unsuccessful. In cases of adjustable errors, the system initially attempts correction through iterative engagement with the LLM. If the LLM fails to resolve adjustable errors after several attempts, then the system automatically resolves these errors.

4   Evaluation

In this section, we evaluate our LLM-based process modeling framework. We integrate the implemented system with state-of-the-art LLMs to demonstrate the feasibility and practical application of our framework.

Research Questions

We structure the evaluation around the following two research questions:

- Q1: How does our framework perform when integrated with state-of-the-art LLMs?
- Q2: How does our framework's performance compare to other LLM-based process modeling systems?

Q1 aims to investigate the capability of our framework to leverage the latest advancements in LLM technology. We used two state-of-the-art LLMs: GPT-4 and Gemini. We focus on the framework's ability to generate accurate and optimized process models based on initial descriptions and through the iterative feedback loop. The assessment considers the quality of the generated models, the efficiency in handling errors, and the effectiveness of integrating user feedback.

Q2 aims to compare our process modeling framework with other existing approaches. Notably, we found no LLM-based techniques that directly produce process models in the literature. The closest related work is the framework proposed in [12], which utilizes LLMs to transform process descriptions in natural language into *textual abstractions* in a pre-defined notation that captures BPMN base components. We use this framework to generate process models with GPT-4, and we manually transform the generated textual abstractions into BPMN models for comparative analysis. We refer to this approach as the TA (Textual Abstraction) framework throughout this paper.

Setup

We implemented an integration of our system with GPT-4 as a web application available at https://promoai.streamlit.app/. As Gemini APIs are not available in Germany, direct integration of our framework with Gemini is not feasible; we used the web interface (https://gemini.google.com/app), and we manually transferred the prompts and responses between Gemini and our framework.

Throughout our experiments, we set a threshold of two iterations for handling adjustable errors through interaction with the LLM before automatically resolving them, and we set a threshold of five iterations for critical errors before terminating the process and marking the model generation as unsuccessful. Each experiment was repeated three times to account for the non-deterministic nature of LLM results.

We used two processes for our evaluation: the process described in [16] for handling orders in an online shop and the hotel service process from the

Table 1. Process description and feedback comments for the online shop process.

Initial Process Description	Consider a process for purchasing items from an online shop. The user starts an order by logging in to their account. Then, the user simultaneously selects the items to purchase and sets a payment method. Afterward, the user either pays or completes an installment agreement. After selecting the items, the user chooses between multiple options for a free reward. Since the reward value depends on the purchase value, this step is done after selecting the items, but it is independent of the payment activities. Finally, the items are delivered. The user has the right to return items for exchange. Every time items are returned, a new delivery is made.
1st Feedback	Model the item selection using an activity "Add Items" that can be repeated.
2nd Feedback	The user may skip the reward selection

Table 2. Process description and feedback comments for the hotel process.

Initial Process Description	The Evanstonian is an upscale independent hotel. When a guest calls room service at The Evanstonian, the room-service manager takes down the order. She then submits an order ticket to the kitchen to begin preparing the food. She also gives an order to the sommelier (i.e., the wine waiter) to fetch wine from the cellar and to prepare any other alcoholic beverages. Eighty percent of room-service orders include wine or some other alcoholic beverage. Finally, she assigns the order to the waiter. While the kitchen and the sommelier are doing their tasks, the waiter readies a cart (i.e., puts a tablecloth on the cart and gathers silverware). The waiter is also responsible for nonalcoholic drinks. Once the food, wine, and cart are ready, the waiter delivers it to the guest's room. After returning to the room-service station, the waiter debits the guest's account. The waiter may wait to do the billing if he has another order to prepare or deliver.
1st Feedback	Include an activity "prepare food".
2nd Feedback	The guest may or may not tip the waiter after receiving the order

Table 3. Number of error-handling iterations needed for the initial model generation and feedback integration for each process. We use * to indicate that adjustable errors were resolved automatically, not through interaction with the LLM. We use - to mark the cases where the model generation was unsuccessful after five error-handling iterations.

Process	Step	GPT-4			Gemini		
		run 1	run 2	run 3	run 1	run 2	run 3
Online Shop	Initial Model	2	1	2	2*	2*	2*
	1st Feedback	0	0	0	0	-	-
	2nd Feedback	0	0	0	-	-	-
Hotel	Initial Model	2	2*	1	5*	-	3*
	1st Feedback	0	2*	0	2*	-	2*
	2nd Feedback	0	2*	0	-	-	2*

PET data set [2]. The process descriptions and feedback comments we used are reported in Table 1 for the online shop process and in Table 2 for the hotel service process. Note that we incorporated the feedback comments into the process description when applying the TA approach.

In Table 3, we report the number of error-handling iterations needed for the initial model generation and feedback integration for each process. We show

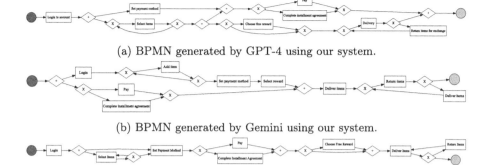

(a) BPMN generated by GPT-4 using our system.

(b) BPMN generated by Gemini using our system.

(c) BPMN corresponding to the textual abstraction generated by GPT-4 using TA.

Fig. 2. BPMN models generated for the order handling process in the first run. Although the models generated using our system show some deviations from the original process description, the model generated by GPT-4 correctly captures complex non-hierarchical dependencies. Unlike the models generated using our system, TA led to an unsound model that is dead after the choice between paying and completing an installment agreement.

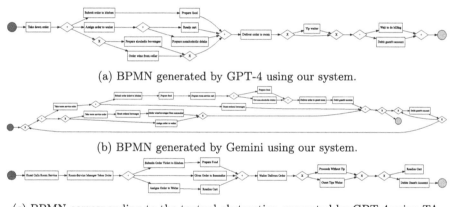

(a) BPMN generated by GPT-4 using our system.

(b) BPMN generated by Gemini using our system.

(c) BPMN corresponding to the textual abstraction generated by GPT-4 using TA.

Fig. 3. BPMN models generated for the hotel process in the first run. The model generated by GPT-4 using our system provides a high degree of conformance with the process description, significantly surpassing the model generated by Gemini. The model generated using TA is unsound as the end event is not reachable after the second instance of "Readies Cart".

the final models generated in the first run by both our framework and the TA framework: Fig. 2 for the online shop process and Fig. 3 for the hotel process. All generated models, along with an example detailing the complete sequence of prompts and responses exchanged between our system and GPT-4 until generating the final model, are available under https://github.com/humam-kourani/LLM-Process-Modeling.

Addressing Q1

GPT-4 demonstrated strong performance in generating process models for both processes. GPT-4 managed to deliver the initial models by the second error-handling iteration at the latest in all cases. Notably, the errors encountered during the generation of the model, which were classified as adjustable errors, were successfully resolved by GPT-4 in five cases. Feedback integration was notably efficient, with all feedback being accurately incorporated without any additional iterations for error handling in all three runs.

The model shown in Fig. 3a provides a high degree of conformance with the process description of the hotel process and the two employed feedback comments, however, some parts of the model can still be improved for better conformance. In the second run for the online shop process, GPT-4 was able to discover an optimal model that fully conforms with the reference model from [16], showcasing its robust understanding and modeling capabilities. This process contains complex non-hierarchical dependencies between selecting the items, setting a payment method, the reward selection, and the payment choice. While conventional hierarchical process modeling languages, such as process trees, are unable to capture such complex dependencies, POWL empowers our framework with the capability to model these complex structures. The other models discovered by GPT-4 show some deviations from the original process. As LLMs continue to evolve, with ongoing advancements and enhancements, we expect future models to offer more consistency in the outcomes.

In contrast to GPT-4, Gemini's performance was significantly weaker. The quality of the models generated by Gemini is markedly inferior to those produced by GPT-4. Gemini struggled to properly resolve adjustable errors, and, although the initial model generation was successful in five of the six cases, this was due to the internal automatic error correction, not a resolution through the interaction with Gemini. Furthermore, Gemini failed to integrate the feedback comments in most cases, leading to the generation of critical errors. These errors included attempting to use non-existent functions, attempting to use external libraries, stopping the return of Python code, and ignoring instructions from the initial prompt. These issues highlight Gemini's limitations in understanding the task requirements and error resolution within our framework.

Addressing Q2

Although some behaviors of the models produced by our framework deviate from the initial process descriptions, all produced models are sound and executable. The TA framework, in contrast, produces unsound models. For example, the model in Fig. 2c shows a choice between paying or completing an installment agreement through an exclusive choice gateway. The process is dead afterward; it requires both activities to be executed to proceed through the following parallel gateway. The model in Fig. 3c is also unsound as the end event is not reachable after the second instance of "Readies Cart". This shows the advantages of employing POWL as an intermediate process representation in ensuring the soundness of all models produced by our framework.

Evaluation Summary

The comparative analysis between GPT-4 and Gemini demonstrates the superior capabilities of GPT-4 within our LLM-based process modeling framework. GPT-4 not only excelled in generating high-quality process models with remarkable efficiency but also showcased its adeptness at effectively resolving errors and seamlessly integrating user feedback. Our framework's comparison with the TA approach highlights its superiority, particularly in producing sound and executable models. This shows the robustness of our methodology and the strategic use of POWL as an intermediate process representation.

5   Limitations and Future Directions

Our approach, while pioneering in leveraging LLMs for process modeling, has limitations. In this section, we outline areas for improvement and propose ideas for addressing them in future work.

Expanding Process Perspectives. Our framework addresses the control-flow perspective of process modeling, omitting the data, resource, and operational perspectives, which are crucial for a comprehensive understanding of business processes. The inherent flexibility and understanding capabilities of LLMs present a significant potential for extending our framework to incorporate additional process perspectives.

Extended Evaluation and User Studies. While our evaluation demonstrates promising results with the datasets and process descriptions employed, we acknowledge the need for a broader investigation to better assess the generalizability of the framework. In our future work, we aim to extend the evaluation to encompass a more diverse set of processes and domains. Moreover, we aim to conduct a user study to evaluate the framework's usability, efficiency, and learning curve for both expert and non-expert users.

Direct BPMN Generation. The implemented system instantiating our framework utilizes POWL for intermediate process representation. A possible direction for future research is the exploration of the direct generation of BPMN models without an intermediate process representation. This approach promises to offer greater flexibility in representing intricate process structures and dynamics and allows for the enrichment of process models with context-rich annotations. However, moving away from the structured guarantees provided by POWL necessitates the development of more advanced process model generation and validation techniques.

Enhanced Interactivity. We intend to enhance the model refinement loop to support more nuanced and interactive feedback mechanisms. For example, we aim to empower users to not only provide textual feedback on generated process models but also to manually edit the generated models.

6   Conclusion

This paper introduces a novel framework that integrates LLMs with process modeling. Our framework leverages the natural language understanding and text generation capabilities of LLMs to generate and refine process models starting from textual descriptions. Our framework employs innovative prompting strategies for LLM utilization, a robust model generation protocol considering safety and quality aspects, and a user feedback mechanism for model refinement. While our framework enhances the accessibility and efficiency of process modeling, we recognize that manual effort remains crucial for validating generated models and providing effective feedback. Through preliminary results, we demonstrated the practicality and effectiveness of our framework, paving the way for future research and development.

References

1. Bellan, P., Dragoni, M., Ghidini, C.: A qualitative analysis of the state of the art in process extraction from text. In: Vizzari, G., Palmonari, M., Orlandini, A. (eds.) Proceedings of the AIxIA 2020 Discussion Papers Workshop co-located with the the the 19th International Conference of the Italian Association for Artificial Intelligence (AIxIA2020), Anywhere, November 27th, 2020, CEUR Workshop Proceedings, vol. 2776, pp. 19–30. CEUR-WS.org (2020)

2. Bellan, P., van der Aa, H., Dragoni, M., Ghidini, C., Ponzetto, S.P.: PET: an annotated dataset for process extraction from natural language text tasks. In: Cabanillas, C., Garmann-Johnsen, N.F., Koschmider, A. (eds.) Business Process Management Workshops - BPM 2022. LNBIP, vol. 460, pp. 315–321. Springer, Cham (2022). https://doi.org/10.1007/978-3-031-25383-6_23

3. Berti, A., Schuster, D., van der Aalst, W.M.P.: Abstractions, scenarios, and prompt definitions for process mining with LLMs: a case study. In: De Weerdt, J., Pufahl, L. (eds.) Business Process Management Workshops - BPM 2023. LNBIP, vol. 492, pp. 427–439. Springer, Cham (2023). https://doi.org/10.1007/978-3-031-50974-2_32

4. Busch, K., Rochlitzer, A., Sola, D., Leopold, H.: Just tell me: prompt engineering in business process management. In: van der Aa, H., Bork, D., Proper, H.A., Schmidt, R. (eds.) Enterprise, Business-Process and Information Systems Modeling, BPMDS 2023, EMMSAD 2023. LNBIP, vol. 479, pp. 3–11. Springer, Cham (2023). https://doi.org/10.1007/978-3-031-34241-7_1

5. Chen, S., Liao, H.: Bert-log: anomaly detection for system logs based on pre-trained language model. Appl. Artif. Intell. **36**(1) (2022)

6. Gonçalves, J.C.D.A.R., Santoro, F.M., Baião, F.A.: Let me tell you a story - on how to build process models. J. Univers. Comput. Sci. **17**(2), 276–295 (2011)

7. Devlin, J., Chang, M.W., Lee, K., Toutanova, K.: BERT: pre-training of deep bidirectional transformers for language understanding. In: Burstein, J., Doran, C., Solorio, T. (eds.) Proceedings of the 2019 Conference of the North American Chapter of the Association for Computational Linguistics: Human Language Technologies, NAACL-HLT 2019, Minneapolis, MN, USA, 2–7 June 2019, Volume 1 (Long and Short Papers), pp. 4171–4186. Association for Computational Linguistics (2019)

8. Anil, R., et al. Gemini: a family of highly capable multimodal models. CoRR, abs/2312.11805 (2023)
9. Brown, T.B., et al.: Language models are few-shot learners. In: Larochelle, H., Ranzato, M., Hadsell, R., Balcan, M.-F., Lin, H.-T. (eds.) Advances in Neural Information Processing Systems 33: Annual Conference on Neural Information Processing Systems 2020, NeurIPS 2020, 6–12 December 2020, virtual (2020)
10. Fill, H.-G., Fettke, P., Köpke, J.: Conceptual modeling and large language models: impressions from first experiments with ChatGPT. Enterp. Model. Inf. Syst. Archit. Int. J. Concept. Model. **18**, 3 (2023)
11. Friedrich, F., Mendling, J., Puhlmann, F.: Process model generation from natural language text. In: Mouratidis, H., Rolland, C. (eds.) Advanced Information Systems Engineering - CAiSE 2011. LNCS, vol. 6741, pp. 482–496. Springer, Heidelberg (2011). https://doi.org/10.1007/978-3-642-21640-4_36
12. Grohs, M., Abb, L., Elsayed, N., Rehse, J.-R.: Large language models can accomplish business process management tasks. In: De Weerdt, J., Pufahl, L. (eds.) Business Process Management Workshops - BPM 2023. LNBIP, vol. 492, pp. 453–465. Springer, Cham (2023). https://doi.org/10.1007/978-3-031-50974-2_34
13. Ivanchikj, A., Serbout, S., Pautasso, C.: From text to visual BPMN process models: design and evaluation. In: Syriani, E., Sahraoui, H.A., de Lara, J., Abrahão, S. (eds.) MoDELS 2020: ACM/IEEE 23rd International Conference on Model Driven Engineering Languages and Systems, Virtual Event, Canada, 18–23 October 2020, pp. 229–239. ACM (2020)
14. Klievtsova, N., Benzin, J.V., Kampik, T., Mangler, J., Rinderle-Ma, S.: Conversational process modelling: state of the art, applications, and implications in practice. In: Di Francescomarino, C., Burattin, A., Janiesch, C., Sadiq, S.W. (eds.) Business Process Management Forum - BPM 2023. LNBIP, vol. 490, pp. 319–336. Springer, Cham (2023). https://doi.org/10.1007/978-3-031-41623-1_19
15. Kourani, H., Schuster, D., van der Aalst, W.M.P.: Scalable discovery of partially ordered workflow models with formal guarantees. In: 5th International Conference on Process Mining, ICPM 2023, Rome, Italy, 23–27 October 2023, pp. 89–96. IEEE (2023)
16. Kourani, H., van Zelst, S.J.: POWL: partially ordered workflow language. In: Di Francescomarino, C., Burattin, A., Janiesch, C., Sadiq, S. (eds.) Business Process Management - BPM 2023. LNCS, vol. 14159, pp. 92–108. Springer, Cham (2023). https://doi.org/10.1007/978-3-031-41620-0_6
17. Leemans, S.J.J.: Robust Process Mining with Guarantees - Process Discovery, Conformance Checking and Enhancement. Lecture Notes in Business Information Processing, vol. 440. Springer, Cham (2022)
18. Li, J., Tang, T., Zhao, W.X., Nie, J.Y., Wen, J.-R.: Pretrained language model for text generation: a survey. In: Zhou, Z.-H. (ed.) Proceedings of the Thirtieth International Joint Conference on Artificial Intelligence, IJCAI-21, pp. 4492–4499. International Joint Conferences on Artificial Intelligence Organization, Survey Track (2021)
19. Martino, A., Iannelli, M., Truong, C.: Knowledge injection to counter large language model (LLM) hallucination. In: Pesquita, C., et al. (eds.) The Semantic Web: ESWC 2023 Satellite Events. LNCS, vol. 13998, pp. 182–185. Springer, Cham (2023). https://doi.org/10.1007/978-3-031-43458-7_34
20. Miyake, D., Iohara, A., Saito, Y., Tanaka, T.: Negative-prompt inversion: fast image inversion for editing with text-guided diffusion models. CoRR, abs/2305.16807 (2023)

21. Muff, F., Fill, H.-G.: Limitations of chatgpt in conceptual modeling: insights from experiments in metamodeling (2024)

22. OpenAI. GPT-4 technical report. CoRR, abs/2303.08774 (2023)

23. Sholiq, S., Sarno, R., Astuti, E.S.: Generating BPMN diagram from textual requirements. J. King Saud Univ. Comput. Inf. Sci. **34**(10 Part B), 10079–10093 (2022)

24. van der Aalst, W.M.P.: Process Mining - Discovery, Conformance and Enhancement of Business Processes. Springer, Heidelberg (2011)

25. van Hee, K.M., Sidorova, N., van der Werf, J.M.E.M.: Business process modeling using Petri nets. Trans. Petri Nets Other Model. Concurr. **7**, 116–161 (2013)

26. Vidan, A., Fiedler, L.H.: A composable just-in-time programming framework with LLMs and FBP. In: IEEE High Performance Extreme Computing Conference, HPEC 2023, Boston, MA, USA, 25–29 September 2023, pp. 1–8. IEEE (2023)

27. Vidgof, M., Bachhofner, S., Mendling, J.: Large language models for business process management: opportunities and challenges. In: Di Francescomarino, C., Burattin, A., Janiesch, C., Sadiq, S.W. (eds.) Business Process Management Forum - BPM 2023. LNBIP, vol. 490, pp. 107–123. Springer, Cham (2023). https://doi.org/10.1007/978-3-031-41623-1_7

28. Von Rosing, M., White, S., Cummins, F., De Man, H.: Business process model and notation - BPMN. In: von Rosing, M., von Scheel, H., Scheer, A.-W. (eds.) The Complete Business Process Handbook: Body of Knowledge from Process Modeling to BPM, Volume I, pp. 429–453. Morgan Kaufmann/Elsevier (2015)

29. Xu, B., et al.: Expertprompting: instructing large language models to be distinguished experts. CoRR, abs/2305.14688 (2023)

30. Zhou, Y., et al.: Large language models are human-level prompt engineers. In: The Eleventh International Conference on Learning Representations, ICLR 2023, Kigali, Rwanda, 1–5 May 2023. OpenReview.net (2023)

Could a Large Language Model Contribute Significantly to Requirements Analysis?

Steven Alter[✉] [ID]

University of San Francisco, 2130 Fulton St., San Francisco 94117, USA
alter@usfca.edu

Abstract. This research-in-progress paper presents a quasi-experiment in which three different ChatGPT-4 prompts (for system structure, analysis, and recommendations) are applied in standard or augmented form to the work system in each of three case studies (automated warehouses, ride hailing platforms, and medication administration systems). The augmented forms (treatments) are based on different sets of ideas. Each case study comprises 3000+ words. The prompts are detailed requests for responses of up to 500 words related to three steps (system structure, analysis, and recommendations) related to those cases. A null treatment serving as a quasi-control uses standard prompts for each case without augmentation. The first actual treatment is a revision of an analysis template used by MBA and EMBA students; the other six are sets of questions based on activity theory, a BPM design space, system principles, and three other approaches The research questions are whether ChatGPT-4 can produce a useful first cut at system structure, analysis, and recommendations and whether various augmentations of ChatGPT-4 prompts improve or extend the outputs significantly.

Keywords: Requirements Analysis · Large Language Model · Systems Analysis and Design

1 Applying Large Language Models Despite Their Known Shortcomings

The enormous wave of attention to large language models (LLMs), especially ChatGPT, combines enthusiasm, fear, and initial applications in many organizations. Strengths of LLM-based chatbots start with their ability to produce text that is grammatical, reasonably well structured, and often approximately correct even if it lacks nuance [1]. Shortcomings of LLMs start with their operation as "stochastic parrots [2] that lack of common sense and other real-world knowledge despite being "excellent at processing longer sequences of data –like text– by using self-attention processes that enable the model to focus on different areas of the input." [3]. They tend to fabricate facts or ideas (to "hallucinate"), as was learned by a lawyer who thought that ChatGPT was a search engine and used it to submit a US federal court legal brief that cited legal precedents that never occurred [4]. The idea of "prompt engineering" [5, 6] arose from the common difficulty in specifying "prompts" (instructions for an LLM) specific enough to obtain

© The Author(s), under exclusive license to Springer Nature Switzerland AG 2024
H. van der Aa et al. (Eds.): BPMDS 2024/EMMSAD 2024, LNBIP 511, pp. 245–255, 2024.
https://doi.org/10.1007/978-3-031-61007-3_19

an adequate answer to a non-trivial question. On the other hand, a Sept. 2023 working paper by a collaboration of authors from leading institutions reported impressive results from a careful experiment involving 758 consultants for a leading consulting firm: On a set of "realistic consulting tasks within the [current] frontier of AI capabilities, consultants using AI were significantly more productive (they completed 12.2% more tasks on average, and completed task 25.1% more quickly), and produced significantly higher quality results (more than 40% higher quality compared to a control group)." [7].

This paper pursues two research questions: 1) Can ChatGPT-4 produce a useful first cut at structure, analysis, and recommendations related to a problematic system in an organization? 2) Can various augmentations of ChatGPT-4 prompts improve or extend its outputs significantly? This paper was inspired by wondering whether ChatGPT could generate reasonably good first cuts at management briefings similar to over 700 produced by MBA and EMBA students. If it could do that, then it might be able to contribute significantly to requirements analysis by students or by real world analysts.

Organization. The next section explains a quasi-experiment in which ChatGPT-4 summarizes system structure, analysis, and recommendations (three separate outputs) for three case studies (automated warehouses, ride hailing platforms, and medication administration systems). Standard ChatGPT prompts requesting responses of up to 500 words are augmented by 7 treatments that add different sets of ideas. A null treatment serving as a quasi-control uses standard prompts for each case without augmentation. Excerpts from prompts and ChatGPT-4 outputs that are available through Dropbox at https://www.dropbox.com/scl/fo/edn6u80h1hdhn1oboaonv/h?rlkey=0qalg6 7hdc5ama8cpd5f9zujn&dl=0. Those quotations provide evidence of both the power and the limitations of using ChatGPT-4 in this context. A concluding section identifies potentially fruitful areas for extending this research. This paper is a shortened version of a longer and more complete paper that was accepted with a requirement that it be reduced to 10 pages. The more complete paper and the cases, prompts, and outputs are available through Dropbox.

2   The Quasi-Experiment

This exploratory paper uses a quasi-experiment to demonstrate the potential usefulness of LLMs for requirements analysis. The quasi-experiment unfolded in two phases. The first phase produced initial results by applying 24 structured ChatGPT-4 prompts to each of three cases. The second phase tried to use ChatGPT-4 to refine those results.

2.1   The Quasi-Experiment's Goal and Form

The initial goal was exploring whether ChatGPT-4 could produce a rough cut at the type of management briefing that 700+ (mostly) MBA and EMBA students or student teams produced during 2003–2017 for proposing improvements in problematic work systems, mostly in their own organizations (e.g., [8, 9]). Initial trial applications of ChatGPT-4 to case studies led to extending the goal by comparing results from using an EMBA analysis template from 2014 along with other identifiable sets of ideas in the IS literature, such system principles, system design spaces, and activity theory.

Three separate cases were used because on a single case seemed insufficient even for illustrative purposes. The cases discuss problems whose solution is nontrivial and that are not simply exercises in programming. Each case was the subject of three separate prompts, one each for structure of the system, analysis of the situation, and recommendations. A standard prompt produced for each purpose was augmented by 7 treatments. Results from using the three standard prompts served as a quasi-control for purposes of comparison with results from using augmented prompts that incorporated ideas from the MBA template or from other identifiable sets of ideas. Ultimately, this generated 72 separate text responses, i.e., 3 cases × 3 types of prompts × 8 different sets of ideas. Those 8 sets of ideas included the control case (no augmentation), the MBA template, and six other sets of ideas from the literature.

2.2 Creation of Usable MS Word Documents Representing Three Cases

Informal searches based on personal awareness of the literature led to three cases that seemed interesting, seemed sufficiently different, contained enough detail to be worthy of analysis, and involved issues or controversies that call for recommendations.

The first case is about a ride hailing system (RDHL) that was extracted from a 2022 article [10] that explored resistance versus control in ride hailing and gig work. The RDHL case removed everything about gig work, organization theory, and other material unrelated to the ride hailing system. The result was 3385 Word document.

The second case concerned a bar code medication administration (BCMA) system (BCMA) in which nurses scan the barcode of a medication and the barcode on the patient's wristband to assure that the right medication is administered to the right patient at the right time. A 2008 article [11] about workarounds in that type of system identified numerous reasons for workarounds. Additional content from more recent articles from 2021 and 2023 [12, 13] extended the coverage from [11].

The third case (AMAZ) involves Amazon's order fulfillment warehouses. Glowing descriptions of these warehouses speak of transforming e-commerce, saving time, cooperation between people and robots doing heavy lifting [14]. Criticisms often say that people are treated like machines, are expected to perform work that causes many injuries, and are evaluated based on exceedingly tight standards. [15, 16]. The 3140 words in the AMAZ case combine excerpts from those three sources.

2.3 The Treatments

The Control. The quasi-experiment uses a control (designated CTL), which is viewed as a "null treatment". The control has 3 prompts that are called "standard prompts" (for system structure, analysis, and recommendations). Those steps are identified as ST, AN, or RE. Thus, the standard CTL prompt for making a recommendation for the AMAZ case is designated as AMAZ-CTL-RE. That format for designating prompts proved quite important for convenient identification of 72 prompts and 72 responses by ChatGPT-4. The longer version of this paper available through Dropbox uses the AMAZ-CTL-RE prompt to illustrate how the CTL operates. That prompt uses the term *scenario* as a synonym of treatment to avoid accidental confusion with medical terms.

The 7 treatments listed below augment the CTL treatment by instructing ChatGPT to use ideas from an MBA template or from one of 6 other sources. The treatments are identified by acronyms: MBA (MBA template), ACT (activity theory), AXM (work system axioms), BPM (business process design space), DSP (design space for work systems), FCT (facets of work), and PRN (work system principles).

MBA: This is an excerpt from a template used by MBA and EMBA students in 2014 for producing management briefings about problematic systems in their own organizations. The MBA prompt reduced that template to a textual form that omitted tables and topics that were not relevant. The MBA treatment asks questions related to work system theory [9]. The lengthy analysis prompt AMAZ-MBA-AN begins similarly to the prompt AMAZ-CTL-RE until the statement *"The suggested questions and ideas begin here."* The AMAZ-MBA-AN adds eight broad questions derived from the 2014 template. Those questions lead to many possible answers. Prompts for all treatments other than CTL use the same approach, i.e., a standard introduction up to the point where suggested questions begin, inclusion of suggested questions that express the treatment, and then continuation of the standard prompt after the suggested questions end. Using a consistent format across all prompts and designating a specific location for the various treatments made it possible to produce and save 72 lengthy prompts without many mistakes. Box 2 in the long paper available through DropBox shows AMAZ–MBA–AN.

ACT: Activity theory is "a broad theoretical framework for describing the structure, development, and context of human activity… [through basic principles]: hierarchical structure of activity, object-orientedness, internalization and externalization, tool mediation, and development. These general principles … are somewhat abstract when it comes to the actual business of working on a design or performing an evaluation." [17, p. 28]. (Also see [18].). The ACT questions are based on an Activity Checklist in [17] focusing on actors, outcomes, tools, activities, rules, community, division of labor, mediation of activity by tools, motives of actors, roles and rules for actors, reward for actors, structure of social interaction, dynamics of interaction, evaluation criteria, conflicts and contradictions, how actors think about norms, rules, and procedures, how much freedom actors have in doing their work, and so on. The prompts for ACT integrate those ideas into questions whose appearance resembles the MBA questions.

AXM: This treatment revises and extends a proposed series of service system axioms presented at ICIS 2017 [19]. Those axioms were updated as 24 axioms meant to apply to any work system. Each axiom brings two or more questions that a business or IT professional might ask about a work system. Prompts for the AXM treatment focus on the main topics of the axioms, i.e., system boundaries, inputs, outputs, system purposes, system beneficiaries, purposeful activities, key resources, regulation, management, subsystems, criteria for success or failure, surrounding environment, internal interactions, external interactions, maintenance activities, goals, performance gaps, alignment and misalignment, conflicts of beneficiaries, goals, relevant trade-offs, operational fit between subsystems, situations beyond the system's design and scope, and issues related to compliance and noncompliance.

BPM: This treatment summarizes a business process design space [20] that overlaps in many ways with a work system perspective despite coming from a different community. It has six layers, five of which are identical to the elements of the work system framework; the other is organization, instead of participants. Those overlaps go back to a BPR framework in a 2005 article on business process redesign [21] that used a similar six-part framework built on the "work centered analysis framework" from a 1999 IS textbook. [20] links the six central layers to 19 dimensions including customer segment, customer experience, customer value, customer, channel, scope of product/service, flow unit, location, temporality, business process, coordination, trigger, and outcome, objectives of the organization, internal participants, revenue model, business partner, etc. The ST prompt for BPM focuses on those dimensions. The AN prompt focuses on a related set of questions in tables in [20]. The RE prompt looks for recommended changes related to those topics.

DSP: This treatment is a summary of a design space published in a 2010 article [22] based on the elements of work system framework at the core work system theory. The ST prompt defines those elements. The AN prompt identifies numerous characteristics and features of those elements that may be problematic. For example, issues related to participants may involve personal knowledge and skills, personal autonomy, personal challenge, and personal growth. The RE prompt asks for ways in which elements of the work system framework might change in a beneficial way for the case.

FCT: This treatment is based facets of work [23], an extension of work system theory that looks at 18 common aspects of processes such as making decisions, communicating, processing information, coordinating, controlling execution, improvising, applying knowledge, and so on. [23] explains that specific facets of work were selected because they apply to sociotechnical and totally automated work systems, are associated with many relevant concepts, bring evaluation criteria and design trade-offs, have sub-facets, and bring open-ended questions for analysis and design. The ST prompt for FCT identifies the 18 facets identified in [23]. The AN and RE prompts contain questions about the current work system or future possibilities for each facet.

PRN: This treatment is a set of 24 proposed principles, each of which applies to one of the elements of the work system framework or to the work system as a whole [24]. Those principles are statements that apply to most work systems but may not apply to all work systems and may be mutually contradictory in some situations. For example, the principle "please the customer" sometimes conflicts with the principle "do the work efficiently." Principles are different from axioms (the AXM treatment) because axioms are meant to apply to all work systems and can be disqualified as axioms by identifying nontrivial work systems to which they do not apply. The ST prompt for PRN identifies elements of the work system framework. The AN prompt asks about ways in which the current work system conforms with or deviates from each of the 24 principles. The RE prompt asks what changes in the work system would increase its conformance with those principles.

2.4 Execution of the Quasi-Experiment

The key to maintaining organization in this quasi-experiment was to identify prompts in a consistent format (e.g., AMAZ-PRN-AN or BCMA-BPM-RE), to produce all of the prompts in advance using a standard format that leaves a space for treatment-related augmentation, and to store all of the prompts in a single Word document with the identification of each prompt formatted as a top-level heading. Specific prompts are found easily in that document by using MS Word's outlining capabilities.

Production of each output generated by ChatGPT-4 was simple because everything was set up in advance: Paste the appropriate prompt into ChatGPT-4's input box, paste the appropriate case at the end of the prompt, and click *enter*. Copy the ChatGPT-4 output (around 500 words) and paste it in a separate Microsoft Word document organized the same way as the prompts were organized. Storing the ChatGPT responses in the same manner made it easy to find and copy any specific text or any group of texts so they could be compared easily (e.g., all RE texts for BCMA), especially since multiple ChatGPT-4 responses can be pasted into a new prompt for comparison purposes, as was done in the second part of the quasi-experiment.

3 Evaluation of Results Generated by ChatGPT-4

Prompts requesting responses of no more than 500 words generated a total output of 34865 words, i.e., averaging 484 words, for 72 responses that cover 3 cases × 3 steps × 8 treatments. Boxes 3, 4, and 5 in the version available at Dropbox illustrate that realistic real-world responses would need to be much longer than 500 words. Another complication is the widely observed phenomenon of LLMs producing different results when trying to answer the same question a second time. The following comments reflect initial observations based on selected examples from the outputs and comparisons that illustrate specific points.

Answers to the Research Questions. Responses produced by ChatGPT-4 led to partially affirmative answers to both research questions. 1) Yes, ChatGPT-4 can produce a limited, but possibly useful first cut at structure, analysis, and recommendations for a problematic system in an organization if it receives sufficient input about that system. Parts of that answer are likely to be unreliable due to the nature of LLMs. 2) Yes, despite reliability caveats, augmentations of ChatGPT-4 prompts can improve or extend those responses if the inputs are sufficient. Selected ChatGPT-4 responses will illustrate those points along with others related to limitations.

System Summaries. Excerpts from system summaries for BMCA-CTL-ST and BMCA-ACT-ST (Boxes 3 and 4 in the version available through Dropbox) illustrate that different treatments yield different summaries. The BMCA-CTL-ST prompt asked for a summary including purpose, participants, activities, and outputs. BMCA-ACT-ST added questions built on activity theory: "*In combination, the actors, outcomes, tools, activities, rules, community, and division of labor are viewed as the activity system in this situation.*" Main topics in both prompts are underlined in those Boxes, illustrating that answers for the same main topics differ. Those Boxes omit similar answers for participants and activities. Treatment-related topics at the bottom of Box 4 (ACT) do not appear in Box 3 (CTL). Reusing the same CTL or ACT prompt returned slightly different answers in each category.

Analysis of the System. The prompt RDHL-MBA-AN produced an analysis based on parts of a template used by MBA and EMBA students. Box 5 available through Dropbox shows the entire response because it illustrates that ChatGPT-4 is able to produce a reasonably coherent first cut at an analysis if it starts with an appropriate prompt applied to a sufficiently informative case. This "analysis" mostly consists of brief and somewhat generic bullet items, largely because ChatGPT-4 has neither common sense nor real-world knowledge that can be applied to this context. A real-world analysis would go much deeper and would recognize social, psychological, and economic nuances that determine what is practical or even defensible. Nonetheless, MBA or EMBA student teams might have used the content of that box as a first cut that they could improve upon, thereby saving time and identifying topics that they might not have considered. A more advanced prompt submitted to a more advanced or better trained LLM might contribute in a similar way to a real-world requirements analysis effort.

Recommendations for Changes in the System. Many of the ChatGPT-4 recommendations were impractical or otherwise highly questionable because they did not reflect a practical understanding of the types of situations that the cases portrayed. Some of the impractical recommendations seemed like excerpts from introductory management courses or generic HR training films that portray typical expectations, rules of thumb, and collegial behavior but are not related to the specific problematic situations in the cases. Box 1 (below) shows three of many questionable recommendations for each case. Many managers would wonder about the competence or seriousness of a person making such recommendations because basic business experience would say that some of those recommendations seem irrelevant to the situations described in the cases and others seem impractical in the type of business settings that are described. Nonetheless, even unreliable recommendations based on better prompts and submitted to a more powerful LLM might point to issues that managers or analysts might overlook otherwise, such as facets of work, work system principles, or ideas from activity theory.

Different Results for Different Treatments. Length limitations prevent including examples that illustrate how the unique ideas in the different treatments appeared in all 3 steps (ST, AN, RE) for all 3 cases. Overall, ChatGPT-4 responses for specific treatments included many of the concepts (e.g., communication or coordination or division of labor) mentioned explicitly by those treatments (see Sect. 2.4). Some treatment-related issues probably would not have been mentioned in typical requirements analysis discussions despite the potential insights that might result. Widely applicable, almost generic ideas such as improving processes, providing incentives, providing training, and providing better technology were identified for all treatments but without supporting details because ChatGPT-4 had no way of understanding the relevance of contextual factors. Thus, an appropriately designed chatbot informed by one or more potentially useful sets of ideas might contribute to deliberation processes in requirements analysis even if the participants believed that LLM responses tend to be unreliable, should not be taken literally, and should not be used mechanically or automatically.

Box 1. Examples of impractical recommendations

AMAZ–MBA–RE: "Redesign processes where human judgment is critical, ensuring a balanced integration of human skills with robotic efficiency." (Additional human judgment does not seem critical for packing items for shipment.)

AMAZ–BPM–RE: Develop specialized processes for handling orders from premium customers. (Not relevant to issues in this case)

AMAZ–PRN–RE: Implement lean management techniques to streamline processes, reducing waste and increasing efficiency (Processes may be too efficient/lean.)

BCMA–BPM–RE: Introduce flexible process variations for emergency situations (Emergency situations were not mentioned.)

BCMA–FCT–RE: Incorporate virtual or augmented reality training modules for staff (Augmented reality is not needed for learning to use bar code scanners.)

BCMA–PRN–RE: Simplify the BCMA interface to reduce the cognitive and physical effort required by users. (Cognitive and physical effort is minimal.)

RDHL–CTL–RE: Educate customers about the impact of their ratings on drivers' livelihoods. (Ride hailing customers are not interested in this type of education).

RDHL–AXM–RE: Adapt to regulatory changes by engaging in proactive dialogue with authorities and seeking collaborative solutions. (Sounds like consultant-speak.)

RDHL–DSP–RE: Involve drivers in decision-making processes related to platform changes, enhancing their sense of belonging and commitment. (Sense of belonging?)

Refining Responses by Combining Results of Different Prompts. Inspecting 72 responses ($3 \times 3 \times 8$) of roughly 500 words led to wondering whether filtering or consolidating those responses might lead to more useful results. Subsequent trials explored alternative approaches for using ChatGPT-4 to filter or consolidate two or more of the 72 responses that it had produced initially. The version of this paper that is available at Dropbox mentions three approaches that were attempted:

1) Consolidate to a single response that builds on treatment-focused responses: A second phase of the quasi-experiment prompted ChatGPT-4 to create a single 500-word response that would represent a unified understanding of each case. Those prompts called for consolidating all 8 of the ST responses or just 7 of them (eliminating CTL) for each case into a single 500-word response. A surprising complication worth noting was that ChatGPT-4 created and used acronyms that appeared in two initial responses for AMAZ but not in other responses. Those acronyms were AES (Automated Efficiency System) and AWS (Automated Warehouse System). Both acronyms appeared in a consolidation, but without any clarity about whether or how they referred to the same or different systems.

2) Produce a longer consolidated response. It seemed likely that a 1000-word consolidated response might allow inclusion of more content from the separate 500-word responses. That approach produced somewhat longer responses (mostly between

570 and 690 words) but typically did not produce substantially deeper results. Several prompts requesting a 1500-word consolidation paradoxically produced shorter responses of 449 and 501 words.

3) <u>Identify unique ideas resulting from the treatments</u>. A prompt asked ChatGPT-4 to identify the most unique ST-related ideas produced by each of the treatments for the AMAZ case. Box 7 in the version available through Dropbox mentions ideas influenced directly by several specific treatments. A repeat of that prompt requesting a 1000-word response expanded on those ideas but was organized as separate sections for each treatment.

4   Conclusions

This research-in-progress paper was designed to explore the possible use of ChatGPT-4 for requirements engineering when augmented by different recognizable sets of ideas related to systems in organizations. Implications for next steps include:

Build Tools Based on the Inherent Strengths and Limitations of LLMs. LLM-based tools should be designed to engage participants in analysis processes, and not to produce precise documentation. Production of different answers by reusing the same tool might introduce beneficial ideas missed initially. Use of similar tools based on different treatments (e.g., ACT vs. AXM vs. BPM, etc.) might uncover issues at design time that would not have been considered before problems arose at run-time. Ideally, issues exposed by extending this research will inspire creation of formats or templates that will be more effective in reflecting specific issues and realities of situations being analyzed.

Use with Caution. This research emerged from imagining possibilities at the intersection of AI and systems analysis. Initial progress reported here illustrates potential benefits of using LLMs in requirements analysis processes but also brings cautionary concerns. Boxes 3 through 7 in the version available through Dropbox do not support suggestions in a 2023 BPM Forum paper [25] implying that an LLM application might be able to redesign a process somewhat autonomously if provided with adequate inputs. ChatGPT responses for all three cases illustrate the substantial distance between redesigning an abstract process model and redesigning the ongoing execution of a real-world process.

Focus on Deliberations, Not Just Tools or Automated Decisions. Sociotechnical consultants who help making workplaces simultaneously more productive and more humane often focus on facilitating human deliberations [26]. Results to date imply that the promise of using LLMs for requirements analysis is greatest in that area and not mainly in producing tools for detailed documentation or automated design decisions.

Disclosure of Interests.   The authors have no competing interests to declare that are relevant to the content of this article.

References

1. Dutta, S., Chakraborty, T.: Thus spake ChatGPT. Commun. ACM **66**(12), 16–19 (2023)

2. Bender, E.M., et al.: On the dangers of stochastic parrots: can language models be too big? In: Proceedings of the 2021 ACM Conference on Fairness, Accountability, and Transparency, pp. 610–623 (2021)
3. Teubner, T., et al.: Welcome to the era of Chatgpt et al. the prospects of large language models. Bus. Inf. Syst. Eng. **65**(2), 95–101 (2023)
4. Weiser, B., Schweber, N.: The ChatGPT lawyer explains himself. New York Times (2023)
5. White, J., et al.: A prompt pattern catalog to enhance prompt engineering with chatgpt. arXiv preprint arXiv:2302.11382 (2023)
6. Meskó, B.: Prompt engineering as an important emerging skill for medical professionals: tutorial. J. Med. Internet Res. **25**, e50638 (2023)
7. Dell'Acqua, F., et al.: Field experimental evidence of the effects of AI on knowledge worker productivity and quality. Harvard Business School Technology & Operations Mgt. Unit Working Paper (24-013) (2023)
8. Truex, D., et al.: Systems analysis for everyone else: empowering business professionals through a systems analysis method that fits their needs. In: Proceedings of ECIS (2010)
9. Alter, S.: Work system theory: overview of core concepts, extensions, and challenges for the future. J. Assoc. Inf. Syst. **14**(2), 72–121 (2013)
10. Cameron, L.D., Rahman, H.: Expanding the locus of resistance: understanding the co-constitution of control and resistance in the gig economy. Organ. Sci. **33**(1), 38–58 (2022)
11. Koppel, R., et al.: Workarounds to barcode medication administration systems: their occurrences, causes, and threats to patient safety. J. Am. Med. Inform. Assoc. **15**(4), 408–423 (2008)
12. Mulac, A., et al.: Barcode medication administration technology use in hospital practice: a mixed-methods observational study of policy deviations. BMJ Qual. Saf. **30**(12), 1021–1030 (2021)
13. Grailey, K.: Understanding the facilitators and barriers to barcode medication administration by nursing staff using behavioural science frameworks. A mixed methods study. BMC Nurs. **22**(1), 378 (2023)
14. Blogger, G.: How robots are transforming amazon – e-commerce warehouses (2022). https://www.sellersnap.io/amazon-robotics-warehouse-automation/. Accessed 26 Nov 2023
15. Evans, W.: Ruthless quotas at Amazon are maiming employees. The Atlantic 5 (2019)
16. Gordon, J.L.: Under pressure: addressing warehouse productivity quotas and the rise in workplace injuries. Fordham Urban Law J. **49**, 149–188 (2021)
17. Kaptelinin, V., et al.: Methods & tools: the activity checklist: a tool for representing the "space" of context. Interactions **6**(4), 27–39 (1999)
18. Allen, D.K., et al.: How should technology-mediated organizational change be explained? A comparison of the contributions of critical realism and activity theory. MIS Q. **37**(3), 835–854 (2013)
19. Alter, S.: Service system axioms that accept positive and negative outcomes and impacts of service systems. In: Proceedings of ICIS (2017)
20. Gross, S., et al.: The Business Process Design Space for exploring process redesign alternatives. Bus. Process. Manag. J. **27**(8), 25–56 (2021)
21. Reijers, H.A., Mansar, S.L.: Best practices in business process redesign: an overview and qualitative evaluation of successful redesign heuristics. Omega **33**(4), 283–306 (2005)
22. Alter, S.: Work systems as the core of the design space for organisational design and engineering. Int. J. Organ. Des. Eng. **1**(1–2), 5–28 (2010)
23. Alter, S.: Facets of work: enriching the description, analysis, design, and evaluation of systems in organizations. Commun. Assoc. Inf. Syst. **49**(13), 321–354 (2021)
24. Alter, S., Wright, R.: Validating work system principles for use in systems analysis and design. In: Proceedings of ICIS (2010)

25. Vidgof, M., Bachhofner, S., Mendling, J.: Large language models for business process management: opportunities and challenges. In: Di Francescomarino, C., Burattin, A., Janiesch, C., Sadiq, S. (eds.) Business Process Management Forum: BPM 2023 Forum, Utrecht, The Netherlands, September 11–15, 2023, Proceedings, pp. 107–123. Springer, Cham (2023). https://doi.org/10.1007/978-3-031-41623-1_7
26. Painter, B.: Sociotechnical systems design: coordination of virtual teamwork in innovation. Team Perform. Manag. **22**(7/8), 354–369 (2016)

Model-driven Engineering & AI 2
(EMMSAD 2024)

Fast & Sound: Accelerating Synthesis-Rules-Based Process Discovery

Tsung-Hao Huang[1]($^{(\boxtimes)}$)(iD), Enzo Schneider[2], Marco Pegoraro[1](iD), and Wil M. P. van der Aalst[1](iD)

[1] Process and Data Science (PADS), RWTH Aachen University, Aachen, Germany
{tsunghao.huang,pegoraro,wvdaalst}@pads.rwth-aachen.de
[2] RWTH Aachen University, Aachen, Germany
enzo.schneider@rwth-aachen.de
http://www.pads.rwth-aachen.de/

Abstract. Process discovery aims to construct process models describing the observed behaviors of information systems. It is an essential step in process mining projects as most process mining techniques assume a process model as input. While various process discovery algorithms exist, few provide desirable properties: soundness and free-choiceness. By exploiting the free-choice net theory, the recently developed Synthesis Miner not only guarantees the two desirable properties but also enables a more flexible representation (non-block structures) of the discovered process models. The flexibility allows the Synthesis Miner to discover process models with potentially higher quality. Nevertheless, applying the Synthesis Miner remains a challenge due to its lack of scalability. In this paper, we identify the bottleneck and address it by introducing various extensions that utilize the log heuristics and extract the minimal sub-net of the process model. The evaluation using real-life event logs shows that the proposed extensions improve the scalability of the Synthesis Miner by reducing the computation time by 82.85% on average.

Keywords: Process Modeling · Process Mining · Process Discovery · Free-choice Workflow Net · Synthesis Rules

1 Introduction

Process mining is an emerging scientific discipline that bridges the gap between process science and data science. It provides organizations with data-driven techniques to improve operational processes. With the use of process models and event data, process mining techniques help to identify and eliminate inefficiencies in processes.

Process discovery plays an essential role when executing process mining projects because the output of process discovery, a process model, is a prerequisite for many other process mining techniques such as checking conformance, detecting concept drift, predicting performance, etc. The goal of process discovery is to automatically construct a process model from event logs describing

H. van der Aa et al. (Eds.): BPMDS 2024/EMMSAD 2024, LNBIP 511, pp. 259–274, 2024.
https://doi.org/10.1007/978-3-031-61007-3_20

the observed behaviors in the corresponding information systems. In general, the quality of a process model can be evaluated by four main criteria—namely fitness, precision, generalization, and simplicity [4]. Additionally, process models with formal guarantees such as soundness and free-choiceness are preferable [4,10]. On the one hand, soundness ensures that the process model does not contain apparent anomalies [4] such as the existence of a dead transition, i.e., a transition that can never be fired. On the other hand, free-choice process models have several benefits. First, a free-choice net has a separate construct for choice and synchronization by definition. Such a construct is also naturally embedded in the widely used process model notation BPMN. Consequently, the property enables easy conversion from free-choice nets to BPMN process models. Moreover, free-choice nets have an abundance of analysis techniques at hand from theory [10].

Despite various algorithms being proposed, few provide the aforementioned two properties. The Inductive Miner (IM) family [15] is one of the few algorithms that ensure such properties. This is achieved by exploiting the representation of process trees, whose converted Petri nets are sound and free-choice by construction. Nevertheless, such a representation is a double-edged sword, as process trees can only represent process models with block structures. Using process trees to represent a process with non-block structures often compromises model quality.

The recently proposed discovery algorithm, the Synthesis Miner [13,14], can discover models with non-block structures while providing the same guarantees by applying the synthesis rules from the free-choice net theory [10]. Adopting an iterative setting, the approach tries to find the best modification (w.r.t. F1-score) to an existing workflow net by generating and evaluating various candidate nets. The generation and evaluation steps require the application of synthesis rules [10] and alignment-based conformance checking [3] respectively. Both operations include expensive computations [3,13]. As a result, adopting the Synthesis Miner remains a challenge due to its scalability problem.

In this paper, we propose various extensions to address the identified bottleneck. The extensions utilize the observation that the modification in each iteration often only affects a subpart of the entire model. The subpart can be extracted and isolated to accelerate the modification. First, log heuristics are exploited to prune the search space even further than the original approach [13,14]. Moreover, the generation and evaluation steps are decomposed into smaller problems by extracting the minimal subnet containing the affected nodes. The extracted subnet can be directly transformed into a sound free-choice WF-net so that the predefined patterns based on synthesis rules can be applied as usual. The experiment using real-life event logs shows that the extensions improve the scalability of the Synthesis Miner by reducing the computation time by 82.85% on average for both generation and evaluation steps.

The remainder of the paper is structured as follows. We review the related work in Sect. 2 and introduce necessary concepts in Sect. 3. Section 4 introduces the approach. Section 5 presents the experiment and Sect. 6 concludes the paper.

2   Related Work

We refer to [7] for a comprehensive overview of process discovery in general. In this paper, we focus on process discovery algorithms that provide formal guarantees, specifically, soundness and free-choiceness. While various discovery algorithms have been proposed throughout the years, only a handful meet the criteria. The Inductive Miner (IM) family [15] exploits the representation of process trees to provide such guarantees. By definition, every process tree represents a sound and free-choice WF-net. Nevertheless, process trees can only represent processes with block structures, i.e., process models that can be separated into parts with a single entry and exit [15]. As a matter of course, discovery algorithms [9,16] using process trees as internal representation also suffer from the same problem. Various algorithms [6,8] can discover process models with non-block structures but cannot guarantee both free-choice and sound properties.

Another group of algorithms [11,13] utilizes the synthesis rules from free-choice net theory [10] to guarantee both properties while having a more flexible representation. The work in [11] adopts an interactive setting where user inputs are required. However, the discovery process involves various steps of back-and-forth application of synthesis/reduction rules without clear indications. In other words, the users need to have extensive knowledge about the control flow of the process to navigate the discovery. Additionally, although a variation of the work in [11] can recommend the most prominent modifications, it still needs to evaluate all possibilities. The exhaustive search of all the possible modifications is computationally expensive and not feasible in practice.

To address the problems, the Synthesis Miner [13,14] automates the discovery procedure used in [11] by introducing an additional synthesis rule and predefined patterns. The additional rule reduces the need for the back-and-forth steps in [11]. Moreover, using log heuristics, a search space pruning strategy is proposed to locate the most likely position to add the respective transition. The pruning strategy is effective in reducing the computation time [13] as opposed to evaluating all possibilities. Nevertheless, the Synthesis Miner is still not scalable for process discovery in practice [13,14]. The problem stems from the generation and evaluation steps of the candidates. First, unlikely/undesirable modifications are still included in the set of generated candidates. Including such candidates implies spending unnecessary computation time for evaluation. In addition, there is room for improvement when evaluating the candidates as the modification typically only concerns a subpart of the whole process.

3   Preliminaries

For some set A, $\mathcal{B}(A)$ denotes the set of all multisets over A. For some multiset $b \in \mathcal{B}(A)$, $b(a)$ denotes the number of times $a \in A$ appears in b. For example, given a set $A = \{x, y, z\}$, $b = \langle x^5, y^6, z^7 \rangle$ is a multiset over A. $b(y) = 6$ as y appears 6 times in b. $\sigma \in A^*$ denotes that σ is a sequence over some set A. For a sequence $\sigma = \langle a_1, a_2, a_3, ..., a_n \rangle$, $|\sigma| = n$ is the length of σ. For $1 \leq i \leq |\sigma|$,

$\sigma(i) = a_i \in A$ denotes the i-th element of σ. Given two sequences σ and σ', $\sigma \cdot \sigma'$ denotes the concatenation.

Next, we introduce the projection function. Let A be a set and $X \subseteq A$ be a subset of A. For $\sigma \in A^*$ and $a \in A$, we define the projection function $\lceil_X \in A^* \to X^*$ recursively with $\langle\rangle\lceil_X = \langle\rangle$, $(\langle a \rangle \cdot \sigma)\lceil_X = \langle a \rangle \cdot \sigma\lceil_X$ if $a \in X$ and $(\langle a \rangle \cdot \sigma)\lceil_X = \sigma\lceil_X$ otherwise.

Definition 1 (Activities, Traces, and Logs). *Let $\mathcal{A}$ be the universe of activities. A trace $\sigma \in \mathcal{A}^*$ is a sequence of activities. A log $L \in \mathcal{B}(\mathcal{A}^*)$ is a multiset of traces.*

Definition 2 (Petri Net and Labeled Petri Net). *A Petri net is a tuple $N = (P, T, F)$, where P is the set of places, T is the set of transitions, $P \cap T = \emptyset$, $F \subseteq (P \times T) \cup (T \times P)$ is the set of arcs. A labeled Petri net $N = (P, T, F, l)$ is a Petri net with a labeling function $l \in T \nrightarrow \mathcal{A}$ mapping transitions to activities. For any $x \in P \cup T$, $\overset{N}{\bullet}x = \{y \mid (y, x) \in F\}$ denotes the set of input nodes (preset) of x and $x\overset{N}{\bullet} = \{y \mid (x, y) \in F\}$ denotes the set of output nodes (postset) of x. The superscript N is dropped if it is clear from the context.*

Note that l can be partial, which means if a transition $t \in T$ is not in the domain of l, it has no label. In such a case, we write $l(t) = \tau$ to denote that the transition is silent or invisible.

Definition 3 (Free-choice Net). *Let $N = (P, T, F)$ be a Petri net. N is a free-choice net if for any $t, t' \in T : \bullet t = \bullet t'$ or $\bullet t \cap \bullet t' = \emptyset$.*

Free-choice nets have separate constructs for choices and synchronizations as any two transitions either have the same preset or don't share any places in their presets.

Definition 4 (Path). *A path of a Petri net $N = (P, T, F)$ is a non-empty sequence of nodes $\rho = \langle x_1, x_2, ..., x_n \rangle$ such that $(x_i, x_{i+1}) \in F$ for $1 \leq i < n$.*

Definition 5 (Workflow Net (WF-net)). *Let $N = (P, T, F)$ be a Petri net. N is a workflow net if it has a dedicated source place $i \in P : \bullet i = \emptyset$ and a dedicated sink place $o \in P : o\bullet = \emptyset$. Moreover, every node $x \in P \cup T$ is on some path between i and o.*

The soundness[1] property is defined for WF-nets [1]. A sound WF-net guarantees that (1) a process can always be finished and (2) a process can be properly completed: once a process reaches the final state, it is not possible to fire any transition (3) no inexecutable transitions exist.

Definition 6 (Incidence Matrix [10]). *Let $N = (P, T, F)$ be a Petri net. The incidence matrix $\mathbf{N} : (P \times T) \to \{-1, 0, 1\}$ of N is defined as*

$$\mathbf{N}(p, t) = \begin{cases} 0 & \text{if } ((p, t) \notin F \wedge (t, p) \notin F) \vee ((p, t) \in F \wedge (t, p) \in F) \\ -1 & \text{if } (p, t) \in F \wedge (t, p) \notin F \\ 1 & \text{if } (p, t) \notin F \wedge (t, p) \in F \end{cases}$$

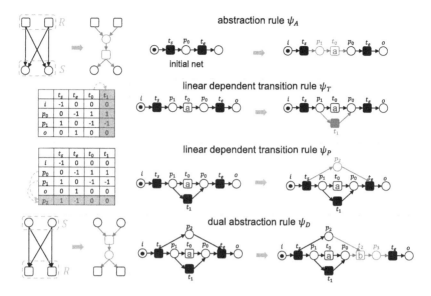

Fig. 1. Examples of the synthesis rules applications, where the highlighted parts (in green) indicate the newly added components. (Color figure online)

Next, we briefly illustrate the synthesis rules introduced in [10,13]. Given a workflow net N, the abstraction rule (ψ_A) allows adding a place p and a transition t between a set of transitions $R \subseteq T$ and a set of places $S \subseteq P$ if they are fully connected, i.e., $(R \times S \subseteq F) \wedge (R \times S \neq \emptyset)$. The linear transition/place rule (ψ_T/ψ_P) allows adding a transition/place (t/p) if it is linearly dependent on the other transitions/places in the corresponding incidence matrix. Lastly, the dual abstraction rule (ψ_D) allows adding a transition t and a place p between a set of places S and a set of transitions R if $(S \times R \subseteq F) \wedge (S \times R \neq \emptyset)$. All four rules[2] preserve sound and free-choice properties [10,13]. Figure 1 (extracted from [12]) shows examples of rules applications. From top to bottom, ψ_A adds p_1 and t_0 with $R = \{t_s\}$ fully connected to $S = \{p_1\}$. ψ_T adds t_1 as it is linearly dependent on t_0. ψ_P adds p_2 as it is a linear combination of p_0 and p_1. ψ_D adds t_2 and p_3 with $S = \{p_0, p_2\}$ fully connected to $R = \{t_e\}$.

4   Approach

In this section, we introduce the extensions that accelerate the computation. As the proposed extensions build on top of the Synthesis Miner [13,14], we briefly discuss the essential steps of the Synthesis Miner and point out limitations that are addressed by the proposed extensions in this paper.

---

[1] The precise definition of soundness is out of scope, we refer to [1].

[2] The formal definition of the rules is out of scope, we refer to [10,13].

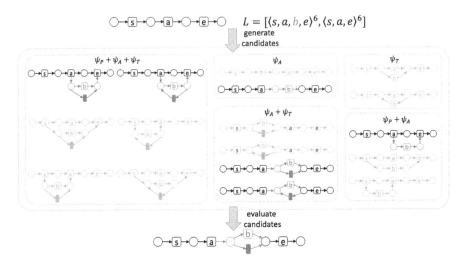

Fig. 2. An example showing the generation and evaluation steps of the Synthesis Miner. First, the candidates are generated using predefined patterns [13] based on synthesis rules, as indicated by the symbols on top of each block. Then, each candidate is evaluated by alignment-based conformance checking to retrieve the F1-score. Note that the figure does not show the complete set of candidates.

4.1 The Synthesis Miner and Its Limitations

Both variations [13,14] of the Synthesis Miner adopt an interactive approach to modify an existing WF-net that is sound and free-choice. The variation in [13] starts with the *initial net* (as indicated in Fig. 1) containing only the artificial start and end transitions whereas [14] starts from a WF-net discovered by IM.

In every iteration, both variations try to modify the existing net to maximize the model quality (F1-score). The modifications consist of adding new nodes and/or removing existing nodes. Both the removal and addition operations preserve soundness and free-choiceness [14]. Nevertheless, the bottleneck appears when adding new nodes to the existing WF-net. In the background, the addition requires generating and evaluating the candidates. Figure 2 shows an example of the generation and evaluation steps. In Fig. 2, a transition labeled as b is to be added to the existing net. First, various candidates are generated based on predefined patterns [13] using synthesis rules. Using information from the log, the generation is constrained to connect the new nodes only to the most likely position (existing nodes). The log in Fig. 2 indicates that activity b is preceded by activity a and followed by activity e. To generate the most prominent candidates, the Synthesis Miner connects the new nodes only to the existing nodes on the path between transitions labeled a and e. Any nets with unlikely connections are not considered. For illustration purposes, such nets are still shown in Fig. 2 but grayed out. Then, the candidates are evaluated and the best one is selected for the next iteration based on the F1-score. In this case, the transition labeled b (with the option to skip) is placed in between transitions labeled a and e. The selected candidate perfectly fits the log (high fitness) and does not allow any unseen behaviors (high precision).

The example in Fig. 2 shows that the pruning strategy used in the existing work [13,14] can reduce the search space to a certain degree. However, the strategy is still unfeasible in real-life scenarios when the event log and the existing net become larger. To discuss the limitations using a concrete example, we consider the following log

$$L_s = [\langle a,b,c,d,e,f,g,h \rangle^{10}, \langle a,b,e,c,d,f,g,h \rangle^{10}, \langle a,b,e,c,f,g,d,h \rangle^{10},$$
$$\langle a,b,e,c,f,d,g,h \rangle^{10}, \langle a,b,c,e,d,f,g,h \rangle^{10}, \langle a,b,c,e,f,d,g,h \rangle^{10},$$
$$\langle a,e,b,c,d,f,g,h \rangle^{10}, \langle a,e,b,c,f,g,d,h \rangle^{10}, \langle a,e,b,c,f,d,g,h \rangle^{10},$$
$$\langle a,b,c,e,f,g,d,h \rangle^{10}].$$

Limitation 1 (Generation): The main problem in generation is that the search space (number of candidates) grows exponentially with the number of nodes that are considered to be connected to the new node. In [13,14], log heuristics are used to narrow down the search space. To be more precise, we first define a few log properties used to determine the preceding and following activities.

Definition 7 (Log Properties [13]). *Let* $L \in \mathcal{B}(\mathcal{A}^*)$ *and* $a, b \in \mathcal{A}$.

- $\#(a, L) = \Sigma_{\sigma \in L} |\{1 \le i \le |\sigma| \mid \sigma(i) = a\}|$ *is the times* a *occurred in* L.
- $\#(a, b, L) = \Sigma_{\sigma \in L} |\{1 \le i < |\sigma| \mid \sigma(i) = a \land \sigma(i+1) = b\}|$ *is the number of direct successions from* a *to* b *in* L.
- $caus(a, b, L) = \begin{cases} \frac{\#(a,b,L)-\#(b,a,L)}{\#(a,b,L)+\#(b,a,L)+1} & \text{if } a \ne b \\ \frac{\#(a,b,L)}{\#(a,b,L)+1} & \text{if } a = b \end{cases}$ *is the strength of causal relation* (a, b).
- $A_\theta^p(a, L) = \{a_p \in \mathcal{A} \mid caus(a_p, a, L) \ge \theta\}$ *is the set of* a's *preceding activities, determined by threshold* θ.
- $A_\theta^f(a, L) = \{a_f \in \mathcal{A} \mid caus(a, a_f, L) \ge \theta\}$ *is the set of* a's *following activities, determined by threshold* θ.

The following sections assume the use of default value $\theta = 0.9$ [13] to determine the preceding and following activities. Once the sets of preceding and following activities are identified using Definition 7, the corresponding labeled transitions can also be found[3]. Then, every node on the path from the set of preceding transitions to the set of following transitions is considered to be connected to the new node [13].

In Fig. 3, a transition labeled e should be added to the net. Since activity e is preceded by a and followed by f in L_s (Definition 7), the set of nodes on the path is $\{t_1, p_2, t_2, p_3, t_3, p_9, t_6\}$. As an example, using the linear dependent transition rule (ψ_T), we have to check the linear dependency of $3^3=27$ vectors

---

[3] For the ease of reading, hereafter, we directly refer to the corresponding labeled transitions of the preceding and following activities as the preceding and following transitions.

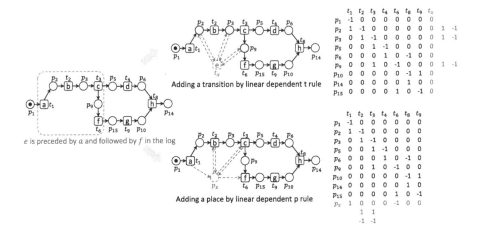

Fig. 3. Adding a transition or a place using the linear dependent rules. The columns and rows outside of the incidence matrix indicate the three possible connections between the new and the existing nodes. Consider the set of nodes $\{t_1, p_2, t_2, p_3, t_3, p_9, t_6\}$ on the path between activity a and f, linear dependency has to be checked on $3^3 + 3^2 = 36$ vectors. Note that we only illustrate the basic linear dependent rules in this figure, the best candidate (not shown) in this case combines the linear dependent place rule ψ_P and the abstraction rule ψ_A.

as there are three connecting possibilities (corresponding to -1, 1, and 0 in the incidence matrix) for every place in $\{p_2, p_3, p_9\}$. In addition, there are $3^2 = 9$ vectors to be evaluated when using the linear dependent p rule (ψ_P) to add a place. Furthermore, the predefined patterns are built based on these rules. The example shows that the number of candidates to be evaluated grows exponentially as the number of nodes that are considered for connection. A clear direction for improvement is to further reduce the number of nodes considered for connection.

Limitation 2 (Evaluation). The alignment-based conformance checking is known to be reliable yet computationally expensive [5]. As alignment-based conformance checking is applied to every single candidate for evaluation in [13,14], it introduces a bottleneck in the evaluation phase. Based on observations in [13,14], the change in every iteration often only affects a subpart of the model. Figure 2 shows an example, where the transition labeled s is not involved in any modification, i.e., no candidates connect new nodes to the transition. The example shows an opportunity to extract and isolate a subnet to speed up the alignment computation.

4.2   Extensions

Extension 1: Log Heuristics. As shown in Sect. 4.1, the most likely position (nodes) to place the new node can be identified using heuristics. Although the search space reduction strategy in [13, 14] already reduces the computation time significantly, we propose to further reduce the search space by only considering the sets of preceding/following transitions (Definition 7) and their post/pre-sets (Definition 2). Once the sets of preceding/following transitions (T_p/T_f) are identified, the set of nodes to be considered for connection would only be $T_p \cup T_f \cup T_p \bullet \cup \bullet T_f$. Hereafter, we denoted the set of nodes pending for connection as $V_s = T_p \cup T_f \cup T_p \bullet \cup \bullet T_f$. The assumption for the extension is that the other nodes are either in an independent or concurrent relationship with the new node. Thus, there is no need to consider the possibility of adding any connection to the rest of the nodes.

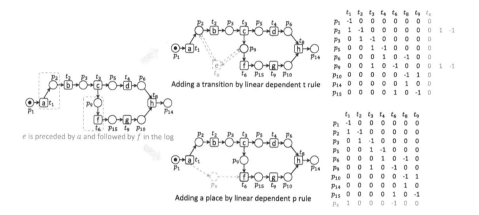

Fig. 4. Considering only the sets of preceding/following activities and their post/pre-set, the number of vectors pending for linear dependency checkup is reduced from 36 to $3^2 + 1 = 10$. In this case, the best candidate (not shown in the figure) applies the abstraction rule ψ_A to the net at the bottom to add another place and a transition labeled e in between $R = \{t_1\}$ and $S = \{p_x\}$.

Using the example in Fig. 4 to illustrate the idea, we know that activity e is preceded/followed by activity a/f respectively in log L_s according to Definition 7. The set of nodes considered for connection is then $\{t_1, p_2, p_9, t_6\}$ as opposed to $\{t_1, p_2, t_2, p_3, t_3, p_9, t_6\}$ from the original strategy shown in Fig. 3. As shown in Fig. 4, the number of vectors pending for linear dependency check is reduced from 36 to 10 for the running example. Moreover, the effect of such reduction in turn reduces the number of candidates.

Extension 2: Minimal Subnet Extraction: As discussed in Sect. 4.1, not every part of the process model is involved in applying synthesis rules due to the use of log heuristics. In other words, the modification often concerns only a subpart of the model. Motivated by such observation, we propose extracting the subnet containing the set of nodes (V_s) that are most likely to connect to the new nodes according to Extension 1. To be precise, we first define the concept of a subnet in the context of this paper.

Definition 8 (Subnet). *Let $N = (P, T, F)$ be a WF-net that is sound and free-choice. $N_s = (P_s, T_s, F_s)$ is a subnet of N if*

- $P_s \subseteq P, T_s \subseteq T, F_s = F \cap ((P_s \times T_s) \cup (T_s \times P_s))$
- *there exist $P_{in} \subseteq P \backslash P_s, P_{out} \subseteq P \backslash P_s, T_{start} \subseteq T_s, T_{end} \subseteq T_s$ such that*
    - $\forall_{p \in P_{in}} (p\bullet = T_{start})$, *the postset of every place in P_{in} equals to T_{start}.*
    - $\forall_{p \in P_{out}} (\bullet p = T_{end})$, *the preset of every place in P_{out} equals to T_{end}.*
    - $\forall_{t \in T_{start}} (\bullet t = P_{in})$, *the preset of every transition in T_{start} equals to P_{in}.*
    - $\forall_{t \in T_{end}} (t\bullet = P_{out})$, *the postset of every transition in T_{end} equals to P_{out}.*
    - $\forall_{p \in P_s} (\overset{N}{\bullet}p \cup p\overset{N}{\bullet} \subseteq T_s)$, *all places in P_s only connects to transition in T_s.*
    - $\forall_{t \in T_s \backslash T_{start}} (\overset{N}{\bullet}t \subseteq P_s)$, *except for T_{start}, the input places of every transition in T_s are in P_s.*
    - $\forall_{t \in T_s \backslash T_{end}} (t\overset{N}{\bullet} \subseteq P_s)$, *except for T_{end}, the output places of every transition in T_s are in P_s.*

The criteria of a subnet in Definition 9 are visualized in Fig. 5a, where N_s meets all the requirements of a subnet as the only incoming connections are through the start transitions T_{start} and the only outgoing connections are through the end transitions T_{end}. Any other nodes inside N_s have no external connections. A subnet $N_s = (P_s, T_s, F_s)$ can be transformed into a WF-net by adding a source place i' connecting to the set of start transitions T_{start} and a sink place o' connecting from the set of end transitions T_{end}. Figure 5b shows the transformed WF-net. Note that the transformed WF-net from subnet N_s is sound and free-choice as the whole net N is also a sound free-choice WF-net. Therefore, we can generate candidates based on the transformed WF-net using synthesis rules as usual.

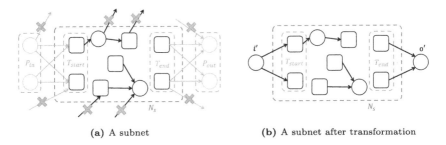

(a) A subnet   (b) A subnet after transformation

Fig. 5. An example showing the criteria of a subnet as defined in Definition 9 and the transformed WF-net.

Since we are only interested in the smallest subnet containing nodes that might be connected to the new nodes, we define the concept of a minimal subnet.

Definition 9 (Minimal Subnet)   *Let* $N = (P, T, F)$ *be a sound and free-choice WF-net and* $N_s = (P_s, T_s, F_s)$ *be a subnet of* N. *Let* $V \subseteq P \cup T$. N_s *is a minimal subnet for* V *if*

- $V \subseteq P_s \cup T_s$ *and*
- *there exists no other subnet* $N'_s = (P'_s, T'_s, F'_s)$ *such that*
  - $V \subseteq P'_s \cup T'_s$
  - $(P'_s \cup T'_s) \subset (P_s \cup T_s)$ *and* $F'_s \subset F_s$.

The minimal subnet can also be transformed into a sound free-choice WF-net so that the standard synthesis rules in [13] can be used to generate candidates. The benefits of extracting minimal sub-subnets are two-fold.

1. Smaller incidence matrix: applying linear dependent t/p rules requires linear dependency checkup using Gaussian elimination, whose computation complexity is polynomial to the size of the matrix. Therefore, performing Gaussian elimination on a smaller incidence matrix indicates faster computation. The WF-net transformed from the extracted minimal subnet has a smaller incidence matrix. The implication is that any modifications following synthesis rules on the minimal subnet ensure the desirable properties as well.
2. Faster conformance checking: since the modifications are only performed on the extracted subnet, the model quality (w.r.t. F1-score) of the subnet can be used as an indicator for the quality of the whole net. Performing conformance checking on a smaller net and a smaller log also leads to faster computation.

To illustrate the idea, consider the running example as shown in Fig. 6, where the transition labeled as g has to be added to the WF-net. As activity g is preceded by activity f and followed by activity h in log L_s (Definition 7), we know that the set of nodes to be considered for connection would be $V_s = \{t_6, p_{10}, t_8\}$. With the constraint of V_s, the minimal subnet can be extracted as shown in Fig. 6 (highlighted in green). The subnet is then transformed into a WF-net before various candidates are generated and evaluated. Finally, the best candidate is selected and connected back to the original net as shown in the last step in Fig. 6. Moreover, the conformance checking can also be decomposed. Specifically, all candidates derived from modifications on the minimal subnet are evaluated using the projected log $L_s\!\restriction_{\{d,f,g,h\}} = [\langle d, f, g, h \rangle^{40}, \langle f, g, d, h \rangle^{30}, \langle f, d, g, h \rangle^{30}]$. Then, the best candidate is selected and connected back to the original net. As shown in Fig. 6, the best candidate places the new transition labeled g in between transitions f and h. By removing the source and sink places i' and o', we connect the selected net back to the other part of the original net. Specifically, we add the arcs $(P_{in} \times T_{start}) \cup (T_{end} \times P_{out})$ back.

5   Experimental Evaluation

In this section, we present the experiments conducted to evaluate the efficiency of the proposed extensions. We start by introducing the setup for the experiments before discussing the experimental results.

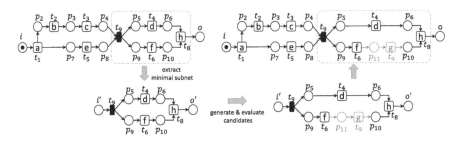

Fig. 6. As activity g is preceded by activity f and followed by activity h in log L_s, the minimal subnet can be extracted. The green dotted line highlights the extracted subnet, where $P_{in} = \{p_4, p_8\}$, $P_{out} = \{o\}$, $T_{start} = \{t_9\}$, $T_{end} = \{t_8\}$ (Color figure online)

5.1   Experimental Setup

The paper aims to improve the time performance of the synthesis-rules-based process discovery approach introduced in [13,14]. Moreover, the model quality should remain at a similar level. Therefore, comparing the computation time and the model quality with/without the extensions is the experiment's focus. In particular, we would like to focus on the generation and evaluation steps. To achieve this, we use publicly available real-life event logs, which are BPI2017[4] and helpdesk[5]. BPI2017 is split into two sub-logs, BPI2017A and BPI2017O, using the event prefixes.

Since we assume the initial model to be sound and free-choice, we apply Inductive Miner - infrequent (IMf) [15] for this purpose as it guarantees both properties and is scalable at the same time. For each event log, we get two model-log pairs by applying the IMf using two different filter values (0.2 and 0.4). In total, we have 6 model-log pairs as the input for the experiment.

For each model-log pair, we apply the approach in [14] with four different experimental settings, depending on whether the two extensions are turned on/off. For each process model, we remove each labeled transition and add it back. Then, we record the time of generating and evaluating the candidate nets. Lastly, the quality of the resulting models is evaluated and documented. The experiment and the code with extensions can be found in an open repository[6].

5.2   Results and Discussion

Table 1 shows the results of the computation time (in seconds) for the generation and evaluation of the candidate nets. Note that the numbers are the average time of adding back every labeled transition in the corresponding process model. As discussed, there are four different settings depending on whether the extensions

---

[4] https://doi.org/10.4121/uuid:3926db30-f712-4394-aebc-75976070e91f.

[5] https://doi.org/10.4121/uuid:0c60edf1-6f83-4e75-9367-4c63b3e9d5bb.

[6] https://github.com/denzoned/AccelarateSynthesisMiner.

are applied. The settings are labeled as *e1* (extension 1 is applied), *e2* (extension 2 is applied), *e1+e2* (both extension 1 and 2 are applied), and *original* (without extensions, correspondent to the original approach in [14]). The model-log pairs are indicated by [log name]_[IMf filter].

Table 1. Computation time (seconds) for generation and evaluation of candidate nets

model-log	generation				evaluation			
	e1	*e2*	*e1 + e2*	*original*	*e1*	*e2*	*e1 + e2*	*original*
BPI2017A_02	0.0990	2.6453	0.0576	31.4863	28.1865	30.2120	11.2979	93.0011
BPI2017A_04	0.0496	0.1566	0.0427	1.3720	17.6582	17.5019	11.9836	36.7301
BPI2017O_02	0.0408	0.0995	0.0325	0.1628	9.2453	5.7846	3.2266	17.6581
BPI2017O_04	0.0559	0.1040	0.0279	0.1514	10.4371	5.5425	2.8860	16.8704
helpdesk_02	0.5753	2.7208	0.0255	3.1770	6.3565	7.1008	2.4854	15.8367
helpdesk_04	0.5131	2.5675	0.0272	2.8994	5.8298	7.2238	2.4993	15.6390

We can see that the computation time is significantly reduced. Figure 7 shows a clearer indication regarding how much time (%) is reduced compared to the original approach [14]. In general, both extensions can reduce the time for generation and evaluation.

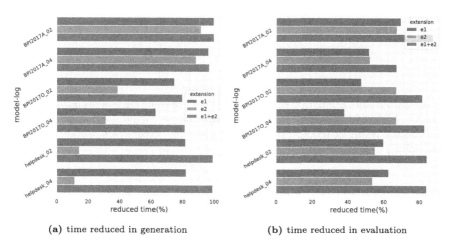

(a) time reduced in generation   (b) time reduced in evaluation

Fig. 7. Bar charts showing the time reduced (%) compared to the original approach [14] (Color figure online)

As shown in Fig. 7a, Extension 1 is more effective in reducing the computation time for generating candidate nets compared to Extension 2. The combination of both extensions reduces the computation time the most, as indicated by the green bars in Fig. 7. On average, both extensions combined reduce the computation time by 82.85% compared to the original approach without any extensions.

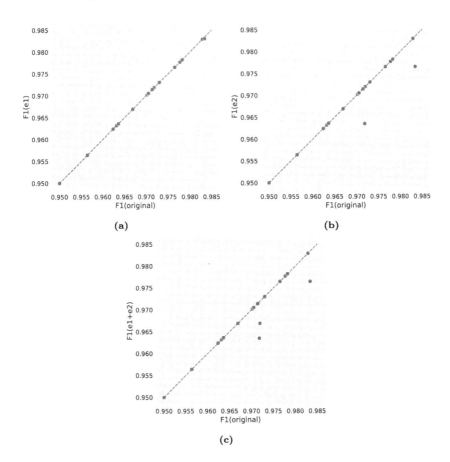

Fig. 8. Scatter plots comparing the quality (F1) of the resulting models using different settings (*e1*, *e2*, *e1 + e2*). The red dashed lines indicate the ideal situation where the quality of the resulting models with/without applying extensions is the same. (Color figure online)

Next, we would like to compare the quality (F1-score) of the resulting process models with/without applying the extensions. Figure 8 shows the result of the comparison. Each scatter plot consists of 49 data points. For each data point, the x coordinate indicates the F1 score of the resulting model using the original approach [14] whereas the y coordinate shows the same using different extensions (*e1*, *e2*, *e1+e2*). Any dot on the red dashed lines indicates the ideal case, where the qualities of the resulting model (when applying the extensions) are the same compared to the original approach. We can see that Setting *e1* always finds the model with the same quality as the original, while settings *e2* and *e1+e2* can do the same for most of the models but with a few outliers.

6 Conclusion

The Synthesis Miner algorithm was developed to discover models featuring non-block structures while maintaining desirable guarantees (free-choiceness and soundness) using synthesis rules based on free-choice net theory. Adopting an iterative setting, the approach tries to find the best modification (w.r.t. F1-score) to an existing Workflow net by generating and evaluating various candidate nets. However, the generation and evaluation steps involve the application of synthesis rules and alignment-based conformance checking respectively, presenting scalability challenges.

To address this, our paper proposes extensions leveraging the insight that modifications often impact only a subpart of the model. By isolating these subparts, we aim to speed up the process. Firstly, we use log heuristics to narrow down the search space. Additionally, we break down the generation and evaluation steps into smaller tasks by focusing on a smaller but most relevant component of the process model. Evaluated using real-life event logs, the experiment indicates that the extensions enhance the scalability of the Synthesis Miner by decreasing the computation time by 82.85% on average.

Several directions can be investigated in future works. Firstly, we are interested in techniques that can help to further reduce the search space. One interesting idea could be to apply the evaluation of place fitness [2] to filter out candidate nets containing non-fitting places before evaluation. Also, the scale of the experiment is relatively small, which poses a potential threat to the validity of the extensions. Thus, we plan to conduct a more comprehensive evaluation including more real-life event logs.

Acknowledgements. We thank the Alexander von Humboldt (AvH) Stiftung for supporting our research.

References

1. van der Aalst, W.M.P.: The application of Petri nets to workflow management. J. Circ. Syst. Comput. **8**(1), 21–66 (1998)
2. van der Aalst, W.M.P.: Discovering the "Glue" connecting activities - exploiting monotonicity to learn places faster. In: de Boer, F., Bonsangue, M., Rutten, J. (eds.) It's All About Coordination. LNCS, vol. 10865, pp. 1–20. Springer, Cham (2018). https://doi.org/10.1007/978-3-319-90089-6_1
3. van der Aalst, W.M.P., Adriansyah, A., van Dongen, B.F.: Replaying history on process models for conformance checking and performance analysis. WIREs Data Min. Knowl. Discov. **2**(2), 182–192 (2012)
4. van der Aalst, W.M.P., Carmona, J. (eds.): Process Mining Handbook. Lecture Notes in Business Information Processing, vol. 448. Springer, Cham (2022). https://doi.org/10.1007/978-3-031-08848-3
5. Adriansyah, A., Munoz-Gama, J., Carmona, J., van Dongen, B.F., van der Aalst, W.M.P.: Measuring precision of modeled behavior. Inf. Syst. E Bus. Manag. **13**(1), 37–67 (2015)

6. Augusto, A., Conforti, R., Dumas, M., Rosa, M.L., Bruno, G.: Automated discovery of structured process models from event logs: the discover-and-structure approach. Data Knowl. Eng. **117**, 373–392 (2018)

7. Augusto, A., et al.: Automated discovery of process models from event logs: review and benchmark. IEEE Trans. Knowl. Data Eng. **31**(4), 686–705 (2019)

8. Augusto, A., Conforti, R., Dumas, M., Rosa, M.L., Polyvyanyy, A.: Split miner: automated discovery of accurate and simple business process models from event logs. Knowl. Inf. Syst. **59**(2), 251–284 (2019)

9. Buijs, J.C.A.M., van Dongen, B.F., van der Aalst, W.M.P.: A genetic algorithm for discovering process trees. In: CEC 2012, pp. 1–8. IEEE (2012)

10. Desel, J., Esparza, J.: Free Choice Petri Nets. No. 40, Cambridge University Press, Cambridge (1995)

11. Dixit, P.M.: Interactive process mining. Ph.D. thesis, Technische Universiteit Eindhoven (2019)

12. Huang, T., van der Aalst, W.M.P.: Comparing ordering strategies for process discovery using synthesis rules. In: Troya, J., et al. (eds.) ICSOC 2022. LNCS, vol. 13821, pp. 40–52. Springer, Cham (2022). https://doi.org/10.1007/978-3-031-26507-5_4

13. Huang, T., van der Aalst, W.M.P.: Discovering sound free-choice workflow nets with non-block structures. In: Almeida, J.P.A., Karastoyanova, D., Guizzardi, G., Montali, M., Maggi, F.M., Fonseca, C.M. (eds.) EDOC 2022. LNCS, vol. 13585, pp. 200–216. Springer, Cham (2022). https://doi.org/10.1007/978-3-031-17604-3_12

14. Huang, T., van der Aalst, W.M.P.: Unblocking inductive miner - while preserving desirable properties. In: van der Aa, H., Bork, D., Proper, H.A., Schmidt, R. (eds.) BPMDS/EMMSAD@CAiSE. LNBIP, vol. 479, pp. 327–342. Springer, Cham (2023). https://doi.org/10.1007/978-3-031-34241-7_23

15. Leemans, S.: Robust process mining with guarantees. Ph.D. thesis, Technische Universiteit Eindhoven (2017)

16. Schuster, D., van Zelst, S.J., van der Aalst, W.M.P.: Incremental discovery of hierarchical process models. In: Dalpiaz, F., Zdravkovic, J., Loucopoulos, P. (eds.) RCIS 2020. LNBIP, vol. 385, pp. 417–433. Springer, Cham (2020). https://doi.org/10.1007/978-3-030-50316-1_25

Navigating the Data Model Divide in Smart Manufacturing: An Empirical Investigation for Enhanced AI Integration

István Koren[1]([✉])(iD), Matthias Jarke[2](iD), Judith Michael[3](iD), Malte Heithoff[3](iD),
Leah Tacke Genannt Unterberg[1], Max Stachon[3](iD), Bernhard Rumpe[3](iD),
and Wil M. P. van der Aalst[1](iD)

[1] Process and Data Science, RWTH Aachen University, Aachen, Germany
{koren,leah.tgu,wvdaalst}@pads.rwth-aachen.de
[2] Information Systems and Databases, RWTH Aachen University, Aachen, Germany
jarke@dbis.rwth-aachen.de
[3] Software Engineering, RWTH Aachen University, Aachen, Germany
{michael,heithoff,stachon,rumpe}@se-rwth.de

Abstract. In engineering informatics, the myriad data types, formats, streaming and storage technologies pose significant challenges in managing data effectively. The problem grows, as new analytics perspectives are emerging from a totally different AI-based tradition. This divide often necessitates the development of custom solutions that link specific data capture methods to particular AI algorithms. Encouraged by the success of object-centric mining models for discrete processes, we look for large clusters of data management practices where novel bridging data models can help navigate the data model divide. We address this question in a two-cycle design science approach. In a first cycle, over 80 actual data model practices from a wide variety of engineering disciplines were analyzed, leading to four candidate fields. In a second cycle, an initial bridging data model for one of these fields was developed and validated wrt some of the found practices. Our findings offer the prospect of significantly streamlining data pipelines, paving the way for enriched AI integration in production engineering, and consequently, a more robust, data-driven manufacturing paradigm.

Keywords: Industry 4.0 · Manufacturing Data Model · Empirical Study · AI Integration · Digital Shadow

1 Introduction

The Industrial Internet of Things (IIoT) and Industry 4.0 have ushered in a new era of opportunities for the manufacturing industry. They promise enhanced operational efficiency, increased productivity, and the potential for innovation in product design and manufacturing processes. Central to realizing these opportunities is the integration of Artificial Intelligence (AI) tools which can provide

H. van der Aa et al. (Eds.): BPMDS 2024/EMMSAD 2024, LNBIP 511, pp. 275–290, 2024.
https://doi.org/10.1007/978-3-031-61007-3_21

intelligent analytics, predictive maintenance, and autonomous decision-making, among other benefits. However, the implementation and optimization of AI in manufacturing hinges on the effective management and integration of vast and varied data generated across the production lifecycle [15]. A predominant challenge in leveraging this data effectively is the heterogeneous nature of data models and pipelines across different use cases in manufacturing. Current common practice involves custom solutions for data management and analytics for each application, owing to the lack of better, standardized approaches. This practice, while solving immediate challenges, consumes significant resources and obstructs cross-domain interoperability and knowledge transfer.

This paper explores innovative solutions to this problem at the data model level. After a review of data management research and practice focused on Digital Twins (DT) in manufacturing, it pursues a two-cycle design science approach [16], contributing to these research questions:

RQ1: Do data model practices within and across engineering disciplines expose sufficient similarity to make the existence of useful standardized data models plausible? Answering such a question is not easy due to the reluctance of many companies to share their practices, let alone the cross-validation of claimed practices by looking at actual data. Fortunately, the research cluster Internet of Production (IoP) at RWTH Aachen University [9] with over 25 different engineering and related natural science disciplines—all actively involved in application-oriented research and practice—offers a unique alternative setting for such a study. In Sect. 3, we report on design, results, and implications of a structured analysis of over 80 such data model practices at both a conceptual and data-example level. The identification of at least four broadly observed candidate clusters of practices indicates an affirmative answer to RQ1.

RQ2: How can a "bridging" data model be derived for such a cluster, and how can it be validated from formal and practice perspectives? Formal requirements for the models were initially derived from both general design principles in database and knowledge graph research, and the insights of pioneering work in object-centric process mining [3]. Subsequently, a bridging model was developed, addressing the commonly observed need to integrate measurements of continuous processes and discrete events with high-level analytics. This model underwent both a formal evaluation and a practical assessment. The practical assessment involved quantifying the effort necessary to generate data from five distinct sensor data practices identified in RQ1, and examining the utility of this data in various analytical processes. The results indicate potential for enhanced analytics and data sharing despite reduced effort, but also show limitations and needs for further research.

This paper is structured as follows. The next section presents background and related work. Subsequently, Sect. 3 describes the empirical study of data model practices. Section 4 introduces and discusses the *Measurement and Event Data* format as the first example of a bridging model. Finally, Sect. 5 concludes this paper.

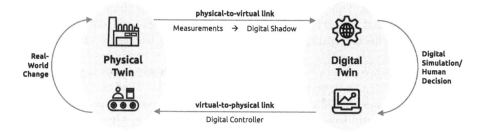

Fig. 1. Digital Twin showing the data model gap between sensor-based metrology and AI-based digital shadows.

2 Background and Related Work

Persistent problems of data availability in manufacturing engineering, operations, and usage [6] as well as in AI generally [15] are well-known. Partial solution proposals come from many areas of Computer Science [8]. Examples include: requirements engineering in manufacturing cases [23]; data lake-based layered metamodel for Computer-Aided Engineering [33]; optimization and security of physical dataflows in the edge-cloud spectrum [27,28].

In industry, leading cloud providers offer their own standard data models on open platforms, such as the Open Manufacturing Platform (OMP) on top of Microsoft's Azure IIoT cloud (cf. https://azure.microsoft.com/solutions/industrial-iot). Several initiatives are standardizing approaches to reduce reliance on vendor-specific solutions and domain-centric modeling languages. AutomationML [1], an XML-based, object-oriented data modeling language, supports the creation, storage, and exchange of engineering models. It serves as a neutral format for data exchange across diverse manufacturing scenarios. The OPC Unified Architecture (OPC UA) offers standardized information models with associated guidelines and best practices, including standard APIs for novel specialized services such as data access or alarms and conditions [26]. In the domain of standards and reference models that enrich the solution space through ontologies, notable examples include the Smart Appliances REFerence (SAREF) ontology [19] and the framework provided by the International Data Spaces Association [4].

The growing complexity of manufacturing systems with multiple conflicting goals, frequently changing boundary conditions and strategies have led to the conclusion that any solution concept must take the essentially decentralized and modular, yet interoperable nature of manufacturing data management into account. Interacting DTs have emerged as a widely accepted abstraction paradigm, often inspired by experiences from multi-agent systems [29]. Recently, also the IIoT community, like Industrie 4.0, re-interpreted their idea of Asset Administration Shell (AAS) as enablers for DTs [22].

Each DT accompanies the life of some real-world object, process, or aggregate Cyber-Physical Production System (CPPS) in a so-called twinning cycle, as illustrated in Fig. 1. This twinning requires a bi-directional connection between the real world and the DT, such that real-world changes and digitally found decisions are reflected transparently with well-defined frequency and faithfulness [13].

The importance of data in DT architectures was already recognized a decade ago [12], recently also in civil engineering [24]. A Digital Shadow (DS), in this context, refers to a digital representation of a physical asset or process, which is essential for data-driven decision-making and analytics. Organized around this DS concept, data management must support two core tasks in a DT-based infrastructure. It focuses on the creation and maintenance of DSs by a wide range of intelligent analytics combining model-based and AI approaches [10, 11]. But DTs are also active cooperating or competing agents that sovereignly share DSs in data spaces [17,32]. From a conceptual modeling perspective, DSs have recently been characterized as materialized views and as shareable, even tradeable data assets [21], but also as software engineering artifacts with a real-world grounding and well-defined provenance information [25].

Figure 1 implicitly showcases a "data model gap". This gap is not merely about the physical and digital representations but also about how data is modeled, structured, and utilized in these two realms. In the physical world, data capture methods are often heterogeneous, reflecting the complex reality of physical processes. Conversely, the digital world, particularly within AI algorithms, requires data to be structured in a highly standardized format for efficient processing and analysis. This discrepancy between the physical "as-is" and the digital "to-be" structured data leads to a data model divide.

Contrary to the often complex semantic structures emphasized in the discussed standards and models, our approach portrayed in this paper aligns more closely with the methodology observed in general AI libraries. As input, these libraries rely on a limited number of standardized data formats, such as CSV or other forms of tabular data, which serve as the basis for parameterizing algorithms and frameworks. By adopting parameterizable data models, we facilitate an amalgamation of both schema and instance data, simplifying the data model complexity while maintaining versatility and effectiveness in the AI-driven analysis and decision-making processes.

3   Stage 1: Empirical Study of Data Model Practices

Our approach is informed by observations in Fig. 1. In their survey of DT approaches, Jones et al. [18] emphasize that the activities involved in the physical2virtual link span two largely disjoint communities of research and practice. The long established engineering theories of measurement (metrology) with the related sensor management IT community (e.g., [31]) must somehow be matched to the explosively growing field of model-driven analytics and data-driven AI for the creation, optimization, visualization, and sharing [20] of purpose-oriented DSs. The challenge arises in managing the multitude of potential $m \times n$ mappings between these two parts. The claim pursued in this paper is that a few

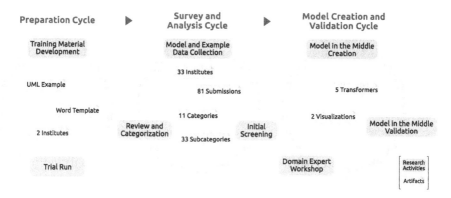

Fig. 2. Research Cycles of the Empirical Study.

(say: b) standardized "models in the middle" could reduce the mapping complexity to $b \times (m+n)$. This could offer scalability, reuse, and cross-enterprise sharing, with the potential for significant reduction in effort, and increased utility.

We conducted an empirical study to investigate how data models are employed across various use cases within the manufacturing domain. Our approach aligns with the Design Science Research Methodology (DSRM) [16], which we adapted to include a survey to gather empirical data and validate our research artifacts. The overall design science process is portrayed in Fig. 2.

3.1 Research Design

Adhering to the DSRM, our initial effort was aimed at understanding the problem domain and the requirements for a potential solution. We selected the highly interdisciplinary engineering team from the IoP research cluster as study participants to obtain meaningful information, considering their diverse backgrounds.

Preparation Cycle: Previous modeling experiences in the research cluster indicated familiarity with modeling languages such as UML, yet there remained a gap between theoretical knowledge and practical application. To address this, we developed training materials illustrating UML class diagram modeling with simple everyday object associations, avoiding mechanical engineering content to mitigate bias. Next, we created a Word template for capturing essential metadata and structuring data models. It was divided into two main sections—a UML class diagram and tables populated with example data—supported by the following metadata: dataset name, contact person, institute name, work package, version number, date, and a brief description. This template design was iteratively refined through pilot trials at two institutes with disparate data management practices. One institute operates legacy machines requiring manual intervention at every step, from process planning to data analysis using MATLAB. The other institute operates a connected ecosystem where industrial machines relay data to a time-series database via a message broker, harnessing visualization tools like Grafana. Feedback from these trials was critical in evolving the training materials and integrating a UML class diagram example directly into the template. Identifying a suitable modeling tool presented significant challenges. Web-based tools, while easily accessible, were limited in functionality, restricting the extent to which they could be utilized for our modeling tasks. Native applications, although potentially more robust, were out of reach due to administrative restrictions within the engineering institutes. Thus, PowerPoint and Visio were recommended for modeling as biggest common denominator.

The feedback gathered from the pilot trials not only informed the iterative improvement of these artifacts but also provided valuable insights into the practical challenges and preferences in data modeling practices across different engineering disciplines. Consequently, the outputs of the preparation cycle, specifically the refined Word template and the updated training materials, became critical inputs for the subsequent cycle.

Survey and Analysis Cycle: The study's design and development phase received strong management endorsement and was promoted at key project events, leading to significant participation over two months. A total of 81 data models were submitted, verified for completeness, and any gaps addressed through follow-up queries. These models were versioned and stored securely in a Git repository, adhering to DSRM principles for traceability and rigorous evaluation. A thorough screening to identify and correct errors preceded a detailed coding and classification process. This ensured a methodical assessment of each submission, with discrepancies resolved collectively, enhancing the study's categorization approach.

Rigorous coding and classification were conducted by a mixed team of senior researchers and PhD students, ensuring a comprehensive and methodical evaluation. Each submission was assigned a first coder. This decision was then reviewed by a second coder. Finally, deviations and conflicts were discussed in the whole group and decided in virtual meetings, ensuring refinement and improvement of the categorization along the iterative nature of DSRM. Thus, the survey led to a valuable repository of empirical data to inform future design science research within the manufacturing domain.

To uphold the confidentiality agreement with participants, which was pivotal in securing 81 submissions, the detailed datasets underpinning our study will not be published. This assurance of confidentiality was essential for participant engagement and the integrity of our research findings.

The classification of data models, enriched by empirical evidence and collaborative refinement, served as a critical input for the next cycle, guiding the design and validation of a model that addresses the identified needs and gaps within data management practices of machine data.

Model Creation and Validation Cycle: In the final phase, the data models were systematically consolidated according to their respective categories, leading

Table 1. Overall data model categorization and subcategories.

Category	#	Description (Examples)
MACHINE		
machine data (measurement)	44	Time-series machine and event data
machine master data	40	Machine type designations, and location
machine configuration	39	(Default) parameters
robot	10	Robot configuration
3D printer	3	3D-printer-specific master data
maintenance	2	Maintenance schedules and configuration
PROCESS		
process steps/operation/measurement	45	Assembly instructions and sequence
process aggregation (case/event/log)	15	Preprocessed event data
experiment	12	Experiment setup
images	10	References to binary image files
process evaluation	6	Evaluation of production processes
MATERIAL		
material properties	41	Material characteristics
Bill of Materials (BoM)	7	Parts and part-of relations
material amount/inventory/stock	1	Inventory and stock of material
SIMULATION & OPTIMIZATION		
CAD/3D models	14	References to 3D model files
simulation	8	Descriptions of simulation experiments
computed results	7	Results of simulation runs
planning	6	Simulation plans
mathematical model/optimization	5	References and descriptions of mathematical models
FACTORY		
factory/machine arrangement	15	Shopfloor layouts
factory master data	8	Factory descriptions
finances	4	Financial information on shopfloor equipment
PRODUCTS		
product (parts)	25	Planning and/or evaluation of product parts
SUPPLY CHAIN		
jobs/sales order	13	Details of orders
delivery	6	Delivery master data like shipping address
supplier	5	Supplier data like origin
purchase order (material)	4	Details of purchases

to the identification of potential candidates for models in the middle. These
candidates were refined with domain experts during a dedicated workshop.

3.2   Results

Our analysis revealed a rich collection of 33 distinct model types, which we
ultimately grouped into 11 categories. Some data models span multiple subcategories, highlighting the interconnected nature of manufacturing processes
while underscoring potential integration points for bridging model design. For

example, time series data frequently coincided with "experiment" or "process" categories, prompting multiple assignments.

Table 1 presents our categorization, listing both the primary categories and their subcategories alongside the count of data models in each. The majority of submissions fell under the MACHINE category, predominantly featuring time series measurements. This was followed closely by models describing PROCESS elements, like experiments or test runs. Due to space constraints, we omitted the four least-represented categories (quantity in brackets): HUMAN RESOURCES (21), METADATA (11), REQUIREMENTS (4), and SURVEY (4). These areas, while not the focus of this paper, represent valuable avenues for future exploration.

The 81 submissions collectively paint a heterogeneous picture, but nevertheless a striking similarity in challenges faced by different mechanical engineering processes across various disciplines. For instance, both aluminum die casting and plastic injection molding displayed a common issue: the internal control logic for pressure values operated at a higher frequency than what could be accessed via external interfaces. These shared challenges across disciplines are insightful for our endeavor to standardize and simplify data models, in particular towards the creation of automated data extractors and transformators. A common issue was handling external data such as 3D models or MATLAB files, which are often intricately integrated into the data models that merely outline their context.

Our analysis underscored not only the diversity of data models in manufacturing, but also common operational challenges such as the mentioned frequency discrepancies. These findings highlight critical caps that the "models-in-the-middle" aim to bridge. Specifically, the observed frequency differences between internal control logic and external data accessibility present a fundamental barrier to real-time AI analysis and decision-making. Before AI algorithms can be effectively applied, data must be synchronized and standardized, ensuring that AI tools can operate on real-time or near-real-time data seamlessly. Additionally, the integration of disparate data types into a cohesive model facilitates the development of automated data extractors and transformers, pivotal for AI's role in predictive maintenance, quality control, and process optimization. Thus, addressing these operational challenges is not merely a prerequisite but a foundational step towards realizing the full potential of AI integration in smart manufacturing.

3.3   Discussion and Implications for Data Model Design

While there is considerable diversity across the categories, a remarkable consistency exists within each category: certain modeling approaches and structures seem to be predominant in specific contexts within the manufacturing domain.

A frequently observed pattern was a triadic relationship encompassing (machine data) *measurements*, *processes*, and *products*. This relationship is a cornerstone in many submissions, albeit manifested differently across various stages of product development. In the inception phase (e.g., product development), this might include plans or sequences for robot movements and machine settings, while in the final stages, it shifts towards quality assessments and measurements.

Most models showcased intricate associations between different object types, yet these relationships were often not mirrored in foreign keys or similar in the example data. This observed discrepancy was made apparent by the fact that the majority of the data models were conceptualized retrospectively as part of the study. Initially, the data files (such as CSV files or database tables) were generated without an accompanying conceptual model. In the ex-post process of conceptual modeling, the modelers' inherent domain knowledge played a crucial role, enabling them to explicitly define relationships that were not initially apparent in the raw data. Inverting this approach—starting with a well-defined conceptual data model before data collection—holds significant potential for streamlining data handling.

Three data models documented cross-institute collaborations and two involved external industrial data, further highlighting the interdisciplinary potential by suitable bridging data models. This scarcity can be attributed to various factors, including NDAs and other confidentiality concerns.

The results provide valuable insights into the common patterns, variance, and limitations observed in the submitted data models. The recurring triadic relationship across models indicates a fundamental structure in manufacturing data modeling, while discrepancies between models and example data highlight a crucial area for improvement. The limited collaboration and external data integration also point to systemic challenges in data sharing and inter-institutional cooperation. These insights not only inform the current understanding but also shape our approach to future research and development in this area, especially in creating more integrated, real-world applicable "models in the middle".

4   Stage 2: Design and Preliminary Evaluation of an Intermediary Machine Data Model

We contribute towards a theory of data modeling by identifying a number of formal criteria that an intermediary model for navigating the data model divide should satisfy. While some of these criteria stem from decades of conceptual data model and model implementation research, others are inspired by specific experiences gained from an early success story in object-centric process mining.

Within this context, we then present a specific bridging model addressing the problem of linking event logs to their measurement data provenance, called MAED (Measurement And Event Data). In addition to testing this proposal with respect to the mentioned criteria, we also offer an initial practical validation through an expert panel from different engineering disciplines, and the experimental development of transformers from actual measurement data to the model. Moreover, we study one exploitation potential of MAED on the AI analytics side, i.e., its potential usage to integrate concepts of the measurement stage into Digital Shadow creation by object-centric process mining via OCEL 2.0.

4.1 Formal and Technical Design Criteria for Bridging Data Models: Insights from OCEL 2.0

Before we embark on the data model design, it seems worthwhile to fix some formal properties such models should have, as well as on the requirements concerning the used database technologies. The requirements formulated here can be seen as a database-centric IS engineering view on experiences gained originally in a process mining context, culminating in the Object-Centric Event Log (OCEL 2.0) bridging model [7]. To follow the subsequent discussion, please also refer to Fig. 3.

The need to include both *static and dynamic aspects* in conceptual modeling and data management goes back to early efforts to combine ideas from Entity-Relationship and relational databases, with Petri net models and transaction processing in the late 1970's. Yet, data-oriented and the process-oriented IS engineering subcommunities remain clearly recognizable in conferences such as CAiSE even today. However, a bridging data model must clearly address both perspectives to enable sufficiently rich and selective analytics. In the process mining community, the quest for a "model in the middle" started with standardized file formats such as IEEE XES [2] which serve as an intermediary format between data extraction from ERP systems, and process analytics software. Only from problematic experiences with early attempts at object-centric process mining, the new OCEL 2.0 has emerged from research to address object-centric process mining use cases [3] which carefully differentiates the *object* concept to a degree that significantly extends the versatility with respect to many different object-focused as well as process-focused types of analysis, based on a growing catalog of reusable analytics tools [7].

Such broad applicability, however, requires two additional formal aspects. First, it is extremely important not just to elaborate the important aspects of objects and events, but also to offer a *rich set of relationships* among them, not just structurally but also positioned with shared context aspects such as time or—in geo-intensive applications—space; filters (qualifiers) enable a more narrow focus of analysis in such relationships. At the implementation level, foreign keys are essential to materialize these relationships – one more reason that their use including underlying *unique identifiers* must be included in more engineering management practice.

Second, the evolving landscape of data and analytical methods necessitates adaptive perspectives on data management, particularly for decision makers seeking diverse viewpoints for strategic analysis. An optimal "model in the middle" must facilitate not only schema evolution but also support the coexistence of multiple schema organizations. This concept, rooted in the innovations of deductive database research from the early 1980s, involves integrating data and its schema within a unified framework. This amalgamation approach, now pivotal in various semantic data management areas, enables dynamic schema modifications and multiple, parallel data representations, enhancing flexibility and responsiveness to changing analytical and operational requirements.

However, most of these attempts required significant algorithmic research to address the *performance challenges* associated with amalgamation. For example, research in [14] employs RDF knowledge graphs for comprehensive modeling (schema) and execution (instance) of Digital Shadow structure and process as in [25]. While it demonstrated many of the needed aspects, massive performance problems have prevented its use in practice. Figure 3 shows how OCEL 2.0 addresses the amalgamation in a relational setting, having tables for both schema and instance data. This approach cannot just profit from long experience with similar methods in SQL servers, but also permits, e.g., special-purpose main memory databases for interactive analytics even with massive event data.

From a practical viewpoint, a bridging data model is only useful if its content can be easily filled using simple, generic, and robust transformation mechanisms from legacy, use-case-specific data models. Such transformers are not only pivotal for integrating diverse data sources but also for ensuring the scalability and adaptability of data models in dynamic industrial settings.

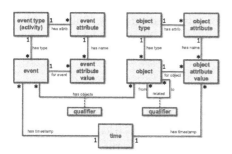 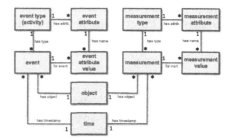

Fig. 3. OCEL 2.0 Metamodel [7].   **Fig. 4.** Measurement and Event Data (MAED) model for Machine Data.

4.2 MAED: A Bridging Data Model for Harmonizing Sensor-Generated Industrial Measurement Data

In manufacturing, the challenge of harmonizing vast streams of sensor-generated data with the analytical needs of CPPS is substantial. We propose the MAED data model for capturing and standardizing time-series data and event records from manufacturing processes (see Fig. 4). For a detailed introduction to the MAED data model, see [30]. Recognizing the pioneering efforts of OCEL 2.0 in establishing a robust framework for object-centric process mining, our approach to MAED was informed and inspired by the foundational principles and structural components of OCEL 2.0. This was a deliberate choice, grounded in the rationale that event-driven data points, central to both OCEL 2.0 and MAED, present a complex domain where prior advancements can significantly accelerate innovation and applicability in related fields. The seamless integration of measurement and event data is pivotal for enriching analytics, enhancing decision-making, and ultimately fostering the development of more responsive and efficient CPPS.

At its core, the MAED format requires minimal, yet critical data attributes for each entry: the precise time of data capture, the nature of the recorded information, and the identification of its physical origin within the manufacturing system. Data points within the MAED schema are categorized as "events" (Fig. 4, left) or "measurements" (Fig. 4, right). Events are singular occurrences that mark transitions or alterations in state, carrying significance even when devoid of detailed data. A simple event like "machine overheated" suffices to signal a system's condition. In turn, measurements are systematically captured and expected readings that depict a machine's operational state through their values, which can reveal normal function or indicate anomalies like sensor faults.

"Time" is central, providing the temporal context and enabling the chronological reconstruction of events and states. The "object" identifier is equally critical, enriching the data with spatial context and relevance.

By consolidating events and measurements into a uniform structure with clear specifications, the MAED metamodel facilitates the assembly of individual data points into comprehensive sequences for advanced analysis. This provides a framework for creating data sets that are more readily comparable and analyzable across different machines or processes.

4.3 Preliminary Evaluation

In accordance with the validation phase of the DSRM, the proposed data model underwent a preliminary user evaluation during a workshop. It convened around 30 engineering researchers from diverse domains, leading to the collective affirmation of the fundamental principles of the proposed model.

Further, we collaborated with five data owners within the IoP and an external partner, on transformers of their datasets into our specified format to test its practical applicability and effectiveness. The original data formats included collections of CSV files, JSON files with complex nestings, untyped text files from a MinIO database export, and a complete PostgreSQL database dump. As a consequence, no two datasets could be processed or visualized using the same methodology or tools initially. However, once the datasets were transformed into the MAED format, they were seamlessly integrated and became compatible with preliminary tooling, underscoring the robustness and versatility of the approach in standardizing and automating data processing for effective analysis and visualization. As initial proofs-of-concept, we created a Python library for handling the data, and two visualization widgets. In this widget, measurement and event types can be specified to be rendered below each other.

The successful transformation of datasets into the MAED format across five distinct examples not only substantiates the feasibility of our approach but also highlights intricacies of data structures at both logical and physical levels. Further easing the transformation process requires foundational prerequisites, like the inclusion of explicit foreign key relationships, thereby streamlining data integration and enhancing effective automation. Looking at the previously specified formal design criteria for such models, the successful transformer experiments and positive workshop feedback offer strong evidence of a good match of MAED to current practices and its potential.

However, the formal criteria are only partially satisfied. While we have rich relationships and schema-instance amalgamation for measurement and event data, and a time concept as in OCEL 2.0, the same has not yet been achieved for the integration of the object concept. Thus, one main usage idea of MAED—embedding extremely fine-grained and massive measurement data from continuous processes into the object-centric process mining world of OCEL 2.0—remains a non-trivial challenge for more sophisticated analyses and thus opens the avenue for significant further technical research.

Regarding the envisioned enhanced AI integration, the "model in the middle" approach enables a seamless and standardized application of advanced AI services across various domains. This standardization unlocks the potential for employing advanced AI methodologies, such as few-shot learning with large language models (LLMs) for domain-specific language (DSL) model generation, where previously, the absence of uniform data models limited the applicability of such technologies [5]. Beyond this, standardized data formats pave the way for AI-driven anomaly detection, predictive maintenance, and optimization algorithms that can now be more readily integrated and operationalized across different manufacturing environments.

5 Conclusions, Limitations, and Future Work

This paper addressed the critical challenge of bridging the divide in Industry 4.0 between a multitude of data models and diverse data-driven analytical technologies. It proposed the use of standardized intermediary models, a strategy that reduces complexity and enhances reuse across various organizational contexts.

In summary, our contributions are manifold. By utilizing empirical methods, we have opened a novel avenue to structure data diversity into categories, provided a practical example of a "model in the middle" in a mechanical engineering context, and yielded positive initial experiences with the new data format. This advancement marks a significant step towards enabling artificial intelligence methods to work more effectively with comprehensive, real-time manufacturing data, leading to smarter, more adaptive, and efficient production systems.

The empirical study of over 80 data model practices in an applied research context confirmed that there are several clusters of sufficiently similar practices within and beyond individual engineering disciplines that could scope the requirements and potential advantages for such models. Further validation directly in industry or from analysis of published case studies should promote deeper understanding and identification of other "high potentials".

Transitioning from a diverse array of data models to a small number of standardized models presents a series of organizational implementation challenges. Organizations may encounter resistance due to existing investments in custom data models. The transition may necessitate significant effort, time, and resources, potentially acting as a deterrent for some stakeholders. Moreover, the absence of established metrics for evaluating the efficiency and effectiveness of the proposed "model in the middle" approach poses another limitation. Without a benchmark, it becomes challenging to quantitatively assess the impact and benefits of our approach, beyond the formal and practice-oriented criteria proposed in this paper.

The integration of the MAED model with additional proposed data models offers substantial benefits, particularly in enhancing AI integration within production engineering. Effectively linking the data dimensions-machine, process, and product-facilitates the creation of comprehensive event logs, which are instrumental for analysis through generic process mining tools. This integration not only requires a more nuanced representation of entities like product types and hierarchies but also marks a critical step towards realizing a holistic and integrated data analysis approach. Such an approach significantly contributes to the advancement of AI applications in production engineering, as it leverages the comprehensive insights provided by the "models in the middle", ensuring that AI algorithms can access a richer, more structured pool of manufacturing data for enhanced decision-making and optimization.

Our "models in the middle" approach strategically positions itself between domain-specific standards, such as OPC-UA Companion Specifications, and general AI frameworks and libraries. This unique placement facilitates a critical linkage, enabling integration of specialized industrial protocols with advanced AI analytical frameworks. Future work will provide interoperability tests with existing IoT platforms and AI analytics tools to validate and refine this connection, aiming to close a significant gap in the current ecosystem.

Furthermore, while our approach offers a promising framework for enhancing AI integration in smart manufacturing, the aspects of scalability and real-time data processing have not been extensively explored in this paper. Future research will need to assess the scalability of our models, identifying computational and architectural optimizations to handle large-scale, real-time data streams effectively. This evaluation is crucial for ensuring that our approach can support the dynamic and expansive nature of smart manufacturing environments.

Acknowledgements. Funded by the Deutsche Forschungsgemeinschaft (DFG, German Research Foundation) under Germany's Excellence Strategy - EXC-2023 Internet of Production - 390621612. We thank the Alexander von Humboldt (AvH) Stiftung for supporting our research. We express our gratitude to all participants in our study.

References

1. Engineering data exchange format for use in industrial automation systems engineering - automation markup language. Standard IEC 62714-1 (2014)
2. IEEE Standard for eXtensible Event Stream (XES) for Achieving Interoperability in Event Logs and Event Streams (2016). iSBN: 9781504424219
3. van der Aalst, W.: Concurrency and objects matter! Disentangling the fabric of real operational processes to create digital twins. In: Cerone, A., Ölveczky, P.C.

(eds.) ICTAC 2021. LNCS, vol. 12819, pp. 3–17. Springer, Cham (2021). https://doi.org/10.1007/978-3-030-85315-0_1

4. Bader, S., et al.: The international data spaces information model - an ontology for sovereign exchange of digital content. In: Pan, J.Z., et al. (eds.) ISWC 2020. LNCS, vol. 12507, pp. 176–192. Springer, Cham (2020). https://doi.org/10.1007/978-3-030-62466-8_12

5. Baumann, N., et al.: Combining retrieval-augmented generation and few-shot learning for model synthesis of uncommon DSLs. Gesellschaft für Informatik e.V. (2024)

6. Bazaz, S.M., Lohtander, M., Varis, J.: Availability of manufacturing data resources in digital twins. Procedia Manuf. **51**, 1125–1131 (2020)

7. Berti, A., Koren, I., Adams, J.N., et al.: OCEL (object-centric event log) 2.0 specification. Chair of Process and Data Science, RWTH Aachen University (2023)

8. Brauner, P., Dalibor, M., Jarke, M., et al.: A computer science perspective on digital transformation in production. ACM Trans. Internet Things **3**(2), 1–32 (2022). Article 15

9. Brecher, C., Padberg, M., Jarke, M., van der Aalst, W., Schuh, G.: The internet of production: interdisciplinary visions and concepts for the production of tomorrow. In: Brecher, C., Schuh, G., van der Aalst, W., Jarke, M., Piller, F.T., Padberg, M. (eds.) Internet of Production. IDEAS, pp. 3–14. Springer, Cham (2024). https://doi.org/10.1007/978-3-031-44497-5_1

10. Brockhoff, T., Heithoff, M., Koren, I., et al.: Process prediction with digital twins. In: Models@run.time Workshop at MODELS 2021 (2021)

11. Correia, J., Abel, M., Becker, K.: Data management in digital twins: a systematic literature review. Knowl. Inf. Syst. **65**, 3165–3196 (2023)

12. Gantz, J., Reinsel, D.: The digital universe in 2020: big data, bigger digital shadows, and biggest growth in the far east. IDC Analyze the Future (2013)

13. Geisler, S., Vidal, M.E., Cappiello, C., et al.: Knowledge-driven data ecosystems towards data transparency. ACM J. Data Inf. Qual. (JDIQ) **14**(1), 1–13 (2022). Article 3

14. Gleim, L., Pennekamp, J., Liebenberg, M., et al.: FactDAG: formalizing data interoperability in an internet of production. IEEE Internet Things J. **7**(4), 3243–3253 (2020)

15. Groeger, C.: There is no AI without data. Commun. ACM **64**(11), 98–108 (2021)

16. Hevner, A.R., March, S.T., Park, J., Ram, S.: Design science in information systems research. MIS Q. Manag. Inf. Syst. **28**(1), 75–105 (2004)

17. Jarke, M.: Data sovereignty and the internet of production. In: Dustdar, S., Yu, E., Salinesi, C., Rieu, D., Pant, V. (eds.) CAiSE 2020. LNCS, vol. 12127, pp. 549–558. Springer, Cham (2020). https://doi.org/10.1007/978-3-030-49435-3_34

18. Jones, D., Snider, C., Nassehi, A., Yon, J., Hicks, B.: Characterizing the digital twin: a systematic literature review. CIRP J. Manuf. Sci. Technol. **29**, 36–52 (2020)

19. Lefrançois, M., Garcia-Castro, R., Bouter, C., Poveda-Villalon, M., Daniele, L., Gnabasik, D.: SAREF: the smart applications REFerence ontology (2020)

20. Lenzerini, M.: Direct and reverse rewriting in data interoperability. In: Giorgini, P., Weber, B. (eds.) CAiSE 2019. LNCS, vol. 11483, pp. 3–13. Springer, Cham (2019). https://doi.org/10.1007/978-3-030-21290-2_1

21. Liebenberg, M., Jarke, M.: Information systems engineering with Digital Shadows: concept and use cases in the Internet of Production. Inf. Syst. **114**, 102182 (2023)

22. Lin, S.W., Watson, K., Shao, G., Stojanovic, L., Zarkout, B.: Digital Twin Core Conceptual Models and Services. Industrial IoT Consortium Framework Publication (2023)

23. Loucopoulos, P., Kavakli, E., Chechina, N.: Requirements engineering for cyber physical production systems. In: Giorgini, P., Weber, B. (eds.) CAiSE 2019. LNCS, vol. 11483, pp. 276–291. Springer, Cham (2019). https://doi.org/10.1007/978-3-030-21290-2_18

24. Merino, J., Xie, X., Moretti, N., Chang, J., Parlikad, A.: Data integration for digital twins in the built environment based on federated data models. In: Smart Infrastructure and Construction, No. 2300002, pp. 1–18. Proceedings of the Institutions of Civil Engineers (2023)

25. Michael, J., et al.: A digital shadow reference model for worldwide production labs. In: Brecher, C., Schuh, G., van der Aalst, W., Jarke, M., Piller, F.T., Padberg, M. (eds.) Internet of Production. IDEAS, pp. 1–29. Springer, Cham (2023). https://doi.org/10.1007/978-3-030-98062-7_3-3

26. OPC-Foundation: The industrial interoperability standard (2023). https://opcfoundation.org/developer-tools/documents/?type=Specification. Accessed 27 July 2023

27. Pennekamp, J., Henze, M., Schmidt, S., et al.: Dataflow challenges in an internet of production: a security & privacy perspective. In: Proceedings of the ACM Workshop on Cyber-Physical Systems Security & Privacy, pp. 27–38. ACM (2019)

28. Plebani, P., Salnitri, M., Vitali, M.: Fog computing and data as a service: a goal-based modeling approach to enable effective data movement. In: Krogstie, J., Reijers, H. (eds.) CAiSE 2018. LNCS, vol. 10816, pp. 203–219. Springer, Cham (2018). https://doi.org/10.1007/978-3-319-91563-0_13

29. Stary, C.: Digital twin generation: re-conceptualizing agent systems for behavior-centered cyber-physical system development. Sensors **21**(1096), 1–24 (2021)

30. Tacke Genannt Unterberg, L., Koren, I., van der Aalst, W.M.: Maximizing reuse and interoperability in industry 4.0 with a minimal data exchange format for machine data. In: Modellierung 2024, pp. 103–118. Gesellschaft für Informatik e.V., Bonn (2024)

31. Vila, M., Sancho, M.R., Teniente, E.: Modeling context-aware events and responses in an IoT environment. In: Indulska, M., Reinhartz-Berger, I., Cetina, C., Pastor, O. (eds.) CAiSE 2023. LNCS, vol. 13901, pp. 71–87. Springer, Cham (2023). https://doi.org/10.1007/978-3-031-34560-9_5

32. Volz, F., Sutschet, G., Stojanovic, L., Uslaender, T.: On the role of digital twins in data spaces. Sensors **23**(7601), 1–21 (2023)

33. Ziegler, J., Reimann, P., Keller, F., Mitschang, B.: A metadata model to connect isolated data silos and activities of the CAE domain. In: La Rosa, M., Sadiq, S., Teniente, E. (eds.) CAiSE 2021. LNCS, vol. 12751, pp. 213–228. Springer, Cham (2021). https://doi.org/10.1007/978-3-030-79382-1_13

A Multi-dimensional Model for the Design and Development of Analytical Information Systems

Maribel Yasmina Santos[1(✉)] and Ana León[1,2]

[1] ALGORITMI Research Centre, University of Minho, Campus de Azurém,
4800-058 Guimarães, Portugal
maribel@dsi.uminho.pt, aleon@vrain.upv.es
[2] Valencian Research Insitute on Artificial Intelligence (VRAIN),
Universitat Politènica de València, Valencia, Spain

Abstract. The design and development of Analytical Information Systems demand efficient techniques and technologies for processing vast amounts of data that arrive at high velocity or that are available in legacy/operational systems. While many advances have been verified in the technological field to deal with the potential volume, velocity, and variety of the data, fewer contributions can be found in the methodological domain. These conceptual and methodological perspectives are key to providing the foundations for designing and developing Analytical Information Systems that also guarantee the veracity and value of the data. Considering three levels of detail, this paper proposes a multi-dimensional model that abstracts the dimensions to be considered, the driving components of the dimensions, and the core concepts of the components with the supporting approaches, techniques, or technologies for designing and developing Analytical Information Systems. We exemplify the proposed model with an instantiation that highlights the decisions or actions to be taken toward the design and development of more effective and efficient systems supporting decision-making in organizations.

Keywords: Big Data Analytics · Data Analytics · Analytical Information Systems · Conceptual Modeling

1 Introduction

As a resource widely available in organizations and society, data play an important role in Analytical Information Systems (AIS) to support decision-making processes. While many advances have been verified in the technological field to deal with volume, variety, and velocity [3,9,18,26], fewer contributions can be found in the conceptual domain to address veracity and value. This motivates the adoption of a design science approach for advancing human and organizational capabilities by proposing an artifact, a model, for the design and development of

H. van der Aa et al. (Eds.): BPMDS 2024/EMMSAD 2024, LNBIP 511, pp. 291–306, 2024.
https://doi.org/10.1007/978-3-031-61007-3_22

AIS. The research process is grounded in the Design Science Research Methodology for Information Systems [24], and has a problem-centred research entry point after reviewing the literature and identifying the lack of a model that supports students and practitioners in the design and development process. The definition of objectives for the solution guided the model's proposal, and an instantiation supported the demonstration phase highlighting the usefulness and effectiveness of the model in a specific problem, the TPC-H dataset [29].

The research objectives include *the identification of the driving dimensions, components and related core concepts to be considered in the design and development of AIS* and *the specification of the relationships between those components and concepts to support a seamless design and development process*. The model aims to aid students and practitioners in the Business Intelligence and Analytics domain by providing a comprehensive view of the actions and decisions involved in the design and development process. Students and practitioners often rely on reference architectures like the National Institute of Standards and Technology (NIST) Big Data Framework [22], as this architecture focuses the technological perspective by handling data at different maturity stages, by setting the data storage needs, and by providing the means for processing and making available data [22]. However, this technological perspective needs to be complemented with the domain and data perspectives including the actors and resources essential for interacting with or executing specific tasks involving data [1]. With this view, value is systematically delivered by supporting the data life cycle aligned with processes, products, techniques, roles, and tools [21], and veracity is ensured in the outcomes by aligning processes with domain knowledge.

The proposed model formalizes dimensions, components, and concepts, facilitating a holistic understanding of the design and development process, and is rooted in three core pillars of data analytics — domain concepts, domain requirements, and domain data — taking a Business Analytics perspective when considering business processes and their indicators to assess business performance. It also considers that an AIS: i) must be grounded in domain knowledge that guides all the design and development process; ii) handles data that are provided or consumed by users or other systems; iii) considers the domain's analytical requirements for providing valuable insights for decision-making; iv) integrates and stores data for analytical purposes; and, v) has processing capabilities throughout the data life cycle. These perspectives point to the five dimensions needed to have a comprehensive design and development model: the Domain Knowledge, the Data Provider and Consumer, the Analytical Requirements, the Data Architecture, and the Data Processing and Analytics.

The Domain Knowledge dimension formalizes the knowledge in terms of the data model (domain semantics) and the rules to map, transform, and verify the quality of the data to be loaded into an AIS. The Data Provider and Consumer dimension is concerned with data collection and the data life cycle needed to make available data at different maturity stages. The Analytical Requirements dimension supports the decision-making process, which must be aligned with the organizational business processes and their activities. The Data Architecture dimension formalizes the logical and physical layers that support an AIS, considering existing data architectures and their different physical implementations. Lastly, the Data Processing and Analytics dimension highlights the data pipelines needed to physically collect, prepare, enrich, access, analyze, and visualize the data.

This paper is organized as follows. Section 2 presents the related work. Section 3 formalizes the proposed model with its five dimensions and associated components, concepts, and interactions expressed as relationships between components and/or concepts. Section 4 instantiates the proposed model. Section 5 concludes with some remarks and guidelines for future work.

2 Related Work

An Information System (IS) is defined in [1] as *a work system whose processes and activities are devoted to processing information, that is, capturing, transmitting, storing, retrieving, manipulating, and displaying information.* AIS are fundamental in organizations to address veracity and value when systematically supporting the data life cycle [21]. Although some relevant related works can be found in the literature, next presented, they do not consider all the dimensions here proposed and do not provide a seamless abstraction that guides the design and development process.

[15] proposes a Model Driven Architecture (MDA) to select the most adequate visualizations for Big Data Analytics according to the user's goals. It combines a requirements model that represents the information goals, a data representation model that abstracts the required information, and a visualization model for representing visualization details. [12] adopts an MDA for streamlining analysis processes, from data preparation to data visualization. This work considers the need to specify i) the user's objectives and the dataset to be visualized, ii) the transformation of this information into a platform-independent visualization type, and iii) the implementation of the suggested visualization, extending the work of [16] that highlighted how analysts can use computation-independent models to define preparation, processing, analysis, and visualization tasks that are associated with a set of platform-independent and platform-specific models of a Big Data platform. A model-driven approach is also proposed in [2], with a methodology for implementing Big Data Analytics-as-a-Service. For this, the approach considers the use of a computation-independent model (declarative model), a platform-independent model (procedural model), and a platform-dependent model (deployment model). MDA has been used for data systems design in terms of data storage, identifying the data schemas to be implemented, and supporting the required extraction, transformation, and loading processes [8]. In multi-model database management systems, [4] addressed open challenges in the logical design of multi-model data warehouses, integrating concerns with querying, storage, and the extraction, transformation, and loading processes. In the field of structured approaches for data modeling, given their relevance to AIS, Data Vault focuses on building business-centred models, aligning the needs

and objectives of the business, and enhancing decision-making processes [10]. For data-driven analytics with Data Mining or other Machine Learning techniques or approaches, the Cross-Industry Standard Process for Data Mining (CRISP-DM) supports these projects with several phases and iterations that guide core activities for business understanding, data understanding, data preparation, modeling, evaluation, and deployment [27].

Due to the complexity of developing and maintaining stable and scalable Big Data applications, [7] analyzed how software engineering concepts associated with the software development project life cycle can support the development of better Big Data application projects. This study also points to the need to address methods, practices, and the development of novel methodologies for *validation/verification and quality assurance*, as there is not a standard life cycle model for the development of Big Data projects [17].

3   Model for the Design and Development of AIS

The proposed multi-dimensional model for the design and development of AIS is a three-level model (Dimensions, Components, Concepts) aimed at supporting the design and development process, guiding students and practitioners and helping them consider the several decisions required during the design and development process. The model is abstracted and represented using an approximation of the Unified Modelling Language (UML) Class Diagram notation. The representation of the classes has been simplified using a square to represent the main concepts and no attributes have been specified to improve the readability of the model. Connections to other models, detailing the dimensions, are represented as squares with a grey background. For the data models presented in Sect. 4, attributes are added to the classes along with attribute properties such as the type of attribute or key.

The proposed dimensions converge to the main component to be considered in an AIS, which is Data. Data assume different roles in the data life cycle. As shown in Fig. 1, the Domain Knowledge dimension includes the Domain Data Model that abstracts the available data (raw data at a high level of detail) and the several domain rules - mapping, transformation, and quality - needed to address veracity in the analytical process and to add value to data. The Data Provider and Consumer dimension addresses the data that can be made available for, or be used in, the decision-making process. The Data Architecture dimension is concerned with storing the data in a physical system that complies with a logical layer of a specific data architecture. This logical layer must consider the Analytical Data Model that addresses the Analytical Requirements identified for the organizational Business Processes. The Data Processing and Analytics dimension handles all the physical data pipelines needed to collect, select, prepare, enrich, access, analyze, and visualize the data. The five dimensions combine the models, goals, and data that ensure that the semantics of the domain drive the analytical tasks needed to support the decision-making process.

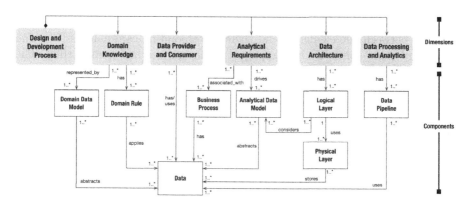

Fig. 1. Dimensions and Components for the Design and Development of AIS.

The components and corresponding concepts emerged from the analysis of the literature, from the identification of the students'/practitioners' main difficulties when facing the design and development of this type of system, from our teaching experience in Business Intelligence and Analytics courses, and from our participation in several research and development projects with academia and industry in this field. In general, when designing and developing an AIS major difficulties are faced in modeling data and requirements, and in having a clear overview of the global design and development process. As mentioned in the introduction, the proposed dimensions emerged to join three foundational pillars of data analytics: domain concepts, domain requirements, and domain data. From understanding domain concepts to achieving domain goals, the model addresses how to manage data and align concepts, requirements, and data effectively. The model highlights in the dimensions *why the design and development process should be done in this way*, the components summarize *how each dimension needs to be addressed*, and the last level considers *what to do*, highlighting concepts (theoretical concepts or techniques/technologies) that detail the design and development process. For using the model, there is a need to consider each dimension starting with the proposed order and instantiate the components and concepts. This order is a design and development road map with several iterations in each dimension and between dimensions, as these are related to each other, as shown in Fig. 1.

3.1 Domain Knowledge Dimension

The Domain Knowledge provides specific and specialized knowledge about the domain and the rules that need to be considered for handling the data and its quality (Fig. 2). The domain knowledge must be able to represent the knowledge needed to understand the domain and its possible analytical requirements and also be able to add and modify the already described knowledge to allow the system to evolve. To such an aim, the use of domain ontologies is encouraged. A Domain Ontology semantically defines the main elements (entities) of

the domain, their corresponding attributes, data types and data values, the relationships between the elements, and their corresponding cardinalities [13]. The
domain rules can specialize in mapping, transformation, and quality rules. The
mapping rules allow the model to model transformations by establishing the cor-
respondences between the entities of a source model and the entities of a target
model. These entities are transformed using the transformation rules to comply
with a specific format when needed. The mapping and the transformation rules
can be used to select the relevant data from the raw data providers and transform them (e.g., normalize, merge, or remove duplicates) to obtain an enriched
and prepared data set to be analyzed. The quality rules contribute to validating
the relevant data associated with the selected and transformed attributes and
play an essential role in verifying data veracity and increasing data value. As
the data go through several maturity stages (see the Data Providers and Consumers dimension), different mapping, transformation, and quality rules can be
considered.

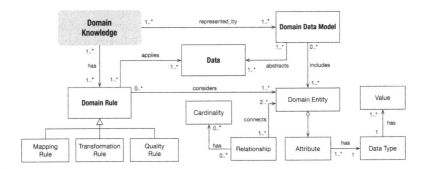

Fig. 2. Domain Knowledge Dimension.

3.2   Data Provider and Consumer Dimension

The Data Provider and Consumer dimension represents the raw data collection,
and the data life cycle or tasks (selection, treatment, preparation, and enrichment) needed to make available data for analytical purposes (Fig. 3). These tasks
are considered crucial for any organization aiming to successfully create value
from analytical data-driven approaches [21]. Data are collected from the data
providers and are supposed to have the rawest state possible. The Raw Data are
the entry point to start the data selection, treatment, preparation, and enrichment process. The Selected Data represents the identification of the relevant
data that will be analyzed and considers the need not to process and analyze
all the available raw data, but only the data that is valuable to achieve the
analytical requirements. The relevant data is selected using the mapping rules
defined in the Domain Knowledge dimension. The selected data are prepared to
move the data one step further toward analytics. To this end, the preparation
and enrichment of the data are guided by the transformation and quality rules,
also defined in the Domain Knowledge dimension. The Prepared and Enriched

Data are processed with the corresponding Data Pipelines (of the Data Processing and Analytics dimension) considering the analytical requirements (in the Analytical Requirements dimension) that drive the data analytics processes. The Raw Data, Selected Data, and Prepared and Enriched Data are physically stored in files or other physical structures defined by the logical and physical layers represented by the Data Architecture dimension. Considering the variety of possible data sources, data providers and consumers may make available or use structured, semi-structured, or unstructured data. In the case of semi-structured and unstructured data, data from documents, social media, weblogs/server logs, sensors, or models are examples of possible sources.

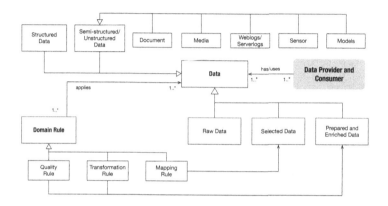

Fig. 3. Data Provider and Consumer Dimension.

3.3 Analytical Requirements Dimension

This dimension (Fig. 4) addresses the components and concepts required to specify the analytical requirements, complementing the Domain Knowledge dimension. The analytical requirements met by an AIS must be aligned with the business processes and activities in which the users are enrolled and for which information or indicators are needed to support their role in the decision-making process. When analyzing the data generated in a business process, there is the need to identify the attributes that represent analytical measures (analytical attributes) for analysis and the ones associated with the analytical dimensions (key-value/descriptive attributes) used to give context to the analytical measures (mainly addressing the context for the analysis of those measures, such as *who, when, where, what*, providing a way of interpreting analytical measures with different perspectives using, for instance, aggregation or filtering operations [26]). This information is crucial for devising the Analytical Data Model that will guide data processing and analytics. For identifying the Analytical Data Model, three approaches can be usually followed. A data-driven approach, in which the available operational data guide the design and development process; a user-driven approach, in which the user (or a set of users) specify the requirements of the analytical system detailing the analytical queries to be answered; or, a goal-driven approach in which strategic requirements are defined for guiding the analysis process. The data-driven is a bottom-up iterative approach, in which the operational data sources are analyzed and used to derive the Analytical Data Model. The user-driven is also a bottom-up approach for requirements elicitation based on several sessions or interviews with the users. The goal-driven approach focuses on the business strategy, also using several sessions or interviews with top managers to identify organizational goals that can be translated into quantifiable Key Performance Indicators (KPIs) [11]. These several approaches can be combined to integrate the different perspectives in an analytical system [30].

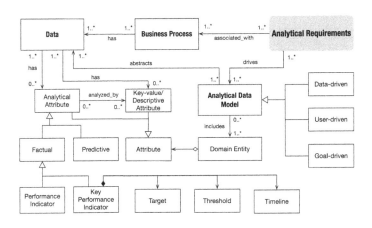

Fig. 4. Analytical Requirements Dimension.

Analytical attributes can be specialized in factual or predictive measures. While factual analytical measures represent evidence of something that happened, predictive measures represent an estimate of what happened or a prediction of something that can occur in the near future. The analysis of factual historical data can be enhanced with predictive data obtained through the use of Machine Learning, Data Mining, or other Data Science approaches [26]. Factual measures can represent indicators of the domain, addressing business processes and their performance, or can address KPIs used to monitor business processes' goals. In this last case, the specification of the analytical requirements must include the Target (goal to be achieved), the Threshold (to classify the value as achieving or not the defined goal), and the Timeline (time to achieve the goal) of KPIs. The current value of a KPI is compared with the target, considering the threshold and the timeline, to continuously monitor a business process [20].

3.4   Data Architecture Dimension

The Data Architecture dimension (Fig. 5) highlights the need to identify both the Logical Layer to be adopted and the Physical Layer that will support the

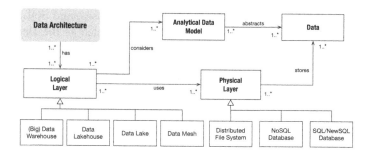

Fig. 5. Data Architecture Dimension.

analytical system. Common data architectures include in their Logical Layer systems such as Data Warehouses [14], Big Data Warehouses [26], Data Lakes [19], Data Lakehouses [3], and Data Mesh [6]. These two last ones represent emerging concepts with ongoing formalization in terms of concepts and methodological approaches for their implementation.

A Data Warehouse is a key organizational asset used for many years now to integrate data from different sources and make available data access, analysis, and presentation, supporting the decision-making process. It handles structured data and is also characterized for handling non-volatile historical data organized by subject (main business processes of the organization) [14]. With increasing volume, variety, and velocity, Big Data Warehouses can be defined as scalable, high-performance, and highly flexible processing systems able to handle ever-increasing volumes of data, accompanied by significant variety and speed [5]. While the data stored in a (Big) Data Warehouse are already cleaned and prepared fitting data quality requirements and user needs for decision support, the architectural paradigm of a Data Lake [28] is based on massive storage of raw data, where the data are stored in their original format and remain in this format until they need to be processed. These are devised for massive amounts of continuously stored data. More recently, the concept of Data Lakehouse [3] emerged as an evolution of the Data Lake architecture, adding principles such as Atomicity, Consistency, Reliability, and Durability (ACID), thus combining the advantages of both the Data Warehouse and the Data Lake. To extend the previously presented data architectures, the Data Mesh concept emerged as a disruptive and innovative concept with the main aim of making organizations truly data-oriented. This data architecture is distributed, requiring governance and standardization as these allow for interoperability among the Mesh nodes [6]. This set of data architectures for the logical layer does not intend to be an exhaustive and complete list. Its objective is to give examples of possible approaches, summarizing and conceptualizing them.

To physically tackle the logical layer, different implementation approaches can be followed. Considering the umbrella data organization strategy that a Data Mesh can give to the logical layer, including data products that can be distributed and decentralized into different data systems, the physical layer can include Distributed File Systems (DFS), NoSQL Databases, and SQL/NewSQL Databases. Overall, different systems can be adopted, such as the Hadoop Distributed File System (HDFS), key-value stores, document stores, column-based stores or graph stores for NoSQL databases, or different relational or relational-oriented databases. The proposed dimension does not further detail them as the choices to be made are highly influenced by the organizational context, available technologies and supporting environment (e.g., on-premises, cloud). This physical layer stores the domain's structured, semi-structured, and/or unstructured data. Data can be stored in a file system or in an indexed storage system for batch or streaming data processing [22], depending on their origin (Data Provider) and their use/destination (Data Consumer).

3.5 Data Processing and Analytics Dimension

The Data Processing and Analytics dimension (Fig. 6) includes the data flows and scripts (Data Pipeline) needed to address three fundamental tasks in an AIS: i) Data Collection, from the data providers; ii) Data Selection, Preparation and Enrichment, to provide analytical value and feed the Physical Layer of the system; and iii) Data Access, Analytics, and Visualization for processing the available data providing valuable insights to the data consumers.

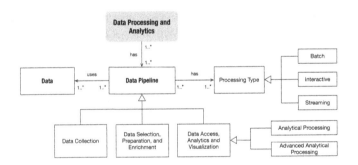

Fig. 6. Data Processing and Analytics Dimension.

For Data Access, Analytics, and Visualization we highlight traditional Analytical Processing with *ad hoc* querying, online analytical processing (OLAP), or exploratory data visualization. Advanced Analytical Processing, with Machine Learning, Data Mining, or other Data Science techniques and technologies, can be used to analyze the data and extract valuable insights. As mentioned in the Analytical Requirements dimension, factual and predictive data can be combined to join the evidence of what happened with predictions of what can happen in the near future. The data pipelines need to consider different types of processing needs as the volume, the variety, or the velocity of data may demand Batch, Interactive, or Streaming processing capabilities. Batch processing usually includes the analysis of vast amounts of historical data, processing complex *ad hoc* queries, or processing intensive Machine Learning or Data Mining algorithms. Interactive processing is useful for exploratory data analytics that may be supported by execution times ranging from milliseconds to a few tens of seconds [26]. Streaming processing is associated with high-velocity systems with data in motion, processed and analyzed in real-time or near real-time [22].

4 Demonstration Case: The TPC-H Data Set

The demonstration case with the instantiation is based on TPC-H [29], a decision support benchmark that includes a set of business-oriented *ad-hoc* queries. The data model includes eight operational tables dealing with sales, customers, and suppliers, modeling a business that manages, sells, and distributes products. This example was chosen for the demonstration case as its operational data model (Domain Data Model) [29] and a possible Logical Layer of a Data Warehouse system (addressing a specific Analytical Data Model) are documented in the literature allowing replicability and the validation of results [23,25].

As we are working on a synthetic example with synthetic data, the analytical requirements that guide the definition of the Analytical Data Model can be identified using a data-driven approach or following a user-driven approach that considers the queries of the benchmark as the analytical queries to be answered by the system. To allow comparison with documented analytical models such as the Star Schema Benchmark (SSB) [23] or a Constellation Schema [25], we follow a data-driven approach that provides a comprehensive set of analyses that are possible based on the available data. Following the components of the Analytical Requirements dimension, the available data from the TPC-H data set is associated with the Orders business process, keeping in mind that an order can include one or more ordered items. This means that for implementing a Data Warehouse system, with a logical layer based on a star schema, only one fact table can be considered, handling all-together the orders and the ordered items. The level of detail, of this domain entity, must be at the item level [23]. A different analytical model could consider a constellation schema with three fact tables, as documented in [25], assuming that the PARTSUPP entity (Fig. 7) supports a fact table that depicts, to our understanding, part of the Inventory business process. As this business process is not fully represented in the Domain Data Model and corresponding data set, the instantiation here documented considers two domain entities with analytical value, ORDER and LINEITEM, one for analyzing the orders and the other for detailing the ordered items.

Taking the Orders business process and its corresponding data, Fig. 7 depicts a possible scenario for the Analytical Data Model, highlighting the analytical attributes, the descriptive or key-value attributes, and the remaining attributes present in the Domain Data Model. For identifying the analytical/descriptive/key-value attributes there is the need to understand the application domain, and the data (meaning and level of detail of each attribute), and foresee their value for the decision-making process or for the data architecture that is going to be selected for implementation. For instance, in the case of key-value attributes such as customer key, order key, part key, or supplier key, these are considered useful natural keys that can be used in filtering or aggregation operations or can support type 2 slowly changing dimensions in Data Warehouse systems [14].

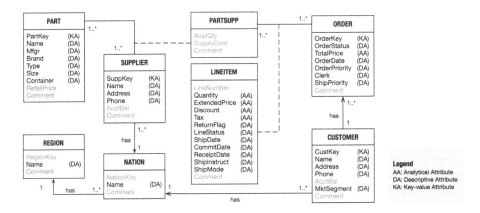

Fig. 7. Possible Analytical Data Model (in context of the Domain Data Model).

With the key elements of the Analytical Data Model is possible to model a constellation schema as the Logical Layer of our Data Architecture that uses a Data Warehouse physically implemented in a SQL Database. Figure 8 depicts a possible constellation schema with two fact tables and ten dimension tables that give context to the indicators to be analyzed. Besides the dimensions directly derived from entities available in the Analytical Data Model, such as Part, Supplier, and Customer, the modeling process allowed the integration of the Date dimension, needed in a Data Warehouse system for keeping track of the historical data, and other conformed dimensions [14], such as Priority, Clerk, Mode, Return Info, Status and Instruct, which can be used by other fact tables in a future evolution of the data model here proposed. These dimensions could be avoided by creating two specific dimension tables for storing the details about the orders (status, ship priority, order priority, clerk) and the details about the ordered items (return info, line order status, ship instruct, ship mode). However, with time, these dimension tables will contain a high number of records impacting the performance of the system when processing the data.

With the Analytical Data Model and the Constellation Schema, it is possible to go back to the Domain Knowledge dimension and define the mapping, transformation, and quality rules. The mapping rules guide the selection of the data. The transformation rules define if the selected data must be modified to comply with the final format required by the system (e.g., format dates, add prefixes, remove special characters, or join different attributes into one). In this demonstration case, several transformations are needed to derive the calculated attributes or to transform data types between the source and the target data

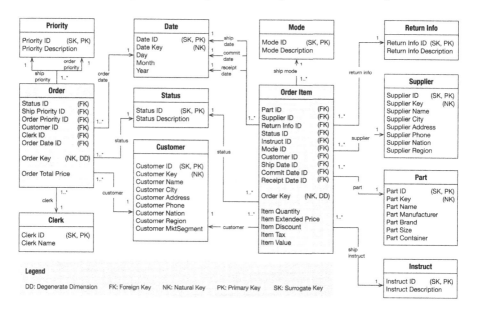

Fig. 8. Possible Constellation Schema for the Data Warehouse.

system. Regarding the quality rules, these contribute to validating the relevant data associated with the selected and transformed attributes and play an essential role in verifying data veracity and increasing data value. For example, the quality rules could define the minimum quality criteria the extracted data must comply with to be included for further analysis (e.g., remove rows with empty values or duplicates). An example of a transformation rule could be deriving the price of an item considering the discount. In this case, the *Extended Price* and the *Discount* attributes of the LINEITEM class (Fig. 7) are used to calculate the *Item Value* attribute by applying the formula: [Item Value] = [Extended Price] * [Discount] (Fig. 8).

For the Data Processing and Analytics dimension, several data pipelines need to be considered for data collection from the data sources, for the selection, preparation, and enrichment of the data, and for data access, analytics, and visualization. In this demonstration case, batch pipelines can handle the historical data that needs to be collected, stored, and analyzed. These pipelines can be developed using different languages or technologies. For analytics, the data available in the Data Warehouse can be analyzed with OLAP tools making available interactive analytical dashboards that provide drill-down, roll-up, slice and dice, and other data operations.

After instantiating the five dimensions, Fig. 9 highlights the components and concepts used in this demonstration case. This overall overview helps in cross-checking the decisions made along the process and helps to see how the proposed dimensions complement each other in the design and development of AIS.

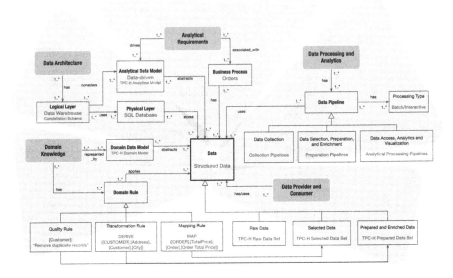

Fig. 9. Instantiation of the TPC-H Demonstration Case.

5   Conclusions

This paper presents a multi-dimensional model for the design and development of Analytical Information Systems (AIS) and is intended to support students and practitioners from information systems and related areas to have a shared understanding of the key dimensions, components, and concepts that need to be considered and addressed in the design and development of AIS. The proposed model integrates five dimensions (Domain Knowledge, Data Provider and Consumer, Analytical Requirements, Data Architecture, Data Processing and Analytics) targeting AIS that handle not only data volume, variety, and velocity, but, also, veracity and value. The Domain Knowledge and Analytical Requirements dimensions provide the concepts and the perspective of the goals, extending more technical and technological perspectives usually followed when implementing these systems. The Data Provider and Consumer, Data Architecture, and Data Processing and Analytics dimensions use this domain knowledge and goals to select, prepare, enrich, and process data.

This proposal leads us to a model where Data is always put into the context of the domain concepts, as the Domain Knowledge and Analytical Requirements provide the knowledge about the concepts of the application domain and the analytical requirements, information used in all the other views to handle the domain data with this knowledge in mind. This is of utmost relevance to effectively extract value from data. In future work, the proposed model will be evaluated with a class of master's students and the results will be used to fine-tune the proposal and report the main findings. Also, the model will be used in complex industrial projects to ease the design and development process. These results will also be analyzed for improving the model and reporting the main findings. Leveraging the insights gathered, the proposed model will be supplemented by a set of guidelines and supportive practices for AIS implementation.

Acknowledgments. This work has been supported by *FCT - Fundação para a Ciência e Tecnologia* within the R&D Units Project Scope: UIDB/00319/2020, and by the Spanish Ministry of Universities and the Universitat Politècnica de València under the Margarita Salas Next Generation EU grant.

References

1. Alter, S.: Defining information systems as work systems: implications for the IS field. Eur. J. Inf. Syst. **17**(5), 448–469 (2008)
2. Ardagna, C.A., Bellandi, V., Ceravolo, P., Damiani, E., Bezzi, M., Hebert, C.: A model-driven methodology for big data analytics-as-a-service. In: 2017 IEEE International Congress on Big Data (BigData Congress), pp. 105–112. IEEE, Honolulu, HI, USA (2017)
3. Armbrust, M., Ghodsi, A., Xin, R., Zaharia, M.: Lakehouse: a new generation of open platforms that unify data warehousing and advanced analytics. In: 11th Annual Conference on Innovative Data Systems Research (CIDR 2021), pp. 1–8. www.cidrdb.org, virtual (2021)
4. Bimonte, S., Gallinucci, E., Marcel, P., Rizzi, S.: Logical design of multi-model data warehouses. Knowl. Inf. Syst. **65**(3), 1067–1103 (2023)
5. Costa, C., Andrade, C., Santos, M.Y.: Big data warehouses for smart industries. In: Sakr, S., Zomaya, A. (eds.) Encyclopedia of Big Data Technologies, pp. 1–11. Springer International Publishing, Cham (2018). https://doi.org/10.1007/978-3-319-63962-8_204-1
6. Dehghani, Z.: Data Mesh: Delivering Data-Driven Value at Scale. O'Reilly, Sebastopol (2022)
7. Dipti Kumar, V., Alencar, P.: Software engineering for big data projects: domains, methodologies and gaps. In: 2016 IEEE International Conference on Big Data (Big Data), pp. 2886–2895. IEEE (2016)
8. El Beggar, O., Letrache, K., Ramdani, M.: DAREF: MDA framework for modelling data warehouse requirements and deducing the multidimensional schema. Requirements Eng. **26**(2), 143–165 (2021)
9. Gandomi, A., Haider, M.: Beyond the hype: Big data concepts, methods, and analytics. Int. J. Inf. Manage. **35**(2), 137–144 (2015)
10. Giles, J.: The Elephant in the Fridge: Guided Steps to Data Vault Success through Building Business-Centered Models (First Edition). Technics Publication (2019)
11. Golfarelli, M.: From user requirements to conceptual design in data warehouse design - a survey. In: Bellatreche, L. (ed.) Data Warehousing Design and Advanced Engineering Applications: Methods for Complex Construction, pp. 1-16. IGI Global (2009)
12. Golfarelli, M., Rizzi, S.: A model-driven approach to automate data visualization in big data analytics. Inf. Vis. **19**(1), 24–47 (2020)
13. Kaiya, H., Saeki, M.: Using domain ontology as domain knowledge for requirements elicitation. In: 14th IEEE International Requirements Engineering Conference (RE 2006), pp. 189–198 (2006)

14. Kimball, R., Ross, M.: The Data Warehouse Toolkit: The definitive Guide to Dimensional Modeling. Wiley, Hoboken, 3rd. edition edn. (2013)
15. Lavalle, A., Maté, A., Trujillo, J.: Requirements-driven visualizations for big data analytics: a model-driven approach. In: Laender, A.H.F., Pernici, B., Lim, E.-P., de Oliveira, J.P.M. (eds.) ER 2019. LNCS, vol. 11788, pp. 78–92. Springer, Cham (2019). https://doi.org/10.1007/978-3-030-33223-5_8
16. Leida, M., Ruiz, C., Ceravolo, P.: Facing big data variety in a model driven approach. In: 2016 IEEE 2nd International Forum on Research and Technologies for Society and Industry Leveraging a better tomorrow (RTSI), pp. 1–6. IEEE (2016)
17. Lin, Y.T., Huang, S.J.: The design of a software engineering lifecycle process for big data projects. IT Prof. **20**(1), 45–52 (2018)
18. Machado, I.A., Costa, C., Santos, M.Y.: Data-driven information systems: the data mesh paradigm shift. In: 29th. International Conference of Information System Development (ISD 2021) (2021)
19. Madera, C., Laurent, A.: The next information architecture evolution: The data lake wave. In: 8th. International Conference on Management of Digital Ecosystems (MEDES 2016), pp. 174–180 (2016)
20. Maté, A., Trujillo, J., Mylopoulos, J.: Specification and derivation of key performance indicators for business analytics: a semantic approach. Data Knowl. Eng. **108**, 30–49 (2017)
21. Michalczyk, S., Scheu, S.: Designing an analytical information system engineering method. In: Proceedings of the Twenty-Eighth European Conference on Information Systems (ECIS2020). Association for Information Systems (2020)
22. National Institute of Standards and Technology: National Institute of Standards and Technology Big Data Interoperability Framework (2015)
23. O'Neil, P., O'Neil, B., Chen, X.: The star schema benchmark (SSB) (2009). https://www.cs.umb.edu/~poneil/StarSchemaB.PDF
24. Peffers, K., Tuunanen, T., Rothenberger, M.A., Chatterjee, S.: A design science research methodology for information systems research. J. Manag. Inf. Syst. **24**(3), 45–77 (2007)
25. Romero, O., Abelló, A.: Automatic validation of requirements to support multidimensional design. Data Knowl. Eng. **69**(9), 917–942 (2010)
26. Santos, M.Y., Costa, C.: Big Data: Concepts. River Publishers, Warehousing and Analytics (2020)
27. Shearer, C.: The CRISP-DM model: the new blueprint for data mining. J. Data Warehous. **5**(4), 13–22 (2000)
28. Terrizzano, I., Schwarz, P., Roth, M., Colino, J.E.: Data wrangling: the challenging journey from the wild to the lake. In: 7th. Biennial Conference on Innovative Data Systems Research (CIDR 2015) (2015)
29. Transaction Processing Performance Council: TPC-H Specification (Decision Support) Standard Specification, Revision 2.17.2 (2017). http://www.tpc.org/tpc_documents_current_versions/pdf/tpc-h_v2.17.2.pdf
30. Vieira, A.A.C., Pedro, L., Santos, M.Y., Fernandes, J.M., Dias, L.S.: Data requirements elicitation in big data warehousing. In: Themistocleous, M., Rupino da Cunha, P. (eds.) EMCIS 2018. LNBIP, vol. 341, pp. 106–113. Springer, Cham (2019). https://doi.org/10.1007/978-3-030-11395-7_10

Modeling and Sustainability (EMMSAD 2024)

Situational Environmental, Social and Governance Accounting: From Ethical Value Elicitation to Sustainability Reporting

Vijanti Ramautar[1]([✉]), Sjaak Brinkkemper[1], Óscar Pastor[2], and Sergio España[1,2]

[1] Utrecht University, Princetonplein 5, Utrecht 3584 CC, The Netherlands
v.d.ramautar@uu.nl
[2] Universitat Politècnica de València, Camí de Vera, Algirós, Valencia 46022, Spain

Abstract. **[Background]** Globally, mandates like the EU Corporate Sustainability Reporting Directive are shaping environmental, social, and governance accounting (ESGA) trends, which is crucial for enhancing organisational sustainability. Our domain-specific, model-driven technology allows creating adaptive tool support for ESGA, requiring a situational ESGA model as input. However, our experience has shown that organisations are rarely capable of expressing the method they need, so modelling the ESGA method is far from the starting point. **[Aim]** The objective of this work is to develop methodological support, given that it concerns a non-traditional requirements engineering process. Therefore, we will engineer a situational meta-method that allows configuring a domain-specific, model-driven technology. **[Method]** To develop this situational meta-method we apply a multi-case study approach and validate the meta-method by means of expert interviews. The situationality in the meta-method is an approach to cope with (a) the variety of situational factors involved in ESGA, and (b) the evolution expected in this domain in the coming years. **[Result]** The situational meta-method, called ESG4Orgs, has allowed us to create six ESGA methods that each align with the sustainability strategy of the case study organisations. Overall, the ESGA experts concur that ESG4Orgs is deemed understandable and useful. Our work is pertinent to policymakers shaping sustainability reporting legislation, managers seeking to enhance organisational impact, and scientists developing support for sustainability reporting.

Keywords: Situational method engineering · environmental social and governance accounting · model-driven engineering · sustainability reporting · meta-method

S. España—Is supported by a María Zambrano grant of the Spanish Ministry of Universities, co-funded by the Next Generation EU European Recovery Plan.

H. van der Aa et al. (Eds.): BPMDS 2024/EMMSAD 2024, LNBIP 511, pp. 309–324, 2024.
https://doi.org/10.1007/978-3-031-61007-3_23

1   Introduction

On 5 January 2023, the new Corporate Sustainability Reporting Directive (CSRD) came into effect within the EU [1]. The new directive defines stricter rules concerning the environmental, social and governance (ESG) information that companies must report on. Compared to preceding policies, the CSRD has broadened the set of organisations that are required to report on their ESG performance. Moreover, the CSRD is just one of many international institutional initiatives for ESG reporting, which are being introduced gradually, each time with a stricter level of compliance. Needless to say, the role of ESG accounting (i.e. assessing, reporting, and auditing sustainability performance) will only become more prevalent in the next decades. The need for ESG reporting standards has been highly debated. However, in the literature, there is consensus on the fact that there should be a level of diversity in ESG reporting [2]. Rather than prescribing organisations to report on a specific set of topics and indicators, there should be standardisation in the underlying processes for collecting, calculating, and validating data [3]. Currently, there is no comprehensive approach that allows organisations to create ESG accounting (ESGA) methods and develop versatile information systems (ISs) that support the ESGA method. As a result, organisations sometimes end up creating methods that do not align with their values and goals [4]. Secondly, when organisations create their own methods, a lack of flexible ISs poses a problem. Most ICT tools for ESGA can only support predefined ESGA methods. Large organisations with plenty of resources usually develop an in-house system. However, for small and medium enterprises that typically allocate fewer resources to ESG accounting, developing an in-house system is unfeasible. Therefore, we have previously developed the openESEA framework [5,6], a domain-specific, model-driven technology that allows developing ESGA ISs. Experts have deemed the technology valuable. However, when applying the technology in practice we noticed that companies have difficulties expressing the ESGA method they need. The role of the ESGA consultant using the openESEA framework cannot be reduced to modeller, since they need to also become method engineers (to be able to assist companies in defining the method), and requirements engineers (to be able to elicit the needs of the company and configure the openESEA technology appropriately). We found that methodological support is necessary. Therefore our main research goal is: **Engineering a situational meta-method that allows configuring a domain-specific, model-driven technology for ESGA information systems.** Application of the meta-method by organisations results in the process and information system necessary to measure ESG performance and impacts.

Our contributions include the situational meta-method, along with its situational factors, for constructing an ESGA method and its supporting IS. The situational meta-method is based on six case studies, performed with different types of organisations in two stages, and it was validated with expert interviews. We consider our work relevant to policymakers who formulate legislation regarding ESG reporting, managers who aim to improve ESG performance of their diverse organisations (e.g. company managers, department boards, conference organisers, research group leaders, etc.), and scientists who aim to develop methods or software support to improve the sustainability of organisations. Note, that we refrain from suggesting concrete ESG topics or indicators in this paper because ESGA is highly dependent on contextual factors (e.g. type of company, geographical location, industry sector). Instead, we provide organisations with a process that they can apply to define their own topics and indicators.

The outline of the paper is the following. Section 2 presents background information on ESG accounting and situational method engineering. The research questions and research method are explained in Sect. 3. We present our situational meta-method (called ESG4Orgs) in Sect. 4. The outcomes of the validation activities are described in Sect. 5. Finally, Sect. 6 presents the discussion and conclusion.

2 Background

2.1 ESG Accounting with Situational Method Engineering

Let us start by clarifying the terminology. An ESGA *method* consists of a process part and a deliverable part, which corresponds to the definition of a method in [7]. The method is typically described in a set of documents that define the method activities and content. In this work, a method *model* is a structured textual file that represents the deliverable part of the method. The model can serve as input to create an *information system* that operationalises the method.

As previously stated, ESGA practices should be more adaptable to different geographical circumstances, social contexts, and industry sectors [2,8]. Hence, it comes as no surprise that several methods for measuring ESG impacts have been developed, e.g. [9–11]. However, some methods positively influence the business' mission, practices, and capacities [8], while other methods do not fit the organisational situation, are rarely used and do not effectuate positive change [12]. This highlights the need for a meta-method that allows organisations to develop an ESGA method (i.e. the activities and content) that takes into account their values, relevant stakeholder groups, and desired impacts, as well as their situational factors.

A meta-model is a model of a model [13] and meta-modelling is "the act and science of creating meta-models, which are a qualified variant of models". In method engineering, the meta-model is a model of a software engineering method [14]. Thus, a meta-method refers to a method meant to create methods. Therefore, the meta-method presented herein is a method that allows engineering ESGA methods and ISs. To clarify the scope of this research, Fig. 1 depicts OMG's multi-level hierarchy [15] and exemplifies how it is operationalised in this research. The M3 level describes the meta-metamodel. In our case, the M3 level consists of the concept **class** (among others). The M2 level defines the metamodel of ESGA models. The metamodel contains instances of classes, such as the **topic** class, **indicator** class, and **survey** class. M1 specifies the ESGA model, i.e. what will be measured. It instantiates the classes on M2. For instance, "**gender** equity" and "environmental impact" are instances of the topic class. Instances of the indicator class are "number of women in management positions", "number of men in management positions", "recycled waste (in kg)", and "CO_2 emission". The M0 level contains the data (e.g. 32 women, 50 men, 1000kg of recycled waste, and 100 tonnes CO_2 equivalents). Our situational meta-method is on the M2 level and can be used to create ESGA methods (including the model) and supporting ISs on the M1 level. Moreover, the meta-method allows the creation of additional relevant elements, such as a sustainability strategy and ethical value hierarchy.

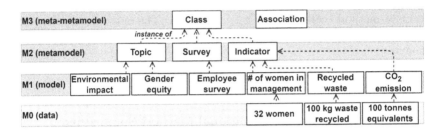

Fig. 1. The ESGA domain positioned on the OMG hierarchy

The literature describes several terms for method parts, e.g. fragments, chunks, parts, or services [16–18]. Our research intensively relies on Process Deliverable Diagrams [19] (as shown here [20]), so we adopt the corresponding terminology; namely, method fragments.

2.2 The OpenESEA Framework for Developing ESGA ISs

We have developed a domain-specific, model-driven technology for engineering ISs that support ESGA methods, called openESEA [5,6]. Figure 2 shows a high-level overview of how the openESEA technology works. OpenESEA consists of a domain-specific language (DSL) and an interpreter. The interpreter requires an ESGA model as input. The ESGA model is a structured representation of the deliverable part of the ESGA method (which defines what should be measured, and how). The ESGA model is created according to the rules in the DSL. The concrete syntax of the DSL is specified as an Xtext grammar [21]. The DSL is supported by an editor, which facilitates the creation of valid ESGA models. These models are uploaded to the interpreter and parsed. The interpreter creates an ESGA IS by displaying the content of the ESGA model and activating the appropriate features. The ESGA IS can then be used to collect, calculate, audit, and visualise ESG information. The meta-method presented in this paper aids organisations in developing an ESGA method that aligns with their sustainability strategy. The result of applying ESG4Orgs at the RCIS conference has resulted in assessing the ESG performance of the conference edition in 2022 [22]. The results of the other case studies can be found in a technical report [23].

3   Research Approach

To achieve our goal of engineering a situational meta-method that allows configuring a domain-specific, model-driven technology for environmental, social and
governance accounting information systems, we formulate the following research
questions.

- RQ1. Which activities should be taken into account when configuring a
  domain-specific, model-driven technology for ESGA information systems?
- RQ2. How should ESG4Orgs ensure that the resulting ESGA method and
  supporting IS align with the sustainability strategy of organisations?
- RQ3. What are the benefits and drawbacks of the situational meta-method
  in terms of usefulness and understandability?

The research method is depicted in Fig. 3. Our domain analysis consists of a
literature review [24] to better understand the domain of ESGA. Afterwards,
we **perform three case studies** where we develop ESGA models and supporting ISs for each organisation. In this work, we chose a diverse set of case study
participants to ensure that the meta-method is useful to a variety of organisations. In the first three case studies, the units of analysis are method engineering

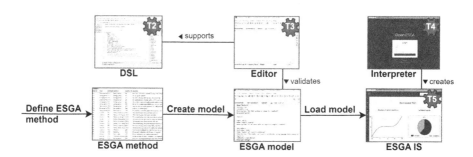

Fig. 2. The coarse-grained, high-level steps for using the openESEA framework. The
cogs identify tool fragments that are discussed later in this paper.

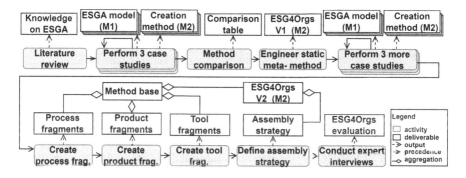

Fig. 3. An overview of the research method

projects in which a tailor-made ESGA method is being created for a university department (Information and Computing Sciences department of Utrecht University), a scientific conference (RCIS 2022) [22], and a network of socially-responsible enterprises in the ICT domain (Fairtrade Software Foundation). The case studies not only yield three ESGA models (models on the M1 level) along with their three supporting ISs, but also the three meta-methods (models on M2) that depict the process and data structures that have allowed us to engineer the ESGA model and ISs. To convert these three M2 models into one common approach for engineering ESGA methods, we conduct a **method comparison** [19]. Based on the comparison we **engineer a static meta-method** for configuring a domain-specific, model-driven technology for ESGA ISs (i.e. openESEA). By *static* we mean that the meta-method cannot be adapted to situational contexts. We call this meta-method ESG4Orgs. While creating the first version (V1) of ESG4Orgs we assumed that a static (i.e. non-situational) meta-method would suffice.

To validate V1 of ESG4Orgs, we **perform three more case studies**. The case study participants are a research group (PROS - Research Centre on Software Production Methods, at Universitat Politècnica de València), a foundation (Refugee Wellbeing & Integration Initiative), and a start-up (GenDelf, we will use this case as a running example). While validating the first version of ESG4Orgs, we soon discovered that a static meta-method would not be suitable for all organisations. Hence, we have opted for a situational meta-method. The case studies result in a set of requirements. An excerpt of the requirements can be found in Table 1.

Table 1. An excerpt of the requirements that were defined as a result of the case studies

ID	Requirement	Source
R1	The meta-method shall include process fragments that support the integral involvement of stakeholders	ICS dept
R2	The meta-method shall allow the development of custom-made ESGA methods to accomodate all types of organisations (e.g. conferences and research groups)	RCIS, PROS
R3	The meta-method shall include the creation of a production chain, in case the organisation does not have a clear vision on its stakeholders and value proposition	GenDelf
R4	The meta-method shall include fragments that enable the creation of a theory of change because this is useful for organisations with a social mission	RWII

The design of ESG4Orgs V2 has been informed by literature on situational method engineering e.g. [16–18,25,26]. Hence, we also adopt the terminology commonly used in situational method engineering. SME typically uses the

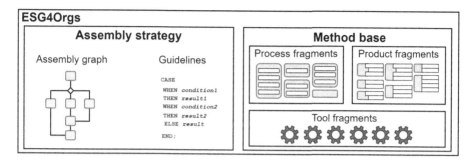

Fig. 4. The SME framework used in this research, based on [18,25,27,28]

notion of *method base*. The method base consists of *conceptual method fragments*. Method fragments are described as "a coherent piece of an IS development method" [7]. In this paper, we extend the definition of method fragment beyond the domain of IS development. We define a method fragment as a coherent piece of a domain-specific technology configuration method. Method fragments can either be *product fragments*, *process fragments*, or *tool fragments*. Method construction is typically guided by *assembly guidelines* (or rules) and *situational factors*. We first **create the process, product, and tool fragments** and then we **define the assembly strategy**, consisting of an assembly graph, which depicts all valid method outlines, and assembly guidelines. The method base and the assembly strategy comprise version V2 of ESG4Orgs. The structure of ESG4Orgs is depicted in Fig. 4.

To evaluate V2 of ESG4Orgs, we **conduct two expert interviews** with a policymaker working with the Dutch Ministry of Interior Affairs and a freelance sustainability advisor. The policymaker works on a project that helps social enterprises build their network. The sustainability advisor has over 15 years of experience with sustainability accounting. Using these preliminary expert interview results, we assess whether the meta-method is useful, applicable, and understandable.

4   A Meta-method for the Creation of Situational ESG Accounting Methods

The purpose of ESG4Orgs is to create an ESGA method and its supporting IS that fit well the needs of an organisation and its context. Such a method and IS need to be aligned with the sustainability strategy of an organisation. When the organisation applying ESG4Orgs has already defined their sustainability strategy, ESG4Orgs helps establish the traceability between ESGA method elements (e.g. topics and indicators) and elements of the strategy (e.g. goals and targets). When the strategy does not yet exist, the application of ESG4orgs helps create a blueprint for it.

ESG4Orgs V1 could not cater to organisational differences, such as maturity, size, or legal entity type. It also did not adapt well to the context of the meta-method application, such as participant background or time constraints. As a result, there were situations in which it could not be applied without major adaptation. Moreover, ESGA methods tend to evolve over time to address contemporary subjects. Therefore, we have transformed it into a situational meta-method [17], ESG4Orgs V2, by creating a method base, adding 14 new process fragments (w.r.t. V1), and defining situational factors for assembling a method.

4.1 Process Fragments

The set of process fragments in the method base is depicted in Fig. 5. The fragments are coded using a letter or a letter and number combination. Some fragments are further deconstructed into sub-processes. Still, the figure only shows an abstracted version of the process fragments. The detailed activities and dependencies within are omitted to reduce the complexity of the method base. Find complex fragments in full detail in an accompanying technical report [23]. Within each of the fragments, there are situational factors that determine how activities are performed. We describe the situational factors within the fragments in the following sections and code each factor with an ID (e.g. SF1).

A: Set-up ESGA Project. The set-up of the method engineering process requires team formation and timeline definition. The company size, measured by the number of full-time employees (SF1), determines team composition. In large organisations, it is more important to have well-structured procedures for compiling diverse and inclusive teams to ensure representation and equal opportunities. We recommend assessing the project's situational context by evaluating each SF, detailed in the technical report's table [23]. In this activity, we recommend assessing the project's context by evaluating each SF, detailed in the technical report [23]. In the case study on GenDelf, the team consisted of four representatives of the start-up and two researchers who helped to apply ESG4Orgs.

B: Create Production Chain. When organisations do not yet have clear and official definitions of their value proposition, market segment, and key stakeholder groups (SF2) they should first create an overview of their production chain. This will provide input for the stakeholder analysis. For GenDelf we drafted the value chain shown at the bottom of Fig. 7a.

C: Stakeholder Analysis. In stakeholder analysis, organisations identify relevant groups for consideration during the ESGA. The complexity of this analysis generally increases with the size of the organisation (SF1). For small entities, stakeholders include employees, customers, suppliers, and society. Medium and large organisations additionally consider works councils, trade unions, shareholders, and trade associations. Various techniques for stakeholder analysis are detailed in the technical report [23]. In subactivity C4, the ESGA team decides which stakeholders will be actively involved in defining the ESGA method content. Examples of stakeholders of GenDelf are genetic advisors, doctors, research

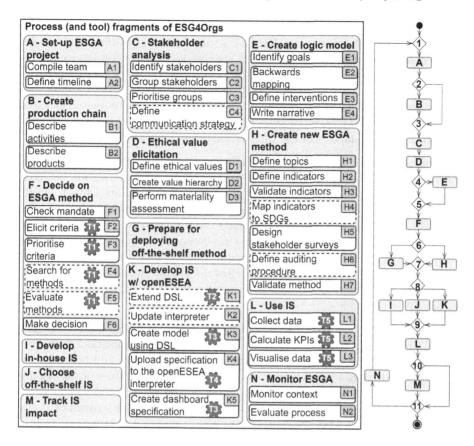

Fig. 5. The process fragments (left) and the assembly graph (right). Some process fragments are supported by tool fragments. The tool fragments are depicted with a gear symbol and identifier.

institutions, and patients. The stakeholders were elicited by discussing the production chain (Fig. 7a) and later further analysed.

D: Ethical Value Elicitation. For organisations that have not yet defined a sustainability strategy, eliciting the ethical values of the organisation helps develop this strategy. In small and medium organisations the value elicitation can be done in plenary sessions. For large organisations (SF1) workshops or focus groups are more suitable. As an example, we organised a workshop and focus groups to define the ESGA method for the 16th Research Challenges in Information Science conference (RCIS 2022[1]). In large corporations/multinationals this step is typically performed top-down, i.e. shareholders and top management determine the core values of the organisation. We recommend that stakeholders on every level of the organisation are involved in this activity, to stimulate cor-

---

[1] https://esea4rcis.sites.uu.nl.

porate democracy [29]. The value hierarchy forms the basis of the materiality assessment. As can be observed in GenDelf's value hierarchy at the top of Fig. 7a, *social equality* and *improved public health* are core values to this start-up. Literature indicates that the industry sector (SF3) significantly shapes the materiality assessment process and the identification of material topics [30]. To ensure consistent quality, organisations are advised to develop a materiality matrix [30] and refer to established taxonomies such as SDG targets, the EU social taxonomy, or the disclosure standards of the International Sustainability Standards Board.

E: Create Logic Model. A logic model is a cause-effect diagram relating organisational inputs (from an enterprise modelling perspective, we can consider these to be resources), activities (i.e. processes), outputs (direct results of the processes), outcomes (indirect, longer-term results brought about by the outputs), and eventually impacts (i.e. main goals related to the organisational mission) [31]. Organisations with a social mission commonly use logic models to articulate desired social impacts and secure funding. Due to its time-intensive nature, we recommend only social enterprises (SF4) undertake this activity. Consequently, we have only performed this step for the Refugee Wellbeing & Integration Initiative.

F: Decide on ESGA Method. There is a multitude of ESGA methods [20]. To save time and improve comparability of ESG reports, organisations can select a pre-existing ESGA method. Pre-existing ESGA methods should be evaluated to discover if there is a method that aligns with the ethical values of the organisations. This can be done systematically using our decision model and decision-support system (DSS) for selecting ESGA methods [4]. Find a screenshot of the DSS in Fig. 7b. If the DSS concludes that there is no good fit, the team should decide to create a new ESGA method. If there is a good fit, the team can decide to adopt this method.

G: Prepare for Deploying Off-the-Shelf-Method. If an off-the-shelf method is selected the team should review the method documentation, register with the network of social enterprises, announce the ESGA project, and possibly complement the method with additional indicators.

H: Create New ESGA Method. Material topics identified in activity D can be detailed into specific topics. For instance, in the case of GenDelf, *social activism* and *responsible procurement* are examples of topics. Indicators to measure these topics are then defined by referencing ESG repositories such as the SDG compass. Validation of indicators occurs with relevant stakeholder groups, following the mode determined in activity C4. Internationally operating organisations (SF5) can align indicators with the globally recognised Sustainable Development Goals (SDGs) set by the United Nations or other widely acknowledged frameworks. ESGA involves survey-based data collection, with surveys tailored to key stakeholder groups from activity C2. This activity includes designing said surveys. To enhance ESG report trustworthiness (SF6), implementing an auditing procedure is recommended to verify the accuracy and truthfulness of collected data. Validation with stakeholders from activity C2 is integral to the entire ESGA process.

I: Develop in-House IS and J: Choose off-the-Shelf IS. In this article, we spotlight our technology stack for developing ISs, but for completeness purposes, we add activities I and J. When a new ESGA method is designed from scratch (activity H), the organisations want to alter their method over time (SF7), or they are concerned about data privacy (SF8), developing an in-house system is a suitable option. Alternatively, an organisation can choose an off-the-shelf IS (J) when the team has selected an off-the-shelf ESGA method (following the decision in activity C) and this method is supported by an off-the-shelf IS.

K: Develop IS with openESEA. The openESEA technology offers several advanced features [6], is more versatile than other tools in the market due to its model-driven nature [5], and is fully open-source. Therefore, it is a fitting choice when an organisation wants to evolve their ESGA method over time (SF7), when more advanced features (e.g. smart auditing, infographic generation, and model management operations) are required (SF9), when an open-source technology stack is desired (SF10), or when the allocated resources for the ESGA project are very low (SF11). The values, logic model elements, material topics, indicators, auditing procedures, and other products resulting from the preceding activities serve as requirements for the openESEA DSL. Though the openESEA DSL design has been informed by the analysis of 19 ESGA methods, new requirements can arise as more organisations start using the technology. Hence, the DSL may have to be extended. For this, the metamodel should first be evolved, before evolving the Xtext grammar. The full evolution approach is described in [21]. After extending the DSL, the interpreter should be updated to ensure that the models created with the new DSL can be properly parsed. Thereafter, the ESGA method model can be created and uploaded to the interpreter. To visualise the ESGA data in a dashboard, a dashboard specification should be created because the dashboard functionality in openESEA is model-driven too. This assures that the organisation can use the same dashboard layout over time to promote their corporate sustainability image.

L: Use IS. The first step in using the IS is collecting data. The organisational structure (SF12) and data storage infrastructure (SF13) determine how data is collected. In general, data collection entails filling in the stakeholder surveys designed in activity E3. After data collection, key performance indicators (e.g. *carbon intensity and gender pay gap*) are calculated, the data is audited, and the results are visualised. If the openESEA framework is used, model-driven infographics and dashboards can be produced automatically.

M: Track IS impact. If an organisation is very passionate about its environmental impact (SF14), it may want to track the energy consumption of the ESGA IS, using one of the numerous energy monitoring systems.

N: Monitor Context. The dynamic ESGA context should be monitored by a task force because it evolves rapidly. For instance, because of changes in legislation. Moreover, the task force should reflect on the current ESGA practices of

Product fragments of ESG4Orgs										

Product fragments of ESG4Orgs						
A	ESGA team	A1	**B**	Prod. chain	B1	**C**
	Project	A2		Activity	B1	

(table of product fragments)

A ESGA team A1 · Project A2

Criterion F1/2 · **F** ESGA method F3 · Mapping F4

G ESGA method G

L Indicator value L1/2 · Charts L3

M Environmental impact M

B Prod. chain B1 · Activity B1 · Product B2

E Logic model E1 · Impact E1 · Outcome E2 · Output E2 · Activity E3 · Input E2 · Narrative E4

I Inform. syst. I

C Stakeholder group C2/3 · Stakeholder C1 · Commun. str. C4

D Value hierarchy D2 · Value D1 · Material topics D3

K DSL (Xtext) K1 · Xtext editor K1 · Interpreter code K2 · Method model K3 · Dashboard spec K5

J Inform. system J

H ESG topics H1 · ESGA method H7 · Indicator H2 · SDG H4 · Survey H5 · Section H5 · Question H5 · Auditing proc. H6

N Context N1 · Evaluation N2

Fig. 6. The product fragments. The letter before the products indicates the process fragment that produces the product. An indent in a product placement can be regarded as an aggregation relationship. For instance, the product *value hierarchy* consists of *values*. We chose this notation for its conciseness.

the organisation. Whenever the task force finds that the current ESGA method definition (or IS) is insufficient because there are new ESG regulations, there is societal awareness about a new ESG topic, or there are clear points of improvement in the current ESGA process, ESG4Orgs can be executed again to create a new more up-to-date ESGA method and IS.

4.2 Product and Tool Fragments

The product fragments are instantiated when a process fragment is executed. The product fragments can be regarded as concepts, comprising attributes. The concept attributes and the relationships between the fragments can be found in the technical report [23]. We have opted to only include the concept names in the product fragment repository in Fig. 6, for the sake of brevity.

Several process fragments are supported by tool fragments. In Fig. 5 we have marked the process fragments that are supported by a tool fragment within the openESEA framework. Screenshots of these tool fragments (marked with the same cogs symbol) can be found in Figs. 2 and 7b. The first tool fragment within the openESEA framework (T1) is the DSS that helps select an ESGA method. T2 represents the Xtext DSL. The accompanying editor Xtext editor is T3. The interpreter is the fourth tool fragment (T4). Finally, the IS that is created by uploading a model to the interpreter is T5. We also use numerous tools outside of the openESEA framework, some of them analogue, such as sticky notes to create the value hierarchy, a drawing tool to sketch the production chain, and survey tools to validate ESGA method questions (depicted in Fig. 7a).

4.3 Assembly Strategy and Good Practices

The assembly strategy coincides with the assembly-based strategy from [25]. First, the requirements of the method are defined, thereafter fragments that meet

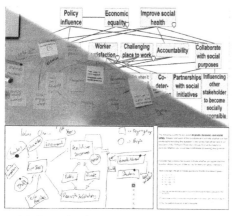 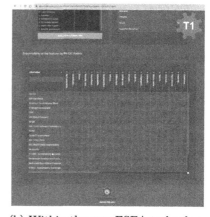

(a) Outside the openESEA technology   (b) Within the openESEA technology

Fig. 7. Example of the usages of (a) manual and (b) automated tool fragments in ESG4Orgs. The value hierarchy (top, left) was first created using sticky notes and later digitised.

Table 2. The assembly guidelines instruct users when making decisions at the XOR-gates. They use situational factors to direct the flow of the meta-method.

XOR ID	Guideline	SF
2	IF input for stakeholder analysis = insufficient THEN B ELSE GATE-3	SF2
4	IF social mission = true THEN E ELSE GATE-5	SF3
6	IF decision = design new method THEN H ELSE G	
8	IF tailor-made tool = required IF resources = low OR open-source technology = desired THEN K ELSE J ELSE I	SF 7, 8, 9, 10, 11
10	IF environmental impact tracking = desired THEN M ELSE GATE-11	SF14

the requirements are retrieved from the method base to compose a new method. The assembly graph (right side of Fig. 5) shows that the method should be constructed using a pre-defined outline (i.e. top-down). The graph displays valid method outlines, incorporating XOR and JOIN gates to adhere to seven process modelling guidelines [32]. We labelled gates, not flows, for brevity. Guidelines (shown in Table 2) are provided to assist ESG4Orgs users in choosing method fragments at XOR-gates. Note that not all SFs influence a decision at an XOR-gate. Instead, some SFs influence *how* activities and subactivities are performed. We found that the M2 methods we created as part of the six case studies, all follow a valid path in the assembly graph [23].

Moreover, based on the case-study experiences we have defined good practices for assembling and executing methods. An example of a good practice is "Involve the data privacy officer when validating indicators to ensure regulatory compliance (e.g. GDPR)". Find all good practices in the technical report [23].

5   ESG4Orgs Evaluation

In this section we report on the preliminary expert interview results. During the interviews, both participants affirmed the **comprehensibility** of ESG4Orgs, expressing confidence in using it after minimal training. To enhance its accessibility in the Dutch market, the policymaker recommended translating the meta-method and supporting documentation into Dutch. The sustainability advisor suggested simplifying the meta-method for small and medium organisations, proposing a more intuitive design for the industrial version. The interviewees suggested adding graphic designs for each process fragment or providing a basic and customisable method outline, possibly in infographic form.

The policymaker expressed that the **usefulness** of ESG4Orgs for organisations depends on how much the ESGA benefits the organisation. A cost-benefit analysis before using ESG4Orgs could provide more insights since usefulness in this domain is instance-based. The sustainability advisor expressed that ESG4Orgs provides a handy overview of the steps that should be taken to perform ESGA. The policymaker stated that ESG4Orgs can serve as a guide for policymakers on the operational level, while the advisor highlighted its utility for the public sector entering the ESGA domain. As a point of improvement, the advisor proposed adding time/effort indicators to each fragment.

In the interviews, semantic changes were noted, which further improved the **completeness** of the meta-method. The materiality assessment was moved from an optional to a mandatory process fragment (D). The term "theory of change" in fragment E was changed to the less ambiguous term "logic model". We have also added subactivity N2, "evaluate process" because the expert explained that after each iteration of ESG4Orgs the team should evaluate the process and identify improvements for the next iteration. In total, 15 new process fragments were added, contributing to the completeness of ESG4Orgs, as affirmed by the experts.

6   Discussion and Conclusion

Outcome 1: We have derived process fragments from six case studies in which we configured our domain-specific, model-driven technology for environmental, social and governance accounting information systems. We complete the method base by adding product fragments, and tool fragments.
Outcome 2: To ensure that the ESGA method and supporting IS align with the sustainability strategy of the organisation we have added several process fragments that address the intricacies of realising sustainable development, such as the ethical value elicitation.
Outcome 3: Experts have concluded that the conceptual fragments are complete and deemed ESG4Orgs understandable and useful, but training on method engineering is required before using ESG4Orgs. Its main benefit lies in the comprehensive ESGA overview and adaptability to organisational traits, but the drawback is the complexity of the meta-method.

A threat to validity is that we have not assessed the syntactic quality of ESG4Orgs. To warrant syntactic quality we have followed state-of-the-art SME approaches. Furthermore, we have not yet tested the meta-method on large organisations, and therefore probably have not yet reached semantic completeness. Lastly, we have interviewed two experts in the validation round. This low number of interviews poses a threat to the external validity. However, we plan more extensive validations in follow-up projects. For future work, we plan to create an industrial version of ESG4Orgs, including graphic designs, explanatory documentation, and example cases, after which we will assess the user-friendliness, completeness, and usefulness of ESG4Orgs again with a set of large organisations. Moreover, we could also assess the quality of the ESGA methods created using ESG4Orgs. All in all, we deem our situational meta-method a success and are optimistic about the contributions of ESG4Orgs for different types of organisations.

References

1. EU: Directive (EU) 2022/2464 of the European Parliament and of the Council of 14 December 2022 amending Regulation. ELI: http://data.europa.eu/eli/dir/2022/2464/oj (2013). Accessed 17 Nov 2023
2. Sridhar, K., Jones, G.: The three fundamental criticisms of the triple bottom line approach: an empirical study to link sustainability reports in companies based in the Asia-Pacific region and TBL shortcomings. Asian J. Bus. Ethics **2**(1), 91–111 (2013)
3. Cort, T., Esty, D.: ESG standards: looming challenges and pathways forward. Organ. Environ. **33**(4), 491–510 (2020)
4. Ramautar, V., España, S.: Decision-Making Criteria for Ethical. ECGIC, Universitat de València, Social and Environmental Accounting Method Selection (2022)
5. España, S., Bik, N., Overbeek, S.: Model-driven engineering support for social and environmental accounting. In: RCIS, pp. 1–12. IEEE (2019)
6. Ramautar, V., España, S.: The OpenESEA modeling language and tool for ethical, social, and environmental accounting. In: CSIMQ, no. 34 (2023)
7. Brinkkemper, S., Saeki, M., Harmsen, F.: A method engineering language for the description of systems development methods. In: Dittrich, K.R., Geppert, A., Norrie, M.C. (eds.) CAiSE 2001. LNCS, vol. 2068, pp. 473–476. Springer, Heidelberg (2001). https://doi.org/10.1007/3-540-45341-5_33
8. Carvalho, B., Wiek, A., Ness, B.: Can B Corp certification anchor sustainability in SMEs? Corp. Soc. Responsib. Environ. Manag. **29**(1), 293–304 (2022)
9. Kolsch, D., Saling, P., Kicherer, A., Grosse-Sommer, A., Schmidt, I.: How to measure social impacts? A socio-eco-efficiency analysis by the SEEBALANCE method. IJSD **11**(1), 1–23 (2008)
10. Zappalà, G., Lyons, M.: Recent approaches to measuring social impact in the Third sector: an overview (2009)
11. Gauthier, C.: Measuring corporate social and environmental performance: the extended life-cycle assessment. J. Bus. Ethics **59**, 199–206 (2005)
12. Flower, J.: The international integrated reporting council: a story of failure. Crit. Perspect. Account. **27**, 1–17 (2015)
13. Kühne, T.: Matters of (meta-) modeling. SoSyM **5**, 369–385 (2006)
14. Engels, G., Sauer, S.: A meta-method for defining software engineering methods. In: Graph Transformations and Model-Driven Engineering, pp. 411–440 (2010)
15. Henderson-Sellers, B., Unhelkar, B.: OPEN modeling with UML. Pearson Education, London (2000)

16. Deneckère, R., Iacovelli, A., Kornyshova, E., Souveyet, C.: From method fragments to method services. EMMSAD **2008**, 80–96 (2008)
17. Henderson-Sellers, B., Ralyté, J.: Situational method engineering: state-of-the-art review. J. UCS 16(3), 424–478 (2010)
18. Harmsen, A.F.: Situational method engineering (1997)
19. van de Weerd, I., de Weerd, S., Brinkkemper, S.: Developing a reference method for game production by method comparison. In: Ralyté, J., Brinkkemper, S., Henderson-Sellers, B. (eds.) Situational Method Engineering: Fundamentals and Experiences. ITIFIP, vol. 244, pp. 313–327. Springer, Boston, MA (2007). https://doi.org/10.1007/978-0-387-73947-2_24
20. España, S., Ramautar, V., Martín, S., Thorsteinsdottir, G., Anneria-Sinaga, Y., Pastor, Ó.: Why and how responsible organisations are assessing their performance: state of the practice in environmental, social and governance accounting. In: COPERMAN, Springer, Cham (2023)
21. Ramautar, V., España, S., Brinkkemper, S.: Task completeness assessments in the evolution of domain-specific modelling languages. In: Indulska, M., Reinhartz-Berger, I., Cetina, C., Pastor, O. (eds.) Advanced Information Systems Engineering. CAiSE 2023, LNCS, vol. 13901, pp. 314–329. Springer, Cham (2023). https://doi.org/10.1007/978-3-031-34560-9_19
22. España, S., Ramautar, V., Le, Q.T.: Assessing the ethical, social and environmental performance of conferences. In: Guizzardi, R., Ralyté, J., Franch, X. (eds.) Research Challenges in Information Science. RCIS 2022, LNBIP, vol. 446, pp. 752–760. Springer, Cham (2022). https://doi.org/10.1007/978-3-031-05760-1_52
23. Ramautar, V., España, S., Brinkkemper, S., Pastor, Ó.: Situational method engineering for ESG accounting (technical report). https://doi.org/10.17632/2z83pvb832.1
24. Garousi, V., Felderer, M., Mäntylä, M.V.: The need for multivocal literature reviews in software engineering: complementing systematic literature reviews with grey literature. In: EASE, pp. 1–6 (2016)
25. Ralyté, J., Deneckère, R., Rolland, C.: Towards a generic model for situational method engineering. In: Eder, J., Missikoff, M. (eds.) CAiSE 2003. LNCS, vol. 2681, pp. 95–110. Springer, Heidelberg (2003). https://doi.org/10.1007/3-540-45017-3_9
26. Brinkkemper, S., Saeki, M., Harmsen, F.: Meta-modelling based assembly techniques for situational method engineering. Inf. Syst. **24**(3), 209–228 (1999)
27. Ralyté, J., Rolland, C.: An approach for method reengineering. In: S.Kunii, H., Jajodia, S., Sølvberg, A. (eds.) ER 2001. LNCS, vol. 2224, pp. 471–484. Springer, Heidelberg (2001). https://doi.org/10.1007/3-540-45581-7_35
28. Ralyté, J., Rolland, C.: An assembly process model for method engineering. In: Dittrich, K.R., Geppert, A., Norrie, M.C. (eds.) CAiSE 2001. LNCS, vol. 2068, pp. 267–283. Springer, Heidelberg (2001). https://doi.org/10.1007/3-540-45341-5_18
29. De Jong, G., Van Witteloostuijn, A.: Successful corporate democracy: sustainable cooperation of capital and labor in the Dutch Breman group. AMP **18**(3), 54–66 (2004)
30. Torelli, R., Balluchi, F., Furlotti, K.: The materiality assessment and stakeholder engagement: a content analysis of sustainability reports. Corp. Soc. Responsib. Environ. Manag. **27**(2), 470–484 (2020)
31. Mayne, J.: Theory of change analysis: building robust theories of change. CJPE **32**(2), 155–173 (2017)
32. Mendling, J., Reijers, H.A., van der Aalst, W.M.: Seven process modeling guidelines (7PMG). IST **52**(2), 127–136 (2010)

Realizing the Accountability of Algorithms in the Public Sector: A Reference Method for Managing Algorithm Registers

Nena Schuitemaker[1]([✉]), Martijn van Vliet[1,2], Sjaak Brinkkemper[1],
Inge van de Weerd[1], and Sergio España[1,3]

[1] Department of Information and Computing Sciences, Utrecht University, Utrecht,
The Netherlands
{n.schuitemaker,m.vanvliet,s.brinkkemper,g.c.vandeweerd,s.espana}@uu.nl
[2] Netherlands Police, Nieuwegein, The Netherlands
martijn.van.vliet@politie.nl
[3] Valencian Research Institute for Artificial Intelligence, Universitat Politècnica de
València, Valencia, Spain

Abstract. The government of The Netherlands has mandated public organizations to disclose an algorithm register in the future. This aligns with the upcoming AI Act of the European Union, as a directive that aims to enhance transparency in algorithmic decision-making and use. This research highlights that the practices are rarely mature and not fully understood, which is characterized by their variability. The novelty of the practices in the industry and the limited research to date, currently make this a chaotic domain. In this research, we explore this domain through a method engineering approach. We conduct six case studies to elicit the process that each organization applies or envisions to manage their algorithm register. We model their processes using Process-Deliverable Diagrams, a meta-modeling technique that integrates dynamic and static perspectives. By applying a systematic method comparison approach, we compare and combine the processes into a single reference method for algorithm register management (RM4AR). This paper documents the process and outcomes of developing such a reference method, demonstrating how method engineering techniques aid in bringing structure into an emerging field.

Keywords: Algorithm register · Reference method · Method engineering · AI accountability · Public sector

1 Introduction

As part of the ongoing digital transformation, organizations worldwide are adopting disruptive technologies in order to benefit from unprecedented technological possibilities [15]. Artificial intelligence (AI) is currently being considered as the main driving force behind the ongoing digital transformation of organizations

H. van der Aa et al. (Eds.): BPMDS 2024/EMMSAD 2024, LNBIP 511, pp. 325–340, 2024.
https://doi.org/10.1007/978-3-031-61007-3_24

[22]. The wish to adopt new disruptive technologies to achieve their benefits has not been limited to the private sector, with governments worldwide already having committed major investments towards the research and development of AI-related technologies [55]. However, inherent challenges of AI as a technology complicate the implementation and adoption of the technology in practice, as a vast majority of AI and data science projects fail to be effectively deployed to achieve a significant positive impact [51]. Even with these challenges, it is expected that AI-driven innovation will have a continued profound impact on public sector employees, citizens, and societies [34]. Inadequately dealing with these challenges in combination with the inherent susceptibility of the technology to lead to privacy and ethical issues, has citizens increasingly expressing their concerns [30]. These increasing concerns have resulted in a push for more regulations and ethics in AI [2].

The AI act that is in development within the European Union among others calls for transparency obligations towards the use of AI systems [48]. More specifically, one of the answers to the calls for regulation from the government of The Netherlands has been the proposal to instate policies for the realization of an algorithm register. An algorithm register is defined as *a governance mechanism that allows organizations to be transparent and to provide accountability to society by providing an overview of (1) the documentation about algorithms, (2) the organization or organizational department responsible for their use, and (3) the goals pursued with their use* [47]. An algorithm register is a new societal phenomenon and a critical concept in the rapidly emerging field of accountability of AI. The mandatory nature of the topic inclined a multitude of government organizations in the Netherlands to figure out how to realize an algorithm register. The National Algorithm Register of The Netherlands currently contains information on 340 algorithms that are used in a total of 116 government organizations [12]. The current iteration of the national register and its available entries can be viewed here. The information available in this national register is divided into three categories:

- **General information:** Provides information such as: the name and short description of the algorithm, the organization using the algorithm, whether it is self-learning or not, the domain that it is deployed in, the launching date, contact information, and links towards external information.
- **Responsible use:** Descriptions about the goal and impact of the algorithm, functional considerations, whether human intervention plays a role, risk management aspects, legal basis, and what impact assessment was applied.
- **Technical references:** Elaborations on the data that are processed by the algorithm, and textual descriptions of its technical design.

This research applies method engineering practices towards the creation of an algorithm register. Based on conducted case studies, a reference method for the management of an algorithm register was created. Method engineering was used to achieve a reference method by analyzing the processes and activities from each individual case study. This paper intends to contribute to the method engineering literature by proposing a detailed process to construct a reference method.

Moreover, it shows how method engineering, and its established practices, can be applied to a unique and chaotic research topic in an emerging field.

In Sect. 2, we provide an overview of the relevant existing literature on the domains of method engineering and algorithm registers and discuss the relevance to the current challenges surrounding the adoption of AI in organizations. In Sect. 3, we present our objectives and discuss our research method and the theory building approach based on the conducted case studies. Section 4 shows the constructed Reference Method for Algorithm Registers (RM4AR). Lastly, in Sect. 5, we discuss the importance of managing the traceability of the research results towards the sources, what the implications of our findings are, their limitations, and the possibilities for future research.

2   Related Work

2.1   Implementation and Adoption of AI in Organizations

Alluring benefits such as improvement in predictions and decision making, reduction in required production time and costs, increased performance and customer satisfaction are important drivers for the adoption of AI in organizations [10]. In the chase to achieve these benefits, AI has emerged as the most critical technological factor influencing organizations structures worldwide [7]. As a result, advanced algorithms are currently transforming the workforce and altering the way that firms operate [20]. Challenges surrounding the implementation and adoption of AI come from many areas. Dwivedi et al. (2021) mention challenges of organizational and managerial kind, issues related to data, legal constraints, ethical concerns, technological nature, social concerns and economical impact [14]. The current lack of realized impact of AI projects illustrate the effects of the many challenges in these seven areas, and that they pose a significant barrier for impactful implementation and adoption of AI [53]. The existing challenges allow for instances to occur where unwanted consequences from the use of AI systems, either intentionally or unintentionally become reality. Therefore, especially in the context of AI, organizations need adequate systems to ensure that their use of AI technologies aligns with the strategies, objectives and values of the organization in the long term [35]. Benbya et al. (2020) state that mechanisms for the management and governance for the adoption of AI in organizations are one of the main directions organizations should focus on, to remove or diminish the barriers that block AI being used to its fullest potential [5].

The awareness within the scientific community that AI is already having a large impact on society and the daily life of people has already been identified [19]. Toreini et al. (2020) state that the area of trustworthy AI reflects the recognition that maintaining trust in AI may be critical for ensuring acceptance and successful adoption of AI driven services and products [45]. In response to the rise of AI, many people have proposed guidelines for the responsible use of AI [23]. Fjeld et al. (2020) discuss eight themes within the field of trustworthy AI such as privacy, accountability, safety and security, transparency and explainability, fairness and non-discrimination, human control of technology, professional responsibility, promotion of human values and international human rights [18]. These themes and their underlying principles however are often considered too high-level and provide few specific recommendations in practice. Hagendorf (2020) and Mittelstadt (2019) mention that AI development lacks proven methods to translate responsible AI principles into practice [25, 37].

2.2 The Necessity of Algorithm Registers

Examples of malpractice of the application of (AI) algorithms are not hard to find. A well-known recent example of inadequate deployment of algorithms in the public sector is that of the Dutch Tax Authorities. The so-called childcare-benefits scandal caused by a discriminating algorithm resulted in more than 20,000 parents being accused of fraudulent conduct, ultimately resulting in the wrongful separation of at least 1,100 children from their families [27].

Currently, citizens and users are not well aware of the hidden complex information that is used to influence their daily lives [36, 42]. Transparency is key in ensuring that the government and its public organizations abide by the law. This includes transparency about the generation, collection, and processing of data which contains information that is used for (AI) algorithms [13]. The algorithm register is proposed as a possible solution for providing sufficient insights into the algorithm usage of public organizations [31].

This upcoming law will require public organizations in The Netherlands to publish information about the characteristics and the use of algorithms. The goal of the upcoming legislation is to raise organizational awareness on critical aspects of the development and use of algorithms within their organizations. By adhering to the guidelines, they want to stimulate organizations to realize unprecedented levels of proactive transparency and accountability and to make them more aware of the development and operational use of algorithms and potential inherent risks. The law requiring public organizations to have an algorithm register is not in effect yet but will be in the coming years [46]. As the algorithm register is a new concept in an emerging field, more research is required to evolve into a complete mechanism that is able to fulfill its intended goals [47].

Various scholarly works assess their perspectives on the effectiveness and limitations of algorithm registers [9, 19, 29]. Floridi (2020) commends the initiative and explains the content of the Helsinki and Amsterdam algorithm registers [19]. Others have a much more critical view of algorithm registers. They critique the registers for lacking contextualization and highlight potential issues in addressing algorithmic aspects adequately [9]. Houtzager, Verbeek, and Terlouw (2022) seem to support this and suggest ethical guidelines but fail to provide any concrete guidelines [29]. Murad (2021) focuses on best practices for Algorithmic Decision-Making systems registers', yet overlooks the organizational perspective [38]. Additional literature briefly touches on algorithm registers' transparency, including a self-reported report with limited scope [8, 24, 39]. Overall, these works offer insights into algorithm registers' benefits and shortcomings, advocating for better contextualization and ethical guidelines but providing limited actionable suggestions.

2.3   Reference Method Construction

Several approaches exist for constructing reference methods. For example, in Business Process Management (BPM) literature, configurable process models were proposed as building blocks for reference modeling [1], and business process reference models were used to capture best practices [17,33]. Research in this domain has a large emphasis on the process side of models and methods, and less so on the data or deliverable side.

Another research area in which reference methods have been constructed is method engineering, for example for game production [50] and partner selection in software ecosystems [4]. Method engineering has been defined as *the engineering discipline to design, construct, and adapt methods, techniques, and tools for the development of information systems* [6]. To properly perform these engineering activities special purpose specification techniques, called meta-modeling techniques, are required. One form of a method meta-modeling technique is process-deliverable diagrams (PDD) [49]. In comparison to BPM approaches, method engineering emphasizes process and data perspectives equally. New methods can be constructed by selecting fragments containing activities as well as deliverables from different methods. Therefore, method fragments are the basic building blocks, which allow us to construct methods in a modular way [41]. Method engineering even allows for a situational adaptation of methods to fit, for example, a specific project [26]. This is especially helpful in the context of algorithm registers for public organizations, as research has shown that the transparency level of these organizations varies considerably [3]. For our research this was relevant to organize the chaotic nature of the emerging field. Furthermore, it allowed us to structure and combine the strong parts of the approaches between the different cases, to make a concrete step towards the development of an effective and efficient method for the management of an algorithm register.

3   Research Approach

This research adopts a design science methodology involving three principal phases: problem investigation, treatment design, and treatment validation [54]. In our research, we specifically focus on theory-building [11]. We conduct a literature review to explore the problem and case studies to investigate and document so-called "theories-in-use" [6,11]. Finally, these theories-in-use are translated into the reference method for managing an algorithm register.

3.1   Problem Investigation: Literature Study and Observations

Our problem investigation focused on two questions: (1) What is known about public registers in general, and algorithm registers more specifically and (2) how are algorithm registers currently used? To answer these questions, we conducted a multivocal literature study encompassing both academic and non-academic resources [21]. The reason for including non-academic literature was the limited availability of academic literature on algorithm registers. We incorporated diverse sources, such as academic papers, blogs, news articles, government reports, and white papers to gather broad knowledge. Additionally, existing algorithm registers were examined as part of the literature study to prepare the case studies.

During the problem investigation, we developed a conceptualization of an algorithm register exploring its potential functionalities and applications. Additionally, we explored the role of algorithms in organizations and identified disparities and similarities between existing management practices and envisioned possibilities.

3.2   Treatment Design: Theory-Building Case Studies and Reference Method Design

Building upon insights garnered from the problem investigation, a treatment strategy was devised. As prescribed in theory-building, case studies were integral during this phase to understand how organizations approach managing an algorithm register [11]. Emphasizing diversity, our comparative case study encompassed seven participants from six different organizations (referred to with the identifiers O1 to O6). The organizations varied in size, tasks, reputation, level of transparency, and the state of their algorithm registers to ensure a robust theoretical foundation. Moreover, the seven participants had varying backgrounds, functions, IT knowledge and experience, and involvement with algorithm registers.

Observations. Observations were first done at the Netherlands Police, where many inquiries regarding the creation and execution of an algorithm register became apparent. Subsequently, two workshops organized by The Netherlands Ministry of Internal Affairs were attended. Here, representatives from other attending governmental organizations of The Netherlands echoed similar inquiries about the algorithm register.

Survey. Before conducting the interviews, all seven participants were asked to fill in a survey. The goal of this survey was threefold: (1) to get an overview of the perceptions of the participants and their organizations on responsible AI and its principles; (2) to get an indication of their beliefs in the algorithm register's capability to help with enforcing these principles; and (3) to prepare participants on the interviews and give them enough time to think about their answers. We structured the first part of our survey questions according to eight common themes describing responsible AI: privacy, accountability, safety and security, transparency and explainability, fairness and non-discrimination, human control of technology, professional responsibility, and promotion of human values [18].

Interviews. Two members of the author team conducted 2-hour interviews with all seven participants in May and July, 2023. All interviews were audio recorded. Our interview guide was divided into three main phases: (1) background information of the participant and the organization; (2) discussion on the survey results in order to find out more about the theory-to-practice gap that is currently present regarding responsible AI principles and to find out how the algorithm register can contribute to this; (3) the discussion of the organizational process of the algorithm register. During the last phase, participants were asked to draw the process, existing or envisioned, of their organization regarding the algorithm register. Participants were asked to draw the process without any input from the researchers, which made the interviewees focus mainly on the activities that have to be performed to realize an algorithm register. Only afterward, we asked questions about their drawings. These questions were especially focused on why certain things were included or excluded from the process and what the reasoning was for this.

Data Analysis. After all interviews were conducted, we analyzed the observation notes, survey results, interview notes, and drawings of the participants. We followed the formal method engineering approach of Hong, Van den Goor, and Brinkkemper (1993) to compare the participants' different algorithm register processes [28]. We coded our notes and drawings with the structural themes of *activities, roles,* and *concepts*, as well as for five content themes *inventory, risk assessment, internal registration, publication,* and *maintenance*.

Our method comparison approach was supported by a meta-modeling technique [49]. We used Process-Deliverable Diagrams (PDDs) to transform the drawings provided by the participants into formal meta-models. The PDD technique was specifically designed for method engineering and consists of two integrated diagrams. The left side of the PDD showcases the process view of a method (comparable to a UML activity diagram). The right side of the PDD showcases the deliverables of a method (comparable to a UML class diagram).

Finally, the method fragments that resulted from the six different case studies were compared with each other. These method fragments were then combined into a reference method for the management of an algorithm register.

3.3 Treatment Validation: Expert Interviews

The goal of the treatment validation was to confirm that the participants' perspectives were accurately captured and to refine and adapt the reference method based on their feedback. We conducted three expert interviews with three research participants. The three participants were selected based on their own experience, their organization's experience with an algorithm register and their availability. All validation interviews were recorded and transcribed.

3.4 Mitigating Threats to Validity

We took several measures to mitigate threats to validity in the different phases of our research project [44]. First, we ensured *construct validity* by gathering data from multiple sources and by triangulating [56]. Multiple case studies were conducted, each at a different public organization.

External validity was improved by selecting case study participants with diversity in mind. Additionally, a cross-case analysis was performed with six organizations where four case studies would already be a good basis for analytical generalization [16].

Reliability was ensured by applying proper research methods. We used a literature research protocol, case study protocol, and interview protocol to perform research in a logical and systematic manner to ensure the reliability of this study. Each step of this study was documented carefully to ensure reliability [56].

4   Reference Method

The research method resulted in method fragments containing activities from the case studies. Each individual activity from each case was discussed and classified as to whether they were relevant to be included in the reference method. The exclusion criteria (EC) that we considered during the construction of the reference method are shown in Table 1. Figure 2 shows A4. Safeguard re-use of data as an example of an activity that was excluded from the reference method based on criteria EC2. The activity is part of the work practices of organization O4. Details about what specific activities were excluded from the reference method can be found in the technical report [43].

Table 1. Exclusion criteria table.

EC	Definition
EC1	Activity was indicative of what was considered a too premature stage to be included in the reference method. Activity was potentially a one-time occurrence and was only relevant during the construction of the initial iteration of the algorithm register.
EC2	Activity was directly related to the development process of an algorithm or a (AI) system. This kind of activity was considered to be out of scope, as it refers to something that predates the process described in the reference method.
EC3	Too case specific. Activity was only deemed relevant for that particular case/organization

The activities were included in the reference model based on the following inclusion criteria: they were explicitly and directly stated as necessary by a participating organization, they were in line with our impression of what is relevant for the algorithm register process, or they were identified recurringly by different organizations. During the construction of the reference process, activities from a more mature organization were given greater consideration for inclusion compared to those who were less mature. Nonetheless, the essence of concepts and process steps that came from less mature organizations were still considered during the construction of the reference method.

4.1   A Reference Method for Managing an Algorithm Register

The reference method (RM4AR) synthesizes the findings and provides a structured approach for the management of an algorithm register. The resulting PDD is shown in Fig. 1.

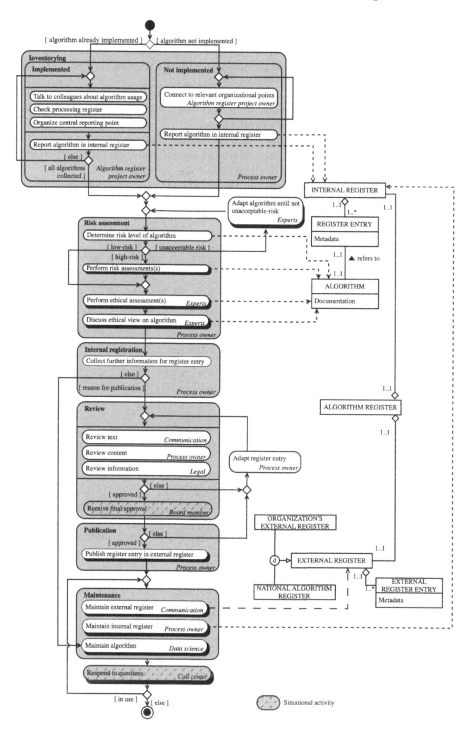

Fig. 1. Model of the RM4AR reference method for managing algorithm registers.

4.2   A Method Comparison

Table 2 shows how the organizations' methods are compared to the reference method. The following notation is used to describe the relationship between the PDDs [50]:

- Blank fields in the comparison table indicate that the particular activity was not present in the PDD of the organization.
- A 'V' indicates that the activity came up during the validation session.
- The '<' symbol denotes that the activity in the reference method constitutes more than the activity found in the PDD of the organization.
- The '>' symbol denotes that the activity in the reference method constitutes less than the activity found in the PDD of the organization.
- The '><' symbol indicates that the activity in the reference method partly overlaps with the activity of the organization's PDD.

Table 2. Activity comparison table

Activity	O1	O2	O3	O4	O5	O6
Inventorying						
Connect to relevant organizational points			V			
Report algorithm in internal register	= A10		= A2			= A8
Talk to colleagues about algorithm usage					>A2, A3, A4	
Check processing register			><A1			
Organize central reporting point			><A1			
Risk assessment						
Determine risk level of algorithm		= A4				<A2
Adapt algorithm until not unacceptable-risk		V				
Perform risk assessment(s)			>A3, A4			<A2
Perform ethical assessment(s)			= A5			<A2
Discuss ethical view on algorithm	= A6					
Internal registration						
Collect further information for register entry	= A8		= A6	= A3	= A6	
Review						
Review text		>A9, A10, A11, A16, A17, A18, A19, A20			<A12, A13	
Review content		>A9, A10, A11, A16			<A12, A13	
Review information		V				
Adapt register entry		= A12, A21	><A10		= A11	
Receive final approval		= A23	= A8		= A14	
Publication						
Publish register entry in external register		= A28	= A9	= A5	>A15, A16, A17	= A9
Maintenance						
Maintain external register		= A30	= A12			<A11
Maintain internal register			= A11			<A11
Maintain algorithm	= A11	><A31		= A2		= A10
Respond to questions		>A33, A34, A35, A36, A37, A38, A39, A40, A41				

4.3   Validation

During the validation interviews, the reference method presented in Fig. 1 was shown to participants. They were asked specific questions, but also given the opportunity to provide questions and remarks of their own. The participants were generally positive about the reference method and acknowledged its applicability. It was recognized that it is especially valuable for organizations that are in the first stages of managing an algorithm register. Even though organizations with a more mature process recognize many elements, it is "not less directive" for them, as stated by one of the participants.

The validation interviews resulted in adding a sub-activity for enhanced inventorying coordination, introducing a new activity to address unacceptable risk, shifting the responsibility for ethical assessments to experts, streamlining documentation by removing a sub-activity, adding legal review to ensure compliance, and incorporating a situational activity to address citizen inquiries.

The National Police of The Netherlands is implementing their Algorithm Register based on the RM4AR method. This gives us additional confidence that our contribution is valuable.

5   Discussion and Conclusion

Organizations require mechanism to govern their AI efforts, to ensure that they stay aligned with their strategies, objectives, and values in the long term [35]. Furthermore, practices are needed that allow responsible AI principles to be applied in practice [25,37]. In this paper, we have proposed a reference method to manage algorithm registers. Six organizations were analyzed that find themselves in different stages of implementing an algorithm register and have different tasks in the public domain. By performing case studies, we were able to create method fragments of all organizations that were subsequently used to configure a reference method. The reference method contains parts of the different participating organizations and integrates the perspectives that were encountered during the case studies.

5.1   Traceability

We have kept the data traceable throughout the research project. This allows now to trace each activity of the reference method to the organizations that have expressed an equivalent practice. A simplified information model of the research results is shown in Fig. 2, including the traceability information. During the method comparison approach, we have managed traceability by recording the identifiers of the activities of the algorithm from interviewed organizations that are mapped to the activities of the reference method (see Table 2). For instance, this allows to trace the activity in the reference method named Publish register entry in external register to activities present in five out of the six organizations (02 to 06); more accurately, in the case of organization 04

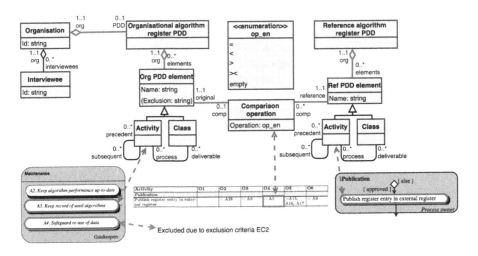

Fig. 2. Simplified information model of the research results and their traceability.

the activity is **A5. Keep record of used algorithms**. This example is also illustrated in Fig. 2. This traceability supports and reinforces the evidence-based nature of the reference method.

5.2 Implications

The lack of scientific literature on algorithm registers shows how this is a relatively new domain where there is still much knowledge to be discovered. Our study is one of the first to dive into the organizational aspects of algorithm registers. The main goal of this research was to contribute to the algorithm register management process, as current research efforts towards the implementation of AI is asymmetrically biased, with little focus on managerial viewpoints [32]. Although some examples of algorithm registers exist, no concrete guidance apart from generic guidelines exist that can help organizations to set up an algorithm register in their organization [52]. With our reference method, we aim to provide this missing guidance for organizations that are working on managing an algorithm register. Moreover, having an algorithm register contributes towards the realization of responsible AI principles [47]. Therefore, we contribute towards addressing the lack of proven methods to translate responsible AI principles into practice and answer the call for closing the AI accountability gap [40].

As discussed above, the domain of AI accountability and algorithm registers is still novel and the existing literature, while providing valuable contributions, remains unstructured. As a result, the current or recommended organizational practices remain implicit or scattered across several publications. The research method we have applied builds upon established techniques in the discipline of method engineering, showing the opportunities they offer to organize research results, so the knowledge can be structured (e.g., as a PDD) and traced back to its sources (e.g., through a method comparison table).

5.3   Limitations

All case studies were performed in the Netherlands, meaning that different regulations and legal environments of other regions were not taken into account affecting the generalizability of this study. Additionally, only a limited number of organizations participated in the study. As algorithm registers are a recent phenomenon, there is a limited number of organizations to include. Moreover, many of these organizations are in the initial phases of implementing an algorithm register and therefore have limited and similar knowledge on the process.

Furthermore, only organizations willing to discuss their algorithmic practices were included, potentially introducing selection bias. However, the interviews were performed with representatives from various organizations and in different roles, therefore facilitating diversity in included perspectives.

Lastly, RM4AR is proposed as a fully assembled method instead of a method component repository. A situational perspective might be more fitted for certain organizations. However, in the current context where organizations often find themselves in the initial stages of managing algorithm registers, a descriptive method such as RM4AR is more fitting.

5.4   Future Research

In future research, the method can be improved as the algorithm register gains more momentum, the knowledge increases and processes behind the algorithm registers develop further. Moreover, future research could look into aligning this perception or changing parts of the algorithm register to further support responsible AI. Finally, this paper provides researchers in the field of method engineering with a guide for developing and recommending reference methods. While the context of algorithm registers is applied in this paper, our approach to construct a reference method can also be applied to other domains.

Acknowledgements. We are thankful to the experts we interviewed, for their time and knowledge. Sergio España is supported by a María Zambrano grant of the Spanish Ministry of Universities, co-funded by the Next Generation EU European Recovery Plan.

References

1. van der Aalst, W.M.P., Dreiling, A., Gottschalk, F., Rosemann, M., Jansen-Vullers, M.H.: Configurable process models as a basis for reference modeling. In: Bussler, C.J., Haller, A. (eds.) BPM 2005. LNCS, vol. 3812, pp. 512–518. Springer, Heidelberg (2006). https://doi.org/10.1007/11678564_47
2. Akinsola, J., Adeagbo, M., Oladapo, K., Akinsehinde, S., Onipede, F.: Artificial intelligence emergence in disruptive technology. In: Computational Intelligence and Data Sciences: Paradigms in Biomedical Engineering, pp. 63–90 (2022)
3. Arellano-Gault, D., Lepore, W.: Transparency reforms in the public sector: beyond the new economics of organization. Organ. Stud. **32**(8), 1029–1050 (2011)

4. Beelen, L., Jansen, S., Overbeek, S.: Are you of value to me? A partner selection reference method for software ecosystem orchestrators. Sci. Comput. Program. **214**, 102733 (2022). https://doi.org/10.1016/j.scico.2021.102733. https://www.sciencedirect.com/science/article/pii/S016764232100126X

5. Benbya, H., Davenport, T.H., Pachidi, S.: Artificial intelligence in organizations: current state and future opportunities. MIS Q. Executive **19**(4) (2020)

6. Brinkkemper, S.: Method engineering: engineering of information systems development methods and tools. Inf. Softw. Technol. **38**(4), 275–280 (1996)

7. Brynjolfsson, E., Mcafee, A.: Artificial intelligence, for real. Harv. Bus. Rev. **1**, 1–31 (2017)

8. Cammers-Goodwin, S., Van Stralen, N.: Making data visible in public space. McGill GLSA Res. Ser. **1**(1), 1–32 (2021). https://doi.org/10.26443/glsars.v1i1.120

9. Cath, C., Jansen, F.: Dutch comfort: the limits of AI governance through municipal registers (2021)

10. Cubric, M.: Drivers, barriers and social considerations for AI adoption in business and management: a tertiary study. Technol. Soc. **62**, 101257 (2020)

11. Dul, J., Hak, T.: Case Study Methodology in Business Research. Routledge (2007)

12. Dutch Government: Het algoritmeregister van de nederlandse overheid (in Dutch: The algorithm register of the Dutch government). https://algoritmeregister.org

13. Dutch Government: I-strategie rijk 2021-2025 (in Dutch: National i-strategy 2021–2025) (2021)

14. Dwivedi, Y.K., et al.: Artificial intelligence (AI): multidisciplinary perspectives on emerging challenges, opportunities, and agenda for research, practice and policy. Int. J. Inf. Manag. **57**, 101994 (2021)

15. Ebert, C., Duarte, C.H.C.: Digital transformation. IEEE Softw. **35**(4), 16–21 (2018)

16. Eisenhardt, K.: Building theories from case study research. Acad. Manag. Rev. 532–550 (1989)

17. Fettke, P., Loos, P., Zwicker, J.: Business process reference models: survey and classification. In: Bussler, C.J., Haller, A. (eds.) BPM 2005. LNCS, vol. 3812, pp. 469–483. Springer, Heidelberg (2006). https://doi.org/10.1007/11678564_44

18. Fjeld, J., Achten, N., Hilligoss, H., Nagy, A., Srikumar, M.: Principled artificial intelligence: mapping consensus in ethical and rights-based approaches to principles for AI. Berkman Klein Center Research Publication (2020-1) (2020)

19. Floridi, L.: Artificial intelligence as a public service: learning from Amsterdam and Helsinki. Philos. Technol. **33**(4), 451–456 (2020). https://doi.org/10.1007/s13347-020-00434-3

20. Foerster-Metz, U.S., Marquardt, K., Golowko, N., Kompalla, A., Hell, C.: Digital transformation and its implications on organizational behavior. J. EU Res. Bus. **2018**(3), 1–14 (2018)

21. Garousi, V., Felderer, M., Mäntylä, M.: Guidelines for including grey literature and conducting multivocal literature reviews in software engineering. Inf. Softw. Technol. **106**, 101–121 (2019)

22. Girasa, R.: Artificial Intelligence as a Disruptive Technology: Economic Transformation and Government Regulation. Springer, Cham (2020)

23. Greene, D., Hoffman, A., Stark, L.: Better, nicer, clearer, fairer: a critical assessment of the movement for ethical artificial intelligence and machine learning. In: HICSS 2019, pp. 2122–2131 (2019)

24. Haataja, M., Van de Fliert, L., Rautio, P.: Public AI registers: realising AI transparency and civic participation in government use of AI (2020)

25. Hagendorff, T.: The ethics of AI ethics: an evaluation of guidelines. Minds Mach. (Dordr) **30**(1), 99–120 (2020)
26. Harmsen, A., Brinkkemper, J., Oei, J.: Situational Method Engineering for Information System Project Approaches. University of Twente (1994)
27. Herderscheê, G.: Ruim 1.100 kinderen van gedupeerden toeslagenaffaire werden uit huis geplaatst (in Dutch: More than 1,100 children of victims of the benefits affair were removed from their homes) (2021)
28. Hong, S., van den Goor, G., Brinkkemper, S.: A formal approach to the comparison of object-oriented analysis and design methodologies. In: Proceedings of the 26th HICSS, vol. 4, pp. 689–698. IEEE (1993)
29. Houtzager, D., Verbeek, S., Terlouw, A.: Gelijk recht doen: Deelrapport sociale zekerheid (in Dutch: Doing equal justice: Social security partial report) (2022)
30. Ingrams, A., Kaufmann, W., Jacobs, D.: In AI we trust? Citizen perceptions of AI in government decision making. Policy Internet **14**(2), 390–409 (2022)
31. Kamminga, R.J.: Kamerstukken: Verslag houdende een lijst van vragen en antwoorden (36200-vii-58) (in Dutch: Parliamentary documents: Report containing a list of questions and answers) (2022). https://www.tweedekamer.nl/kamerstukken/detail?id=2022Z21400&did=2022D46208
32. Kitsios, F., Kamariotou, M.: Artificial intelligence and business strategy towards digital transformation: a research agenda. Sustainability **13**(4), 2025 (2021)
33. Küster, J.M., Koehler, J., Ryndina, K.: Improving business process models with reference models in business-driven development. In: Eder, J., Dustdar, S. (eds.) BPM 2006. LNCS, vol. 4103, pp. 35–44. Springer, Heidelberg (2006). https://doi.org/10.1007/11837862_5
34. Madan, R., Ashok, M.: Ai adoption and diffusion in public administration: a systematic literature review and future research agenda. Gov. Inf. Q. **40**(1), 101774 (2023)
35. Mäntymäki, M., Minkkinen, M., Birkstedt, T., Viljanen, M.: Defining organizational AI governance. AI Ethics **2**(4), 603–609 (2022)
36. Ministry of Justice and Security: Richtlijnen voor het toepassen van algoritmen door overheden en publieksvoorlichting over data-analyses (in Dutch: Guidelines for the application of algorithms by governments and public information about data analyses) (2021)
37. Mittelstadt, B.: Principles alone cannot guarantee ethical AI. Nat. Mach. Intell. **1**(11), 501–507 (2019)
38. Murad, M.: Beyond the black box: enabling meaningful transparency of algorithmic decision-making systems through public registers (2021)
39. Nouws, S., Janssen, M., Dobbe, R.: Dismantling digital cages: examining design practices for public algorithmic systems. In: Janssen, M., et al. (eds.) EGOV 2022. LNCS, vol. 13391, pp. 307–322. Springer, Cham (2022). https://doi.org/10.1007/978-3-031-15086-9_20
40. Raji, I.D., et al.: Closing the AI accountability gap: defining an end-to-end framework for internal algorithmic auditing. In: ACM FAccT 2020, pp. 33–44 (2020)
41. Ralyté, J., Rolland, C.: An assembly process model for method engineering. In: Dittrich, K.R., Geppert, A., Norrie, M.C. (eds.) CAiSE 2001. LNCS, vol. 2068, pp. 267–283. Springer, Heidelberg (2001). https://doi.org/10.1007/3-540-45341-5_18
42. Schraagen, J., Lopez, S., Schneider, C., Schneider, V, Tönjes, S., Wiechmann, F.: The role of transparency and explainability in automated systems. In: HFES Annual Meeting, vol. 65, pp. 27–31. SAGE (2021)

43. Schuitemaker, N., Van Vliet, M., Brinkkemper, S., España, Van de Weerd, I.: Transparency and accountability in an ever-changing world: a framework for algorithm registers in public organizations. Technical report (2024). https://drive.google.com/file/d/1XP6soWI7EQn6oiy560YHu5BNfFzeL8pK. Submitted to OSF Preprints after acceptance
44. Shenton, A.: Strategies for ensuring trustworthiness in qualitative research projects. Educ. Inf. **22**(2), 63–75 (2004)
45. Toreini, E., Aitken, M., Coopamootoo, K., Elliott, K., Zelaya, C.G., Van Moorsel, A.: The relationship between trust in AI and trustworthy machine learning technologies. In: Proceedings of the 2020 ACM FAccT, pp. 272–283 (2020)
46. Van Huffelen, A.: Kamerbrief over het algoritmeregister (in Dutch: Letter to parliament about the algorithm register) (2022). https://www.rijksoverheid.nl/documenten/kamerstukken/2022/12/21/kamerbrief-over-het-algoritmeregister
47. Van Vliet, M., Schuitemaker, N., Brinkkemper, S., Espana, S.: Defining and implementing algorithm registers: an organizational perspective (2023). Manuscript submitted for publication
48. Veale, M., Zuiderveen Borgesius, F.: Demystifying the draft EU artificial intelligence act–analysing the good, the bad, and the unclear elements of the proposed approach. Comput. Law Rev. Int. **22**(4), 97–112 (2021)
49. van de Weerd, I., Brinkkemper, S.: Meta-modeling for situational analysis and design methods. In: Handbook of Research on Modern Systems Analysis and Design Technologies and Applications, pp. 35–54. IGI Global (2009)
50. van de Weerd, I., de Weerd, S., Brinkkemper, S.: Developing a reference method for game production by method comparison. In: Ralyté, J., Brinkkemper, S., Henderson-Sellers, B. (eds.) Situational Method Engineering: Fundamentals and Experiences. ITIFIP, vol. 244, pp. 313–327. Springer, Boston (2007). https://doi.org/10.1007/978-0-387-73947-2_24
51. Weiner, J.: Why AI/Data Science Projects Fail: How to Avoid Project Pitfalls. Springer, Cham (2022)
52. Werkgroep Algoritmeregister: Algoritme rrgister. https://algoritmeregister.org
53. Westenberger, J., Schuler, K., Schlegel, D.: Failure of AI projects: understanding the critical factors. Procedia Comput. Sci. **196**, 69–76 (2022)
54. Wieringa, R.: Design Science Methodology for Information Systems and Software Engineering. Springer, Cham (2014)
55. Wirtz, B.W., Weyerer, J.C., Geyer, C.: Artificial intelligence and the public sector–applications and challenges. Int. J. Public Adm. **42**(7), 596–615 (2019)
56. Yin, R.: Case Study Research and Applications: Design and Methods. Sage (2017)

Requirements for a Digital Twin
for Energy, Social, and Governance Data
of Commercial Buildings

Joseph Chungath and Simon Hacks$^{(\boxtimes)}$ (iD)

Department of Computer and Systems Sciences, Stockholm University,
Stockholm, Sweden
`simon.hacks@dsv.su.se`

Abstract. A Green building is well-managed in its technical and managerial senses. To achieve a Green Building standard, real estate developers should have frameworks in place to monitor and provide information regarding the sustainable aspects of the building. Energy, Social, and Governance (ESG) data is related to the impact made by a building during its operations. A standardized and scalable digital twin to monitor this data will allow developers to achieve a Green Building status easily. This work aims to gather the requirements for such a digital twin that allows the management of the ESG data of a commercial building, enabling real estate developers to monitor and manage the building more sustainably with improved transparency.

Keywords: Green Building · Energy, Social, and Governance Data · Commercial Real Estate · Building Information Model

1 Introduction

Global warming is one of humankind's most significant threats, caused by global carbon emissions [17]. The building sector consumes 40 percent of all energy and emits up to 30 percent of the greenhouse emissions [23]. Thus, governments and institutions should quantify emissions to inform climate actions [2]. Commercial buildings are one significant contributor to this emission. At the same time, there is minimal source for the environmental performance of these buildings [19].

Due to these reasons, more investors are gaining green building certifications as part of their Corporate Social Responsibility (CSR) [16]. In fact, for every 10 percent decrease in energy consumption of buildings, there is a 1 percent increase in the value of the building [16]. Moreover, a building with a green label positively affects the rent. Several Green Building Rating Systems (GBRS) are used to achieve the "green building" status to verify the relative sustainability of their projects [24]. Commercial buildings' most popular rating systems include Energy STAR, LEED (Leadership in Energy and Environmental Design), Green Globes, BREEAM (Building Research Establishment Environmental Assessment Method), and HQE (High-Quality Environmental Standard) [24,25].

H. van der Aa et al. (Eds.): BPMDS 2024/EMMSAD 2024, LNBIP 511, pp. 341–351, 2024.
https://doi.org/10.1007/978-3-031-61007-3_25

Collecting relevant data for these rating systems must be carried out in every property. This process can be time-consuming and repetitive if carried out manually. While smart utility meters exist, they are not often used [32]. Issues like varying measuring equipment in portfolios are also challenging, as the capabilities of each piece of equipment may vary. This limits data availability, and decisions take longer. This could be tackled by standards to collect, store, and process data. This work explores the requirements for a standardized Digital Twin model to manage commercial buildings' Energy, Social, and Governance (ESG) data. A digital twin is a model that not only simulates the behavior of the physical entity based on real-time status data but also makes operational instructions to the entity so that the product can be controlled under guidance [31]. Accordingly, we formulate our research question:

"What are the requirements for a scalable Digital Twin model to effectively manage ESG data in commercial buildings?"

The rest of this work is structured as follows. The next section presents the background of this work needed to understand the domain in which the digital twin shall be developed. Next, the research method is presented, and interviews with employees of a case company are conducted. This is followed by presenting the results and their discussion before concluding the work.

2   Background

2.1   Building Information Systems

While monitoring energy consumption is relevant to real estate developers, the mechanisms are relatively new. Most companies manually collect such data, leading to lower analysis frequencies [27]. This is one of the reasons why digitalizing the real estate industry has become a crucial requirement [22]. To this end, Business Information Models (BIM) are used to visualize geo-referenced data.

The Associated General Contractors of America defines "a building information model [as] the process of generating and managing a building information model through the use of three-dimensional, intelligent design information" [1]. Using BIM will increase the efficiency of building processes by reducing the laborious and error-prone manual data collection [8]. A BIM is managed at the building level and provides a holistic overview of the building's operations.

Building Performance Analysis (BPA) is aimed at analyzing the operational performance of a building, focusing on sustainability data and tenant satisfaction. Implementing a BIM can help simulate different iterations to realize the most optimal configurations and input required [33].

2.2   Adoption of Building Information Systems

The COVID crisis resulted in an accelerated adoption of digital technology in the real estate industry. However, 58 % of them express a lack of integration of existing resources [6]. The current real estate ecosystem utilizes a siloed approach based on software from different external vendors. One challenge related to adopting a BIM system is the lack of standards [12] causing interoperability issues [15]. While few global and regional standards exist, like the IFC (Industry Foundation Classes) data model, these models have become overly complex and have resulted in the lack of semantic integrity of data in the models [3].

Bolshakov et al. [7] analyzed the adoption of BIM in facility, property, and asset management, highlighting its benefits, such as improved location, real-time data access, and maintenance optimization. Digital twins display limited, actionable data to avoid confusion despite the potential for data overload. Such systems reduced energy consumption by 30 % and improved the prediction of mechanical failures in large properties. Asset management has become more predictable, with modern, improved assets increasing property value. Automated systems reduce costs and enhance profits, while real-time data accelerates decision-making and meets investor demands for operational data involvement.

Property management ensures the property's tenants have the best experiences. The social aspects of a property are also collected and analyzed. Research in this area is limited but is fostered by increasing working from home due to COVID. Space utilization has become even more crucial lately. More and more tenants are scaling down their spaces due to lesser space utilization. Monitoring such parameters can lead to better predictability of such situations [21].

3   Research Method

Design science research (DSR) is a research approach that seeks to design and evaluate an artifact. This methodology is appropriate when the aim is to develop IT systems and improve IT practices [20]. Hence, DSR is the most suitable option for this research. The design process will include gathering requirements, understanding different edge cases, and finally, realizing the artifact in a concrete organization. This work reports on gathering the requirements.

DSR has various variants based on the methods used and outcomes expected from the research. Following Venable et al. [29], we opted for Action Design Research (ADR) [26] as the final artifact developed is related to an industry problem. The research outcomes will be verified by intervention within an industry client and improved by feedback from their side. The research evaluation will be ex-ante as the feedback will be based on forecasts.

Semi-structured interviews were conducted with relevant stakeholders to meet the requirements for a digital twin model. These stakeholders were the heads of departments from a leading real estate company managing assets totaling over 8 million square feet. The organization is based in Boston, USA, and owns over 20 commercial properties in over six countries. A complete list of participating interviewees is presented in Table 1. The questions for the interview were framed in such a way that understanding their involvement in developing the digital twin concerning their job roles was essential. The questions were also aimed at understanding each use case once the system is designed.

The meetings were partially in-person, if possible; otherwise, via Zoom. Each interview lasted close to 30 min. The meetings started with a self-introduction

Table 1. Interview details

Identifier	Role in Organization
IP 1	Head of Technical Facilities (Sweden)
IP 2	Director of Sustainability (Boston)
IP 3	Director of Business Operations (San Fransisco)
IP 4	VP of Technology (Dublin/Boston)
IP 5	Director of Investments (Sweden)
IP 6	Head of Technical Facilities for Feedback (Sweden)

Table 2. Identified Requirements for the Digital Twin

Requirement	Description	Inter.	Lit.
Centralized Data Management	The system must aggregate and manage data from diverse sources, ensuring data integrity and accessibility. This integration should be automated	IP2, IP3	[9,34]
Real-time Data Processing	Ability to process and analyze data in real-time to support decision-making and operational efficiency	IP2, IP3	[4,28]
Data Security and Privacy	Implement robust security measures to protect sensitive tenant and operational data	IP3, IP5	[13]
Interoperability	Ensure compatibility with various BIM and external data sources without compromising data integrity	IP2, IP3, IP6	[10]
Optimization	The digital twin must identify potential in energy reduction and be integrated with the utility provider	IP1, IP2, IP3	

of the interviewers and interviewees, followed by the purpose of the meeting and the research goals. The interview questions were then posed to the interviewees, and they were given time to lead the discussions to areas they found were more critical. The interview transcripts were cleaned from confidential data and then analyzed by two researchers independently using a qualitative analysis [14]: (1) Familiarizing with the data; (2) Generating initial codes; (3) Searching for themes; (4) Reviewing themes; (4) Defining and naming themes; (5) Producing the report. The analysis results using thematic methods on the interview transcripts are then used to identify the theoretical requirements to build the digital twin.

4   Results

We identify five requirements for an ESG Data Digital Twin for commercial buildings (c.f. Table 2) that are further detailed following.

4.1   Baseline

The first step towards designing the digital twin was understanding the current operations and processes and the stakeholders involved. The interview questions aimed to understand the existing IT landscape and the requirements for adopting the new model. Understanding the pace of digitalization was crucial to gathering the requirements. According to IP5:

> "I think the digitalization is happening. At different paces in the real estate industry, depending on the domain, in certain areas, it's happening very quickly, particularly around sustainability and construction. That is primarily because up until now, there have been a number of property technology companies that have tried to offer a one-size-fits-all solution".

Even though digitalization is happening at a decent pace, it is often not developed by organizations organically; instead, different solutions are bought to fit individual problems. This software is usually standalone and carries fewer functionalities for collaborating or sharing data with other vendor software.

This type of siloed approach led to non-compatibility between the different existing systems. The non-compatibility could range from just different types of measurement systems used to non-functionality due to fewer provisions to share data. Spending thousands of dollars of investment on third-party vendors' software and even more on consulting expenses to connect these systems has become a norm in the industry. Since the particular organization operates in different regions, the connections between these regional systems become even more troublesome. For example, every building/property uses a very different BIM. Different vendors develop these systems and do not follow a fixed framework for the data that would be stored.

The systems being used differ from building to building and have various levels of sophistication. This is because some of these systems were constructed years ago, and the system they use was never upgraded. In other cases, the building may have been acquired from other developers. This means that accessing data from these systems will be a painfully long process or might not even be possible. IP3, who works on designing standardized business processes at the corporate level, mentioned that she does not even possess a list of different systems the organization uses:

> "(We) don't have a list of the BIM systems being used at each property"
> - IP3

The company does not use a fixed solution or system to manage ESG data. Most operations are carried out by feeding data into Excel sheets and sending them to the required stakeholders.

4.2   Drivers for Change

The organization had been comfortable working for an extended period before moving to modern systems. One primary reason driving the internal transformation was how companies' carbon goals had become prevalent. These carbon goals were planned in gradual increments, with the final goal of becoming carbon neutral. This goal required the organization to monitor the progress. GRESB benchmarking is done individually once every year for each property. The need to file this data repetitively decreased the efficiency of the business process.

Another way the system would bring value to the organization is by managing utility bills and identifying equipment replacements that can help reduce energy consumption. Currently, the process is very manual and requires people to read the meter values manually from each piece of equipment and update documents.

Finally, once the data collection process becomes more uniform, actionable business insights could be derived from this data. The organization can use real-time analytics to detect energy surges and equipment working in less desirable conditions. The corporation will also understand how the portfolio performs and how much value the assets produce. Using a digital twin makes the process more automated, and hidden inefficiencies can surface in the current processes.

4.3   Requirement Gathering

The first important requirement was to connect the system to different data sources, including the organization's ERP system. The ERP system will provide the digital twin with more information about the properties, tenants, and rental data. The second important data source that was identified was utility consumption data. This would include data from machinery used in shared spaces and tenant-specific consumption data. Predictive maintenance, intelligent allocation of resources, and sustainability surveillance are some of the use cases for storing this data. Most tenant utility data are updated manually. Ideally, the possibility of seeing this data on a real-time basis will make the supervision easier.

While dealing with data, an important consideration is protecting the intellectual and private data of the organization and its tenants. Some of the steps taken to ensure this are stripping out tenants. Data transfer from the different data sources must be done using a secure connection to prevent data leakage.

Normalizing the data to a single format for further analysis is essential. This is crucial as assets from different regions may have different measurement systems. Accordingly, data should have two views: corporate and regional.

4.4   Change Management

It is important to navigate change and ease the adoption among the users in the organization. The interviewees explained some methods they would use to adopt the new digital twin in the organization and how to make the tool an integral part of their daily processes. One of the interviewees identified that

"The biggest challenge is getting people to understand the importance of the tool and why they should want to use it and keep it up to date." - IP3

This interviewee also identified that the system can only reach its full potential if the right inputs are fed regularly. This way, the system users will have the platform ready for use and actionable.

The second task in managing change is identifying the players and making them understand how the digital twin can bring value to them. If the value is not reflected accordingly, the chances of adopting the tool would be reduced:

"Because we have so many different players, we need to help them understand why this tool matters for them. If there's nothing in it for the users, they won't use the tool. And if they don't use the tool and they're not keeping certain things updated, that has to be done manually. Then it's useless" - IP3

Finally, to manage the change, one should follow a gradual and steady incremental approach to achieve adoption throughout the organization. The interviewees explained that the process would be to initially roll out the digital twin in only certain assets and then implement it in further assets once the issues are fixed. This is done to manage the manual adoption challenges and address issues related to building custom connectors for each property.

5   Discussion

5.1   Baseline

According to the interviews, most digitalization projects are influenced by a few early adopter organizations. Technologies get faster adopted in the European real estate industry [30], increasing process effectiveness through automation, scale, and uniformity [4]. While this digitalization is happening rapidly, IP5 mentions the need for a more centralized approach as most current solutions have a siloed approach to reduce the localized complexity of systems [9]. Most system architectures were not designed to be discretely operating, but over time, led to the compartmentalization of such systems [5]. The challenge of continually using such systems would need new ways of thinking and technologies to address future problems, which eventually adds to the technical debt.

Developing a centralized digital twin faces technical issues like data incompatibility, security risks like data leaks, and business disruption when different applications are involved. A solution is to develop custom data connectors that fetch data from these systems and store them in a central data warehouse in a standardized format for further processing.

5.2   Drivers for Change

The interviews gave an understanding of three primary change drivers. The most important reason is to reduce carbon emissions. The real estate and related construction industries are some of the most significant contributors to carbon emissions in the world [11], and more and more organizations are setting carbon emission goals in their strategic visions.

To enable landlords and real estate investors to achieve carbon neutrality, specific steps are recommended [18]. Moreover, the organizations should be more transparent about reporting this data by increasing the submetering of buildings and tenants' energy and emissions. While benchmarking and certifications can increase reporting transparency and help make better decisions, the process is often repetitive and time-consuming. It was mentioned that data was collected manually. This process is affected by delays in data collection. This is yet another reason why having a digital twin is essential. Such a digital twin would oversee data without or with minimum manual supervision. The repetitive processes could be automated. Such a system also positively impacts data availability as the data will be collected more quickly.

5.3   Requirement Gathering

A requirement mentioned for the digital twin is retrieving data from multiple data sources. The ERP system provides information about the leased spaces and tenant details. Specific details like the type of leased space, materials used for construction, etc., are also available in the ERP system. Other data sources include BIMs, which could be different in every building. The system should be able to access the data from the BIM effortlessly. The BIM would provide energy consumption, heating, and cooling usage data. Some modern-day BIMs also allow for connection to IoT sensor data, providing information about space utilization, air quality measurement, and energy consumed for lighting. In combination, these data are then utilized for simulations to optimize the building consumption, thus enabling important benefits of a digital twin. Utility data is another essential information that must be warehoused provided by energy providers. The billing is done chiefly weekly or monthly based on region. Potentially, the system would aim to provide insights from the tenant level.

Since the tenant data is sensible, the digital twin should prevent leaks. This could not just affect the trust of the tenants but can also result in attracting hefty fines from the governing bodies. Most real estate organizations cannot develop the digital twin internally due to lacking technical knowledge and resources, so they may have to depend on third-party software products. Careful due diligence should be taken on the vendors and consultants to prevent leakage. The system should allow the creation of reports and deliver them to the certification and benchmarking bodies in an automated manner.

5.4   Change Management

The interviews highlighted that the most crucial challenge when implementing the digital twin is making the users understand its value. Since using the digital twin adds more steps to the stakeholders' day-to-day activities and omits specific older tasks, its value needs to be justified to achieve maximum stakeholder involvement. The interviewees suggest a slow and structured gradual adoption. The process should be iterative, the stakeholders should accept continuous feedback, and changes must be implemented to make the digital twin more effective.

6   Conclusions

The real estate industry significantly contributes to carbon emissions, and organizations are setting goals to reduce their impact. Benchmarking tools are helping to track progress and identify opportunities for decarbonization.

To measure and monitor the impacts, a centralized and integrated solution is essential for efficiency, accuracy, and faster decision-making. A centralized system is preferable as it can automate data collection, improve data availability, and enable real-time decision-making. Even more so if the organizations have multiple properties requiring different management levels. This study elicits the requirements for building such a centralized digital twin. The work contributes to digital twin technology, sustainable real estate management, and information systems integration, offering a comprehensive perspective on applying advanced technologies to enhance sustainability and efficiency in commercial buildings.

This research has limitations as only one organization was studied in detail. In the future, we aim to explore the requirements of other similar organizations and carry out more systematic literature reviews of published works. The research also seeks to create an actual implementation of such a system once the requirements elicitation process is finished.

References

1. AGC: Building information modelling (2023). https://www.agc.org/education/building-information-modeling/building-information-modeling. Accessed September 2023
2. Albert, O.O.K., Marianne, T., Jonathan, L., Nino, J.L., Dario, C.: Tracking the carbon emissions of Denmark's five regions from a producer and consumer perspective. Ecol. Econ. **177**, 106778 (2020)
3. Amor, R., Jiang, Y., Chen, X.: BIM in 2007–are we there yet? In: Proceedings of CIB W78 Conference on Bringing ITC Knowledge to Work, pp. 26–29 (2007)
4. Andrew, B.: Proptech 3.0, the Future of, Real Estate. University of Oxford (2017)
5. Bannister, F.: Dismantling the silos: extracting new value from it investments in public administration. Inf. Syst. J. **11**(1), 65–84 (2001)
6. Bolden: What you need to know about property technology adoption. EY (2021). https://www.ey.com/en_us/esg-in-real-estate-hospitality-and-construction/what-you-need-to-know-about-property-technology-adoption
7. Bolshakov, N., Badenko, V., Yadykin, V., Celani, A.: As-built BIM in real estate management: the change of paradigm in digital transformation of economy. In: IOP Conference Series: Materials Science and Engineering, vol. 940 (2020)
8. Borrmann, A., König, M., Koch, C., Beetz, J.: Building information modeling: why? what? how? In: Borrmann, A., König, M., Koch, C., Beetz, J. (eds.) Building Information Modeling. Springer, Cham (2018). https://doi.org/10.1007/978-3-319-92862-3_1

9. Bygstad, B., Hanseth, O., Truong Le, D.: From it silos to integrated solutions. A study in e-health complexity (2015)
10. Calimbahin, C.M., Pancho-Festin, S., Pedrasa, J.R.: Mitigating data integrity attacks in building automation systems using denoising autoencoders. In: International Conference on Ubiquitous and Future Networks (2019)
11. Chua, S.C., Oh, T.H.: Green progress and prospect in Malaysia. Renew. Sustain. Energy Rev. **15**(6), 2850–2861 (2011)
12. Criminale, A., Langar, S.: Challenges with BIM implementation: a review of literature. In: 53rd ASC Annual International Conference, pp. 329–335 (2017)
13. Dees, K., Rahman, S.: Enhancing infrastructure security in real estate. arXiv Computers and Society (2015)
14. Denscombe, M.: EBOOK: The Good Research Guide: For Small-Scale Social Research Projects. McGraw-Hill Education, UK (2017)
15. Edirisinghe, R., London, K., et al.: Comparative analysis of international and national level BIM standardization efforts and BIM adoption. In: Proceedings of the 32nd CIB W78 Conference, pp. 27–29 (2015)
16. Eichholtz, P., Kok, N., Quigley, J.M.: Doing well by doing good? Green office buildings. Am. Econ. Rev. **100**(5), 2492–2509 (2010)
17. Huisingh, D., Zhang, Z., Moore, J.C., Qiao, Q., Li, Q.: Recent advances in carbon emissions reduction. J. Clean. Prod. **103**, 1–12 (2015)
18. Initiative, C.B.: Aligning buildings with the Paris climate agreement: insights and developments from the green bond market. Climate Bonds Initiative (2020)
19. Kahn, M.E., Kok, N., Quigley, J.M.: Carbon emissions from the commercial building sector. J. Public Econ. **113**, 1–12 (2014)
20. March, S.T., Smith, G.F.: Design and natural science research on information technology. Decis. Support Syst. **15**(4), 251–266 (1995)
21. Mattarocci, G., Scimone, X.: The evolution of proptech. In: Mattarocci, G., Scimone, X. (eds.) The New Era of Real Estate, pp. 7–44. Springer, Heidelberg (2022). https://doi.org/10.1007/978-3-031-16731-7_2
22. Peeters, M.: The added value of smart product-service systems to real estate developments. Ph.D. thesis, University of Antwerp (2021)
23. Programme, U.N.E.: Buildings and climate change: summary for decision makers (2009). https://wedocs.unep.org/20.500.11822/32152
24. Reeder, L.: Guide to Green Building Rating Systems: Understanding LEED, Green Globes, Energy Star, the National Green Building Standard, and more, vol. 12. Wiley (2010)
25. Sánchez Cordero, A., Gómez Melgar, S., Andújar Márquez, J.M.: Green building rating systems and the new framework level (s). Energies **13**(1), 66 (2019)
26. Sein, M.K., Henfridsson, O., Purao, S., Rossi, M., Lindgren, R.: Action design research. MIS Q. 37–56 (2011)
27. bin Syed Mustapa, S.A.H., Adnan, H., Jusoff, K.: Facility management challenges and opportunities in the Malaysian property sector. J. Sustain. Dev. **1**(2), P79 (2008)
28. Yu, T., Wang, X.: Real-time data analytics in internet of things systems. In: Tian, Y.C., Levy, D.C. (eds.) Handbook of Real-Time Computing, pp. 541–568. Springer, Singapore. (2022). https://doi.org/10.1007/978-981-287-251-7_38
29. Venable, J.R., Pries-Heje, J., Baskerville, R.L.: Choosing a design science research methodology (2017)
30. Vigren, O., Kadefors, A., Eriksson, K.: Digitalization, innovation capabilities and absorptive capacity in the Swedish real estate ecosystem. Facilities **40**(15/16), 89–106 (2022)

31. Wang, W., Hu, H., Zhang, J., Hu, Z.: Digital twin-based framework for green building maintenance system. In: IEEE International Conference on Industrial Engineering and Engineering Management, pp. 1301–1305 (2020)
32. Wang, Y., Chen, Q., Hong, T., Kang, C.: Review of smart meter data analytics. IEEE Trans. Smart Grid **10**(3), 3125–3148 (2018)
33. Wong, J.K.W., Zhou, J.: Enhancing environmental sustainability over building life cycles through green BIM. Autom. Constr. **57**, 156–165 (2015)
34. Yesin, V.I., Karpinski, M., Yesina, M., Vilihura, V.V., Veselska, O., Wieclaw, L.: Approach to managing data from diverse sources. In: Intelligent Data Acquisition and Advanced Computing Systems: Technology and Applications (2019)

Enterprise Modeling (EMMSAD 2024)

Understanding Capability Progression: A Model for Defining Maturity Levels for Organizational Capabilities

Ginger Korsten$^{(\boxtimes)}$ ⓘ, Baris Ozkan ⓘ, Banu Aysolmaz ⓘ, Daan Mul,
and Oktay Turetken ⓘ

Eindhoven University of Technology, De Rondom 70, 5612 AP Eindhoven, The Netherlands
g.korsten@tue.nl

Abstract. The pressure for organizations to gain and keep their competitive advantage necessitates continuous assessment and improvement of their capabilities. Maturity modeling has emerged as a management approach to guide organizations in developing and improving their capabilities, following a structured path for improvement within a specific domain. Existing research lacks a theoretically grounded model for defining maturity levels, particularly concerning organizational capabilities. This paper addresses this gap by introducing a model for defining maturity levels for organizational capabilities. Drawing on the Dreyfus model of skill acquisition, the model defines the characteristics of organizational capabilities across six maturity levels. The model is developed following design science research and demonstrated and evaluated in the development of a data analytics maturity model. The findings of the expert survey provided positive evidence regarding the validity, relevance, completeness, clarity, and utility. We emphasize the distinction between capability-based and process-based maturity levels and propose our model as a tool to support the development of capability-based maturity models in various domains.

Keywords: Capability Maturity Models · Organizational Capabilities · Maturity Levels

1 Introduction

Assessing and developing organizational capabilities is essential for organizations to enhance their performance [1]. Given the importance of organizational capabilities, many researchers have investigated the elements that form an organizational capability [2]. An organizational capability defines how people and resources are brought together to accomplish work [3]. They represent the ability of an organization to join resources and information to support a strategic goal [4].

Maturity modeling has emerged as a management approach to guide organizations in developing and improving their organizational capabilities regarding a target domain [5]. A maturity model consists of a sequence of maturity levels for a class of objects. It represents an anticipated, desired, or typical evolution path of these objects shaped as discrete stages [5, 6]. In characterizing maturity, maturity models can take different concepts as their units of analysis, such as processes, capabilities, projects, products, or the organization as a whole [7]. One widely recognized example of a maturity model is the Capability Maturity Model Integration (CMMI), which utilizes a *process* maturity perspective with maturity levels such as initial, repeatable, defined, managed, and optimizing, which are common in process improvement practice (SEI, 2010). A *capability-based-maturity model,* such as the BPM Capability Framework [8], is a model with an organizational capability as its unit of analysis.

It is important to align the maturity level characterizations with the underlying concept that a maturity model is built upon (i.e., process, capability, organization). However, numerous capability-based maturity models have incorporated maturity level characterizations originally devised for *processes* [9], such as the BPM Capability Framework [8], CPMM [10], SAFeMM [11], and ADA-CMM [12]. This approach poses a significant challenge, as capabilities often evolve differently from processes, potentially leading to a misalignment in reflecting their true progression. Furthermore, existing research lacks a theoretically grounded model for defining maturity level characteristics for organizational capabilities, which is imperative for ensuring that a maturity model captures all relevant indicators of a certain maturity level [13].

Therefore, the main objective of this research is to develop a *generic and theoretically grounded maturity level characterization model for organizational capabilities.* The model provides capability maturity level characteristics and indicators and can be used as a template to facilitate the development of effective capability-based maturity models across various domains.

We utilized the Dreyfus model of skill acquisition [14] as the basis for defining capability maturity levels for organizations. We adapted the characteristics of the Dreyfus model per level to the organizational context and provided maturity level descriptions for organizational capabilities. The well-established and widely recognized nature of the Dreyfus model in skill acquisition contributes to the theoretical foundation of our model. In developing the model, we followed the design science research (DSR) paradigm [15], adopting the research process proposed by Peffers et al. [17]. Accordingly, we identified the problem, research gap, and solution objectives. Next, we iteratively designed and developed a capability maturity level model. We applied the model in developing a capability-based maturity model for advanced data analytics. We evaluated the capability maturity level characterization model with a survey among 10 experts; the results confirm its validity, relevance, completeness, clarity, and utility.

The paper is organized as follows: Sect. 2 provides the theoretical background for organizational capabilities and the capability maturity level model. Section 3 outlines the research design, while Sect. 4 presents the model. Section 5 presents an application of the model. The results of the evaluation and conclusion are presented in Sect. 6 and Sect. 7, respectively.

2   Background and Related Work

This section introduces the concepts of maturity, organizational capabilities, and individual skill development, which are relevant to this study.

Maturity can be defined as a state of being complete, perfect, or ready [17]. In general, there are two approaches to the development of maturity levels: the top-down approach and the bottom-up approach. The top-down approach initiates with defining maturity levels across capabilities, which are later articulated to level characteristics and assessment items. This approach, as exemplified by [6], establishes a framework where the levels guide the subsequent detailing of characteristics and assessments. In contrast, the bottom-up approach, as illustrated by [20], starts with the identification of level characteristics or assessment items, which are then grouped to derive levels, presenting an overall perspective on the evolutionary path of maturity.

According to [4], an organizational capability has the following elements: resource, (business) goal, (enterprise) context, process, knowledge, and actor/role. To realize a capability, *resources* are needed. These represent all the elements required for the capability to achieve its goals, such as technologies, HR, budget, and personnel. As an organization represents a goal-oriented system, every capability should be assigned to a certain *goal* from a logical perspective. The goal indicates the outcomes or achievements the capability is expected to enable or support. The *context* relates to the specific conditions or environment in which the capability is applied. A capability is executed using a sequence of activities, i.e., the *process*, to achieve the capability goal. Although *knowledge* might be classified as an immaterial resource, it is considered a distinct concept as it can be understood and interpreted in multiple ways or from various perspectives. It relates to the collective insights and expertise the organization needs to apply the capability effectively. The *actor/role* represents a single person or an organizational unit defined by its roles and corresponding responsibilities, decision authorities, and financial capital for a specific capability. The existence or status of each of these capability elements plays a vital role in identifying the maturity of an organizational capability. The definition of the capability elements, as described in the literature on capability engineering, serves as the basis for defining the capabilities in our capability maturity level model.

Organizational learning and dynamic capabilities literature offer concepts contributing to an organization's overall effectiveness. They provide different perspectives to organizational capabilities. For example, the capability lifecycle framework defined by [27] outlines the stages of capability evolution: founding, development, and maturity, with various paths such as retirement, retrenchment, replication, renewal, redeployment, or recombination. However, a framework of this generality cannot provide detailed explanations of how a specific capability will evolve in a particular setting [19]. Dynamic capabilities emphasize adaptability in a changing environment, while organizational learning involves the structures and processes that enable an organization and its members to learn and adapt. On the other hand, capability maturity levels are focused on the assessment and improvement of particular organizational capabilities, including ordinary capabilities [19], using a structured model. Hence, we can draw implications from these concepts for the capability maturity level model; however, direct adaptation of these concepts to capability maturity levels is not feasible.

The literature on individual skill development highlights three notable approaches: the four stages of competence model [20], Bloom's taxonomy [21], and the Dreyfus model of skill acquisition [14]. Although these models are not directly applicable to organizational capability maturity, they could serve as inspiration for developing maturity level characterizations, e.g., [22]. The four stages of the competence model outline stages from unconscious incompetence to unconscious competence, emphasizing self-awareness in competence development and not considering any other elements [20]. Bloom's taxonomy categorizes learning objectives into cognitive domains, aiding in understanding competency development [21]. The taxonomy has been used in the domain of education to investigate the development of student competencies e.g., [23, 24]. The Dreyfus model describes skill acquisition from novice to expert [14], focusing on experience and tacit knowledge. The model is particularly relevant for providing a maturity level characterization for organizational capabilities because it offers a framework for understanding how individuals acquire and develop skills over time, which can be adapted to understand and assess an organization's evolution of capability maturity over time [25]. We adopted the Dreyfus model of skill acquisition as the theoretical foundation of the capability maturity levels and their characterizations, in line with [25, 26]. This model was chosen due to its clear progression, alignment with capability evolution, and recognition of the role of experience in skill development [27]. This aligns with the idea that organizational capabilities mature through experience and iterative improvement [2]. For example, establishing a specific organizational culture cannot be solely developed by implementing process improvement practices but is developed by shared experiences [28]. Furthermore, the Dreyfus model is widely recognized, has a strong theoretical foundation [14], practical applicability, and can be adapted to various domains [29], making it suitable for developing widely understood maturity levels for organizational capabilities.

Dreyfus et al. [11] developed a five-stage model to analyze the development process of acquiring complex skills. The various levels reflect changes in four general aspects of competence development: from abstract rules to concrete experiences, situations that are considered relevant pieces to seeing the complete whole, rule-based decisions to an intuitive understanding, and change from a remote observer to an involved participant. The characterizations of the levels of individual skill acquisition by Dreyfus [27] are described as follows:

1. At the *novice* level, individuals have no skill experience and rely heavily on rules and guidelines to act. They lack the ability to interpret and apply knowledge in unique situations.
2. At the *advanced beginner* level, individuals have some experience, are beginning to recognize patterns, and are able to make decisions based on concrete examples. They still rely on the rules but may start using their own judgment in certain situations.
3. At the *competent* level, individuals have gained considerable experience and can begin to see the full picture of competence. They can use a combination of rules and intuition to guide actions, set goals, and make plans.
4. At the *proficient* level, individuals intuitively understand their abilities and can respond effectively to new situations. They can make decisions based on a deep understanding of their skills and effectively communicate their knowledge to others.

5. At the *expert* level, individuals have developed a very intuitive understanding of their abilities and can effortlessly perform complex actions without consciously thinking about them. They are able to innovate and find new ways to practice their skills and can mentor and teach others effectively.

While the Dreyfus model of skill acquisition interchangeably employs the terms 'stage' and 'level', we will adhere to using 'level' throughout this study, as it is the prevailing term within the domain of maturity modeling.

3 Research Design

The objective of this study is to develop a capability maturity level model to support the development of capability-based maturity models. To this end, the research design depicted in Fig. 1 was followed.

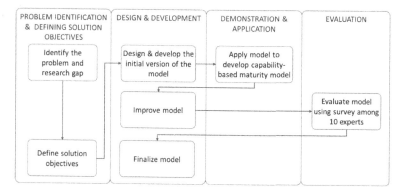

Fig. 1. Research design for the development of capability maturity level model

For our research, we followed the DSR paradigm to develop the proposed artifact [15]. In DSR, an artifact refers to "a thing that has or can be transformed into material existence as an artificially made object (e.g., model) or process (e.g., method or software)" [15]. We followed the DSR process proposed by Peffers et al. [16], which consists of the following steps: problem identification, the definition of the solution objectives, design, and development, demonstration of the artifact in a suitable context, evaluation, and communication. This paper serves as the communication step of the research process.

The solution objectives (SOs) are determined based on the problem definition presented in Sect. 1 and the literature review presented in Sect. 2. As we discuss in Sect. 2, a maturity level characterization model should comprehensively define what elements constitute a capability and what the characteristics of a capability are at each maturity level. Hence, we propose that the artifact should define the elements of an organizational capability and specify the characteristics of those elements at each maturity level (SO1). It is important for maturity levels to have a logical progression from one level to the next, having detailed definitions and distinct characteristics at each level [30]. Accordingly, we propose that the artifact should define a logical progression from one maturity level to the other and have clear and unambiguous definitions and distinct characteristics for each level (SO2). Finally, we expect that the artifact should be applicable across diverse organizational domains, ensuring that the capability maturity levels can be adapted to the emergence, development, and progression of various types of capabilities (SO3).

For the iterative design and development, we used the Dreyfus model of skill acquisition as the foundation for our model. We conceptually mapped the organizational capability elements (i.e. context, resources, knowledge, processes, goal, and actors [4]) to the five stages of skill acquisition of the Dreyfus model (i.e., Novice, Advanced Beginner, Competent, Proficient, and Expert [27]), by analyzing the organizational capability elements and the relations to the Dreyfus model. We iteratively mapped the capability elements to the maturity levels to represent how each capability element contributes to the overall maturation of the capability. Section 4 presents the final mapping. Each level of maturity represents a particular degree of competence that advances from *unaware* to *expert* and is aligned with the behavior and decision-making approach of individuals in an organization. We expanded the original 5 stages of the Dreyfus model of skill acquisition [14] by incorporating an additional level entitled *unaware*. This is because their model emphasizes the skill acquisition process and assumes an initial level of awareness regarding the skill to be acquired. However, this assumption does not align with capability maturity progression, which typically commences with *unconscious incompetence* or *unawareness* [20].

In the demonstration and application stage of DSR, we applied the model to demonstrate its utility in developing maturity levels for a set of capabilities in the domain of Advanced Data Analytics (ADA). The capability maturity model for ADA capabilities was developed through iterative rounds with a panel of experts. For the development of this model, a maturity grid structure was adopted. A maturity grid approach typically contains a written description of the performance characteristics at each maturity level [9]. Initially, we defined the relevant capabilities and their definitions for ADA based on existing literature. Based on these definitions and related literature, we instantiated relevant capability elements of *context, resources, knowledge, processes, goal, and actors*. In the generic maturity levels, we replaced the text referring to the capability elements with the instantiated capability elements. This way, the progression remained the same across the capabilities, but the capability-specific elements were adapted to the specific capability. In total, 15 panelists participated in the expert panel. The panelists provided feedback on the capabilities and the instantiated maturity levels, leading to refinements of the generic and applied maturity levels. During the instantiation, we improved the maturity level descriptions to increase the model's utility.

To evaluate the maturity levels, a survey was conducted. Experts were selected for their experience and knowledge of capability maturity models and ADA. Out of 15 experts contacted via email through authors' contacts, 10 participated in the survey. One expert had more than 10 years of experience with *capability maturity models,* five between 1–5 years of experience with *capability maturity modeling,* and the other four participants had between 2–13 years of experience in the *domain for which the capabilities are defined.* For the evaluation of the artifact, we used specific attributes that are suggested for the evaluation of design artifacts in DSR. These evaluation attributes were translated into statements in the context of an individual maturity level or the maturity levels in general (Table 1). We used a 5-point Likert scale to understand the level of agreement of a participant concerning a particular statement, for which "1" represents 'strongly disagree' and "5" represents 'strongly agree'.

Table 1. Overview of the evaluation attributes and statements used in the survey

Evaluation Attributes	Ref.	Statement
Validity/Relevance	[15, 31]	- The maturity level definition accurately captures the key characteristics that an organization exhibits at this level in the context of an organizational capability (e.g., an ADA-related capability)
		- The maturity level definitions and their organization accurately reflect the progression path of the maturity of an organizational capability (e.g., an ADA-related capability)
		- The maturity level definitions and their organization are relevant and applicable to a broad spectrum of organizational capabilities
Completeness	[32]	- The maturity level definition adequately covers the characteristics associated with the corresponding level of capability development in the context of an organizational capability
		- The maturity level definitions and their organization adequately cover the full range of characteristics associated with capability development in the context of an organizational capability
Clarity/Understandability	[33]	- The maturity level definition is presented in a clear and understandable manner
		- The maturity level definitions and their organization are presented in a clear and understandable manner
Usefulness	[34]	- The maturity level definitions and their organization can be adapted to reflect the characteristics of a specific ADA capability

4 Capability Maturity Level Model

Drawing upon [11], we conceptually analyzed the organizational capability elements as defined by [4] and associate them with the elements of the Dreyfus model. Table 2 presents the overview of the Dreyfus Five stages of skill acquisition model. The following sections describe how the Dreyfus model elements *components, perspective, decision, and commitment* and their characteristics throughout the maturity levels *novice, advanced beginner, competent, proficient,* and *expert,* are associated with the organizational capability elements *context, resources, knowledge, processes, goal, and actors.* The result of the conceptual mapping led to the final maturity level characterization model, as presented in Table 3.

Table 2. Overview of Dreyfus Five Stages of Skill Acquisition model [27]

Skill level	Components	Perspective	Decision	Commitment
1. Novice	Context free	None	Analytic	Detached
2. Advanced beginner	Context free and situational	None	Analytic	Detached
3. Competent	Context free and situational	Chosen	Analytic	Detached understanding and deciding: involved outcome
4. Proficient	Context free and situational	Experienced	Analytic	Involved understanding: detached deciding
5. Expert	Context free and situational	Experienced	Intuitive	Involved

Components is about facts and features the learner is able to recognize. In the *novice* level, these are only context-free features, referring to objective facts and features [27] In this level, the organization is only able to use *context-free* or explicit *knowledge*, so-called generic best practices. Furthermore, the organization does not take into account the organizational *context* when applying this capability. For example, an organization may engage a specialized analytics service provider to develop a data governance management capability, leveraging their expertise and experience in deploying similar data governance management capabilities for other organizations. While such external knowledge may shape initial aspirations, the organization would need to identify deviations with respect to organizational context [35], in this case, specific data governance requirements. In the *advanced beginner* level, the organization delves into the *situational* aspects of the capability, developing an initial understanding of both the *knowledge* needed for this capability and the *context* in which it is applied. The organization gains some experience and is able to use implicit knowledge that is not captured in rules and features [36]. The organization learns the situation-specific aspects of the context in which the capability is applied and tailors the best practices to its needs. In the maturity levels following the advanced beginner level, the experience and understanding of the capability and context gradually improve.

Table 3. Overview of the final maturity level characterization model

Mat. Level	Description
0. Unaware	The organization is unaware or in a state of unconscious incompetence regarding this capability. There is no understanding of the need for it
1. Novice	The organization lacks experience and has very basic knowledge regarding this capability. The capability is applied sporadically and in silos. Those who apply, mostly rely on generic best practices, and apply the capability without a formal process. The organization operates without a clear goal for this capability. No specific team or actor is responsible for this capability and ensures the availability of resources
2. Advanced Beginner	The organization has some experience and knowledge regarding this capability. There is an initial understanding of the capability and the context in which it is applied. There is awareness of the capability being applied in different ways in some parts of the organization. When applying the capability, there is no formal process, but those who apply typically follow and understand the best practices and tailor them depending on the context. The organization operates without a clear goal for this capability. No specific team or actor is responsible for the capability and ensures the availability of resources
3. Competent	The organization has sufficient experience and knowledge regarding this capability. The capability is applied in most parts of the organization in various situations and contexts. The organization follows and chooses best practices, tailors, and incorporates them into process definitions. A specific team or actor has defined a specific goal for this capability. They are involved in achieving the goal and ensuring the availability of resources for its achievement
4. Proficient	The organization has further extended its experience and knowledge regarding this capability. The capability is applied across the entire organization with an integrated approach. The best practices are tailored and incorporated into process definitions. A specific team or actor is involved in achieving the goals for this capability. They quantitively manage, understand how to apply the capability, and ensure the availability of resources
5. Expert	The organization has a wide range of experience and continuously updates its knowledge regarding this capability. The capability is intuitively applied across the entire organization. The organization reflects and improves the best practices that are tailored and incorporated into process definitions. Taking a holistic perspective, a specific team or actor is involved in achieving the goals for this capability. They quantitively manage it, understand how to apply the capability, adapt it as necessary, and ensure the availability of resources

Perspective is about the components the learner chooses to focus on [27]. In the *novice* level, the perspective is *none*, meaning that the elements of the situations to be treated as relevant are so clearly and objectively defined that they can be recognized without reference to the overall situation [27]. In this level, the capability is applied without reference to the rest of the organization or the *context* of the organization, i.e., applied sporadically and in silos. The organization is not able to identify the components to focus on, such as goals and processes. With increasing experience, the organization becomes aware of the different applications of this capability within the organizational context, with ad hoc applications becoming more prevalent. In the *competent* level, this requires a *chosen* perspective or plan [27]. This entails the selection of a specific *goal* and *processes* for applying the capability. The identification of goals is important as it guides the strategy, vision, change, and the development of the capability [2]. At the *proficient* level, the learner moves from a chosen perspective to an *experienced* perspective. The organization with the experienced perspective develops plans based on those who have worked in the past and anticipate similar issues [27]. Whereas in the competent level, the capability is applied in most parts of the organization in various situations and contexts, in the proficient level, the organization has further extended its experience and *knowledge* on how to apply the capability across the entire organization with an integrated approach. It is the organization's experienced perspective on the attributes of deployment, coordination, and integration of the capability that are the ultimate source of competitive advantage [37].

Decision relates to how the learner acts, based on either analytical reasoning or intuitive decision-making based on their experience and understanding of the situation [27]. In the *novice* level, the learner develops rules based on facts and uses generic rules and guidelines (*analytical* reasoning) because there is no set way of doing things [27]. For capabilities to generate outcomes, they must be deployed within organizational *processes* [37]. The *competent* organization incorporates a selection of tailored *knowledge* or best practices into process definitions. The *proficient* organization, while intuitively organizing and understanding the task, will still explicitly consider what to do analytically [27]. The organization executes the sequence of activities based on tailored best practices which are incorporated into process definitions. If exercised regularly, the capability becomes more deeply embedded in the memory structure of the organization. Routines may become more habitual, requiring less and less conscious thought [19]. While most expert performance is ongoing and nonreflective, when time permits, and outcomes are crucial, an expert will deliberate before acting. This deliberation does not require calculated problem-solving but rather involves critically reflecting on one's intuitions [27]. Only at the *expert* level, does the organization *intuitively* reflect and improve the best practices that are tailored and incorporated into process definitions. The organizational context may initiate the organization to reflect on the current capability and rethink the capability into other strategies such as retirement (death), retrenchment, renewal, replication, redeployment, or recombination of the capability [19].

Commitment describes the degree of immersion of the learner in the learning situation, including the understanding, decision-making, and outcome of their actions [27]. In the *novice* and *advanced beginner* level, the organization does not have a dedicated *team or actor* responsible for this capability, there is no defined *goal* or available *resources*. The *competent* performer, while understanding and deciding in a detached manner, becomes intensely involved in the outcome. Successful outcomes are deeply satisfying, leaving a memory of the chosen plan and the situation viewed from that perspective. Conversely, disasters are not easily forgotten [27]. At this level, a dedicated team or actor has defined a specific goal and is committed to achieving its outcome. They ensure the availability of resources for success. Actors need to be committed to the accomplishment of organizational goals and to the goal of learning [38]. Prolonged failure to attain the goal pulls aspirations downward, eventually leading to the abandonment of the capability learning effort [35]. The *proficient* learner is involved in the outcome and intuitively understands its task, followed by detached decision making [27]. In the proficient level, the dedicated team or actor is involved not only in achieving the goal, but also quantitively managing and understanding how this capability can be applied to achieve the goal. Quantitatively managing goals contributes to the understanding of the gap between the goal and the current state and overcoming that gap [38]. The organization can understand the outcome of its actions. At the *expert* level, the learner has experience in a wide variety of situations. At this point, a situation is understood not only when seen as similar to a prior one but also when the associated decision, action, or tactic comes to mind simultaneously [27]. In contrast to the proficient level, the dedicated team or actor directly knows the required action or tactic to improve the capability. They adapt this capability as necessary and ensure the availability of resources.

5 Application of the Model

We applied the maturity level characterization model to demonstrate its utility in developing maturity levels for a specific set of capabilities within the ADA domain. As described in Sect. 3, we refined the capability maturity model through iterative rounds with experts. Feedback from the expert panel led to refinements, enhancing the model's utility for ADA capabilities. We used a survey to evaluate the artifact based on selected design science evaluation constructs. Table 4 presents the application of the generic model to the ADA capability *data architecture management.*

Table 4. Model application to capability 'Data Architecture Management' in the ADA domain

Mat. Level	Description
0. Unaware	The organization is unaware or in a state of unconscious incompetence regarding Data Architecture Management. There is no understanding of the need for it
1. Novice	The organization lacks experience regarding Data Architecture Management and applies it sporadically and in silos. The organization has very basic knowledge of data modeling, cloud computing, database management, data architecture principles and requirements, and business requirements and context. Those who apply the capability mostly rely on generic best practices, but there is neither a formal process, a clear goal, nor a specific actor responsible for this capability and ensuring the availability of resources
2. Advanced Beginner	The organization has some experience regarding Data Architecture Management, and there is an initial understanding and awareness of how it is applied differently in some parts of the organization. The organization has some knowledge of data modeling, cloud services, database management, data architecture principles and requirements, and business requirements and context. Those who apply the capability typically follow and understand the best practices and tailor them depending on the context, but there is neither a formal process, a clear goal, nor a specific actor responsible for this capability and ensuring the availability of resources
3. Competent	The organization has sufficient experience regarding Data Architecture Management and applies it in most parts of the organization in various situations and contexts. The organization has sufficient knowledge of data modeling, cloud services, database management, data architecture principles and requirements, and business requirements and context. The organization follows and chooses best practices, and tailors and incorporates them into the processes of designing, implementing, and maintaining a data architecture. Data architects and engineers, and ADA management have defined and are involved in achieving a specific goal for establishing a scalable and efficient data architecture that explicates how data should come together conceptually and enables the storing, processing, and serving of the data in support of a single source of truth. The actors ensure the availability of infrastructure technology, including servers and storage solutions, and budget for architecture design and implementation
4. Proficient	The organization has further extended its experience regarding Data Architecture Management and applies it across the entire organization with an integrated approach. The organization has further extended its knowledge of data modeling, cloud services, database management, data architecture principles and requirements, and business requirements and context. The best practices are tailored and incorporated into the processes of designing, implementing, and maintaining a data architecture. Data architects and engineers, and ADA management are involved in establishing a scalable and efficient data architecture that explicates how data should come together conceptually and enables the storing, processing, and serving of the data in support of a single source of truth. The actors quantitatively manage and understand how to apply the capability. They ensure the availability of infrastructure technology, including servers and storage solutions, and budget for architecture design and implementation
5. Expert	The organization has a wide range of experience regarding Data Architecture Management and intuitively applies it across the entire organization. The organization continuously updates its knowledge of data modeling, cloud services, database management, data architecture principles and requirements, and business requirements and context. The organization reflects and improves the best practices that are tailored and incorporated into the processes of designing, implementing, and maintaining a data architecture. Taking a holistic perspective, Data architects and engineers, and ADA management are involved in establishing a scalable and efficient data architecture that explicates how data should come together conceptually and enables the storing, processing, and serving of the data in support of a single source of truth. The actors quantitatively manage, understand how to apply, and adapt the capability as necessary. They ensure the availability of infrastructure technology, including servers and storage solutions, and budget for architecture design and implementation

6   Evaluation Results

This section presents the results of the evaluation performed on the capability maturity level model. Table 5 and Table 6 illustrate the results of the responses to the survey on the validity, relevance, completeness, clarity, understanding, and usefulness of each maturity level and the entire model, respectively. The results show that the clarity/understanding of each maturity level and the model, in general, is more often scored 'Strongly Disagree' or 'Neutral' compared to the other evaluation constructs. The validity/relevance of each maturity level and the model more often scored 'Agree' or 'Strongly Agree' compared to the other evaluation constructs. All evaluation constructs received scores between 'Neutral' to 'Strongly Agree', except for the clarity/understandability, which received scores for 'Strongly Disagree'. This supports the achievement of solution objectives SO1, SO2, and SO3 (Sect. 3). Below we will discuss the feedback we received per maturity level and the model in general.

Table 5. Responses to the survey on the maturity levels' validity/relevance, completeness, clarity/understanding and usefulness.

* 1 Strongly Disagree *2 Disagree, *3 Neutral, *4 Agree, and *5 Strongly Agree

Evaluation Construct	Statement	Maturity Level	1	2	3	4	5
Validity/ Relevance	... accurately captures the key characteristics that an organization exhibits at this level in the context of an organizational capability (e.g., an ADA-related capability).	0. Unaware	0	0	0	5	5
		1. Novice	0	0	0	5	5
		2. Advanced Beginner	0	0	2	3	5
		3. Competent	0	0	0	7	3
		4. Proficient	0	0	0	8	2
		5. Expert	0	0	0	5	5
Completeness	... adequately covers the characteristics associated with the corresponding level of capability development in the context of an organizational capability	0. Unaware	0	0	1	4	5
		1. Novice	0	0	0	5	5
		2. Advanced Beginner	0	0	2	3	5
		3. Competent	0	0	1	7	2
		4. Proficient	0	0	0	8	2
		5. Expert	0	0	0	7	3
Clarity/ Understanding	... is presented in a clear and understandable manner.	0. Unaware	0	0	1	3	6
		1. Novice	1	0	4	2	3
		2. Advanced Beginner	1	0	4	2	3
		3. Competent	1	0	3	5	1
		4. Proficient	1	0	3	4	2
		5. Expert	1	0	4	2	3

Table 6. Responses to the survey on model's validity/relevance, completeness, clarity/understanding and usefulness

* 1 Strongly Disagree *2 Disagree, *3 Neutral, *4 Agree, and *5 Strongly Agree

Evaluation Construct	Statement	1	2	3	4	5
Validity	... accurately reflect the progression path of the maturity of an organizational capability (e.g., an ADA-related capability).	0	0	1	5	4
Relevance	... are relevant and applicable to a broad spectrum of organizational capabilities	0	0	0	6	4
Completeness	... adequately cover the full range of characteristics associated with capability development in the context of an organizational capability.	0	0	1	8	1
Clarity/ Understanding	... are presented in a clear and understandable manner.	1	1	4	3	1
Usefulness	... can be adapted to reflect the characteristics of a specific ADA capability	0	0	2	4	4

The *unaware* level received no additional comments during the evaluation. At the n*ovice* level, concerns were raised about clarity regarding goals and generic rules, leading to modifications to clarify these points. The *advanced beginner* level received feedback about its added value compared to the previous level, prompting explicit distinctions and adjustments in wording to accommodate diverse organizational structures. The *competent* level underwent revisions to enhance clarity regarding the experience and knowledge, with adjustments to minimize repetition and highlight application in diverse situations. The *proficient* level prompted suggestions for incorporating processes to stay updated with advancements. Therefore, the distinctions between proficient and expert levels were refined to emphasize reflection and a holistic perspective at the expert level. Similar adjustments were made at the e*xpert* level, emphasizing the unique aspects of intuition, reflection, and holistic perspective that differentiate it from lower levels.

In terms of overarching considerations, recommendations were made to enhance formatting, especially the use of bold and italics for clarity. A notable proposal was to expand the general explanation to include key capability concepts, which was integrated into the model in this paper. Descriptions were refined to improve readability and eliminate redundancy.

7 Conclusion

The main contribution of this research is a theoretically grounded model that facilitates the development of capability-based maturity models, addressing a significant gap in the literature regarding the characterization of capability maturity levels. The research represents a level 2 design science contribution, providing a new solution to a known problem [15]. We demonstrate the functional feasibility of the model through a proof of concept by applying it to develop a capability-based maturity model for ADA. We evaluate the capability maturity level model as a proof of value [39]. The model supports the definition of six maturity levels in a progressive way, from unaware to expert.

Our findings align with existing research emphasizing the importance of selecting appropriate units of analysis for maturity [7], and leveraging skill acquisition models for defining capability maturity levels [25, 26]. However, our research also highlights the need to differentiate between capability and process-based maturity level characterizations. Existing maturity models are often procedural in nature, striving to enhance efficiency with the goal of improving organizational performance. In contrast, Dreyfus's model of skill acquisition and the concepts of organizational capabilities suggest that principles and intuitive understanding play a more significant role in achieving success than strictly following procedures [40]. In the development of maturity models, specific design processes are typically followed, e.g., [5]. Within these processes, it is recognized that a crucial step involves selecting appropriate maturity levels that show logical progression and are theoretically grounded. However, there is a lack of explicit guidance on how to accomplish this task. This paper presents a template for designing and developing maturity levels for capability-based maturity models. This model could be used in the development of capability-based maturity models across various domains, providing a theoretical foundation for enhancing organizational capabilities.

The limitations of our study include its application on a single domain and a relatively small sample size for model evaluation, potentially limiting the generalizability and robustness of our findings. Future research should aim to address these limitations by applying the model across diverse domains and employing larger samples to ensure broader utility and validity.

Disclosure of Interests. The authors have no competing interests to declare that are relevant to the content of this article.

References

1. Eisenhardt, K.M., Schoonhoven, C.B.: Resource-based view of strategic alliance formation: strategic and social effects in entrepreneurial firms. Organ. Sci. **7**(2) (1996). https://doi.org/10.1287/orsc.7.2.136
2. Wang, X., Zeng, Y.: Organizational capability model: toward improving organizational performance. J. Integr. Design Process Sci. **21**(1) (2017). https://doi.org/10.3233/jid-2017-0005
3. Ulrich, D., Smallwood, N.: Capitalizing on capabilities. Harv. Bus. Rev. (2004)
4. Wißotzki, M.: The capability management process: finding your way into capability engineering. In: Simon, D., Schmidt, C. (eds.) Business Architecture Management. MP, pp. 77–105. Springer, Cham (2015). https://doi.org/10.1007/978-3-319-14571-6_5
5. Becker, J., Knackstedt, R., Pöppelbuß, J.: Developing maturity models for IT management. Bus. Inf. Syst. Eng. **1**(3), 213–222 (2009). https://doi.org/10.1007/s12599-009-0044-5
6. Tarhan, A., Turetken, O., Reijers, H.A.: Business process maturity models: a systematic literature review. Inf. Softw. Technol. **75**, 122–134 (2016). https://doi.org/10.1016/j.infsof.2016.01.010
7. Mettler, T.: Maturity assessment models: a design science research approach. Int. J. Soc. Syst. Sci. **3**(1/2) (2011). https://doi.org/10.1504/ijsss.2011.038934
8. de Bruin, T., Rosemann, M.: Using the Delphi technique to identify BPM capability areas. In: ACIS (2007)

9. Maier, A.M., Moultrie, J., Clarkson, P.J.: Assessing organizational capabilities: reviewing and guiding the development of maturity grids. IEEE Trans. Eng. Manage. **59**(1), 138–159 (2012). https://doi.org/10.1109/TEM.2010.2077289

10. Schriek, M., Turetken, O., Kaymak, U.: A maturity model for care pathways. Undefined (2016)

11. Turetken, O., Stojanov, I., Trienekens, J.J.M.: Assessing the adoption level of scaled agile development: a maturity model for scaled agile framework. J. Softw.: Evol. Process **29**(6), e1796 (2017). https://doi.org/10.1002/SMR.1796

12. Korsten, G., Aysolmaz, B., Turetken, O., Edel, D., Ozkan, B.: ADA-CMM: a capability maturity model for advanced data analytics. In: HICSS (2022). https://doi.org/10.24251/hicss.2022.032

13. Thordsen, T., Bick, M.: A decade of digital maturity models: much ado about nothing?. Inf. Syst. e-Bus. Manage. (2023). https://doi.org/10.1007/s10257-023-00656-w

14. Dreyfus, S.E., Dreyfus, H.L.: A five-stage model of the mental activities involved in directed skill acquisition. Oper. Res. Cent. (1980)

15. Gregor, S., Hevner, A.R.: Positioning and presenting design science research for maximum impact. MIS Q. **37**(2), 337–355 (2013). https://doi.org/10.2753/MIS0742-1222240302

16. Peffers, K., Tuunanen, T., Rothenberger, M.A., Chatterjee, S.: A design science research methodology for information systems research. J. Manage. Inf. Syst. **24**(3) (2007). https://doi.org/10.2753/MIS0742-1222240302

17. Simpson, J.A., Weiner, E.S.C.: The Oxford English Dictionary, 2nd edn. Clarendon Press/Oxford University Press, New York/Oxford (1989)

18. Lahrmann, G., Marx, F., Winter, R., Wortmann, F.: Business intelligence maturity: development and evaluation of a theoretical model. In: HICSS 2011 (2011)

19. Helfat, C.E., Peteraf, M.A.: The dynamic resource-based view: capability lifecycles. Strategic Manage. J. **24**(10 SPEC ISS.), 997–1010 (2003). https://doi.org/10.1002/smj.332

20. De Phillips, F.A., Berliner, W.M., Cribbin, J.J.: Management of Training Programs. Richard D. Irwin, Homewood (1960)

21. Bloom, B., Krathwohl, D.: Taxonomy of Educational Objectives, The Classification of Educational Goals, Handbook I: Cognitive Domain, no. 4 (1956). https://doi.org/10.1177/001316445701700420

22. Thomson, K.L., von Solms, R.: Towards an information security competence maturity model. Comput. Fraud Secur. **2006**(5) (2006). https://doi.org/10.1016/S1361-3723(06)70356-6

23. Ching, H.Y., Da Silva, E.C.: The use of Bloom's taxonomy to develop competences in students of a business undergrad course. Acad. Manage. Proc. **2017**(1) (2017). https://doi.org/10.5465/ambpp.2017.10153abstract

24. Reeves, M.F.: An application of Bloom's taxonomy to the teaching of business ethics. J. Bus. Ethics **9**(7) (1990). https://doi.org/10.1007/BF00383217

25. Stelzl, K., Röglinger, M., Wyrtki, K.: Building an ambidextrous organization: a maturity model for organizational ambidexterity. Bus. Res. **13**(3) (2020). https://doi.org/10.1007/s40685-020-00117-x

26. Huber, R.X.R., Renner, J., Stahl, B.: Combining individual and organizational capabilities: an integrated maturity model for ambidexterity. In: HICSS (2021). https://doi.org/10.24251/hicss.2021.699

27. Dreyfus, S.E.: The five-stage model of adult skill acquisition. Bull. Sci. Technol. Soc. **24**(3) (2004). https://doi.org/10.1177/0270467604264992

28. Bellot, J.: Defining and assessing organizational culture. Nurs. Forum **46**(1) (2011). https://doi.org/10.1111/j.1744-6198.2010.00207.x

29. Silva Mangiante, E.M., Peno, K., Northup, J.: Teaching and learning for adult skill acquisition: applying the Dreyfus and Dreyfus model in different fields (2021)

30. de Bruin, T., Freeze, R., Kulkarni, U., Rosemann, M.: Understanding the main phases of developing a maturity assessment model. In: ACIS 2005 (2005)
31. Rosemann, M., Vessey, I.: Toward improving the relevance of information systems research to practice: the role of applicability checks. MIS Q.: Manage. Inf. Syst. **32**(1) (2008). https://doi.org/10.2307/25148826
32. Prat, N., Comyn-Wattiau, I., Akoka, J.: A taxonomy of evaluation methods for information systems artifacts. J. Manage. Inf. Syst. **32**(3) (2015). https://doi.org/10.1080/07421222.2015.1099390
33. Thompson, R.L., Higgins, C.A., Howell, J.M.: Personal computing: toward a conceptual model of utilization. MIS Q. Rev. **15**(1), 125–143 (1991)
34. Davis, F.D.: Perceived usefulness, perceived ease of use, and user acceptance of information technology. MIS Q.: Manage. Inf. Syst. **13**(3) (1989). https://doi.org/10.2307/249008
35. Winter, S.G.: The satisficing principle in capability learning. Strateric Manage. J. **21**(10), 981–996 (2000)
36. Bhardwaj, M., Monin, J.: Tacit to explicit: an interplay shaping organization knowledge. J. Knowl. Manage. **10**(3) (2006). https://doi.org/10.1108/13673270610670867
37. Duhan, S., Levy, M., Birkbeck, P.P.: IS strategy in SMEs using organizational capabilities: the CPX framework. In: ECIS, Regensburg (2005)
38. Goh, S.C.: Learning capability, organization factors and firm performance. In: OLKC, Athens (2014)
39. Nunamaker, J.F., Briggs, R.O., Derrick, D.C., Schwabe, G.: The last research mile: achieving both rigor and relevance in information systems research. J. Manag. Inf. Syst. **32**(3), 10–47 (2015). https://doi.org/10.1080/07421222.2015.1094961
40. Kaul, P., Joslin, R., Brand, C.: Maturity models with 'inflection points' directly support organizational adaptability and innovation. In: IRNOP (2018)

Using Enterprise Modeling to Analyze and Design a "Fit" Between Activities in an Enterprise

Ilia Bider[1,2]([⊠]) [iD] and Erik Perjons[1] [iD]

[1] DSV, Stockholm University, Postbox 7003, 16407 Kista, Sweden
{ilia,perjons}@dsv.su.se
[2] ICS, University of Tartu, Narva Mnt 18, 51009 Tartu, Estonia

Abstract. Michael Porter introduced several concepts related to business strategy and how the latter can be attained. The strategy roughly can be defined as achieving a "competitive advantage," which is one of the concepts he introduced. Additionally, he introduced the concept of "fit," which could be roughly understood as aligning various internal and external activities to achieve a chosen competitive advantage. This paper investigates the potential usability of enterprise modeling for analyzing the attainment of "fit" or designing enterprise activities to achieve it. This is a work-in-progress paper; we focus only on the service enterprises and use only one enterprise modeling technique, a so-called Fractal Enterprise Model. At the same time, our final goal is to develop a methodology for using enterprise modeling for analyzing and designing activities so that they fit the chosen strategy of achieving and sustaining a competitive advantage.

Keywords: competitive advantage · fit · enterprise modeling · fractal enterprise model · FEM

1 Introduction

In 1985, Michael Porter introduced several concepts related to enterprise strategy in his book "Competitive Advantage" [1]. These concepts provide a framework for businesses to strategically position themselves in the market and outperform competitors, fostering sustained profitability. One of the last concepts introduced in [1] is "fit", which can roughly be defined as aligning all internal and external activities of the enterprise to achieve and sustain the chosen or adaptively attained competitive advantage. This concept is discussed in more detail in [2].

This paper is devoted to analyzing whether the fit exists or understanding how to achieve and sustain it in a new enterprise, or in an enterprise where the fit does not exist or is broken at some point in the enterprise's history. The differential point in our endeavor is that we use enterprise modeling for this task. Though other concepts presented in [1], such as value chain, have been connected to enterprise modeling, e.g. [3, 4], to the best of our knowledge, this was not systematically done in regards to "fit".

H. van der Aa et al. (Eds.): BPMDS 2024/EMMSAD 2024, LNBIP 511, pp. 372–387, 2024.
https://doi.org/10.1007/978-3-031-61007-3_27

As we are at the beginning of our work, we start with testing the hypothesis that enterprise modeling can be useful for diagnosing or designing the fit by using examples, some of which are abstract and some concrete. More precisely, we take a business example and build an enterprise model to see how to obtain the fit having a particular competitive advantage in mind. Alternatively, we take a real example in which the fit was broken at some time and then restored. In contrast to [1], we concentrate on service enterprises, leaving manufacturing outside our consideration. As the number of service enterprises is increasing, a solution for only this type could be useful, even if the solution would be impossible to adjust to manufacturing.

In [2], M. Porter introduced three types of fit: first-order fit, second-order fit, and third-order fit. In this paper, we present and analyze the examples related to the second-order fit, which is when activities reinforce each other. This type of fit is more difficult to discover than the first-order fit, which is related to each activity being aligned with an overall strategy.

As we are at the beginning of our research, the choice of an enterprise modeling technique does not matter much as long as it satisfies the main criteria, which can be formulated in the following manner. As we are concerned with the alignment of enterprise activities, they and their connections should be possible to represent in a model. This requirement will exclude a number of modeling techniques, such as business process modeling techniques. The latter, while representing activities, does not have standardized means to connect activities that belong to different processes, at least not without using more complex modeling practices.

We start our investigation using an enterprise modeling technique called Fractal Enterprise Model (FEM) [5, 6]. FEM has a form of a directed graph with two main types of nodes, *processes* and *assets*, where the arrows (edges) from assets to processes show which assets are used in which processes and arrows from processes to assets show which processes help to have specific assets in "healthy" and working order. The arrows are labeled with meta-tags that show how a given asset is used, e.g., workforce, reputation, infrastructure, etc., or how a given process helps to have the given assets "in order", i.e., acquire, maintain, or retire.

The rationale behind the decision to use FEM is: (1) it satisfies the general requirement formulated above, as all activities (processes in the terminology of FEM) are connected via assets that are used in or managed by the activities, (2) FEM is our invention, and thus we have enough experience of using it. If FEM shows not useful for the task, we could try another modeling technique, e.g., ArchiMate [7], unless our investigation shows that enterprise modeling is useless for the task of diagnosing or designing the "fit".

If the initial investigation gives positive results, our long-term goal is to *develop a methodology* for analyzing and designing a fit using *enterprise modeling*. This goal corresponds to the Design Science (DS) methodology accepted for this work and the works that might follow the initial investigation.

The rest of the paper is structured according to the following plan. In Sect. 2, we give a background to our research, i.e., research approach, knowledge base, and introduction to FEM. In Sect. 3, we consider examples that illustrate how the fit can be established or designed with the help of FEM models. In Sect. 4, we present a historical example of the fit established, broken, and restored once more. Section 5 summarizes our findings and presents plans for the future.

2 Background

2.1 Research Approach

The research presented in this paper belongs to the Design Science (DS) paradigm [8, 9], which focuses on looking for generic solutions for known and unknown problems. The result of a DS research project can be a solution to a problem in the terminology of [6] or an artifact in the terminology of [5]; alternatively, the result can be in the form of "negative knowledge," stating that a particular approach is not appropriate for solving certain kind of problems.

The ultimate goal of this research is to develop a methodology for diagnosing and designing the fit between internal and external activities that can support organizations in achieving a competitive advantage using enterprise modeling. However, at this stage of our research, we do not know whether enterprise modeling can be of use for this purpose. Thus, our first task can be formulated as follows. Based on the abstract and concrete examples: (1) try to verify the hypothesis that enterprise modeling can be of help for the purpose in general, and (2) establish whether FEM can be used for the purpose in particular. In case of a negative result, we obtain some knowledge that might set a stop for trying to develop a methodology. In case of a positive outcome, we will continue to pursue our goal.

2.2 Michael Porter's View on Competition and Strategy

Competitive advantage emerges as the cornerstone of strategic success [1]. According to Michael Porter, it denotes a firm's ability to outperform its rivals by delivering greater value to customers or creating comparable value at a lower cost [1].

In [2], Porter distinguishes between operational effectiveness and strategic positioning. Operational effectiveness is about performing similar activities better than competitors, focusing on efficiency and execution. Strategic positioning involves deliberately selecting a unique set of activities that deliver a distinct mix of values to the customer. It is precisely this strategic choice—the selection and execution of a differentiated set of activities—that underpins a firm's competitive advantage, marking strategic positioning the essence of strategic choice.

According to Porter, the focus has been too much on operational effectiveness for achieving competitive advantage [2]. For example, managers have embraced tools such as total quality management, benchmarking, outsourcing, reengineering, and change management. Porter argues that operational effectiveness, although necessary for superior performance, is not sufficient because its techniques are easy to imitate. In contrast, the essence of strategy is choosing a unique and valuable position rooted in systems of activities that are much more difficult to match.

The concept of 'fit' among a company's activities is a critical mechanism for reinforcing competitive advantage and ensuring its sustainability. Porter presents three types of fit [2]:

- *First-order fit*: Simple consistency between each activity and the overall strategy.
- *Second-order fit*: Activities reinforce each other, making the strategy more effective or efficient.
- *Third-order fit*: Optimization of effort, where activities are so well coordinated that they create unique value and efficiency.

According to Porter, the interplay among these activities, characterized by their complementary and reinforcing nature, solidifies the strategic foundation, enabling the firm to achieve and sustain a superior competitive stance.

2.3 Fractal Enterprise Model

As FEM is not a widely spread enterprise modeling technique, in this section, we will present the basic concepts and relations of this technique based on an example. The example concerns the model of a consulting company, e.g., a management consulting company or a software consulting company, that will be used in the next section for presenting the ideas of how the fit can present itself in a FEM of an enterprise. The model is presented in Fig. 1.

The upper put of the model shows that the primary service that the company provides is solving the customer's problems. To be able to do it repetitively, the company needs to have certain assets that can roughly be divided into three categories: (1) *Beneficiary* (customers), (2) *Workforce* (consultants), and (3) *EXecution Template* (*EXT*) and *Tech & Info Infrastructure*, which represents methods and tools used when finding/developing solutions. The rest of the model shows how to get and maintain these assets.

FEM has two main concepts for describing the internals of a company; a process – that is, a repetitive behavior – represented as an oval, and an asset – a set of things or actors that are needed for the behavior to become repetitive – represented as a rectangle. A relation between a process and an asset is represented by an arrow. FEM differentiates two main types of relations between processes and assets. The first – *used-in* relation – is a relation of a process "using" an asset; in this case, the arrow points from the asset to the process and has a solid line. The second – *managed-by* relation – is a relation of a process managing the asset, e.g., adding elements; in this case, the arrow points from the process to the asset and has a dashed line.

In FEM, a label inside an oval names the given process, and a label inside a rectangle names the given asset. Arrows are also labeled to show the meaning of relations between the processes and assets. A label on an arrow pointing from an asset to a process identifies the role the given asset plays in the process, for example, *workforce* or *infrastructure*. A label on an arrow pointing from a process to an asset identifies how the process manages (i.e., changes) the asset. In FEM, an asset is considered as a pool of entities capable of playing a given role in a given process. Labels leading into assets from processes reflect how the pool is affected; for example, the label *Acquire* identifies that the process can/should increase the pool size. Note that having more than one label on an arrow is possible; it shows that the asset fulfills several roles or that the process manages the asset in several ways.

Labels inside ovals (representing processes) and rectangles (representing assets) are not standardized. They can be set according to the terminology accepted in the given domain or be specific to a given organization. Labels on arrows (which represent the relations between processes and assets) are standardized. This is done by using a relatively limited set of abstract relations, such as *Workforce* or *Acquire*, which are clarified by the domain- and context-specific labels inside ovals and rectangles. Standardization improves the understandability of the models. While there are several types of relations that show how an asset is used in a process (see example in Fig. 1), there are only three types of relations that describe how a process manages an asset – *Acquire*, *Maintain*, and *Retire*.

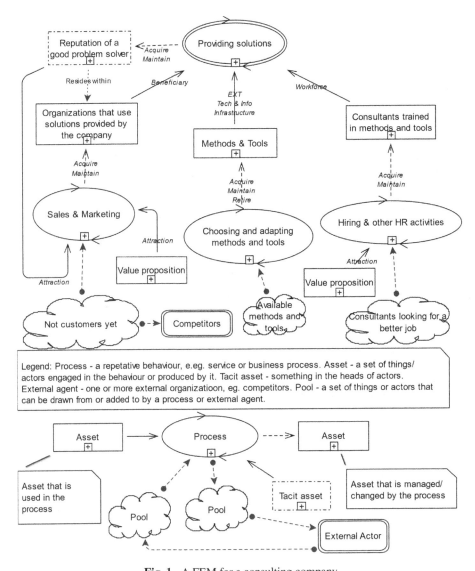

Fig. 1. A FEM for a consulting company

Processes and assets have some properties, several of which are presented visually. For example, an oval with a double border (see Fig. 1) means that the process it represents is a so-called primary process, the one that has a *Beneficiary* for whom it provides some value. It also means that the enterprise gets money for the service provided, e.g., from the beneficiary or somebody else. Another example is a dashed-dotted border of an asset (see Fig. 1), which means that the asset is a tacit asset that resides in the heads of some agents. In which heads it resides is shown by a blue dashed arrow (a general asymmetric association) with the label *Resides within*.

There are two other concepts in FEM; they represent the business context of the enterprise and connect it to specific processes [6]. These are as follows:

- *External pool*, which is represented by a cloud shape, see Fig. 1. An external pool is a set of things or agents of a particular type, e.g., a pool of potential customers. The label inside the pool describes its content.
- *External actor*, which is represented by a rectangle with rounded corners. An external actor is an agent (or group of agents), like a company or person, acting outside the enterprise boundary. The label inside the external actor describes its nature. If the shape represents a set of external actors, it has a double line border; see Fig. 1, which has one external actor of this kind.

External pools and external actors may be related to each other and other elements of the FEM diagram. Such a relation is shown by a dashed arrow that has a round dot start. Some examples of using these relations are shown in Fig. 1:

- An external pool may be connected to a business process with an arrow from the pool to the process. In this case, the process needs to be an *Acquire* process for one or more assets, see *Acquire arrows* in Fig. 1. Such an arrow means that the process uses the external pool to create new elements in the assets based on the elements in the pool.
- An external pool may be connected to an external actor with an arrow directed from the pool to the external actor. In this case, the arrow shows that the external actor uses the pool as a basis for one of its own *Acquire* processes, meaning there might be competition.

There are some other types of relations that are not used in this paper. The readers interested to know more about FEM and why the model is called fractal are referred to [5, 6, 10].

2.4 How Our Approach Differs from Others

In [11], the authors defined strategy as "a pattern in a stream of actions". They also discuss that the actual strategy can be (1) intended and realized or (2) emergent and realized, as shown in Fig. 2. It means that the authors do not just see strategy as a well-formulated plan or a linear process. Instead, they see strategy as a dynamic and organic process that evolves. From our perspective, in the case of intended and realized strategy, there might be documents that describe the strategy and how it is supposed to be achieved. In the case of emergent strategy, there might be no such documents, as the strategy has been achieved in an evolutionary process. In this case, it is a pattern that emerges from daily activities and decisions made at different levels that constitute an organization's strategy. Note that the intended strategy may be substituted by an emergent one without management explicitly accepting this fact.

Porter's discussion on fit in [2] corresponds more to the first kind of strategy, the intended one. In [2], the author uses a special modeling technique called Activity System Map (ASM) to model the strategy. An ASM model consists of a set of interconnected nodes. Though the name of the technique uses the term activity, the nodes, as a rule, represent not activities completed in the enterprise but goals or constraints on the activities. For example, the node *Modular furniture design* in the IKEA ASM from [2] represents a constraint or goal on the design process. This goal/constraints-oriented set of presenting the strategy was accepted as the mainstream in enterprise modeling; see, for example, [12]. Another example is ArchiMate, which has a special strategic layer to deal with the intended strategy. This layer is then connected to the business layer using the realization relation.

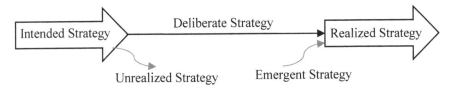

Fig. 2. Type of strategy (adapted from [11]).

In the case of emergent strategy, the goals and constraints are not explicitly defined. Thus, the strategy needs to be derived from the "pattern in the stream of actions". The patterns become evident when actions, decisions, or behaviors are repeated. If we have an enterprise model that presents interconnected actions completed by the organization on a recurrent basis, we can try to discover the strategy from the model. Therefore, we have constraints on the type of enterprise model to use; namely, it should not contain meta-type elements, like goals. Firstly, they are not known in the case of emergent strategy. Secondly, it isn't easy to know in advance whether the intended strategy has been realized and has not been substituted by an emergent one. This requirement differentiates our approach from the mainstream approach that uses languages with meta-type concepts, like goals or requirements, such as ArchiMate [7] or iStar [13].

As we see from Sect. 2.3, FEM does not have concepts that represent meta-type elements, like goals. However, it has enough concepts to represent the environment essential for completing activities, like assets or pools. For example, with the help of the *EXT* label, a modeler can connect manuals or policy documents that affect how a process is executed. Another example is the *Attraction* label that can be used to connect a value proposition in the written form when attracting stakeholders, see Fig. 1. Note, however, that the value proposition is not the only element that can be used as an attraction. The attraction can be the type of customers the organization has or the office's convenient location; examples of such attractions will be shown in the following sections. FEM also has a means for presenting the tacit knowledge, which can be essential for detecting the fit.

3 How the Fit Can Be Analyzed Using an Enterprise Model

In this section, we consider two different strategies for obtaining a competitive advantage by a consulting company, whose generic model is presented in Fig. 1. We discuss what fit is required for each and how it can be represented in an enterprise model.

3.1 Competitive Advantage: Having the Best Consultants

In this section, we consider the strategy of a consulting company to have the best possible consultants. This attracts the top enterprises to become customers. Having top customers allows to ask for higher consulting fees, and thus get enough profit. In short, the competitive advantage is achieved by focusing on *Workforce* and adjusting all other activities to this goal. This strategy is represented in Fig. 3, which is based on the model in Fig. 1. Note, however, that the model in Fig. 3 does not depict all company components; it represents only those that are relevant to show the fit between activities related to the assets in focus, in this case, the workforce, methods, and tools.

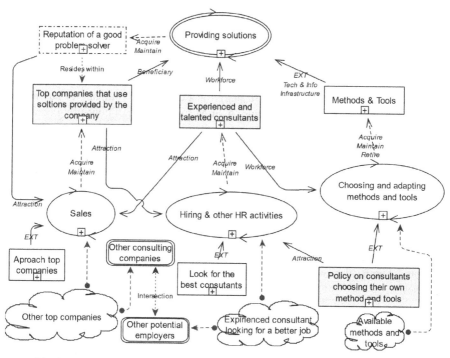

Fig. 3. A model based on the competitive advantage of having the best consulters

In the model presented in Fig. 3, the assets important for the fit are highlighted by the blue (grey in no-color print) background. The fit/alignment is achieved by having the best consultants asset functioning as an attraction for acquiring and keeping the top enterprises as customers. At the same time, having the top companies as customers serves as an attraction for acquiring and retaining the best consultants. Here, we do not discuss how this strategy is achieved, but consider only how it is made sustainable.

The company also needs the fit related to choosing methods and tools. As the chosen strategy is to have the best consultants, it is difficult to assume they want to use the same methods and tools. They may have the method and tools they like or choose them based on a particular consulting assignment. Thus, it is essential that consultants themselves choose methods and tools, which is shown by them being *Workforce* in the process of selecting methods and tools (see Fig. 3). The policy of consultants choosing tools themselves also serves as *EXT* – steering document – for the process. This policy also serves as *Attraction* for the process of acquiring and keeping the best consultants.

Based on the model in Fig. 3, the company has achieved a fit between different activities. This can be tested by removing any indirect connections between the activities and investigating how it would affect the company. For example, if we stop getting top companies as customers and are satisfied with less prestigious customers, we will lose the attraction for hiring and keeping the best consultants. In addition, we will get paid less and thus be unable to keep them. If we stop hiring the best consultants, we will lose the attraction of getting the top customers. Moreover, if we start choosing and adopting methods and tools in a standardized fashion, we may lose the best consultants who value the freedom of selecting tools and methods themselves.

3.2 Competitive Advantage: Having the Best Methods and Tools

This section considers an alternative strategy for a consulting company of having the best/most fashionable methods and tools. A FEM for this type of consulting company is presented in Fig. 4. The strategy is based on the idea that the company can adopt the best or most fashionable methods and tools that are known to their actual and potential customers. This is why the methods and tools asset has a blue background.

As follows from Fig. 4, *Methods & Tools* serves as *Attraction* to sales, and thus it is used to obtain and keep the customers, which are not mandatory the top ones (as in the previous model). At the same time, *Methods & Tools* serves as an attraction for hiring and keeping good consultants (not mandatory, the best one who might not like the fashionable methods and tools). This strategy does not aim to get the top customers and top consultants. Still, it can create enough profit by exploiting fashionable methods and tools for both sales and HR, as the methods and tools serve as an attraction for these processes.

3.3 Summary of the Two Examples

As follows from the two examples of this section, fractal models that depict the consulting companies can show the alignment between different activities. In these examples, the models show that sales, HR, and choosing methods and tools, being activities not directly connected, still need to be aligned. This is because the asset that one of the activities manages serves as an **attraction** for other activities. If the asset cannot be used as an attraction, the alignment is broken, and the strategy chosen to have a competitive advantage may not be attainable.

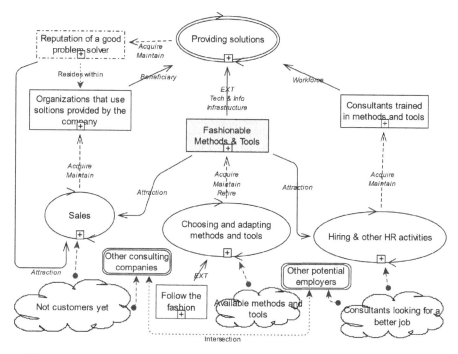

Fig. 4. A model based on competitive advantage of having the best methods and tools

The examples demonstrate that an enterprise model can help analyze the fit between activities that are not directly connected. Therefore, we can preliminarily conclude that the usage of an enterprise model of a certain kind can be useful for analyzing and, maybe, designing the fit.

From the point of view of the ideas of M. Porter [2], the examples of this section present the second-order fit, as aligned activities reinforce each other.

4 A Historical Example

This section considers a historical example of an American software consulting company for which the first author worked from 1996 to 1997 as a consultant. At this stage, the company's business activities were arranged around a software development tool called Prolifics, which has the same name as the company – Prolifics, Inc. The tool was developed inside the company, and the company supported it, including creating new versions. The tool helped the developers build business applications with the minimum of coding, and it worked in both Windows and Unix graphical environments. Thus, an application developed under one platform could be easily migrated to another. The company also had a WEB version, but it was not developed to the level of the graphical versions. A special version of the tool could also work with the most advanced middleware at the time – Tuxedo.

Prolifics, Inc. Sold licenses to companies engaged in developing business applications and provided experts to help their customers start using the tool, especially at the beginning of their projects. At the same time, besides the tool development department, it had a large consulting department engaged in developing business applications with the help of the tool for external customers. Therefore, the company has three sources of earning money: (1) tool license sales, (2) providing expertise for tool customers to start the project, and (3) creating applications for the customers that did not have a development department, using Prolifics as a tool.

A FEM depicting the business activities of Prolifics, Inc. at the time is presented in Fig. 5. The model's central point is the tool software that the company developed and supported. This asset is highlighted by having a thicker border. It is used in almost all processes in Fig. 5. In particular:

- The *Tool software* is used in the process *Tool and expertise sales* as an attraction for getting and keeping customers that acquire licenses. The attraction here is the properties of the tool, including the possibility of having an application run under several different OS. We have bundled tools and expertise sales together, as many new customers require some help at the start of their first project, e.g., a training class. In this case, they order licenses and help in one package.
- The process of *Providing tool licenses* used the tool software package to copy it and ship the copy to the customers who bought licenses. Most of the customers also purchased support, which included getting the new versions of the tool. This was done periodically when a new version appeared and was requested by the customer.
- The *Tool software* is used in the process *Customer development project*. For a customer who has bought a license and expertise, e.g., help to start its development project, the process of *Providing expertise* creates a small consulting team. This team participates in the process *Customer development project* that uses the *Tool software* as an asset. This process has a blue border (thicker border in non-colored print) to show that the process does not belong to Prolifics, Inc. (being the customer's process).
- The *Tool Software* is used twice in the part of the model that concerns in-house projects (the rightmost part). Firstly, it is used as an attraction to get customers, see process *Software development sales*; this is done when bidding to get a commission to develop an application for a customer. Secondly, it is used as an asset of the type *Tech & Info Infrastructure* in the development project itself, see the process *In-house software project*.

The sales and development project activities are aligned via the tool asset. The sales presents attractive features of the tool, and the tool is used in software development by the customer's developers or Prolifics' consultants. This also creates the tacit asset of Prolifics being a good tool that can be used in the sales processes. The alignment of the activities is based on Prolifics being an excellent tool, and the customers understand this fact. If the situation changes, i.e., superior tools appear, or there are big companies that aggressively market their tools, and potential customers do not understand the difference, then the strategy of Fig. 5, relying on the superiority of the tool, will not work.

In 1997, signals came that the strategy started to break down. They came from the department that completed the in-house projects. They were losing business opportunities because they put Prolifics as a tool in the bidding processes. They also got some indications that they could have gotten some projects if they had suggested another,

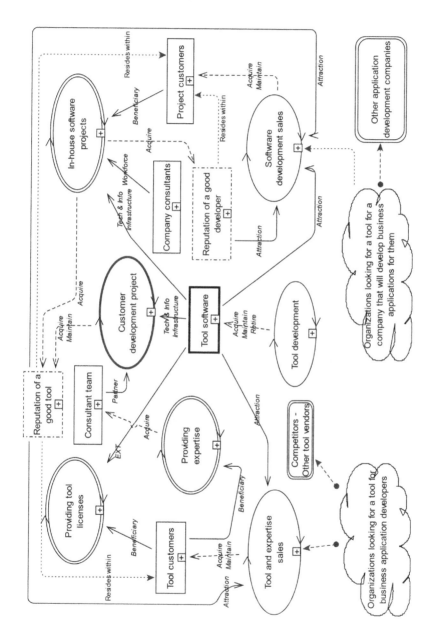

Fig. 5. A model of Prolifics business activities

more known, or popular tool. The department manager came to the company management with a proposal to allow using other tools when bidding. Such a change would result in new relations between business activities in the company. These relations are presented in a FEM of Fig. 6. As we see from the model, the in-house projects became separated from other activities in the company. Moreover, this could affect the tool's reputation negatively, as it would look like a part of the company has abandoned it (even if partially).

At this point, the management of Prolifics, Inc. Strongly believed in the competitive advantage of their tool and decided to sell the in-house software projects business activity rather than lose the fit between different activities in the company. It took about a year to complete the decision. After that, the remaining consultants worked only in projects that used the company's tool. In this situation, the company activities could be described by the left part of the model in Fig. 6.

Note that the management's decision is consistent with Porter's suggestions [2] that a company should have only one strategy. As Fig. 5 shows, remaining in this situation means the company would have two strategies.

5 Discussion and Plans for the Future

Analyzing the examples of alignment/fit presented in Sects. 3 and 4, we can see that the fit between activities we have considered is obtained by an asset (best consultant or best methods and tools) that is used for two purposes. One purpose concerns the direct usage of the asset, e.g., as *Beneficiary, Workforce,* or *Tech & Info Infrastructure*. The other purpose is *Attraction* in the process of acquiring and maintaining some other asset(s), such as customers. The importance of having this type of fit/alignment is confirmed by a historical example. The management of Prolifics, Inc. Perfectly understood that a transformation from the business situation depicted in Fig. 5 into the business situation depicted in Fig. 6 would break the fit. Thus, a radical decision was made to sell a part of their business to avoid having business activities that did not fit each other.

Summarizing our preliminary investigation of using enterprise modeling to detect fit/nonfit between a company's activities, we can draw two conclusions:

1. A fit related to an asset used in one activity that is also used in acquiring/maintaining activity related to another asset can be seen in an enterprise model of a certain kind. This fit belongs to the second-order fit, according to [2], as the results of one activity reinforce another activity. Moreover, the reinforcement may work in both directions in some cases. If the fit has a tendency to be broken, radical decisions should be made, as our historical example shows.
2. FEM is equipped for detecting and designing the described above type of fit. It has a special role for an asset, called *Attraction*, that is used in processes that draw elements from external pools in situations of competition. FEM allows to use any type of assets as an attraction, e.g., customers, tools, etc. FEM also has enough concepts for describing a competitive situation - external pools and agents.

We can now give a theoretical explanation of the conclusions above. A process of acquiring new elements for an asset from an external pool belongs to the group of

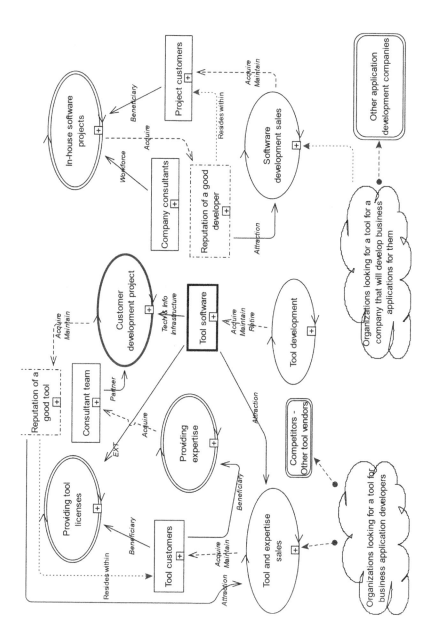

Fig. 6. Suggestion to the management

processes responsible for the autopoiesis of the enterprise. The term autopoiesis comes from biological cybernetics, first introduced in [14, 15] to identify the particulars of living systems that differentiate them from other types of systems. The term means that a living system constantly reproduces itself. More precisely, an autopoietic living system/organism, according to the original authors who coined the term, consists of a network of molecular processes that constantly reproduce the components of the system.

Though autopoiesis was introduced to describe biological systems, it was soon reinterpreted for other types of systems, such as sociological ones [16]. In paper [17], we argue that an enterprise is an autopoietic system, as it needs to constantly renew its assets, e.g., substitute retired people or equipment that no longer could be used. In the paper [17], we also have used FEM to present an enterprise as an autopoietic system.

The label *Attraction* was introduced in FEM for the processes that acquire stakeholders, i.e., assets that fulfill the role of *Workforce, Partner,* or *Beneficiary*. These assets cannot be reproduced inside an organization, and they need to be acquired from outside. As these types of assets represent agents making their own decisions, and there can be competition for the agents, attracting them to the enterprise is necessary. At least some of the attractions should be related to intrinsic properties of the enterprise, such as the type of customers or fashionable tools. Note, however, that these properties should not distract the company from making a profit; otherwise, it will not survive. Best of all, these properties should make their own contribution to profit.

Note that it is doubtful that the type of second-order fit found in our preliminary investigation is the only type of fit that should exist in an enterprise to ensure a competitive advantage. However, according to Porter [2] and the theory of autopoiesis, this is an important type of fit. This paper shows that this type of fit can be discovered or designed using enterprise modeling. Therefore, enterprise modeling can be useful for this task, even if only partially. In addition, as discussed in Sect. 4, an enterprise model can show that an organization has more than one strategy and the strategies are not connected, which is not a good situation, according to Porter [2].

Our plans for the future include finding out what other types of fit can be discovered and/or designed using enterprise modeling in general and using FEM in particular. One of the directions is to pay attention to first-order fit, which, according to [2], is aligning activities to a strategy. If the strategy elements are not directly presented in the model, this type of fit can be investigated as a fit between the directly connected activities. For example, it can be a fit between the hiring activity and the activities (processes) in which the hired person should participate. Some ideas of how to investigate this type of fit using FEM are presented in [18].

Note that so far, we have not discovered that FEM lacks some concepts to be useful for the task of analyzing or designing a "fit". Thus, our attention is still on creating a methodology for using FEM for the purpose rather than extending FEM with new concepts.

Acknowledgment. The authors are thankful to Patrick Hoverstadt, who raised our attention to the works of Mickael Porter on competitive advantage. The first author's work was partly supported by the Estonian Research Council (grant PRG1226). The authors also thank anonymous reviewers whose questions and comments helped improve the text.

References

1. Porter, M.: Competitive Advantage. Free Press, New York (1985)
2. Porter, M.: What is strategy? Harv. Bus. Rev. **74**(6), 61–78 (1996)
3. Frank, U.: Multi-perspective enterprise modeling (memo) conceptual framework and modeling languages. In: Proceedings of the 35th Annual Hawaii International Conference on System Sciences, IEEE, pp.1258–1267 (2002)
4. Giannoulis, C., Petit, M., Zdravkovic, J.: Modeling competition-driven business strategy for business IT alignment. In: Salinesi, C., Pastor, O. (eds.) CAiSE 2011. LNBIP, vol. 83, pp. 16–28. Springer, Heidelberg (2011). https://doi.org/10.1007/978-3-642-22056-2_3
5. Bider, I., Perjons, E., Elias, M., Johannesson, P.: A fractal enterprise model and its application for business development. SoSyM **16**(3), 663–689 (2017)
6. Bider, I., Perjons, E., Klyukina, V.: Tool support for fractal enterprise modeling. In: Karagiannis, D., Lee, M., Hinkelmann, K., Utz, W. (eds.) Domain-Specific Conceptual Modeling, pp. 205–229. Springer, Cham (2022). https://doi.org/10.1007/978-3-030-93547-4_10
7. Wierda, G.: Mastering Archimate Edition 3.1. P&A (2022)
8. Hevner, A., March, S.T., Park, J.: Design science in information systems research. MIS Q. **28**(1), 75–105 (2004)
9. Bider, I., Johannesson, P., Perjons, E.: Design science research as movement between individual and generic situation-problem-solution spaces. In: Baskerville, R., De Marco, M., Spagnoletti, P. (eds.) Designing Organizational Systems, vol. 1, pp. 35–61. Springer, Heidelberg (2013). https://doi.org/10.1007/978-3-642-33371-2_3
10. Fractalmodel.org: Fractal Enterprise Model. https://www.fractalmodel.org/. Accessed October 2023
11. Mintzberg, H., Waters, J.A.: Of strategies, deliberate and emergent. Strateg. Manage. J. **6**(3), 257–272 (1985)
12. Roelens, B., Steenacker, W., Poels, G.: Realizing strategic fit within the business architecture: the design of a process-goal alignment modeling and analysis technique. Softw. Syst. Model. **18**, 631–662 (2019)
13. Dalpiaz, F., Franch, X., Horkoff, J.: iStar 2.0 Language Guide. https://arxiv.org/pdf/1605.07767. Accessed April 2024
14. Varela, F., Maturana, H.R., Uribe, R.: Autopoiesis: the organization of living systems, its characterization and a model. BioSystems **5**(4), 187–196 (1974)
15. Maturana, H.R., Varela, F.J.: Autopoiesis and Congnition: The Realization of the Living, Reidel, Dordrecht. Holland (1980). Reidel, Dordrecht, Holland (1980)
16. Luhmann, N.: The autopoiesis of social systems. In Geyer, F., van der Zouwen, J., (eds.) Sociocybernetic Paradoxes. Sage, London (1986)
17. Bider, I., Regev, G., Perjons, E.: using enterprise models to explain and discuss autopoiesis and homeostasis in socio technical systems. CSIMQ **22**, 21–38 (2020)
18. Bider, I., Perjons, E.: Using fractal enterprise model to assist complexity management. In: BIR Workshops 2018, CEUR, Stockholm, vol. 2218, pp.233–238 (2018)

Technology-Aware Enterprise Modeling: Challenging the Model-Driven Architecture Paradigm

Irina Rychkova[1(✉)], Eddy Kiomba Kambilo[1], Nicolas Herbaut[1], Oscar Pastor[2], Rene Noel[2], and Carine Souveyet[1]

[1] University Paris 1 Pantheon-Sorbonne, Paris, France
{irina.rychkova,eddy.kiomba-kambilo,
nicolas.herbaut,carine.souveyet}@univ-paris1.fr
[2] Universitat Politècnica de València, València, Spain
opastor@dsic.upv.es, rnoel@pros.upv.es

Abstract. We propose a holistic design approach that extends a traditional Model Driven Architecture paradigm with the bottom-up constraint analysis and propagation. We define a Unified Feature Model that represents the organizational goals and the technical properties of the solution, and use model-checking to reason about the constraints that arise from their interplay. In the illustrative example, we show how the technical decisions specified in a Feature Model can be formalized, validated, and translated into strategic limits of a Goal Model for further redesign of both business and technical enterprise models.

Keywords: MDA · Enterprise Modeling · Feature Model · model-checking

1 Introduction

The Model-Driven Architecture (MDA) provides a fundamental framework for the design and development of enterprise information systems, prioritizing the top-down design process. It introduces three levels of model abstraction and a model transformation process, ensuring a traceability and alignment between the high-level business goals and developed technological components [10]. In this methodology, the selection of technological platforms and components is deferred to lower levels of the MDA design hierarchy. This approach is justifiable under the assumption that technological choices have primarily local effects. However, the emergence of disruptive technologies, such as blockchain challenges the established principles of MDA by exerting a broader influence on processes and goals of the enterprise as a whole [9].

The intrinsic properties of blockchain not only create efficiencies locally, but also introduce strategic limits extending beyond the initially targeted areas of implementation. Consequently, the adoption of such technologies requires a holistic analysis of their potential impacts on the business processes and objectives

H. van der Aa et al. (Eds.): BPMDS 2024/EMMSAD 2024, LNBIP 511, pp. 388–396, 2024.
https://doi.org/10.1007/978-3-031-61007-3_28

enterprise-wide. Moreover, this analysis cannot be postponed to the later design stages, but accompany the whole design process, increasing the technology-awareness already at the early design stages.

We propose an approach for Technology-Aware Enterprise Modeling (TEAEM) that extends the MDA paradigm with the bottom-up constraint propagation and analysis. We depart from the idea that technical properties defined at the lower MDA abstraction levels can create implicit 'side effects' in the higher MDA levels. This position paper introduces TEAEM and presents the first results of its implementation. Some of the TEAEM steps are supported by the well known modeling tools. We developed several modules for model transformation, model unification and interpretation of results. The current version of TEAEM supports only goal - feature model unification. The component modeling will be integrated in the nearest future. We illustrate our approach on a theoretical example of an Organization seeking to implement a blockchain solution for its processes. The results of this analysis provide the ground for a technology-aware business (re)design and decision-making for the Organization.

In Sect. 2, we provide a brief reminder on the MDA and discuss its challenges; in Sect. 3, we introduce the TEAEM approach; in Sect. 4, we present our illustrative example; in Sect. 5, we provide a road-map for the future development of TEAEM and present our conclusions.

2   Background

Model Driven Architecture (MDA) is a software design approach that provides a set of guidelines for structuring specifications expressed as models, supporting traceability and business-IT alignment. MDA defines three primary types of models: *Computation Independent Model* (CIM) represents the system's requirements and business context without detailing the structure or processing; *Platform Independent Model* (PIM) specifies the system's structure and functionality but abstracts away the details of any specific implementation platform; *Platform Specific Model* (PSM) provides the technical details on system implementation using a particular technology or platform.

Methods and approaches for enterprise system design grounded on MDA are discussed in research literature for several decades. Alignment between enterprise models at different MDA abstraction levels is addressed in [5,17,21,22]. Numerous works focus on validation and analysis of alignment between business processes and goals [1,3,4]. Formal methods are proposed for alignment verification in [18]. To acknowledge the constantly changing business environment, integration of organizational strategy and structure into MDA is addressed in [13]. In [14], a semi-automated *strategy-to-code* approach that integrates organizational, business process, and information system modeling is introduced. This approach is grounded on LiteStart modeling method [12] and ensures traceability across modeling levels.

The research presented in [9,11,16] acknowledges the rapid evolution and complexity of technological solutions and their impact on organizational strategy and processes. While technological solutions may initially excel in addressing specific business goals, their implementation can introduce strategic limits in other areas. This necessitates the evolution of design approaches, including MDA, and motivates the TEAEM approach presented in this work.

3   Technology-Aware Enterprise Modeling

TEAEM is a holistic approach that extends the (top-down) MDA design paradigm with the bottom-up traceability and constraint propagation analysis.

3.1   TEAEM: Steps

Figure 1 illustrates the TEAEM approach. We use goal modeling [20], feature modeling [23] and component modeling [19] to represent an enterprise solution at the three MDA abstraction levels.

The top-down *Model Design* follows the MDA paradigm and consists of developing a Goal Model (CIM), a Feature Model (PIM) and a Component model (PSM) and their respective model transformations. The bottom-up *Constraint Analysis* represents our main theoretical contribution and consists of Model unification and Model checking/Impact analysis steps.

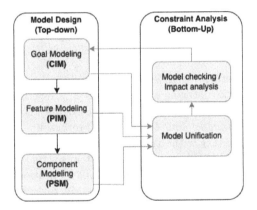

Fig. 1. TEAEM approach

Goal Modeling (CIM). A goal model representing the high-level business goals, requirements, and domain concepts is created in this step. This model correspond to CIM - the highest level of abstraction within MDA. It outlines the dependencies between goals and intended outcomes ensuring alignment with broader organizational context. These dependencies are explored in the further constraint analysis.

Feature Modeling (PIM). A feature model is defined in this step. This model specifies the hierarchical structure of abstract technical functionalities (features) of the prospective solution and corresponds to PIM. The dependencies and constraints between the features define alternative configurations for the technical solution.

Component Modeling (PSM). A component model is created in this step. This model specifies technological components and platform-specific details necessary for implementation of the features defined in PIM. Technical constraints between the components provide the information about alternative implementations of the designed solution.

Model Unification. In this step, business goals, technical features, and components are specified within a single Unified Feature Model (UFM). For further impact analysis, we use logical expressions to formalize the mappings between the model elements defined at different MDA abstraction levels.

We define the following mapping types: *Goal to Feature Mapping* associates the business goals with the technical features satisfying these goals. This mapping reflects technical assumptions made by system engineers. *Feature to Goal Mapping* associates the technical features with the goals that can be possibly compromised or inhibited by implementation of these features. *Feature to Component Mapping* associates the features with the specific technological components implementing these features. *Component to Feature Mapping* explicitly defines possible restrictions or incompatibilities between the features and the components. *Component to Goal Mapping* indicates possible restrictions between the (soft) goals and the components such as quality, feasibility, performance issues etc. We combine these mappings with the constraints defined in the previous TEAEM steps to form the UFM.

Model Checking/Impact Analysis. We use model-checking to validate the UFM and to identify inconsistencies (if any) in its specification. A solver finds possible configurations of a solution and/or shows the conflicts between the elements of the unified model. We propose a domain-specific interpretation of these conflicts and recommendations for their resolution.

The Constraint Analysis can be performed at different stages of Model design and serve to: (a) identify and propagate the effect of design decisions specified in PIM on CIM; (b) identify and propagate the effect of design decisions specified in PSM on PIM and/or on CIM.

3.2   TEAEM: Implementation

In this work, we illustrate a semi-automated model unification and constraint analysis between CIM and PIM abstraction levels of MDA.

To implement the approach, the following three modules are developed[1]:

1. *Generation of the Unified Feature Model (UFM)*: The unified model comprises the goal model, features model, and constraints. *For the top-down model design,* we use the i* modeling language [2] and the PiStar tool [15] for Goal Modeling, and the feature modeling environment FeatureIDE [7]. The mapping for different MDA abstraction levels is added manually with an external file using logical expression notation. We develop an automated Python module [transform.py] which takes as input the goal model, the feature model, and

---

[1] https://github.com/Eddykams/TEAEM_develop.

the provided constraints, and automatically transforms them into a unified model.

2. *Extraction of the constraints from the UFM:* We use FeatureIDE and its bundled Sat4j solver [8] to retrieve the constraints from the UFM. We generate an output in JSON that is further used for the constraint analysis step.

3. *Interpretation of the solution (constraints violation and their implication bottom-up):* We develop a Python module [interpretation.py] that uses the .json list of constraint violations extracted from the UFM in FeatureIDE as an input and produces the domain-specific interpretations of these violations that can be further used for enterprise models redesign.

The current version of our tools is semi-automated. The goal model is designed with piStar tool, the feature model is designed with FeatureIDE. The mapping between goal model and feature model is formalized using logical expressions in an external text file. This file is used as an input to generate our Unified Model. The model-checking of the unified feature model is automatically applied by FeatureIDE. The model-checking results are extracted and interpreted by the developed module. We are working to provide a fully automated mapping process for the next version.

4   Illustrative Example

We illustrate the TEAEM approach on a simple example of the Organization that seeks to enhance transparency and auditability of its processes. The Organization considers blockchain technology as a platform for its enterprise solutions. In particular, the Organization needs to choose between two blockchain platforms (PublicBC_X and PrivateBC_Y). Further, in the design, it will configure the selected blockchain platform and its components. Since the Organization is also concerned with the GDPR compliance, more detailed analysis of the abstract capabilities and technical functionality of the prospective blockchain solution is required. We illustrate how TEAEM can support the analysis of technical constraints and their impact on the defined business goals of the Organization.

Goal Modeling (CIM): The goal model illustrated in Fig. 2(a) defines the two goals of the Organization: 'GDPR Compliance' and 'Auditability' that have to be achieved. We specify this dependency with the i* And-refinement link that corresponds to the logical conjunction:

```
Business Goals => GDPR Compliance AND Auditability
```

Feature Modeling (PIM): The feature model illustrated in Fig. 2(b) specifies the abstract functionalities associated with blockchain technology. The prospective Technical Solution of the Organization (modeled as a root feature) will be grounded either on the functionalities of a 'PublicBC_X' or a 'PrivateBC_Y'. We specify this with the alternative feature group in FeatureIDE that corresponds to exclusive OR expression:

```
Technical Solution => PublicBC_X XOR PrivateBC_Y
```

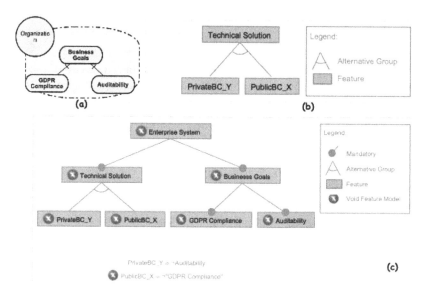

Fig. 2. (a): Goal Model of the Organization; (b): Feature Model with a proposition of alternative blockchain solutions; (c): Unified Feature Model that merges (a) and (b).

Once the goal model and solution proposition are formalized, we proceed with the (bottom-up) constraint propagation and analysis.

Model Unification. We create a unified feature model that specifies the 'Enterprise System' of the Organization (Fig. 2.(c)). Our UFM represents the goals (from CIM) and the features (from PIM) using the feature modeling formalism. Here we model 'Technical Solution' and 'Business Goals' as mandatory features of the 'Enterprise System' root feature.

To formalize the mapping between the created MDA models, We assume the following assumptions: we consider generic properties of Public blockchain X and Private blockchain Y. The Private blockchain Y limits the auditability of the blockchain because their nodes are controlled by a single (private) entity and the immutability is contingent upon the trustworthiness of this entity. The Public blockchain X does not face this immutability issue because any node can participate in the consensus and validation processes, ensuring that operations are conducted fairly and transparently. Nevertheless, this immutability of public blockchains prevents from implementation of a fundamental GDPR's 'right to be forgotten' - an alteration/deletion of data on demand. We map the technical features defined in PIM to the goals that can be compromised by implementation of these features using the following logical expressions:

```
PublicBC_X => NOT GDPR Compliance;
PrivateBC_Y => NOT Audit
```

Goal model, Feature model and Feature to Goal mapping presented above are documented as XML files and are used for semi-automated generation of the UFM.

Model Checking/Impact Analysis. The FeatureIDE automatically executes the model-checking on the generated UFM. In our example, the UFM is invalid (i.e., the model is void), meaning that no Enterprise System satisfying actual constraints can be configured. We identify and trace the sources of conflicting constraints to the model elements defined at different MDA levels (PIM and CIM in our example). Using our developed Extraction and Solution Interpretation modules, we provide the domain-specific constraint interpretation, aiming to assist business users in redesign (Fig. 3).

```
Logical constraints:
 ['Enterprise System ⇒ Technical Solution', 'Enterprise System ⇒ Businesss Goals', 'Techni
cal Solution ⇒ PrivateBC_Y v PublicBC_X', 'Businesss Goals ⇒ GDPR Compliance', 'Businesss
Goals ⇒ Auditability']
*********************************

Domain-specific constraint analysis & interpretation:
-----------------------------------------------------
To correct your UFM, you have the following options:
-----------------------------------------------------
Make constraint 'GDPR Compliance' non-mandatory, OR Remove constraint 'GDPR Compliance'.
Make constraint 'Auditability' non-mandatory, OR Remove constraint 'Auditability'.
```

Fig. 3. Domain-specific constraint analysis & interpretation.

In this example, the business expert faces the problem where any choice of blockchain solution compromises one of the business goals defined by the Organization. Along with modification or refinement of the prospective Technical Solution, this analysis calls for redefinition or re-prioritization of the Business Goals in response of the bottom-up constraint propagation.

5   Conclusion and Future Work

We presented TEAEM approach that contributes to design of enterprise systems within the MDA paradigm. While existing approaches support traceability and alignment between goals and technical solutions top-down, they often fall short in guiding stakeholders through the decision-making process and analysis of inconsistencies bottom-up. Our approach enables reconciliation between business goals, technical capabilities and specific solutions through formal analysis and propagation of constraints.

We outlined the TEAEM steps (illustrated in Fig. 1). Model unification and Model checking/Impact analysis are the two steps that extend the MDA providing constraint propagation and analysis. We developed a technique for the semi-automated generation of the Unified Feature Model (UFM) and used the feature modeling environment FeatureIDE for automated model-checking.

In this article, we illustrated the propagation of constraints from PIM to CIM. Identification and propagation of the effect of design decisions specified in PSM on PIM and/or on CIM, and the automated mapping between the elements at different MDA levels of abstraction will be addressed in our future work.

We illustrated our approach on a short theoretical example. Developing a realistic example is an important next step. We plan to conduct a case study on the design and analysis of a Supply Chain Management solution based on blockchain technology. In this case study, propagation and impact of technical properties related to specific blockchain solutions on the organizational supply chain management process and strategic goals will be examined. In particular, we will focus on trustworthiness goals addressed in our previous work [6].

References

1. Cortes-Cornax, M., Matei, A., Dupuy-Chessa, S., Rieu, D., Mandran, N., Letier, E.: Using intentional fragments to bridge the gap between organizational and intentional levels. Inf. Softw. Technol. **58**, 1–19 (2015)
2. Franch, X., López, L., Cares, C., Colomer, D.: The i* framework for goal-oriented modeling. Domain-Specific Conceptual Model. Concepts, Methods Tools, 485–506 (2016)
3. Gröner, G., Asadi, M., Mohabbati, B., Gašević, D., Bošković, M., Parreiras, F.S.: Validation of user intentions in process orchestration and choreography. Inf. Syst. **43**, 83–99 (2014)
4. Guizzardi, R., Reis, A.N.: A method to align goals and business processes. In: Johannesson, P., Lee, M.L., Liddle, S.W., Opdahl, A.L., López, Ó.P. (eds.) ER 2015. LNCS, vol. 9381, pp. 79–93. Springer, Cham (2015). https://doi.org/10.1007/978-3-319-25264-3_6
5. Horita, H., Honda, K., Sei, Y., Nakagawa, H., Tahara, Y., Ohsuga, A.: Transformation approach from KAOS goal models to BPMN models using refinement patterns. In: Proceedings of the 29th Annual ACM Symposium on Applied Computing, pp. 1023–1024 (2014)
6. Kambilo, E.K., Rychkova, I., Herbaut, N., Souveyet, C.: Addressing trust issues in supply-chain management systems through blockchain software patterns. In: Nurcan, S., Opdahl, A.L., Mouratidis, H., Tsohou, A. (eds.) RCIS 2023. LNBI, vol. 476, pp. 275–290. Springer, Cham (2023). https://doi.org/10.1007/978-3-031-33080-3_17
7. Kastner, C., et al.: Featureide: a tool framework for feature-oriented software development. In: 2009 IEEE 31st International Conference on Software Engineering, pp. 611–614. IEEE (2009)
8. Le Berre, D., Parrain, A.: The sat4j library, release 2.2. J. Satisfiability, Boolean Model. Comput. **7**(2–3), 59–64 (2010)
9. Marques, L., Pereira, R.: Creating value with blockchain for organizations. In: Pereira, R., Bianchi, I., Rocha, Á. (eds.) Digital Technologies and Transformation in Business, Industry and Organizations, vol. 497, pp. 17–41. Springer, Cham (2023). https://doi.org/10.1007/978-3-031-40710-9_2

10. Mellor, S.J.: MDA Distilled: Principles of Model-driven Architecture. Addison-Wesley Professional, Boston (2004)
11. Morkunas, V.J., Paschen, J., Boon, E.: How blockchain technologies impact your business model. Bus. Horiz. **62**(3), 295–306 (2019)
12. Noel, R., Panach, I., Ruiz, M., Pastor, O.: The litestrat method: Towards strategic model-driven development. In: Proceedings of the 29th International Conference on Information Systems Development (2021)
13. Noel, R., Panach, J.I., Pastor, O.: Challenges for model-driven development of strategically aligned information systems. IEEE Access **10**, 38237–38253 (2022)
14. Pastor, O., Noel, R., Panach, I.: From strategy to code: achieving strategical alignment in software development projects through conceptual modelling. In: Hameurlain, A., Tjoa, A.M. (eds.) Transactions on Large-Scale Data- and Knowledge-Centered Systems XLVIII. LNCS, vol. 12670, pp. 145–164. Springer, Heidelberg (2021). https://doi.org/10.1007/978-3-662-63519-3_7
15. Pimentel, J., Castro, J.: pistar tool–a pluggable online tool for goal modeling. In: 2018 IEEE 26th International Requirements Engineering Conference (RE), pp. 498–499. IEEE (2018)
16. Rajnak, V., Puschmann, T.: The impact of blockchain on business models in banking. IseB **19**, 809–861 (2021)
17. Ruiz, M., Costal, D., España, S., Franch, X., Pastor, O.: GoBIS: an integrated framework to analyse the goal and business process perspectives in information systems. Inf. Syst. **53**, 330–345 (2015). https://doi.org/10.1016/j.is.2015.03.007
18. Rychkova, I.: Formal semantics for refinement verification of entreprise models (2008). https://doi.org/10.5075/EPFL-THESIS-4210, http://infoscience.epfl.ch/record/126002
19. Trinidad, P., Cortés, A.R., Pena, J., Benavides, D.: Mapping feature models onto component models to build dynamic software product lines. In: SPLC (2), pp. 51–56 (2007)
20. Van Lamsweerde, A.: Goal-oriented requirements engineering: a guided tour. In: Proceedings fifth IEEE International Symposium on Requirements Engineering, pp. 249–262. IEEE (2001)
21. de la Vara, J.L., Sánchez, J., Pastor, O.: On the use of goal models and business process models for elicitation of system requirements. In: Nurcan, S., et al. (eds.) BPMDS/EMMSAD -2013. LNBIP, vol. 147, pp. 168–183. Springer, Heidelberg (2013). https://doi.org/10.1007/978-3-642-38484-4_13
22. Wegmann, A., Regev, G., Rychkova, I., Lê, L.S., De La Cruz, J.D., Julia, P.: Business and it alignment with seam for enterprise architecture. In: 11th IEEE International Enterprise Distributed Object Computing Conference (EDOC 2007), pp. 111–111. IEEE (2007)
23. Yu, Y., Lapouchnian, A., Liaskos, S., Mylopoulos, J., Leite, J.C.S.P.: From goals to high-variability software design. In: An, A., Matwin, S., Raś, Z.W., Ślęzak, D. (eds.) ISMIS 2008. LNCS (LNAI), vol. 4994, pp. 1–16. Springer, Heidelberg (2008). https://doi.org/10.1007/978-3-540-68123-6_1

Author Index

H. van der Aa et al. (Eds.): BPMDS 2024/EMMSAD 2024, LNBIP 511, pp. 397–398, 2024.
https://doi.org/10.1007/978-3-031-61007-3